THE KOVELS' COLLECTORS' SOURCE · BOOK

THE KOVELS' COLLECTORS' SOURCE BOOK

BY RALPH & TERRY KOVEL

CROWN PUBLISHERS, INC.   NEW YORK

In memory of
Noah L. Butkin,
a true friend
who knew the "sources" of the greatest
art in the world,
as well as the "source" for
marble-tipped clock dials, bicycle wheels, and whatever . . .
and, of course,
to
Kim and Lee,
who know the source for everything

Published by Crown Publishers, Inc., One Park Avenue,
New York, New York 10016, and simultaneously in Canada by
General Publishing Company Limited
Manufactured in the United States of America

Library of Congress Cataloging in Publication Data
Kovel, Ralph M.
The Kovels' collectors' source book.
1. Antiques. I. Kovel, Terry H. II. Title.
NK1125.K67   745.1   82-5153
ISBN 0-517-54846-1 (cloth)   AACR2
ISBN 0-517-54791-0 (paper)

10 9 8 7 6 5 4 3 2 1
First Edition

CONTENTS

PART II: GENERAL INFORMATION AND SOURCE LISTS 273

INTRODUCTION

Each year we are asked by collectors, other authors, editors, librarians, and our readers literally thousands of questions about antiques and collectibles. How do I join the Barber Pole Collectors Club? What does "marvered" mean? Where can I buy a flushcup? What *is* a flushcup? (Our question.) What is the address of the American Society of—well, you name it?

Whenever possible, we have tried to answer these questions, but quickly this service—which we very much wanted to provide—was becoming a full-time job for at least one member of our staff. The world of collectors was sometimes confused, needed information, and we wanted to address the problem.

This book, *The Kovels' Collectors' Source Book,* is our attempt to respond to those thousands of questions. To compile this directory, we sent out more than 5,000 letters to companies, clubs, individuals, and others who offered a service or product that might be of interest to collectors. Quite simply, we included only those sources that responded *in writing* to our inquiry. This, of course, was a somewhat arbitrary way of deciding who would be included in the book, but by using this as our criterion, we were sure of providing the most up-to-date information possible. What's more, we felt that if the source did not respond to our inquiry, it probably would not respond to yours.

In addition, we would like to state up front that no charge was made to anyone listed here. In other words, the listings are neither advertisements nor endorsements. We cannot guarantee that you will have excellent service or a problem-free relationship with any of the sources listed here, but we are fairly certain these sources will be useful. Keep in mind, though, that this is a reference book only. We have made every effort to be complete and accurate in our sources and their addresses. Some sources might not have been included and some addresses might have changed. We apologize and will be pleased to make the necessary corrections in any future editions.

HOW THIS BOOK IS ORGANIZED

If you turn to the Contents, you will quickly see that there is a reasonable order to *The Kovels' Collectors' Source Book.* First, in **Part I: The Collectibles,** we have arranged, alphabetically, more than 80 categories of antiques and collectibles. These include everything from common antiques (Dolls, Furniture, Glass) to fascinating collectibles (how about Stoves), to the trendy (Movie Memorabilia is currently extremely popular), to the sometimes bizarre (take a look in Odds and Ends). In each chapter we have included clubs, publications, books of marks or other identification information, how-to-fix-it books, sources for parts and supplies, repair services, price guides, appraisers, auction houses, and any other category of information regarding a particular collectible that seemed useful.

In **Part II: General Information and Source Lists,** we have compiled sources for buying by mail, auction houses, mail order information, general publications and price guides, booksellers, and others who provide general information and services to virtually every kind of collector. We have also included special information on security, displaying collectibles, and associations because we find this information always to be of use.

Finally, at the back of the book, you will find a very detailed index, and we strongly suggest that you refer to it often. Many sources provide multiple services. Although we have made a concerted effort within each chapter to be as comprehensive as possible, and in many cases we have referred you to other entries, the index will give you every possible entry. Check it frequently, both to solve problems you may have or to find additional information that might be important to you.

HOW TO CONTACT THOSE WE HAVE LISTED

When you write to learn more about a service or a publication, remember that some of these organizations are very small firms with a limited staff available to answer letters. If a catalogue is offered, be sure to ask if you must pay a fee. When contacting a publication or club, ask for the subscription or membership price. We have not included fees because prices change so frequently and it seemed better not to include a price than to include one that was wrong. Always ask.

In your letter, explain your problem completely so that your *first* letter can be answered appropriately. If any object needs repair, include a photograph of it. Be sure to give an accurate, detailed description, including the type of material, size, and manner in which the surface is decorated. Be patient. The mails are often slow, and some of the companies are slower. Allow at least four weeks before writing a second letter.

Every address and title has been checked for accuracy, but changes are reaching us at the rate of five per week. By the time you read this book, some companies will have moved, or, unfortunately, gone out of business. We tried!

Finally, if you want advice or information, it is helpful to include a long, stamped, self-addressed envelope. That often will hasten a reply.

HOW TO LOCATE BOOKS

We have included bibliographies for many different kinds of books depending upon the category. These include reference books, price guides, and how-to-fix-it-yourself books.

In all cases, we have listed the books with the name of the publisher. For privately printed pamphlets or books, we have included the address. Thus, you can write for further information. The addresses of larger publishers can be found at your local library in *Books in Print*. Ask your librarian. Many of these books can be borrowed from the library through interlibrary loans, and most books can be purchased from your local bookstores through a special order. A few may have to be ordered from specialists who sell particular kinds of books, and the addresses of these specialists are included here.

THE LANGUAGE PROBLEM

Throughout this book we have tried to use the vocabulary of the average collector. For example, although a "conservator," "restorer," and "repairer" are technically different, we did not attempt to be absolutely precise in our use of these terms. In addition, sources are listed according to the title they provided when answering our inquiry. We have made no effort to qualify any given talent or skill based on ability or college degrees.

Our short comments about the publications and services are based on the information sent to us in response to our initial inquiries. We discovered that some newsletters simply listed events and are of no interest to the outside collector, whereas others are treasures of research that should be included in most libraries. Some, unfortunately, have been guilty of spreading misinformation.

We have tried to indicate the contents of the publications and newsletters, but you may want to request a sample copy before ordering a year's subscription. Many newsletters are available only to members, so you may have to join the club to get the information. Be aware that some collectors' newsletters are commercial selling tools or advertisements promoting retail sales under the guise of a newsletter.

Finally, the major language problem we found in writing this book is one we have struggled with in all of the books we have written. Should "paper can label" information be listed under *paper, store,* or *advertising?* We hope the index will help you to find the items that are difficult to categorize.

A FEW FINAL COMMENTS

In the process of deciding what to include in this book, we had to make several arbitrary decisions. For example, we have included only the auction houses that publish catalogues that can be ordered by mail. Thousands of other auction galleries are active in the United States, but we intend this book for the widest possible audience so we decided a catalogue and the ability to bid-by-mail were a must. All specialized auction houses—those that sell just dolls, just bottles, or whatever particular antique or collectible—are listed in the special subject entry; general auction houses are listed in the back of the book.

Most price guides listed are books published after 1979. We purposely did not include the material of interest to collectors of coins, stamps, cars, or restoring old houses because these areas at once are very broad and very specialized. Many books exist that address themselves solely to these areas. In addition, we have not listed local experts and shops; to find these, consult the Yellow Pages of your telephone book. Club publications are listed as part of the information about the clubs and are not listed again under publications.

We always welcome all comments or suggestions, good and bad. Let us know if you have a problem with any source listed. We cannot correct it, but we will assure you that the firm will not be listed again. Serious problems should be brought to the attention of the United States Post Office to determine if there has been any mail fraud. Let us know too if an address has changed or a company has moved. Finally, write to us about companies and services that are not listed here but should be included in our next edition.

Ralph and Terry Kovel
October 1982

PART I

THE COLLECTIBLES

1. ADVERTISING ART

The country store and its contents have delighted collectors for years. Around 1950 the first big group of serious collectors of advertising materials began searching for signs, containers, bottles, store bins, and other objects that could be found in an old country store. It became the vogue to decorate restaurants, homes, and shops with the nostalgia collectibles from these old stores, and prices rose as the supplies dwindled.

There are many facets to advertising collecting. Coca-Cola, Planters Peanuts, Campbell Soup, and other national brands have created enough interest for some groups to have produced books and started clubs on the product. Some collectors want only nationally known brands; some want tobacco ads, advertising dolls, etc. The specialized clubs and publications are listed here. Many current companies have books or pamphlets on past history that would interest the collector and are available from the companies. Repair information must be found under the proper heading, such as paper, tin, glass, dolls, clocks, and so on.

Beware of reproductions in this field of collecting.

CLUBS

The Cola Clan   3306 Yellowstone Drive, Lawrence, Kansas 66044   (913) 842-3929
The Cola Clan puts out two publications: *The Cola Call,* a magazine showing old and new Coca-Cola items, and *Cola Call Classifieds,* which advertises Coca-Cola items that are for sale.

Peanut Pals (Planters)   Box 4465, Huntsville, Alabama 35802   (205) 881-9198
Peanut Pals publishes *Peanut Papers,* a newsletter about Planters Peanuts' history and collectibles.

PUBLICATIONS

Kiddieland Souper Special (Campbell Kids)   11892 Bartlett Street, Garden Grove, California 92645   (714) 892-5686
This is a newsletter about the Campbell Kids issued 6 times a year.

The Tole House Newsletter   P.O. Box 8091, Erie, Pennsylvania 16505   (814) 838-9180
The Tole House Newsletter is published 6 times a year for serious collectors and dealers of commercial collectibles.

BOOK OF MARKS

Kovel, Ralph and Terry. *Kovels' Know Your Collectibles.*
New York: Crown Publishers, 1981.

PRICE GUIDES

Bull, Donald. *A Price Guide to Beer Advertising Openers and Corkscrews.*
Privately printed, 1981 (P.O. Box 106, Trumbull, Connecticut 06611).

Cope, Jim. *Old Advertising.*
Austin, Texas: Great American Publishing, 1980.

Goldstein, Shelly and Helen. *The Index to Coca-Cola Collectibles.*
Privately printed, 1980 (P.O. Box 301, Woodland Hills, California 91364).

Hogan, Bill and Pauline. *Canadian Country Store Collectables.*
Privately printed, 1979 (16 Haynes Avenue, St. Catherines, Ontario L2R 3Z1 Canada).

Hyman, Tony. *Handbook of Cigar Boxes.*
Privately printed, 1979 (R.D. 2, Watkins Glen, New York 14891).

Kaduck, John M. *Advertising Trade Cards.*
Privately printed, 1976 (P.O. Box 02152, Cleveland, Ohio 44102). The 1982–1983 price guide is available.

———. *Collecting Advertising Mirrors.*
Privately printed, 1973 (P.O. Box 02152, Cleveland, Ohio 44102). The 1982–1983 price guide is available.

Munsey, Cecil, and Petretti, Allan. *Official Coca-Cola Collectibles Price Guide,* 1980–1981 ed.
Hackensack, New Jersey: Nostalgia Publishing, 1980.

Richardson, Charles G. and Lillian C. *The Pill Rollers: A Book on Apothecary Antiques and Drug Store Collectibles.*
Fort Washington, Maryland: Old Fort Press, 1979.

Russo, James D. *Cracker Jack Collecting for Fun and Profit.*
Privately printed, 1976 (MLR 38 West 5th Street, Cincinnati, Ohio 45202).

Spanier, Jeff. *Gasoline Pump Globes.*
Privately printed, 1979 (2644 East 22nd Street, Tulsa, Oklahoma 74114).

Tumbusch, Tom. *The Illustrated Radio Premium Catalog and Price Guide.*
Dayton, Ohio: Tomart Publications, 1977.

Weinberger, Marty and Don. *Coca-Cola Trays from Mexico and Canada.*
Privately printed, 1979 (P.O. Box 50, Willow Grove, Pennsylvania 19090).

INFORMATION

If you want to know more about your collectibles you may be able to get information from the following companies. When requesting information, be sure to include a self-addressed, stamped envelope.

The Coca-Cola Company Archives   310 North Avenue N.W., Atlanta, Georgia 30313

Dr Pepper Company   Harry E. Ellis, Historian/Librarian, P.O. Box 225086, Dallas, Texas 75265

H. J. Heinz Company   P.O. Box 57, Pittsburgh, Pennsylvania 15230

The Nabisco Gallery   World Headquarters, River Road & DeForest Avenue, East Hanover, New Jersey 07936

Pepsi-Cola Company   Anderson Hill Road, Purchase, New York 10577

Procter & Gamble Archives   Ed Rider, Archivist, P.O. Box 599, Cincinnati, Ohio 45201
Mr. Rider will help people date products but will not give values.

2. AMERICAN INDIANS AND OLD WEST

Indian baskets, pottery, rugs, jewelry, beadwork, and leatherwork have become increasingly popular with collectors. Interest is especially keen in the West, where American Indian culture is more evident.

PUBLICATIONS

American Indian Basketry Magazine   P.O. Box 66124, Portland, Oregon 97266   (503) 771-8540
This magazine is published irregularly, approximately 4 times a year.

The Indian Trader   P.O. Box 867, Gallup, New Mexico 87301
This is a monthly newspaper with articles about both old and new Indian art and artifacts. It includes sections for buying and selling collectibles as well as ads for new items.

Native Arts/West   P.O. Box 31196, Billings, Montana 59107
This is a monthly newspaper.

Old West   700 East State Street, Iola, Wisconsin 54990   (715) 445-2214
This publication is issued quarterly.

PARTS AND SUPPLIES

Grey Owl Indian Craft Company, Inc.   113-15 Springfield Boulevard, Queens Village, New York 11429   (212) 464-9300
Indian craft supplies and jewelry findings are available. The firm has an illustrated catalogue for $1.00.

L"Eagle" Feathers by Jumping Bull   Division of Western Originals, Inc., 758 East Yale Street, Ontario, California 91764   (714) 988-6127
A price list is available.

REPAIR SERVICES

The Arizona Turquoise and Silver Company, Ltd.   7086 Fifth Avenue, Scottsdale, Arizona 85251   (602) 945-2118 or 947-8610
This company offers full service repair and custom jewelry production, specializing in Indian goods.

Havran's Navajo Rug Cleaners   48 West Main, Cortex, Colorado 81321   (303) 565-7977
This firm specializes in professional Navajo rug cleaning and stain removal. It is fully insured and guarantees prompt return. Please note troublesome areas and send rugs by insured mail.

Salvatore Macri   5518 East Pinchot Avenue, Phoenix, Arizona 85018   (602) 959-1933
Salvatore Macri specializes in (but is not limited to) the restoration of fine art porcelain and Indian artifacts (not rugs or baskets) of a prehistoric, historic, and contemporary nature. His services are available to anyone in the U.S. and he will answer questions by mail.

White Deer Indian Traders   1834 Red Pine Lane, Stevens Point, Wisconsin 54481
White Deer Indian Traders specializes in the repair of American Indian material culture items. Its services include restoration, appraisals, and opinions on conservation and are available to anyone in the U.S. Write and describe needs first enclosing a self-addressed, stamped envelope for a reply.

PRICE GUIDE

Barry, John. *American Indian Pottery: An Identification and Value Guide.*
New York: Crown Publishers, 1981.

BUYING BY MAIL

American Indian Artifact Catalog & Price List   P.O. Box 1005, Watsonville, California 95076
(408) 476-9579
There is a charge for this publication. When writing for information, be sure to include a self-addressed, stamped envelope.

APPRAISERS

American Indian Basketry Magazine   P.O. Box 66124, Portland, Oregon 97266   (503) 771-8540
This is a full appraisal service of American Indian traditional arts: basketry, beadwork, carving, stonework, trade goods, pottery, rugs, blankets, weaponry, etc. Special rates are offered for native American organizations and antiques dealers. For an appraisal by mail, send a good photo accompanied by the size of the item and a statement of its condition.

Salvatore Macri   5518 East Pinchot Avenue, Phoenix, Arizona 85018   (602) 959-1933
Salvatore Macri specializes in (but is not limited to) the restoration and appraisal of fine art porcelain and Indian artifacts (not rugs or baskets) of a prehistoric, historic, and contemporary nature. His services are available to anyone in the U.S. and he will answer questions by mail.

BOOKSELLER

Grey Owl Indian Craft Company, Inc.   113-15 Springfield Boulevard, Queens Village, New York 11429   (212) 464-9300
Books on Indians and Indian crafts are available. The firm has an illustrated catalogue for $1.00.

3. AUTOGRAPHS

It's not only the signature on the bottom of a check that is worth money. Autographs are enthusiastically collected by many and have a value all their own. The most valuable of them are those written as part of a historic personal letter. Be careful of fakes and of machine-written autographs used by many politicians.

CLUBS

The Franklin Autograph Society   National Bank Building, 8 Broad Street, Hatfield, Pennsylvania 19440   (215) 362-0976
The Society publishes *The Franklin Autograph Society Gazette* 4 times a year. This newspaper contains news about collections and autographs for sale. A catalogue of available autographs is also offered.

Universal Autograph Collectors Club   P.O. Box 467, Rockville Centre, New York 11571   (516) 766-0093
The Pen and Quill is a bimonthly publication.

PUBLICATION

Charles Hamilton Galleries, Inc.   25 East 77th Street, New York, New York 10021
(212) 628-1666
The free booklet, *How to Sell Your Autographs,* explains how you can turn old letters and documents into brand new dollars.

AUCTION HOUSES

Charles Hamilton Galleries, Inc.   25 East 77th Street, New York, New York 10021
(212) 628-1666
This firm sells autographs and manuscripts on a consignment basis. Catalogues are available.

Harmers of San Francisco   49 Geary Street, Suite 217, San Francisco, California 94102
(415) 391-8244
Harmers primarily offers stamp auctions, but it occasionally auctions autographs, maps, and postcards. Catalogues are available by subscription and include prices realized.

NASCA (Numismatic and Antiquarian Service Corporation of America)   265 Sunrise Highway, Suite 53, Rockville Centre, New York 11570   (516) 764-6677
Auction bids are accepted in person or by mail. Coins, paper money, tokens and medals, bonds, stocks, certificates, and related items are most commonly auctioned. Stamps and autographs are offered occasionally. Catalogues are available in single copies or by subscription.

BUYING BY MAIL

Each of these firms has a catalogue or list available and there is a charge for some. When writing for information, be sure to include a self-addressed, stamped envelope.

Robert F. Batchelder   1 West Butler Avenue, Ambler, Pennsylvania 19002   (215) 643-1430
Autographs, letters, documents, and manuscripts are available.

The Collector   Walter R. Benjamin Autographs, Inc. P.O. Box 255, Scribner Hollow Road, Hunter, New York 12442   (518) 263-4133

The Franklin Autograph Society   National Bank Building, Hatfield, Pennsylvania 19440
(215) 362-0976

4. AUTOMOBILE PARTS

There are many collectors of old automobiles and automobile parts, instruction books, and memorabilia. This collecting field has been covered at length in many other publications. Check at your library for more information about local clubs and events.

CLUBS

Antique Automobile Club of America   501 West Governor Road, Hershey, Pennsylvania 17033 (717) 534-1910
This club publishes *Antique Automobile,* a bimonthly magazine.

Automobile License Plate Collectors Association, Inc.   P.O. Box 712, Weston, West Virginia 26452   (304) 842-3773
The *ALPCA Newsletter* is published bimonthly.

Contemporary Historical Vehicle Association   P.O. Box 40, Antioch, Tennessee 37013 (615) 776-2424
The magazine *Action Era Vehicle* is published 6 times a year and is about collectors' cars.

Hubcap Collectors Club   P.O. Box 54, Buckley, Michigan 49620
The *Hubcap Collector Newsletter* is published 3 times a year. It is an illustrated, mimeographed 10-page letter about hubcaps.

Spark Plug Collectors of America   P.O. Box 2229, Ann Arbor, Michigan 48106 (313) 994-3101
The club newsletter, *The Ignitor,* contains articles, pictures, original spark plug ads, members' want ads, etc. The club also publishes *Spark Plug Brand Names, 1890–1980,* a list of all known spark plug brand names. It is available for $5.00.

REPAIR SERVICE

J & J Chrome Plating & Metal Finishing Corporation   101 Orange Avenue, West Haven, Connecticut 06516   (203) 934-8510
This firm specializes in antique car, motorcycle, and boat work. Their services include triple plating show chrome as well as plating, polishing, and buffing copper, nickel, and chrome. For estimates by

mail send complete details and enclose a photo or sketch of the piece including its measurements and condition. Also include a self-addressed, stamped envelope.

PRICE GUIDE
Kruse Classic Auction Company *Kruse Professional Price Guide to Collector Cars,* 2nd ed. Orlando, Florida: House of Collectibles, 1980.

5. BARBED WIRE AND INSULATORS

The first barbed wire was patented by Lucien Smith of Kent, Ohio, in 1867. Over 1,500 different varieties of barbed wire are known to collectors, who prefer pieces 18 inches long. Telephone and telegraph insulators have been collected since the 1960s by serious collectors who know the makers, use, and patent histories of the various insulators. Don't ever try to take an insulator from the top of a pole. Often you will find old insulators buried at the base of the pole, left by repairmen. *See also* Chapter 75, Telephone Collectibles.

CLUBS
California Barbed Wire Collectors Association 1046 North San Carlos Street, Porterville, California 93257   (209) 784-9105
California Barbs is a monthly newsletter for members listing club events.

International Barbed Wire Collectors Historical Society   c/o Jack Glover, Sunset Trading Post, Sunset, Texas 76270
International Barbed Wire Gazette is a monthly magazine for members. It includes articles and buy-and-sell ads.

New Mexico Barbed Wire Collectors Association   2816 Camino Principe, Santa Fe, New Mexico 87501
Wire Barb & Nail is a bimonthly newsletter to members including articles and ads.

PUBLICATION
Insulators, Crown Jewels of the Wire   Route 1, P.O. Box 475, Chico, California 95926
This monthly magazine includes listings for conventions, shows, articles, and buy-and-sell ads.

DECODING ADVERTISING COPY

Reading ads for antiques and collectibles often takes special knowledge. Two collectors will speak a certain jargon in the same way that two doctors have a vocabulary known only by those in their profession. To identify barbed wire see Jack Glover's *The "Bobbed Wire" II Bible* (privately printed in 1971 by Sunset Trading Post, Sunset, Texas 76270), which lists pictures and numbers 488 styles of barbed wire. These numbers are used in the ads.

6. BARBER POLES

The barber pole is said to have been made to represent the blood-soaked rags wrapped around the pole in earlier days. The red and white striped pole has been a symbol of the pharmacist or barber since the eighteenth century. Today, the old barber pole is considered folk art.

PARTS AND SUPPLIES

William Marvy Company   1540 St. Clair Avenue, St. Paul, Minnesota 55105   (612) 698-0726
This is the last remaining company in North America that manufactures barber poles and barber pole replacement parts. Parts include glass outer cylinders, paper inner cylinders, replacement lamps, domes, motors, etc. Price lists are available.

7. BAROMETERS

The barometer was invented by Evangelista Torricelli in Florence, Italy, in the 1640s. It measures the change in air pressure and helps indicate changes in weather. Many eighteenth- and nineteenth-century barometers still exist and, like all sensitive scientific instruments, often need repair.

PARTS AND SUPPLIES

Century Glass & Mirror, Inc.   1417 North Washington, Dallas, Texas 75204   (214) 823-7773
Services include custom beveling, sandblast etching, and glass molding. Send patterns for price quotes.

John Morgan   443 Metropolitan Avenue, Brooklyn, New York 11211
John Morgan offers bent glass replacement parts for barometers.

REPAIR SERVICES

Den of Antiquity   138 Charles Street, Boston, Massachusetts 02114   (617) 367-6190
This firm repairs antique mercury barometers. Call or write for more information.

John N. Lewis   156 Scarboro Drive, York, Pennsylvania 17403   (717) 848-1080
Services include mechanical repair and complete restoration of antique barometers. Barometers are also bought and sold.

Santa Fe Glass & Mirror Company, Inc.   P.O. Box 2002, Santa Fe, New Mexico 87501
(505) 982-3828
This firm supplies beveled glass replacements for antique clocks, barometers, and other instruments. If necessary, it will custom form pieces to replace curved or convex glass. Submit a detailed description of the work needed, or ship the article needing repair to the company for an accurate price estimate.

Henry F. Witzenberger   15 Po Lane, Hicksville, New York 11801   (516) 935-7432
Mr. Witzenberger repairs all types of mercury and aneroid barometers. He asks that the barometer be carefully packed in a case in which the repaired instrument can be returned, but, if possible, the customer should pick up the repaired barometer in person to prevent further damage. Clock repair is also available. Allow ample time for restoration.

BUYING BY MAIL

The Compass   Kenneth Nebenzahl, Inc., 333 North Michigan Avenue, Chicago, Illinois 60601
A catalogue is available. When writing for information, be sure to include a self-addressed, stamped envelope.

8. BASEBALL CARDS AND RELATED ITEMS

Baseball cards and other sports cards have been collected since they were first distributed in the 1880s. The first cards were put in a pack of cigarettes or tobacco, a free advertising promotion piece. From 1910 to 1915 the cards were made by the millions; then few were made until the 1930s. The second interest in baseball cards came with candy and gum companies. The modern baseball card really started in 1933 with the Goudey Gum Company. Then the war caused paper shortages and cards were not made. In 1948 the Bowman and Leaf Companies made cards. In 1951 Topps Gum Company cards were introduced.

Although baseball cards are the favorites of collectors, there are cards for other sports figures. Value is determined by condition and rarity and the popularity of the player pictured.

There are special shows and publications for the sports card collectors. Most major cities have card shows on a regular basis. Ask anyone you see selling cards where the nearest shows will be held. They are often not announced in the general publications.

Cards should be stored so that they will be dirt and insect free. Plastic holders made to hold the cards are sold through the shows and publications. You may find baseball cards at any flea market, garage sale, or rummage sale, or even in your own attic.

CLUB

Society for American Baseball Research   P.O. Box 323, Cooperstown, New York 13326
The *Baseball Research Journal,* published annually, is about the historical and statistical aspects of baseball rather than memorabilia.

PUBLICATIONS

Baseball Cards   700 East State Street, Iola, Wisconsin 54990   (715) 445-2214
Baseball cards, other sports cards, and related collectibles are covered in this full-size magazine with articles, ads, show schedules, etc.

Baseball Hobby News   P.O. Box 128, Glen Cove, New York 11542
This is a monthly newspaper with buy and sell ads and articles about old and new baseball cards.

Sports Collectors Digest   P.O. Box E, Milan, Michigan 48160   (313) 439-8733
This magazine is published bimonthly.

Card Prices Update   P.O. Box 500, Selden, New York 11784   (800) 645-1054
This is a monthly newspaper listing prices and events.

The Trader Speaks   3 Pleasant Drive, Lake Ronkonkoma, New York 11779   (516) 981-6915
This is a monthly magazine featuring ads of cards for sale and a few articles.

The Wrapper   309 Iowa Court, Carol Stream, Illinois 60187   (312) 668-2696
The Wrapper is a newsletter published 8 times a year and is available by subscription.
It is for collectors of nonsports cards, sports and nonsports wrappers, and related ephemera.

PRICE GUIDES

Beckett, James, and Eckes, Dennis W. *Sport Americana Baseball Card Price Guide,* No. 3.
Privately printed, 1981 (P.O. Box 606, Laurel, Maryland 20810).

Erbe, Ron. *The American Premium Guide to Baseball Cards, Identification and Values 1880–1981.*
Florence, Alabama: Books Americana, 1982.

————. *Pocket Guide to Baseball Cards, 1960–81.*
Florence, Alabama: Books Americana, 1982.

Official 1983 Pete Rose Price Guide to Baseball Cards, The.
Orlando, Florida: House of Collectibles, 1982.

Sikes, Richard and Mark. *1981 Non Sports Cards.*
Privately printed, 1981 (P.O. Box 3092, Springfield, Massachusetts 01101).

Sugar, Bert Randolph. *The Sports Collectors Bible,* 3rd ed.
Indianapolis: Bobbs-Merrill, 1979.

BUYING BY MAIL

Each of these firms has a catalogue or list available and there is a charge for some. When writing for information, be sure to include a self-addressed, stamped envelope.

Baseball Advertiser   1000 North Division Street, Peekskill, New York 10566   (914) 739-0161

Den's Collectors Den   P.O. Box 606, Laurel, Maryland 20707
A catalogue is issued twice a year.

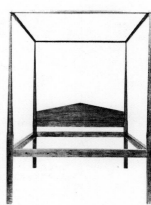

9. BEDS AND BED HANGINGS

Some people hesitate to buy antique beds because they worry about technical problems such as special mattresses and special restoration techniques, but these can be solved in a number of ways.

1. Measure your antique bed carefully before buying it. Make sure the bed is not too high for your ceiling, because surgery on the bedposts reduces the value of the bed.

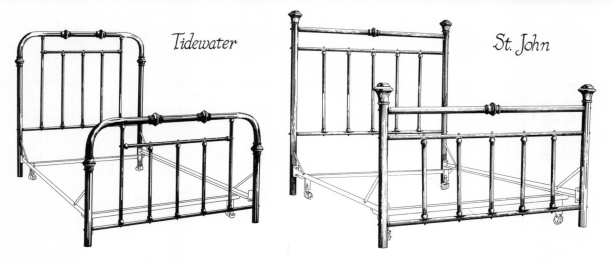

Tidewater   *St. John*

2. Rope "springs" are satisfactory, but they must be properly laced and tightened periodically. A box spring can also be used so long as it is supported by metal brackets. Standard brackets can be screwed to the frame, but the best solution is to have six or eight hanging supports custom made by an ornamental ironworker. These do not harm the frame or reduce the value of the bed. If the box spring combined with a standard mattress is too high, a thinner foam rubber mattress can be substituted.

3. Odd-size mattresses and box springs can be custom made in most major cities, or ordered by mail.

4. Antique-style bed hangings and rope springs are also available.

It is best to be sure your bed is one of the standard sizes in use today if you plan to use easily available sheets and bedspreads.

Brass beds require special care; restoration for these is discussed in Chapter 43, Metal Antiques and Collectibles. *See also* Chapter 30, Furniture—General, Chapter 43, Metal Antiques and Collectibles, and Chapter 76, Textiles.

PARTS AND SUPPLIES

Austin Farm House   P.O. Box 815, Richmond, Virginia 23207   (804) 353-2349
The Austin Farm House specializes in hand-tied fishnet canopies for tester beds, custom handmade bedspreads and dust ruffles, and authentic reproductions of colonial designs. Send appropriate bed measurements.

The Bedpost   R.D. 1, Box 155, Pen Argyl, Pennsylvania 18072   (215) 588-3824
The Bedpost specializes in brass beds, scroll bending, brass tubing, finials, post caps, and other ornaments. A brochure and a price list are available.

Nancy Borden   P.O. Box 4381, Portsmouth, New Hampshire 03801   (603) 436-4284
Nancy Borden sells hand-sewn replicas of eighteenth- and nineteenth-century bed hangings, curtains, and upholstering made from museum-documented reproduction prints and woven fabrics using period construction trims and hanging techniques. Consultation by appointment.

Cohasset Colonials   502EX Ship Street, Cohasset, Massachusetts 02025   (617) 383-0110
Cohasset Colonials is the original manufacturer of reproduction Colonial American furniture kits. It also sells accessories, including fabrics, canopies of hand-tied cotton, and trundle mattresses. For custom fitting send a sketch with dimensions. A catalogue is available; send $1.00 to the above address.

Mary K II

Queen Anne

The Country Bed Shop   P.O. Box 222, Groton, Massachusetts 01450   (617) 448-6336
The Country Bed Shop specializes in re-creating the bedsteads and bed hangings of the seventeenth and eighteenth centuries. Rope, straining wrenches, and pins are available, as well as hardware for other types of springs. Bed hangings and matching window curtains are made to order in documented styles and fabrics. Phone ahead before visiting the shop. A catalogue is available for $3.00.

Laura Copenhaver Industries, Inc.   "Rosemont," Marion, Virginia 24354   (703) 783-4663
Hand-tied fishnet canopies for tester beds, coverlets, and quilts (including reproductions of authentic designs) can be ordered by mail. A catalogue is available. When writing for information, be sure to include a self-addressed, stamped envelope.

Paxton Hardware Company   Upper Falls, Maryland 21156   (301) 592-8505
Bolt covers, rail fasteners, bed bolts, spring supports, and bed bolt wrenches are available from Paxton. Send $1.50 for a catalogue.

Sleep Tite Mattress Company   8 Moore Street, Middletown, Ohio 45042   (513) 422-9206
Mattresses and box springs of any size are made to order in soft, medium, firm, or extra firm. Call or write for more information.

Splendor in Brass Ltd.   123 Market Street, Havre de Grace, Maryland 21078   (301) 939-1312
This firm manufactures solid brass beds. Included are the Victoria, Empire, Queen Anne, and the Regency. All beds are available with marble or porcelain inserts, and headboards may be ordered with or without the frame. Most beds are available in twin, double, queen, and king sizes. Catalogues are available.

Truman Boyle Mattress Company   600 South Washington Street, Alexandria, Virginia 22314 (703) 548-6722
The Truman Boyle Mattress Company specializes in mattresses and box springs in hard-to-fit sizes and shapes. A choice of ticking is available. Send specifications or call for prices. Factory showroom hours are: Weekdays 8:30 A.M. to 5:30 P.M., Saturdays 9:30 A.M. to 3:30 P.M.

REPAIR SERVICE

Abercrombie & Company   8227 Fenton Street, Silver Spring, Maryland 20910   (301) 585-2385
Abercrombie & Company repairs various metal items including brass beds.

10. BEER CANS AND BREWERIANA

The way collectors organize themselves into special interest factions with shows, publications, and clubs is often confusing. There are collectors of early tin containers (like tobacco cans) who consider themselves tin collectors and attend advertising shows. There are collectors of beer bottles who are bottle collectors, and go to bottle shows. Beer can collectors usually buy at beer can shows or flea markets. Books about beer often discuss the cans as well as the bottles and all of the brewery history that is available under a broad term of *breweriana*.

If you are interested in beer cans, be sure to check the other beer-related activities because you might find just the right sign or some "go-with" item in an unexpected place.

Care and repair of beer cans are almost the same as the repair of any commercial tin container, and more information about this can be found in Chapter 78, Tin and Toleware. Suggestions for repairing, restoring, or even making beer cans from metal can company flats can be found in the book *The Beer Can* by the Beer Can Collectors of America. Lists of beer makers and variations in can designs can be found in many books, including a series by the Beer Can Collectors of America, books by World Wide Beer Can Collectors, a series by Thomas Toepfer (L-W Promotions, Gas City, Indiana 46933), and several books by Jack Martells (Great Lakes Living Press, 3634 West 216th Street, Matteson, Illinois 60443). A two-volume *Register of United States Breweries 1876–1976* by Donald Bull (P.O. Box 106, Trumbull, Connecticut 06611) lists the companies that may have made your beer cans.

CLUBS

Beer Can Collectors of America   747 Merus Court, Fenton, Missouri 63026
Beer Can Collectors News Report is this club's publication.

Breweriana Openers Collectors Club   63 October Lane, Trumbull, Connecticut 06611
(203) 261-2398
Just for Openers includes news and pictures in a newsletter format.

The Eastern Coast Breweriana Association   961 Clintonville Road, Wallingford, Connecticut 06492

National Association of Breweriana   c/o Gordon B. Dean, Willson Memorial Drive, Chassell, Michigan 49916   (906) 523-4111
Breweriana Collector, the publication for this club, is a small magazine with articles about the history of beer companies and other breweriana.

National Pop Can Collectors (NPCC)   3014 September Drive, Joliet, Illinois 60435
(815) 436-2115
National Pop Can Collectors, a monthly, mimeographed newsletter, lists events, new issues of cans, and a few ads.

World Wide Beer Can Collectors   P.O. Box 1852, Independence, Missouri 64055
World Wide Beer Can Collectors' Newsletter is composed almost entirely of advertisements for cans.

PUBLICATIONS
The American Can Collector   P.O. Box 608-K, Mount Home, Arkansas 72653   (501) 449-5447
The American Can Collector is a monthly newspaper about beer and soda pop cans, events, and other news of interest to can collectors.

The Beer Can Advertiser & News Report   P.O. Box 373, Independence, Missouri 64051
This publication is a monthly newsletter.

Beer Cans Monthly   P.O. Box 43, Colmar, Pennsylvania 18915   (215) 699-3014
This is a monthly magazine with articles, pictures, and ads of interest to the collector.

SUPPLIES AND RESTORATION
Can World   Ridgecrest Drive, Goodlettsville, Tennessee 37072   (615) 859-5236
Can World will clean and de-rust old cans and is a source for books and supplies including steel display shelves, cleaner, and can brightener.

PRICE GUIDES
Bull, Donald. *A Price Guide to Beer Advertising Openers and Corkscrews.*
Privately printed, 1981 (P.O. Box 106, Trumbull, Connecticut 06611).

Byrne, Thomas. *The U.S. Beer Coaster Guide,* vol. 1.
Privately printed, 1980 (P.O. Box 173, East Hanover, New Jersey 07936).

BUYING BY MAIL
R. L. Dabbs-Cantique   P.O. Box 27, Walnut Hill, Illinois 62893   (618) 533-5000
This firm is a mail order beer can dealer. A catalogue is available. When writing for information, be sure to include a self-addressed, stamped envelope.

BOOKSELLER
Can World   Ridgecrest Drive, Goodlettsville, Tennessee 37072   (615) 859-5236
Can World sells books on beer can collecting and breweries.

11. BICYCLES AND MOTOR BIKES

In 1839, when the roads were rough and the way long, a blacksmith named Kirkpatrick Macmillan invented the bicycle. It weighed 57 pounds and sported a carved horsehead at its front. The years have seen many improvements including motors, steering, and rubber tires. Today, collectors of vintage motorcycles and bicycles both collect and ride the antique models.

CLUBS

Historic Motor Sports Association   P.O. Box 30628, Santa Barbara, California 93105
(805) 966-9151
Vintage Racer is a quarterly magazine for members of the Historic Motor Sports Association.

Vintage Motor Bike Club   330 East North Street, Coldwater, Ohio 45828   (419) 678-3347
The *Vintage Motor Bike Club* newsletter includes membership news and information to interest collectors—such as how to service a Whizzer transmission. It also features ads and diagrams.

The Wheelmen   Mrs. Marge Fuehrer, Treasurer, 1708 School House Lane, Ambler, Pennsylvania 19002
The Wheelmen Magazine is issued twice a year, and *The Wheelmen Newsletter* is issued quarterly, featuring want ads, events, book reviews, and short articles. *The Wheelmen Bulletins* are available to members upon request and cover a variety of topics of interest to collectors of antique bicycles.

PUBLICATION

Motorcycle Trader   P.O. Box 73-K, Folly Beach, South Carolina 29439
The *Motorcycle Trader* is an adsheet featuring items to buy, sell, or swap.

12. BOOKS AND BOOKPLATES

Books and bookplates are collected by specialists who usually find most of their collection at special sales devoted primarily to old books. Many universities and libraries run yearly sales of old or unwanted books. These sales are rarely listed in the usual antiques publications. Large flea markets and white elephant sales have used book sections where bargains can sometimes be found.

Paperback books are among the more recent interests of collectors and they can be found at the flea markets. Comic books are bought and sold at regular special sales in many cities. These sales are best found by contacting local collectors or shops that sell old comics.

Rebinding antique books reduces their value and should be avoided unless absolutely necessary. However, if you must, there are bookbinders in many cities. They are listed in the telephone book under "Bookbinders" or you can learn about them from some of the better bookstores or decorating studios.

Bookstores that sell old books can usually appraise your old books. Dealers in old or rare books are listed in the telephone Yellow Pages under "Book Dealers—Used & Rare."

CLUBS

American Society of Bookplate Collectors and Designers 1206 North Stoneman Avenue, Alhambra, California 91801
Bookplates in the News is its scholarly publication that includes information about bookplate artists and actual tipped-in bookplates.

Horatio Alger Society 4907 Allison Drive, Lansing, Michigan 48910
Newsboy is its newsletter about Horatio Alger stories and other related material including club news.

The International Society of Bible Collectors P.O. Box 2485, El Cajon, California 92021
(714) 440-5871
The Bible Collector is a newsletter for members that features club news and a few articles.

The International Wizard of Oz Club 220 North 11th Street, Escanaba, Michigan 49829
The Baum Bugle is a magazine for members that is published 3 times a year and includes stories of Oziana and the life of Frank Baum.

Manuscript Society 350 North Niagara Street, Burbank, California 91505
Manuscripts is a publication for members of the Society.

CHARLES DICKENS.

Masthead Society   P.O. Box 1009, Marblehead, Massachusetts 01945
Masthead: A Journal for Teaching History with Old Newspapers is a newspaper for members.

PUBLICATIONS
AB Bookman's Weekly   P.O. Box AB, Clifton, New Jersey 07015   (201) 772-0020
This is a weekly, 3-part magazine for the book trade and libraries that includes: editorials, articles, and news about the trade (including book auctions); books wanted by dealers and libraries (this is the largest section of the magazine); and books for sale.

The Book-Mart   P.O. Box 72, Lake Wales, Florida 33853   (813) 676-7035
This is a monthly magazine about old books and includes ads for buying and selling books.

Fine Print   P.O. Box 7741, San Francisco, California 94120
This quarterly newsletter announces newly issued books of private presses as well as news notes on hand bookbinding, calligraphy, papermaking, and anything pertaining to the history of books.

Geographic Collectors' Newsletter   c/o Edwin C. Buxbaum, P.O. Box 465, Wilmington, Delaware 19899
This is the newsletter of *National Geographic* magazine and lists additional books, magazines, and newspapers.

Illustration Collectors Newsletter   Illustration House, 53 Water Street, South Norwalk, Connecticut 06854   (203) 838-0486
This newsletter is published 1 to 3 times a year and is an illustrated report of original illustrators' art sold during the preceding year. Auction prices are included.

HOW-TO-FIX-IT BOOKS
Horton, Carolyn. *Conservation of Library Materials: Cleaning and Preserving Bindings and Related Materials.* Chicago: American Library Association, 1969.

Muir, David. *Binding and Repairing Books by Hand.*
New York: Arco Publishing, 1977.

Rare Book and Paper Repair Techniques. American Association for State and Local History, 708 Berry Road, Nashville, Tennessee 37204. Leaflet.

Waters, Peter. *Procedures for Salvage of Water-Damaged Library Materials.*
Washington, D.C.: Library of Congress, 1975.

REPAIR SERVICES
Adolphus Bindery   P.O. Box 2085, Austin, Texas 78768   (512) 444-6616
This is a hand bindery specializing in restoration. Questions are answered by mail for a fee.

Archival Conservation Center, Inc.   8225 Daly Road, Cincinnati, Ohio 45231   (513) 521-9858
This firm restores Bibles, paper documents, prints, and does hand bookbinding. A brochure is available.

The Bindery   Julie B. Stackpole, Polpis Road, Route 3, Nantucket, Massachusetts 02554
(617) 228-4003
Julie B. Stackpole specializes in bookbinding and rare book restoration. There is an hourly fee for restoration work, examination of book, and time spent on giving an estimate or opinion. There is a 3-year waiting list for this work.

Linda A. Blaser   9200 Hawkins Creamery Road, Gaithersburg, Maryland 20760   (301) 774-2267
Linda A. Blaser specializes in the restoration of books and bookbindings. Estimates are free and general advice is given over the phone or by letter. There is a fee for all services performed. She has cleaned private libraries after smoke damage and offers classes on basic bookbinding at the Smithsonian, as well as privately.

The Book Doctor   984 High Street, P.O. Box 68, Harrisburg, Ohio 43126   (800) 848-7918
The Book Doctor does handcrafted custom bookbinding. Family Bible restoration is a specialty. In addition to restoring books, it offers a complete library maintenance program featuring its own leather care products made of 100 percent natural ingredients. The firm is a library binder and will duplicate fine leather bindings from the sixteenth century to the present time.

Custom Book Binding   1618 West Main Street, New Lebanon, Ohio 45345   (513) 687-1105
This firm binds hard backs and flexible back books using cloth, English Morocco leather, or cowhide. If the spine is worn and the covers are good, only the spine is replaced. A price list is available.

Jacqueline Gilliam   The Fort Worth Art Museum, 1309 Montgomery Street, Fort Worth, Texas 76107   (817) 738-9215
Jacqueline Gilliam's restoration services are available anywhere in the U.S. Works of art on paper, historical documents, globes, and articles made of papier-mâché, vellum, and parchment are restored. No estimates are given without examination.

B. & B. Gimelson Inc.   Bernard Gimelson, 96 South Limekiln Pike, Chalfont, Pennsylvania 18914   (215) 822-1393
Bernard Gimelson specializes in custom binding of books and presentation folders. A brochure is available.

Harcourt Bindery   9 & 11 Harcourt Street, Boston, Massachusetts 02116   (617) 536-5755
The Harcourt Bindery offers all types of portfolios and slipcases. Fallback or dropover boxes can be made in cloth or leather. Blank book journals, diaries, and albums are made to order. Price quotations and recommendations are given without obligation and a catalogue is sent upon request.

Carolyn Horton & Associates, Inc.   430 West 22nd Street, New York, New York 10011 (212) 989-1471
This firm specializes in the restoration of books, manuscripts, maps, and works of art on paper. All work must be examined before an opinion can be given and questions will be answered by mail. A fee of $45.00 is charged even if the work is not done. Services are available to anyone in the U.S.

James Macdonald Company, Inc.   25 Van Zant Street, East Norwalk, Connecticut 06855 (203) 853-6076
This firm restores old and rare books and executes slipcases, fine bindings, and falldown boxes for rare items.

J. Franklin Mowery   201 East Capitol Street, S.E., Washington, D.C. 20003   (202) 544-4600
J. Franklin Mowery will restore rare books, manuscripts, prints, and fine design bindings. Services are available to anyone in the U.S. and questions will be answered by mail.

Stella Patri   1828 Mason Street, San Francisco, California 94133   (415) 982-2595
Stella Patri does restoration and appraisals of books and manuscripts.

Kathleen Wick   41 West Cedar, Boston, Massachusetts 02114
Kathleen Wick does bookbinding and some repair work.

PRICE GUIDES

Cameron, Robert, and Hamaker, Charles. *Price Guide to Rare and Desirable Photography Books and Albums.*
Morris, Connecticut: Robert Shuhi Books, n.d.

Leab, Katherine and Daniel, eds. *American Book Prices Current.*
New York: Dodd, Mead, 1981.

McCulloch, Lou. *Children's Books of the 19th Century.*
Des Moines: Wallace-Homestead, 1979.

Overstreet, Robert M. *The Comic Book Price Guide #12.*
New York: Harmony Books, 1982.

Resnick, Michael. *The Official Price Guide to Comic and Science Fiction Books.*
Orlando, Florida: House of Collectibles, 1980.

Rodger, William. *The Official Price Guide to Old Books and Autographs,* 2nd ed.
Orlando, Florida: House of Collectibles, 1979.

Standard Value Guide Old Books, The, 2nd ed.
Paducah, Kentucky: Collector Books, 1979.

EX·LIBRIS
EDWARD
P·EDKINS
CLARKE

BUYING BY MAIL

Hundreds of dealers and collectors buy and sell old books by mail. Lists of books available are advertised in most of the publications about books (see Chapter 12, Books, Publications; Chapter 99, General Publications; and Chapter 91, Booksellers). For dealers and auction houses, see Chapter 89, Auction Houses; Chapter 90, Auctions by Mail; and Chapter 92, Buying by Mail.

APPRAISERS

Ingeborg R. Baum, ASA   1733 Sixteenth Street, N.W., Washington, D.C. 20009
Ingeborg R. Baum appraises rare books.

Fletcher's Books and Antiques   P.O. Box 65, Salado, Texas 76571
This firm appraises and sells old books.

James Neill Northe   115 South Hudson, Oklahoma City, Oklahoma 73102   (405) 232-1066
James Neill Northe does appraisals of single books or libraries (by special arrangement). Send full information and $3.00 with a stamped, self-addressed return envelope. You will receive the requested information, or your $3.00 and information will be returned with a notice of any further charge, depending on the research required.

Stella Patri   1828 Mason Street, San Francisco, California 94133   (415) 982-2595
Stella Patri does restoration and appraisals of books and manuscripts.

Princeton Antiques Bookservice   2915-17 Atlantic Avenue, Atlantic City, New Jersey 08401 (609) 344-1943
This firm does appraisals for estates, insurance, and taxation purposes, etc. A brochure is available.

Sam Yudkin & Associates   Booksellers, Book & Print Auctions, 1125 King Street, Alexandria, Virginia 22314   (703) 549-9330
This firm appraises any paper items including stamps and money. Its fee is usually 5 percent of the appraised value. Minimums depend on items and locations.

BOOKSELLERS

Books about how to buy and sell old books can be found in a good bookstore or library. Many of these books are available through the mail order antiques book dealers listed in Chapter 91 or through dealers listed in the specialized publications about books (see Chapter 12, Books, Publications).

13. BOTTLES AND GO-WITHS

Bottle collecting is a family hobby. Some of the best bottles are dug from old dumps, construction sites, old privies, or pulled from river bottoms. Like many other hobbies, bottle digging requires the proper equipment and training. Do not try to dig before learning the basic rules. Digging is fun but can be dangerous to the inexperienced. Local bottle clubs always welcome members and bottle shows are filled with collectors who delight in talking about their hobby and the bottles they have found.

There are all types of old bottles including inkwells, flasks, bitters, medicines, poisons, and whiskeys. Many collectors search for recent bottles such as milk bottles, fruit jars, and the new bottles which include the figural whiskeys such as Jim Beam, Ezra Brooks, or Ski Country. Some manufacturers of bottles now have their own publications and books which are usually available at the bottle shows. Check our club and publication lists carefully to determine the type of bottle you want to collect.

"Go-withs" are the accessories that can "go with" a bottle and delight a bottle collector. They include openers, corkscrews, advertising materials, and even the fruit jar rubber rings that were used on the closures.

Never display glass bottles in a sunny window. The sun may color the glass, or the combination of the glass and sun may cause a fire. Beware of "sick" bottles. The inside of one is usually etched and the bottle appears cloudy. It is possible to polish the inside of a bottle but it is very expensive, requires talent, and is a risky repair. Watch out for bottles repaired with the new plastics. Some of these repairs are invisible except under black light. *See also* Chapter 87, Writing Utensils, for inkwells.

CLUBS

American Collectors of Infant Feeders   540 Croyden Road, Cheltenham, Pennsylvania 19012 (215) 379-2323
Keeping Abreast is the quarterly newsletter for this club.

Bud Hastin's National Avon Collector's Club   P.O. Box 12088, Overland Park, Kansas 66212
The *Avon Times* is 16 pages of Avon collector gossip and ads for buying or selling Avon bottles.

The Federation of Historical Bottle Clubs   10118 Schuessler, St. Louis, Missouri 63128
(314) 843-7573
The Federation Letter is a pamphlet featuring events in the bottle world, chapter activities, and a few articles about bottles.

International Association of Jim Beam Bottle & Specialties Club   c/o Mrs. Shirley Clark, 5120 Belmont Road, Suite D, Downers Grove, Illinois 60515   (312) 963-8980
Beam Around the World is a newsletter with ads for new bottles, events, books, and information about club activities.

Lionstone Bottle Collectors of America   P.O. Box 2418, Chicago, Illinois 60690
Lionstone Collector is a company-produced newsletter about recently released bottles. It includes large pictures.

Michter's National Collectors Society   P.O. Box 481, Schaefferstown, Pennsylvania 17088
The Michter's Collector is a company-produced newsletter with information of interest to employees and Michter bottle collectors.

Milkbottles Only Organization (MOO)   P.O. Box 5456, Newport News, Virginia 23605
The Milking Parlor, the organization's chatty, mimeographed newsletter, includes membership news, facts about milk bottles and the dairy industry, and some ads to buy or sell milk bottles.

National Ezra Brooks Bottle & Specialties Club   420 West First Street, Kewanee, Illinois 61443
This club offers information about new Ezra Brooks releases.

National Grenadier Bottle Club   3108A West Meinecke Avenue, Milwaukee, Wisconsin 53210
This manufacturer's club offers information regarding new releases.

National Ski Country Bottle Club   1224 Washington Avenue, Golden, Colorado 80401
(303) 279-3373
The Ski Country Collector, the club's publication, includes pictures of new Ski Country bottles and information about releases.

P.O.P.S. (Procurers of Painted-label Sodas)   P.O. Box 8154, Houston, Texas 76104
(713) 523-4346
POPS is a monthly newsletter for members.

Western World Avon Club   P.O. Box 27587, San Francisco, California 94127
Western World Avon Collectors Newsletter is a good source for buying and selling Avon bottles. The newsletter also includes a few other articles and club news.

World Wide Avon Collectors Club   44021 Seventh Street East, Lancaster, California 93534 (805) 948-8849
World Wide Avon News is a newspaper completely filled with buy and sell ads of interest to Avon collectors.

PUBLICATIONS

Antique Bottle Collecting   85 Cartway, Bridgnorth, Salop, England
This is a monthly magazine about English bottle collecting.

Antique Bottle World   5003 West Berwyn, Chicago, Illinois 60630   (513) 236-2165
This publication includes articles about old bottles, ads to buy and sell old bottles, and listings of shows and events.

Fruit Jar Newsletter   7 Lowell Place, West Orange, New Jersey 07052
Fruit Jar Newsletter has collector information about old jars including pictures, trademarks, patent information, and buy and sell information.

Milk House Moosletter   The Time Travelers, P.O. Box 366, Bryn Mawr, California 92318
This newsletter has articles about old dairies, bottles, and other facts of the dairy business as well as buy and sell ads.

The Milk Route   4 Ox Bow Road, Westport, Connecticut 06880
The Milk Route is a newsletter on milk bottles and go-withs. It includes a bottle exchange column and informative articles about the entire dairy industry.

The Miniature Bottle Collector   P.O. Box 2161, Palos Verdes Peninsula, California 90274
This is a magazine for collectors of modern and old miniature bottles. It is illustrated and lists local clubs for miniature bottle collecting.

Miniature Bottle Mart   24 Gertrude Lane, West Haven, Connecticut 06516
This illustrated monthly newsletter includes articles and ads for old and new miniature bottles.

Old Bottle Magazine   P.O. Box 243, Bend, Oregon 97701
This illustrated monthly magazine lists events and shows and includes articles and many ads. It also sells books about bottles.

The Opener   95 Apple Valley Road, Stamford, Connecticut 06903   (203) 329-9961
This is a quarterly newsletter for the collector of bottle openers.

Pictorial Bottle Review   P.O. Box 2161, Palos Verdes Peninsula, California 90274
This illustrated monthly magazine is for collectors of modern bottles. It includes ads and listings for events and local clubs.

DECODING ADVERTISING COPY

Reading the ads for antiques and collectibles often takes special knowledge. Two collectors will speak a special language in the same way two doctors have a vocabulary known only to their profession. When looking up bottles it might help to know these terms and abbreviations. Some abbreviations consist of numbers used in particular authoritative books on special types of bottles. Also, look up the abbreviations listed in Chapter 31, Glass.

ABM. Automatic bottle machine, a twentieth-century bottle made by machine.

B-xx refers to medicine bottles listed in *A Collector's Guide to Patent and Proprietary Medicine Bottles of the Nineteenth Century* by Joseph K. Baldwin (New York: Thomas Nelson, 1973).

B-xx can also refer to milk glass found in *Milk Glass* by E. M. Belknap (New York: Crown Publishers, 1969).

BIMAL. Blown in mold, applied lip.

BIMALOP. Blown in mold, applied lip, open pontil.

C-xx refers to ink bottles listed in *Ink Bottles and Inkwells* by William E. Covill, Jr. (Taunton, Massachusetts: William S. Sullwold Publishers, 1971).

Coffin. A shape, often for a poison bottle or a flask.

Dug. This bottle was dug from the ground.

FB. Free blown.

McK G-xx refers to flasks listed in *American Bottles & Flasks and Their Ancestry* by George L. and Helen McKearin (New York: Crown Publishers, 1959).

OP. Open pontil.

Owl. Usually refers to a bottle used by the Owl drugstore although some figural bottles are shaped like owls.

Picnic. A bottle shape.

Pumpkinseed. A special flaw, a bubble formed in the making of the bottle.

R-xx refers to bottles listed in *For Bitters Only* by Carlyn Ring, privately printed, 1981 (59 Livermore Road, Wellesley, Massachusetts 02181).

SC. Sun-colored; the bottle was exposed to the sun and changed color.

SCA. Sun-colored amethyst.

Van R-xx refers to flasks listed in *Early American Bottles & Flasks,* revised edition by Stephen Van Rensselaer, privately printed, 1969 (J. Edmund Edwards, 61 Winton Place, Stratford, Connecticut 06497).

W-xx refers to bitters bottles listed in *Bitters Bottles* and *Supplement to Bitters Bottles* by Richard Watson (Camden, New Jersey: Thomas Nelson & Sons, 1965 and 1968).

Figural bottles are sometimes described with a reference to the book *American Pressed Glass and Figure Bottles* by A. Christian Revi (New York: Thomas Nelson & Sons, 1964).

BOOK OF MARKS

Toulouse, Julian Harrison. *Bottle Makers and Their Marks.*
Camden, New Jersey: Thomas Nelson, Inc., 1971.

PARTS AND SUPPLIES

Abercrombie & Company   8227 Fenton Street, Silver Spring, Maryland 20910   (301) 585-2385
This firm supplies metal tops for shakers and bottles.

PRICE GUIDES

Cembura, Al, and Avery, Constance. *A Guide to Jim Beam Bottles.*
Privately printed, 1981 (139 Arlington Avenue, Berkeley, California 94707).

————. *Jim Beam Regal China Go-Withs.*
Privately printed, 1979 (139 Arlington Avenue, Berkeley, California 94707).

Cleveland, Hugh. *Bottle Pricing Guide,* rev. 3rd ed.
Paducah, Kentucky: Collector Books, 1980.

Creswick, Alice M. *The Red Book of Fruit Jars, No. 4.*
Privately printed, 1982 (0-8525 Kenowa S.W., Grand Rapids, Michigan 49504).

Hastin, Bud and Vickie. *The 1981 Bud Hastin's Avon Bottle Encyclopedia.*
Privately printed, 1981 (P.O. Box 8400, Ft. Lauderdale, Florida 33310).

Kay, Robert E. *Miniature Beer Bottles & Go-Withs.*
Batavia, Illinois: K & K Publishers, 1981.

Kovel, Ralph and Terry. *The Kovels' Bottle Price List,* 6th ed.
New York: Crown Publishers, 1982.

Montague, H. F. *Montague's Modern Bottle Identification and Price Guide,* 2nd ed.
Privately printed, 1980 (H. F. Montague Enterprises, P.O. Box 4059, 7919 Grant, Overland Park,
Kansas 66204).

Ohio Bottles, 10th Anniversary Edition.
Barberton, Ohio: Ohio Bottle Club, 1981.

Roberts, Mike. *Price Guide to All the Flasks.*
Newark, Ohio: Walker Press, 1980.

Sellari, Carlo and Dot. *Bottles Old and New,* 4th ed.
Orlando, Florida: House of Collectibles, 1979.

————. *Hutchinson Bottles.*
Covington, Tennessee: Sellari Publishing Company, 1981.

Toulouse, Julian Harrison. *Fruit Jars, Collectors' Manual with Prices.*
Hanover, Pennsylvania: Everybodys Press, 1977.

Triffon, James A. *The Whiskey Miniature Bottle Collection.*
Privately printed, 1981 (P.O. Box 1900, Garden Grove, California 92640).

Tutton, John. *Udder Delight.*
Privately printed, 1981 (Route 1, Box 261, Marshall, Virginia 22115).

Weiss, Joe. *Avon 6.*
San Francisco: Western World, 1981 (P.O. Box 27587, San Francisco, California 94127).

BUYING BY MAIL

Hundreds of dealers and collectors buy and sell bottles by mail. Lists of bottles available are advertised in most of the bottle publications (see Chapter 13, Bottles, Publications). Lists may be free or about 50¢ to $2.00 to cover postage.

BOOKSELLERS

Recently published bottle books are found in most bookstores. Privately printed books about bottles are sold by most major mail order book dealers (see Chapter 91, Booksellers). Several of the major publications about bottle collecting offer books through the magazine or newspaper (see Chapter 13, Bottles, Publications).

14. BUTTONS

If you find an old box of buttons, look carefully at its contents. You may have a button string, a special group of buttons that are strung together on one piece of thread. These have special value to collectors. Other buttons are saved for their beauty, rarity, or intrinsic value.

CLUBS

The National Button Society   2733 Juno Place, Akron, Ohio 44313
The National Button Bulletin is published 6 times a year for members.

The Buttonhook Society   83 Loose Road, Maidstone, Kent ME15 7DA England
The Boutonneur is a newsletter with articles, history, and buying information.

PUBLICATION

Creative Button Bulletin   26 Meadowbrook Lane, Chalfont, Pennsylvania 18914
This newsletter offers modern buttons for sale and has articles about old buttons.

15. CARROUSELS

The carrousel animal has become an accepted part of American folk art. Museums and collectors are adding the horses, carvings, crestings, chariots, and musical mechanisms to their collections.

It is best to keep most of these wood carvings in unrestored condition unless the finish has deteriorated or been badly damaged. There are restorers who remove the old finish and repaint the animals, or who restore damaged wood and finish. Have as little done as possible and do not restore one of these figures yourself unless you are talented and trained. A bad restoration can destroy the resale value.

CLUB
American Carousel Society c/o Joy Smith, 1785 South Forest Hill Road, Troy, Ohio 45373 (513) 335-6833
The society publishes a newsletter and booklets at random for its members.

PUBLICATION
Carrousel Art Magazine P.O. Box 992, Garden Grove, California 92642 (714) 534-1700
This is a quarterly magazine with articles on collecting, restoring, and displaying carrousel figures, illustrations, and ads for those interested in merry-go-rounds and associated memorabilia.

REPAIR SERVICES
Carrousel Midwest Highway 83, Box 97, North Lake, Wisconsin 53064 (414) 966-2182
Restoration costs from $400.00 to $1,000.00 per animal, depending on its condition and size. New twisted brass stands for carrousel figures are available for standing or prancing figures and jumpers.

Gray Sales, Inc. Amusement Equipment, P.O. 4732, Surfside Beach, South Carolina 29577 (803) 238-0251
This firm does carrousel figure restorations.

APPRAISER
Gray Sales, Inc. Amusement Equipment, P.O. Box 4732, Surfside Beach, South Carolina 29577 (803) 238-0251
This firm appraises carrousel figures.

16. CASH REGISTERS

The old brass cash register is now wanted by both collector and shopkeeper. Many are in use in stores that feature nostalgia. The machines made by NCR or other companies still in business can often be restored by the company. Call the local salesman to see if it is possible. Remember that inflation has had many influences; early machines register only to $10.00 or perhaps $100.00, not the high numbers seen today.

RESTORATION, PARTS, AND SUPPLIES

Play It Again Sam 5343 West Devon, Chicago, Illinois 60646 (312) 763-1771
This firm restores antique cash registers and supplies parts. A brochure is available.

The Vintage Cash Register & Slot Machine Company 13448 Ventura Boulevard, Sherman Oaks, California 91403
This firm restores antique brass National Cash Registers. It maintains a large inventory and also carries cash register parts. Send a self-addressed, stamped envelope for a price list.

17. CHAIRS

Our ancestors seem to have delighted in surrounding themselves with chairs. Inventories of homes from the late eighteenth century list over a dozen chairs even in small bedrooms. We often wonder how they found room for all of them. Whatever their reason, the chair is still one of the most popular and numerous pieces of furniture in a home. An odd chair from a different period can often be placed in a room as a special accent as well as a useful place for people to sit.

Refinishing and restoring chairs can be handled by most amateurs. Recaning, upholstering, and some more complicated parts of refinishing may require a few special lessons, but many adult education centers and schools offer this type of instruction. Libraries are filled with books that will furnish detailed refinishing information. Most of these services are available through local decorating shops or services. Look in the Yellow Pages of the telephone book under "Caning," "Furniture Repairing and Refinishing," and "Upholsterers." *See also* Chapter 30, Furniture—General.

HOW-TO-FIX-IT BOOKS

Blanchard, Roberta Ray. *How to Restore and Decorate Chairs in Early American Styles.*
New York: Dover, 1981.

Cane Seats for Chairs.
Ithaca: Cornell University, Media Services Distribution Center (7 Research Park, Ithaca, New York 14850), n.d. Leaflet.

Hong Kong Grass, Rope and Twine Seats of Chairs.
Ithaca: Cornell University, Media Services Distribution Center (7 Research Park, Ithaca, New York 14850), n.d. Leaflet.

Perry, L. Day. *Seat Weaving: A Manual for Furniture Fixers.*
New York: Charles Scribner's, 1977.

Rush Seats for Chairs.
Ithaca: Cornell University, Media Services Distribution Center (7 Research Park, Ithaca, New York 14850), n.d. Leaflet.

Sober, Marion Burr. *Chair Seat Weaving for Antique Chairs.*
Privately printed, 1964 (P.O. Box 294, Plymouth, Michigan 48170).

Splint Seats for Chairs.
Ithaca: Cornell University, Media Services Distribution Center (7 Research Park, Ithaca, New York 14850), n.d. Leaflet.

PARTS AND SUPPLIES

Alexandria Wood Joinery   George and Judy Whittaker, Plumer Hill Road, Alexandria, New Hampshire 03222   (603) 744-8243
The Alexandria Wood Joinery offers chair seats of handwoven cane, press-in cane, splint, natural and fiber rush, and Shaker tape. They also do furniture repair and refinishing. No price list or literature is available as all work is done on a custom basis.

Barap Specialties   835 Bellows, Frankfort, Michigan 49635
Barap offers flat reed, fiber rush, cane webbing, and cane and reed spline for replacing worn seats on chairs. The flat reed comes in ⅜-inch and ½-inch sizes and is sold in 1-pound hanks. The fiber rush is made from a tough grade of kraft paper twisted into a strand to resemble rush. The fiber will wear as well as the genuine rush, yet it is easier to work with because it is supplied in a continuous piece. Cane webbing is offered in a fine open weave or a close modern weave. Cane comes in 5 different sizes from superfine (1/16 inch wide) to common (5/32-inch wide). A catalogue is available for 50¢.

Bedell Manufacturing Company P.O. Box 626, 2704 Dorr Avenue, Merrifield, Virginia 22116 (703) 573-7090
This company manufactures replacement springs for Victorian platform rockers as well as helical springs for porch and outdoor furniture.

Cane and Basket Supply Company 1238 South Cochran Avenue, Los Angeles, California 90019 (213) 939-9644
This firm offers supplies needed for caning, from instruction booklets to tools and kits. Machine-woven cane is also available. The catalogue is $1.00.

The Canery 224 South Liberty Street Annex, Winston-Salem, North Carolina 27101 (919) 724-9361
The Canery sells chair caning supplies and instruction booklets. Call or write for more information.

The Cane-ery P.O. Drawer 17113, Nashville, Tennessee 37217
This firm handles cane, fiber rush, rattan, Oriental seagrass, and other supplies for chair caning. Tools and instruction books are also available. Price lists are sent upon request.

Carolina Caning Supply P.O. Box 2179, Smithfield, North Carolina 27577 (919) 934-0291
Cane, reed, rush, cane webbing, reed spline, round reeds, and seagrass are available for chair caning. For a price list send a self-addressed, stamped envelope.

Chem-Clean Furniture Restoration Center U.S. Route 7, Arlington, Vermont 05250 (802) 375-2743
Chair caning supplies, medium and fine cane, hardwood pegs, instruction booklets, and brochures are available.

Connecticut Cane and Reed Company P.O. Box 1276, Manchester, Connecticut 06040 (203) 646-6586
This is primarily a mail order business and offers over 50 varieties of imported cane, reed, and rattan. There are step-by-step booklets available containing instructions for almost any type of seat weaving. Prewoven cane is also available. The brochure (with price list) is 50¢.

Finishing Products and Supply Company, Inc. 4611 Macklind Avenue, St. Louis, Missouri 63109 (314) 481-0700
Seven different widths of cane and 16 different cane webbing designs are offered by this firm. A catalogue is available for $2.00.

The Finishing Touch 5636 College Avenue, Oakland, California 94618 (415) 652-4908
The Finishing Touch offers pressed leather seats made of oak tanned hides. All seats are reproductions of original designs and are available by catalogue and shipped UPS. Machine cane products, spline, and machine cane wedges are also available along with instructions. A catalogue is available upon request.

Frank's Cane and Rush Supply   7244 Heil Avenue, Huntington Beach, California 92647
(714) 847-0707
This firm carries an assortment of caning and rattan products. Natural strand cane, binder cane, flat fiber, fiber rush, Oriental seagrass, and natural cane webbing are offered. Tools and implements are also available. A catalogue is sent upon request.

Furniture Revival and Company   P.O. Box 994, 580 Southwest Twin Oaks Circle, Corvallis, Oregon 97330   (503) 754-6323
This company offers cane webbing, reed spline, accessories, and replacement chair seats. A catalogue is available for $2.00.

Jack's Upholstery and Caning Supplies   52 Shell Court, Oswego, Illinois 60543   (312) 554-1045
This company offers a line of upholstery and caning supplies. Included in its selection are button machines, snap molds, pivot molds, foam, glue, books, springs, tacks, tools, strand cane, plastic cane, cane webbing, reed spline, rush, and more. A catalogue is available for $1.25, which is refunded after the first purchase.

Keystone   P.O. Box 3292, San Diego, California 92103   (714) 280-1337
Services include caning, spindle turning, and reproduction of wood parts. Caning materials and pressed fiber seat panels are offered. Price lists and other publications are available for a small fee.

Newell Workshop   19 Blaine Avenue, Hinsdale, Illinois 60521
Newell Workshop offers a caning kit that includes the tools, caning material, and instructions to hand cane one average chair. This kit was primarily developed for the beginner so no previous knowledge is necessary. Write or call for more information.

Nu-Cane Seat Company   P.O. Box 995, Lawrence, Massachusetts 01842
This firm manufactures replacement seats using a heavy grade of ½-inch open weave cane webbing that is cut to shape and bound with a cane-color vinyl binding. The seats come in 17 sizes. The customer is supplied with decorative nails to apply to the chair. A brochure is available for $1.00, which is credited to your first purchase.

Old Hotel Antiques   68 Main Street, P.O. Box 94, Sutter Creek, California 95685   (209) 267-5901
This firm manufactures solid oak replacement trays, which are made to fit any type of old high chair. Preassembled and sanded, they are ready to stain to match your chair. There are 14 inches between arms. $24.50 each, plus shipping and handling.

Pat's Etcetera Company, Inc. (PECO)   P.O. Box 777, Smithville, Texas 78957   (512) 237-3600
PECO manufactures fiber replacement seats pressed from original dies of the 1890s. Gross dimensions on oversize embossed border seats are 14¾ inches square, and they can be smoothly cut to the desired size with a utility knife or shears. There are 8 designs available. Send a self-addressed, stamped envelope for literature.

Paxton Hardware Company   Upper Falls, Maryland 21156   (301) 592-8505
Woven cane, cane, reed, rush, seagrass cord, and spline are offered in assorted sizes. A catalogue is available for $1.50.

Peerless Rattan   45 Indian Lane East, P.O. Box 8, Towaco, New Jersey 07082   (201) 334-2867
This firm is a supplier to chair caners, furniture manufacturers, designers, and craftsmen. It offers strand cane, cane webbing, caning tools, and a chair caning kit. Several books and instruction booklets are also offered through their catalogue.

The H. H. Perkins Company   10 South Bradley Road, Woodbridge, Connecticut 06525
(203) 389-9501
The H. H. Perkins Company carries the necessary materials for chair caning. Cane, rush, Oriental grass, tools, kits, and instruction booklets are available. Catalogues and price lists are sent upon request.

E. W. Pyfer   218 North Foley Avenue, Freeport, Illinois 61032   (815) 232-8968
E. W. Pyfer manufactures chair seat replacements that are woven from natural rush, reed, and hickory splint. Chair cane and instruction books are also available. By appointment only.

Squaw Alley Incorporated   106 West Water Street, Naperville, Illinois 60540   (312) 357-0200
This firm offers caning supplies and pressed fiber chair replacement seats made of top quality birch plyboard. Seat boards are untrimmed so that you can trim and shape them to fit your chair. Two catalogues are available: caning supplies, $2.00; pressed fiber replacement seats, $1.00.

The Waymar Company   1165 First Capitol Drive, Saint Charles, Missouri 63301   (314) 946-5811
This company manufactures reproduction wood and fiber chair seats. The seats are sold untrimmed so they can be adapted to any style chair or, if desired, can be cut to specifications. Fiber chair replacement seats are pressed from original brass dies of the 1890s. Their normal color is tan and they can be painted, stained, sealed, or used as is. Wood seats can be sealed with a clear sealer to retain the natural look or stained and sealed as desired. A variety of caning supplies including prewoven cane webbing and tools are also offered in their catalogue.

Noel Wise Antiques   6503 Saint Claudia Avenue, Arabi, Louisiana 70032   (504) 277-7551
This firm handles chair caning supplies.

The Woodworkers' Store   21801 Industrial Boulevard, Rogers, Minnesota 55374
(612) 428-4101
The Woodworkers' Store carries over 3,000 useful products for the woodworker, including caning and upholstery supplies, tools, and books. A catalogue is available for $1.00.

REPAIR SERVICES
Most of these companies offer supplies as well as repair services.

Alexandria Wood Joinery   George and Judy Whittaker, Plumer Hill Road, Alexandria, New Hampshire 03222   (603) 744-8243
The Alexandria Wood Joinery offers chair seats of handwoven cane, press-in cane, splint, natural and fiber rush, and Shaker tape. They also do furniture repair and refinishing. No price list or literature is available as all work is done on a custom basis.

The Anderson-Williams House   47 Mohican Road, Cornfield Point, Old Saybrook, Connecticut 06475   (203) 388-2587
Joseph Williams does seat weaving using natural rush, cane, splint, Shaker tape, and other seat coverings.

The Copper Horse   81 Racine Street, Menasha, Wisconsin 54952   (414) 725-3756 or 725-4880
The Copper Horse specializes in furniture refinishing and caning, including splint and rush.

Ed's Antiques, Inc.   422 South Street, Philadelphia, Pennsylvania 19147   (215) 923-4120
This firm refinishes, repairs, and canes antique furniture.

Richard W. Fiedler   Voth Road Feed Store, 3383 Concord Road, Beaumont, Texas 77703
(713) 832-2121 or 755-2568
Mr. Fiedler makes cowhide-covered chairs, rockers, and stools. He also does repair work, putting new bottoms on old chairs. All the hides used are rawhide treated with Borax. They are selected for color and grain.

Kenneth R. Hopkins 3001 Monta Vista, Olympia, Washington 98501 (206) 943-1118
Mr. Hopkins restores furniture and does stenciling and decoration. He also does distressing, rawhide chair seats, etc. Services are available to anyone in the U.S. and he will answer questions by mail.

Keystone P.O. Box 3292, San Diego, California 92103 (714) 280-1337
Services include caning, spindle turning, and reproduction of wood parts. Caning materials and pressed fiber seat panels are offered. Price lists and other publications are available for a small fee.

MATCHING SERVICE

Roder's Antiques 160 Cokato Street East, Cokato, Minnesota 55321 (612) 286-5081
Roder's Antiques specializes in antique pressed back chairs. Send a photo of the chair you would like to match; there is a large selection in stock.

APPRAISER

Kenneth R. Hopkins 3001 Monta Vista, Olympia, Washington 98501 (206) 943-1118
Mr. Hopkins does appraisal of furniture. Services are available to anyone in the U.S. and he will answer questions by mail.

18. CHRISTMAS COLLECTIBLES

Christmas, Easter, and Halloween collectibles are extremely popular. Of special interest are early Christmas decorations, old Santa Claus figures, and pressed cardboard pumpkins.

PUBLICATION

Spirit of Christmas   P.O. Box 1255, Santa Ana, California 92701
The *Spirit of Christmas* is a quarterly newsletter that includes color photographs of rare Christmas collectibles, articles, and features of interest. The newsletter has a limited number of subscriptions available. The first issue appears in March each year and the fourth in December as a special Christmas issue.

BOOKS

Rogers, Maggie, and Hawkins, Judith.
The Glass Ornament: Old and New.
Forest Grove, Oregon: Timber Press, 1977.

Snyder, Phillip V. *The Christmas Tree Book.*
New York: Viking, 1976.

19. CLOCKS AND WATCHES

Clocks can range from an eighteenth-century tall case style to the twentieth-century animated "electric." Repairing clockworks is a job for an expert, so it is best *not* to try to fix the inside of a broken clock unless you have the required talent. Clock face and dial repainting and reverse glass painting for clock doors also require a specialist. Refinishing a clock case can be done at home. The materials and information found in Chapter 30, Furniture—General, will explain the methods. Clocks with pendulums need special adjustments to keep accurate time and sometimes they must be leveled on a shelf or floor. A local clock repair service will do this or you may be able to correct the swing by following the directions available in various books.

If you acquire an electric clock that is more than 20 years old, always have the wiring checked and replaced.

CLUBS

Antiquarian Horological Society   New House, High Street, Ticehurst, Wadhurst, Sussex TN5 7AL United Kingdom
Antiquarian Horology is its quarterly magazine.

International Wristwatch and Cigarette Lighter Club   832 Lexington Avenue, New York, New York 10021   (212) 838-4560
Old Flames & Old Timer is its monthly newsletter for members.

National Association of Watch and Clock Collectors, Inc.   514 Poplar Street, P.O. Box 33, Columbia, Pennsylvania 17512
The *Bulletin of the National Association of Watch and Clock Collectors* has regular articles about repair and construction of clocks and lists activities and national meetings.

PUBLICATION

Clockwise Magazine   1236 East Main Street, Ventura, California 93001   (805) 648-6655
This is a quarterly magazine.

DECODING ADVERTISING COPY

Reading the ads for antiques and collectibles often takes special knowledge. Two collectors will speak a special language in the same way two doctors have a vocabulary known only to the profession. When looking up watches it might help to know these terms and abbreviations.

ADJ. Adjusted (to heat and cold).
BASE. Base metal used in cases; e.g., silveroid.
BRG. Bridge plate design movement.
COIN. Coin silver.
DMK. Damaskeened.
DS. Double sunk dial.
DR. Double roller.
DWT. Pennyweight: 1/20 Troy ounce.
FULL. Full plate design movement.
¾. ¾ plate design movement.
1F brg. One finger bridge design and a ¾ plate.
2F brg. Two finger bridge design.
3F brg. Three finger bridge design.
GF. Gold filled.
GJS. Gold jewel settings.
G#. Grade number.
HC. Hunter case.
HCI P. Adjusted to heat, cold, isochronism, and positions; e.g., HCI 5P.
J. Jewel; e.g., 21J.
K. Karat; e.g., 14k solid gold—not gold filled.
KS. Key set.

KW. Key wind.
LS. Lever set.
MD. Montgomery type dial.
MRR. Montgomery railroad dial.
M#. Model number.
NI. Nickel plates or frames.
OF. Open face.
P. Position (5 positions adj).
PS. Pendant set.
RGP. Rolled gold plate.
RR. Railroad.
S. Size.
SB & B. Screw back and bezel case.
SS. Single sunk dial.
S#. Serial number.
SW. Stem wind.
TP. Total production.
WGF. White gold filled.
WI. Wind indicator (also as up and down indicator).
YGF. Yellow gold filled.

BOOKS OF MARKS

Baillie, G. H. et al. *Britten's Old Clocks and Watches and Their Makers.*
New York: Bonanza Books, 1956.

de Carle, Donald. *Watch & Clock Encyclopedia.*
London: N.A.G. Press Ltd., 1978.

Palmer, Brooks. *The Book of American Clocks.*
New York: Macmillan, 1950.

Shugart, Cooksey. *The Complete Guide to American Pocket Watches.*
New York: Harmony Books, 1981.

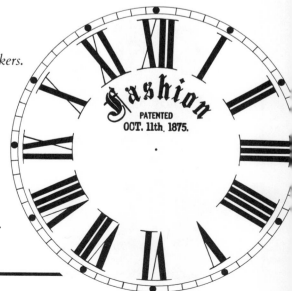

HOW-TO-FIX-IT BOOKS

Britten, F. W. *Horological Hints and Helps.*
Suffolk, England: Antique Collectors' Club (5 Church Street, Clopton, Woodbridge, Suffolk 1P12 1BR England), 1977.

Caring for Clocks.
American Association for State and Local History (708 Berry Road, Nashville, Tennessee 37204), 1968. Leaflet.

400-Day Clock Repair Guide.
Bronxville, New York: The Horolovar Company, 1978.

Smith, Eric P. *Repairing Antique Clocks: A Guide for Amateurs.*
New York: Arco Publishing, 1974.

Tyler, E. J. *American Clocks for the Collector.*
New York: Elsevier-Dutton, 1981.

Whiten, Anthony J. *Repairing Old Clocks and Watches.*
London: N.A.G. Press Ltd., 1979.

PARTS AND SUPPLIES

B. & L. Antiqurie   6217 South Lake Shore Road, Lexington, Michigan 48450   (313) 359-8623
This firm supplies glass for clocks. For information call Tuesday through Saturday 10:00 A.M. to 3:00 P.M.

Fred Catterall   54 Short Street, New Bedford, Massachusetts 02740   (617) 997-8532
Mr. Catterall does replacement pictures for banjo clocks. All pictures are done from original glasses and are mounted on card stock precut to the proper sizes for spring-driven banjos. Neck sections or bottom pictures may be bought separately. Mr. Catterall also repairs antique clocks. Send a self-addressed, stamped envelope for more information. Brochures are available for $1.00.

Century Glass & Mirror, Inc.   1417 North Washington, Dallas, Texas 75204   (214) 823-7773
This firm does custom beveling, sandblast etching, and glass molding. Send patterns for quotes.

Clock Wheel Cutting   1039 Route 163, Oakdale, Connecticut 06370   (203) 848-9127
For those who repair clocks, this is a firm that cuts clock wheels and makes clock parts. Write or call for more information.

Albert Constantine and Son, Inc.   2050 Eastchester Road, Department A11, Bronx, New York 10461   (212) 792-1600
This firm offers clock dials and clock movements, electric or battery operated. A catalogue is available for $1.00.

18th Century Hardware Company, Inc.   131 East 3rd Street, Derry, Pennsylvania 15627 (412) 694-8421

This firm carries finials, hands, keys, and other clock hardware. A catalogue and price list are available.

Fendley's Antique Clocks   Gerald Fendley, C.M.C., 2535 Himes Street, Irving, Texas 75060 (214) 254-2834

This firm does repair and restoration. Wheel and pinions can be cut to your sample or specification. Spring barrels are repaired or made new. Mr. Fendley is a Certified Master Clock maker. Parts and brochures are available.

Gaston Wood Finishes, Inc.   3630 East 10th Street, P.O. Box 1246, Bloomington, Indiana 47402   (812) 339-9111

This company carries a small line of clock movements and related materials. Weighted movements or movements that chime are not available. All clockworks are guaranteed for 1 year against defects in materials and workmanship. A catalogue is available.

Heritage Clocks of Massachusetts   P.O. Box 336, Sturbridge, Massachusetts 01566 (617) 347-7773

This firm offers clock parts and movements. Call or write for more information.

Ron Hoyt   14 Jerome Drive, Glen Cove, New York 11542   (516) 676-5653

Mr. Hoyt sells tools for clock repair by mail order. A price list is available.

S. LaRose, Inc.   234 Commerce Place, Greensboro, North Carolina 27420   (919) 275-0462

This firm carries clock and watch parts, tools, supplies, and books for the horologist as well as replacement movements, motors, birds, and bellows for cuckoo clocks. In addition to its regular catalogue, which is in newspaper form, it publishes a series of catalogues called *Keep Books* for the watch and clockmaker. The 1982 *Keep Book* is available for $2.50.

Merritt's Antiques   R.D. 2, Douglassville, Pennsylvania 19518   (215) 689-9541

Merritt's Antiques stocks all kinds of clock parts including hands, keys, pulleys, springs, pendulums, and dials, also tools, supplies, and books on clocks. They have a large mail order business and a catalogue is available.

Modern Technical Tools and Supply Company   211 Nevada Street, Hicksville, New York 11801   (516) 931-7875

This company offers the clockmaker, watchmaker, technician, and hobbyist a wide selection of clock movement materials for servicing current and antique clocks, repair parts for specific models of current and obsolete movements, and precision tools and supplies. A catalogue is available for $3.50, refundable with the first order.

John Morgan   443 Metropolitan Avenue, Brooklyn, New York 11211

Mr. Morgan makes bent glass replacement parts for clocks and barometers.

D. E. Myers   430 Virginia Avenue, Sanford, Florida 32771
D. E. Myers does reverse glass painting for antique clocks of the mantel variety: ogee, steeple, cottage, and wood works clocks. No restoration work is done. Send $2.00 and a self-addressed, stamped envelope for a brochure.

Santa Fe Glass & Mirror Company, Inc.   P.O. Box 2002, Santa Fe, New Mexico 87501
(505) 982-3828
This firm carries beveled glass replacements for antique clocks. Submit detailed descriptions of the work needed or ship the article needing repair to them for an accurate price estimate.

Selva-Borel   P.O. Box 796, Dept. A, 347 13th Street, Oakland, California 94604   (415) 832-0355
Selva-Borel carries German clock parts including dials, hands, ornaments, tools, and movements. Write for a color catalogue, $2.00.

Nateli Stoddard   Shawenon Studio, North Egremont, Massachusetts 01252
Nateli Stoddard does reverse glass painting for clocks and mirrors. Each painting is taken from an old original and hand painted in oil. Brochures are available for $1.00.

Tec Specialties   P.O. Box 909, Smyrna, Georgia 30081   (404) 952-4842
Tec Specialties creates antique, unique, and modern-style clock dials in Yello-aged, Antique Stained, Attic-aged, High-gloss, Semi-gloss, and Metal Gray. The dials are available with several different styles of numbers with manufacturer's name and trademark: plain, bold, long narrow, and short-style Roman numerals as well as plain, bold, and antique-style Arabic numerals. Combination calendar/ time dials can be purchased also. Decals in gold, silver, and color are also offered. A catalogue is available.

Time Mart   425 Madison Avenue, New York, New York 10017   (212) 753-9284
Time Mart offers leather and Swiss braided nylon watch straps for men and women.

Timesavers   P.O. Box 171A, Wheeling, Illinois 60090   (312) 394-4818
This company carries a complete line of clock and watch parts, such as movements, pendulums, dials, hands, bobs, cuckoo accessories, decals, decorative hardware, keys, and much more. Tools and supplies for repairing clocks and watches are also offered. A catalogue is available.

Warden's Antique Clock Shop   103 North Boling, Claremore, Oklahoma 74017   (918) 341-1770
This firm carries clock supplies and does repair and restoration work. Hours are Monday through Saturday 9:00 A.M. to 5:00 P.M. Catalogues are available for $1.00, which is refundable with the first order.

REPAIR SERVICES
Be sure to check the Yellow Pages of your telephone book under "Clock Repairing" to find a local shop.

Antiques Olde and Nue   6960 North Interstate Avenue, Portland, Oregon 97217   (503) 289-2922
Clock repair and restoration is done by appointment only.

Dorothy Briggs   410 Ethan Allen Avenue, Takoma Park, Maryland 20012   (301) 270-4166
Dorothy Briggs specializes in the restoration of painted clock dials, reverse painted clock door glass, and many other objects. Phone or write for information.

Fred Catterall   54 Short Street, New Bedford, Massachusetts 02740   (617) 997-8532
Mr. Catterall does replacement pictures for banjo clocks. All pictures are done from original glasses and mounted on card stock precut to the proper sizes for spring-driven banjos. Neck sections or bottom pictures may be bought separately. Mr. Catterall also repairs antique clocks. Send a self-addressed, stamped envelope for more information. Brochures are available for $1.00.

Clock Dial Restoration   Joe Louis, R.D. 1, Box 184, Fulton, New York 13069   (315) 593-6053
Mr. Louis specializes in refinishing antique clock dials of every description: wood, cast iron, zinc, tin, etc., and replacing numerals and ornamentation. Because his work is necessarily slow, repainting may be backed up several weeks, but he welcomes inquiries by phone or letter with self-addressed, stamped envelope.

The Clock Shop   806 Main Street, Lake Geneva, Wisconsin 53147   (414) 248-3736
The Clock Shop repairs complicated watches and quality clocks.

The Clock Shop   6207 South Oak Street, Kansas City, Missouri 64113   (816) 333-0542
The Clock Shop repairs and restores antique clocks and watches.

The Clock Shop of Vienna   109 Church Street N.W., Vienna, Virginia 22180
This firm restores the movement of most quality clocks. All work is done in house.

Clock Wheel Cutting   1039 Route 163, Oakdale, Connecticut 06370   (203) 848-9127
Aside from cutting clock wheels and making clock parts, this business will also restore clocks. Write or call for more information.

The Dial House   Martha & Richard Smallwood and Daughters, Buchanan Highway, Route 7, Box 532, Dallas, Georgia 30132   (404) 445-2877
This firm specializes in the restoration of clock dials. Call or write if you are interested in having work done. The firm will enter your name in its reservation file and send you a numbered mailing label to keep with your dial. When they are ready to work on your dial, you will be called. The reservation list is about 3 to 6 months long. It usually takes about a month to complete the work on your dial, once started. A brochure with prices is available.

Dialcraft   305 North High Street, Columbus Grove, Ohio 45830
Dialcraft refinishes antique clock dials, reproducing the original design as closely as possible. All work is hand painted. Specify background colors (white or cream) and flower colors. Roman numerals only at this time. A free brochure and price list are available.

Dolls, Inc.   Route 3, Box 64C, Sandpoint, Idaho 83864

Invisible repairs on china and wood are done. It is requested that the customer mail the item to be repaired, which will be invoiced at that time for the exact cost. Write for more information.

Fendley's Antique Clocks   Gerald Fendley, C.M.C., 2535 Himes Street, Irving, Texas 75060 (214) 254-2834

This Certified Master Clock maker does repairs and restorations, cuts wheels and pinions to your sample or specification, and repairs or makes spring barrels. A brochure is available.

Heritage Clocks of Massachusetts   P.O. Box 336, Sturbridge, Massachusetts 01566 (617) 347-7773

This firm specializes in clock restoration. Call or write for additional information.

International Antique Repair Service, Inc.   8350 Hickman, Suite 14, Des Moines, Iowa 50322 (515) 278-2518 or 278-2515

Clocks and watches with wooden, porcelain, and metal cases are repaired regardless of age or condition. Unobtainable parts in the movements will be manufactured to assure you of an accurate timepiece. All work is guaranteed for 5 years. 90 percent of this firm's work is done by mail order throughout the United States and a brochure is available.

Ithaca Calendar Clock Company   202 Taughannock Boulevard, Ithaca, New York 14850

Ithaca Calendar Clock Company repairs, cleans, and restores old clocks. They also carry replacement parts and reproductions of the original models.

Thomas R. John, Antique Clock Repairs   Western Road, Warren, Maine 04864 (207) 273-3070

Clocks and watches are repaired and cases restored.

Johnson Watch Repair   P.O. Box 121D, Keenesburg, Colorado 80643   (303) 536-9235

This firm specializes in restoring high-grade antique American pocket watches, $15.00 and up. Worn cases are goldplated and polished, $12.00 for open face, $15.00 for hunting. A pamphlet is offered that includes approximate production dates of the most common antique American pocket watches by serial numbers, and a section on identifying watches by characteristics of the different companies. It is available for $3.50.

Just Enterprises   2790 Sherwin Avenue, Unit 10, Ventura, California 93003   (805) 644-5837

This firm repairs clock cases.

Arthur F. Newell   18 Elm Street, Newport, Rhode Island 02840   (401) 849-6690

Mr. Newell restores antique clocks.

The "Olde Timer" Watch & Clock Shoppe   3401-C Mt. Diablo Boulevard, Lafayette, California 94549   (415) 284-4720

Complete restoration services are available for antique clocks and watches. The shop also offers a locating service. Write for more information.

Rosene Green Associates, Inc.   1622A Beacon Street, Brookline, Massachusetts 02146 (617) 277-8368
This firm restores art objects including clockfaces, woodwork, glass, and porcelain.

Santa Fe Glass & Mirror Company, Inc.   P.O. Box 2002, Santa Fe, New Mexico 87501 (505) 982-3828
This firm carries beveled glass replacements for antique clocks. Submit detailed descriptions of the work needed or ship the article needing repair to them for an accurate price estimate.

Paul N. Smith   408 East Leeland Heights Boulevard, Lehigh Acres, Florida 33936   (813) 369-4663
This firm specializes in the repair of clocks (both antique and modern) and other curious or unusual devices. Send a letter briefly describing the problem and enclose a stamped, self-addressed envelope for a reply. Cost estimates are given after an examination of the mechanism. The company makes many special parts such as gears, springs, levers, etc.

Brian J. Tuck   18 Elm Street, Newport, Rhode Island 02840   (401) 847-0310
Among the many antiques Brian Tuck restores are clock cases and dials.

Walker's Antique Clock Repair   351 Mears Street, Martinez, Georgia 30907   (404) 863-3938
This shop will completely restore clocks, from the movement to moldings or carvings on the case. It will clean and oil the clock, repair or reproduce parts, and restore the case. Contact the shop for further information and shipping instructions. It offers its services nationwide.

Warden's Antique Clock Shop   103 North Boling, Claremore, Oklahoma 74017   (918) 341-1770
This shop repairs and restores clocks and carries parts and supplies. Hours are Monday through Saturday 9:00 A.M. to 5:00 P.M. Catalogues are available for $1.00, which is refundable with the first order.

Henry F. Witzenberger   15 Po Lane, Hicksville, New York 11801   (516) 935-7432
Clock repairs are available. All clocks must be carefully packed in a case in which the repaired clock can be returned. If possible, the customer should pick up the repaired clock in person to prevent further damage. Allow ample time for repair.

The Yankee Drummer Antiques   Antique Clock Refurbishment/Restoration, 23 Burnham Road, Route 111, Hudson, New Hampshire 03051   (603) 889-1415
This firm specializes in the restoration, refurbishment, and refinishing of antique clocks, watches, and clock cases.

PRICE GUIDES

Ansonia Clock Co. 1979 Price Guide.
Ironton, Missouri: American Reprints, 1979.

Ehrhardt, Roy. *American Pocket Watch 1979 Price Indicator.*
Kansas City, Missouri: Heart of America Press, 1979.

————. *Clock Identification and Price Guide,* Book 2.
Privately printed, 1979 (P.O. Box 9808, Kansas City, Missouri 64134).

Kaduck, John M. *Collecting Watch Fobs.*
Privately printed, 1973 (P.O. Box 02152, Cleveland, Ohio 44102). The 1982–1983 price guide is available.

Schorsch, Anita. *The Warner Collector's Guide to American Clocks.*
New York: Warner Books, 1981.

Shenton, Alan and Rita. *The Price Guide to Clocks, 1840–1940.*
Suffolk, England: Antique Collectors' Club (5 Church Street, Clopton, Woodbridge, Suffolk 1P12 1BR, England), 1977. A revised price list was published in 1981.

Shugart, Cooksey, and Engle, Tom. *The Complete Guide to American Pocket Watches*, No. 2.
New York: Harmony Books, 1982.

BUYING BY MAIL

Many dealers sell clocks by mail in the United States and Canada. They advertise in the general antiques publications in the section about clocks, furniture, or miscellaneous. (See Chapter 99, General Publications.) Some have catalogues or price lists available at a minimal fee.

APPRAISERS

Antiques Olde and Nue   6960 North Interstate, Portland, Oregon 97217   (503) 289-2922
Clock appraisal is by appointment only.

D. E. Myers   430 Virginia Avenue, Sanford, Florida 32771
D. E. Myers will research the history of your American pocket watch. Send serial number, maker, description, a self-addressed, stamped envelope, and $5.00 for each watch to be researched.

BOOKSELLERS

Books about clocks can be found in every good bookstore or library. Most stores will special order the books for you. Many of these are available through the mail order antiques book dealers listed in

Chapter 91. A few dealers listed here specialize in books about clocks. If you cannot find the books, or if they are privately printed, write to the address listed to buy a copy.

Adams Brown Company   P.O. Box 399, Exeter, New Hampshire 03833

American Reprints Company   111 West Dent, Ironton, Missouri 63650

Arlington Book Company   P.O. Box 327, Arlington, Virginia 22210

Edmonds Book Sales   P.O. Box 143, Ledbetter, Kentucky 42058   (502) 898-6716

Ron Hoyt   14 Jerome Drive, Glen Cove, New York 11542   (516) 676-5653

Movements in Time   Box 6629, Station A, Toronto, Ontario M5W 1X4, Canada

National Association of Watch & Clock Collectors   514 Poplar Street, P.O. Box 33, Columbia, Pennsylvania 17512

20. CLOTHING AND ACCESSORIES

Collecting vintage clothing is a fairly recent hobby. Many cities have shops that specialize in selling old clothing that can be worn everyday. A few bridal shops and antiques shops also sell old fabrics, lace, or dresses. Check in the Yellow Pages of the telephone book under "Clothing Bought & Sold" or "Second Hand Stores" to locate the dealers who sell and repair old clothes. If you have a good eye and the ability to sew, you can always find bargains in antique clothing at the thrift shops such as the Salvation Army, Goodwill, or others.

Dirt and sunlight do more harm to old fabrics than cleaning. Most fabrics can be gently washed in pure soap or carefully dry-cleaned. The rules for old fabrics are the same as for modern ones. Some stains may be permanent but the overall soil should be cleaned away. Repairs to rips should be made before the pieces are cleaned. This will avoid more damage.

See also Chapter 76, Textiles.

CLUB

Costume Society of America   Costume Institute, Metropolitan Museum of Art, Fifth Avenue and 82nd Street, New York, New York 10028   (212) 879-5500

The Costume Society publishes a newsletter 3 times a year and a journal (*Dress*) once a year. All current publications are included in the membership dues for that year.

PARTS AND SUPPLIES
Brandywine Battlefield National Museum, Inc.   Box 265, Route 1, Chadds Ford, Pennsylvania 19317   (215) 388-1134
The museum has a mail order catalogue offering military collectors' items from the Revolutionary War to World War II including equipment, books, and reproduction clothing.

Past Patterns Replicas   2017 Eastern, S.E., Grand Rapids, Michigan 49507   (616) 245-9456
This firm carries authentic reproductions of turn-of-the-century ladies' and gentlemen's fashions. Patterns are available so you can sew your own. Ready-to-wear items can be purchased and custom service is offered. For more information write for a brochure or call.

REPAIR SERVICE
Marc King   Route 5, Box 48, Bluntville, Tennessee 37617   (615) 323-8766 or 246-2111, Ext. 2378
Marc King repairs and restores umbrellas and parasols.

21. COIN-OPERATED MACHINES

"Coin-ops" include jukeboxes, slot machines, arcade and amusement machines, vending machines, and a special group of odd machines called "trade stimulators." The trade stimulators were games that encouraged the sales of cigarettes, cigars, drinks, and many other products or services. Some just offered free games. A slot machine was made to pay out with money from the machine, while the trade stimulator required no money. It was an easier machine to make but often had many of the other features of a slot machine.

Jukeboxes gained favor as collectibles during the 1970s. There are several good books listing the history, models, and stores that sell parts or repair existing machines.

Buying any of the coin-operated machines requires some ingenuity. Some machines are found in special shops and shows, but most of the best buys are made by knowing collectors who follow the local newspaper classified section. It takes regular visits to flea markets and garage sales to find one. The condition of the machine is very important. Ideally, it should be all original, but repairs and replaced parts are often necessary. If a machine has more than one-third replaced parts, it is of a much lower value.

There are clubs and publications that can help you with repairs or finding parts. *See also* Chapter 63, Radio and Phonograph Collectibles.

CLUB
The Society for the Preservation of Historical Coin Operated Machines   100 North Central Avenue, Hartsdale, New York 10630   (914) 428-2600

PUBLICATIONS
The Coin Slot Review   P.O. Box 612, Wheatridge, Colorado 80033
This monthly magazine features antique mechanical devices, counter games, pinball machines, jukeboxes, slot machines, coin pianos, arcade games, etc.

Electronics Trader   P.O. Box 73, Folly Beach, South Carolina 29439   (803) 588-2344
This twice monthly newsletter includes buy-sell-swap ads for old and modern radios, phonographs, records, movies, and jukeboxes.

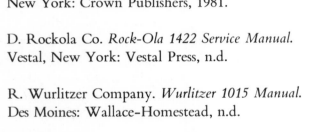

Gumball Gazette   P.O. Box 272, Sun Prairie, Wisconsin 53590   (608) 846-4507
This is a monthly newsletter for the gumball machine collector, featuring diagrams, articles, buy and sell ads, and services.

Jukebox Collector   2545 S.E. 60th Court, Des Moines, Iowa 50317
This informal monthly newsletter is filled with repair information, ads, reprinted articles, and much more.

Loose Change   21176 South Alameda Street, Long Beach, California 90810   (213) 549-0730
Antique coin-operated devices, slot machines, pinballs, trade stimulators, gumball vendors, etc. are discussed in this monthly magazine.

Salveson's Coin Machine Trader   P.O. Box 602, Huron, South Dakota 57350   (605) 352-3870
This monthly newsletter features buy and sell ads and pictures of all types of coin-operated machines.

HOW-TO-FIX-IT BOOKS
Ayliffe, Jerry. *American Premium Guide to Coin Operated Machines.*
New York: Crown Publishers, 1981.

D. Rockola Co. *Rock-Ola 1422 Service Manual.*
Vestal, New York: Vestal Press, n.d.

R. Wurlitzer Company. *Wurlitzer 1015 Manual.*
Des Moines: Wallace-Homestead, n.d.

PARTS AND SUPPLIES

The Antique Apparatus   13355 Ventura Boulevard, Sherman Oaks, California 91403
(213) 995-1169
This firm offers replacement parts for 1940s models of Wurlitzer jukeboxes. Plastic sets, bubble tubes, chassis parts, decals, and so on are available.

Automatic Music Roll Company   P.O. Box 3194, Seattle, Washington 98114   (206) 633-3664
Original rolls, original literature, and parts for player pianos, jukeboxes, phonographs, and radios are for sale. A catalogue is available.

The Jukebox Junkyard   P.O. Box 181, Lizella, Georgia 31052   (912) 935-2721
This firm carries parts and accessories for jukeboxes. It also does minor repairs and complete restoration. Call or write for more information.

Keith Parry   17557 Horace Street, Granada Hills, California 91344   (213) 363-1914
Authentic replica parts for jukeboxes are for sale. A flyer is available.

The Vintage Cash Register & Slot Machine Company   13448 Ventura Boulevard, Sherman Oaks, California 91403
A large inventory of parts is maintained. Send a stamped, self-addressed envelope for a price list.

Bob Zwicker Company   P.O. Box 2739, Youngstown, Ohio 44507   (216) 743-9733
Tailor-made slot machine covers are made of durable cotton and Dacron with the logo of each manufacturer printed on the cover. A "key compartment" is on the back so that your key is always handy. Covers are $9.50 postpaid. Phone orders are shipped on your VISA or MasterCard.

REPAIR SERVICES

The Antique Apparatus   13355 Ventura Boulevard, Sherman Oaks, California 91423
(213) 995-1169
The Antique Apparatus specializes in Wurlitzer jukebox restorations, sales, and replacement parts for 1940s models.

Inzer Pianos, Inc.   John & Hazel Inzer, 2473 Canton Road, Marietta, Georgia 30066
(404) 422-2664
This firm restores antique keyboard instruments, player pianos, grand pianos, pump organs, and nickelodeons. Custom woodworking, mechanical rebuilding, and refinishing are also offered. There are over 3,500 piano rolls in stock. Restoration of reproducers is a specialty. A catalogue of hard-to-find parts for pianos, player pianos, and reed organs is $2.00.

Jukebox Junction, Inc.   P.O. Box 1081, Des Moines, Iowa 50311   (515) 981-4019 or 274-4308
Restoration parts, supplies, and literature for 1940s era jukeboxes are available. Restoration services include total machine restoration, restoration of the mechanism or amplifier, and custom-made Wurlitzer wood parts. Literature, publications relating to jukeboxes, and a catalogue are available.

The Jukebox Junkyard   P.O. Box 181, Lizella, Georgia 31052   (912) 935-2721
This firm does minor repairs and complete restoration of jukeboxes. It also offers parts and accessories. Call or write for more information.

Mariani Enterprises   P.O. Box 5126, Lancaster, Pennsylvania 17601   (717) 569-4339
This firm restores and repairs slot machines. Call or write for more information.

Mechanical Music Center, Inc.   25 Kings Highway North, Box 88, Darien, Connecticut 06820
(203) 655-9510
This firm carries antique mechanical musical instruments including music boxes, player pianos, musical clocks, Wurlitzers, etc. Services include repair and restoration. A catalogue is available.

The Vintage Cash Register & Slot Machine Company   13448 Ventura Boulevard, Sherman Oaks, California 91403
This company offers complete restorations of vintage slot machines.

Jack Weber   434 Nold Avenue, Wooster, Ohio 44691
Mr. Weber does slot machine restoration. A base price of $150.00 includes taking the machine completely apart, sanding and refinishing the case, polishing castings and cabinet parts, repairing, cleaning, lubricating and adjusting the mechanism. Parts are extra, if needed. Send a photo with a self-addressed, stamped envelope if you have any questions about the repair.

PRICE GUIDES
Ayliffe, Jerry. *American Premium Guide to Coin Operated Machines.*
New York: Crown Publishers, 1981.

Bueschel, Richard M. *An Illustrated Price Guide To The 100 Most Collectible Slot Machines,* vol. 2.
Wheatridge, Colorado: Coin Slot Books, 1981. (P.O. Box 612, Wheatridge, Colorado 80033)

Reddock, Richard D. and Barbara. *Wallace-Homestead Price Guide to Antique Slot Machines.*
Des Moines: Wallace-Homestead, 1981.

Wilker, Stan and Betty, comp. *The Official Loose Change Blue Book of Antique Slot Machines.*
Long Beach, California: Mead Publishing, 1982.

———. *The Official Loose Change Red Book of Antique Trade Stimulators and Counter Games.*
Long Beach, California: Mead Publishing, 1980.

BUYING BY MAIL
Each of these firms has a catalogue or list available and there is a charge for some. When writing for information, be sure to include a self-addressed, stamped envelope.

Karl Frick   940 Canon Road, Santa Barbara, California 93110   (805) 682-3006
Mr. Frick sells phonograph parts, supplies, and accessories. Catalogues are available for $2.00.

Jukebox Junction, Inc.   P.O. Box 1081, Des Moines, Iowa 50311   (515) 981-4019 or 274-4308
A catalogue of reproduction parts and literature is available.

BOOKSELLERS

Books about coin-operated machines can be found in some bookstores or libraries. Most stores will special order the books for you. Books can also be ordered from mail order book dealers (see Chapter 91, Booksellers). Some of the publications about coin-operated machines offer books by mail (see Coin-operated Machines, Publications). If you cannot find the books, or if they are privately printed, write to the address listed to buy a copy.

Coin Slot Library   P.O. Box 612, Wheatridge, Colorado 80033

Mead Publishing Corporation   21176 South Alameda Street, Long Beach, California 90810
(213) 549-0730
A catalogue is available for $1.00.

22. COMIC ART

Collectors have recently become serious about comic art. The original art for movie cartoons and comic strips has been surprisingly ignored although comic books have been collected. Most of these materials are now of enough historic importance to be found in many universities and museums.

If you are interested in old comics you should realize that many of the newspaper syndicates and comic book publishers who offered the old strips are still in business. An inquiry about dates or history to these firms may bring you further information. Walt Disney Productions, 55 South Buena Vista Street, Burbank, California 91521, has an archive, and history questions are often answered. *See also* Chapter 47, Movie Memorabilia; Chapter 54, Paper Collectibles and Ephemera; and Chapter 57, Photographs and Photographic Equipment.

CLUB
Mouse Club   13826 Ventura Boulevard, Sherman Oaks, California 91423   (213) 981-5325
A bimonthly newsletter, *The Mouse Club,* is published for members only. It contains informative articles about Mickey Mouse and other Disneyana.

PUBLICATIONS
American Cartoon Quarterly   P.O. Box 425, Lodi, New Jersey 07644   (201) 925-2458
This magazine is about all forms of comic art.

The Buyer's Guide for Comic Fandom   15800 Route 84 North, East Moline, Illinois 61244 (309) 496-2353
This is a weekly newspaper.

Funnyworld   P.O. Box 1633, New York, New York 10001   (212) 427-3139
This magazine on comic art and animated films is published several times a year.

REPAIR SERVICES
Ron Stark, S/R Project   ASIFA/Hollywood, 1258 North Highland Avenue, Suite 102, Hollywood, California 90038
The Search and Rescue Team is a group of members of the International Animated Film Society (ASIFA/Hollywood) who repair and restore animation artwork. Their service is available to anyone. Charges are made for materials used but the labor is donated by the members. A brochure is available.

PRICE GUIDES
Overstreet, Robert M. *The Comic Book Price Guide, 1982–1983, 12th Edition.*
New York: Harmony Books, 1982.

Resnick, Michael. *The Official Price Guide to Comic and Science Fiction Books.*
Orlando, Florida: House of Collectibles, 1980.

BUYING BY MAIL
Each of these firms has a catalogue or list available and there is a charge for some. When writing for information, be sure to include a self-addressed, stamped envelope.

HERE IT IS PAL!

Cartoonerville   P.O. Box 445, Wheatley Heights, New York 11798   (516) 643-8279
A Catalog of Original Comic Art is published quarterly.

Little Nemo Shop & Gallery   108-30 Ascan Avenue, Forest Hills, New York 11375
Original illustrative, graphic, and comic art are sold.

Disneyana can often be purchased by mail. For further information, see Part II, Chapter 90, Auctions by Mail, and Chapter 92, Buying by Mail.

BOOKSELLERS
Books about comic art can be found in every good bookstore or library. Most stores will special order the books for you. If you can't get the books locally, you can write to the mail order antiques book dealers listed in Chapter 91, Booksellers. If the books are privately printed, you can write to the address listed to buy a copy.

23. DECOYS

Decoy collectors are often as interested in modern decoys of top quality as they are in older, used decoys. This is a very special field of collecting with clubs, publications, auctions, and many other events that are separate from the general antiques market. Talk to local collectors to learn about events in your area.

PUBLICATIONS
The Decoy Hunter   901 North 9th Street, Clinton, Indiana 47842   (317) 832-2525
This is a small bimonthly magazine about old and new decoys. It features show lists, ads, and price information.

Decoy Magazine (formerly Toller Trader & Decoy World)   P.O. Box 1900, Montego Bay Station, Ocean City, Maryland 21842   (301) 524-0989
This is a quarterly magazine about modern decoys.

Decoy World   R.F.D. 1, Box 5, Trappe, Maryland 21673   (301) 476-3092
This is a quarterly magazine.

National Directory of Decoy Collectors   c/o Gene & Linda Kangas, Carrollton, Ohio 44615

North American Decoys   Spanish Fork, Utah 84660
This magazine is not published regularly at the present time.

AUCTION HOUSES

Richard A. Bourne Company, Inc.   Corporation Street, Hyannis, Massachusetts 02647
(617) 775-0797
Richard A. Bourne Company, Inc., is a general auction house which has decoy auctions several times a year.

William Doyle Galleries, Inc.   175 East 87th Street, New York, New York 10028
(212) 427-2730
This is a general auction house which has decoy auctions occasionally.

BOOKSELLERS

Books about decoys can be found in every good bookstore or library. Most stores will special order the books for you. Many of these books are available through the mail order antiques book dealers listed in Chapter 91. Publications about decoys may also list sources for books. If you cannot find the books, or if they are privately printed, write to the address listed to buy a copy.

24. DOLLS

Doll collectors judge their collection by beauty, rarity, age, and condition. Examine your old doll carefully. Has it been repainted? Is the body original? Are the arms and legs undamaged? Is the surface of the face uncracked? Doll heads can be professionally mended. Many of the same restorers who mend porcelains will repair a china-headed doll (see Chapter 61, Pottery and Porcelain). Composition dolls and doll heads often crack with age and heat but can be restored. Bodies for dolls can be restored or replaced. Old and new clothing is available. Patterns are still available for period doll dresses. A restored doll is worth more than a damaged doll but much less than an all original doll.

The general rules for buying or selling dolls are the same as for other collectibles and antiques. There are a few auction houses that specialize in this field.

If you are taking a doll to be repaired, there are a few rules that must be followed to assure you and the doll hospital of a happy transaction. Photograph the doll and the damaged parts. Take pictures of the marks, body, hair, etc. Get an estimate of the cost of the repair and the work that is to be done *in writing* before agreeing to the work. It is often easy to remember an old doll as more glamorous than it actually is and sometimes when the restored doll is returned it appears unfamiliar. We often hear complaints that a head or body was replaced or that the repairs were more extensive than expected. The pictures and estimate will solve any problems.

CLUBS

Doll Artisan Guild   35 Main Street, Oneonta, New York 13820   (607) 432-4977
The Doll Artisan is a bimonthly magazine for members.

Ginny Doll Club   305 West Beacon Road, Lakeland, Florida 33803   (813) 687-8015
Ginny Doll Club News is an illustrated newsletter for members. It features 6 pages of information about new Ginny dolls, old Ginny dolls, and club notes.

International Doll Makers' Association   3364 Pine Creek Drive, San Jose, California 95132
(408) 926-3077
The Broadcaster is a newsletter with membership news. It is published every 4 months.

The International Rose O'Neill Club   P.O. Box 668, Branson, Missouri 65616
The Kewpiesta Kourier is a newsletter published 3 or 4 times a year.

Madame Alexander Fan Club   P.O. Box 146, New Lenox, Illinois 60451
Membership dues include 4 issues of fan club newsletters and 10 issues of *Madame Alexander Shopper* each year. The *Shopper* is devoted exclusively to the buying and selling of Madame Alexander dolls and accessories.

United Federation of Doll Clubs   Mrs. Edward Buchholz, Membership Chairman, 2814 Herron Lane, Glenshaw, Pennsylvania 15116
The Federation publishes a monthly newsletter, *Doll News.* A glossary of standardized terminology for collectors is available.

PUBLICATIONS

Bambini   P.O. Box 33, Highland, Illinois 62249   (618) 675-3497
This slick paper magazine, issued 10 times a year, includes photographs, autograph reports, articles of interest to collectors, show and sale lists, and paper dolls.

Celebrity Doll Journal   5 Court Place, Puyallup, Washington 98371   (206) 845-0340
This is a quarterly mimeographed publication with pictures and valuable information for collectors of advertising and celebrity items or dolls.

Collectors United: A Master Key to the World of Dolls   P.O. Box 1160, Chatsworth, Georgia 30705
This monthly newspaper is filled with buy and sell ads and listings of shows and sales.

Costume Quarterly for Doll Collectors   c/o May Wenzel, 38 Middlesex Drive, St. Louis, Missouri 63144
Each issue of this 8-page quarterly newsletter features a clear pattern for a doll dress, instructions, and a photograph of the finished costume.

Doll Castle News   P.O. Box 247, Washington, New Jersey 07882   (201) 689-7512
Dolls, dollhouses, and miniatures are subjects for articles and advertisements in this bimonthly magazine.

Doll Chronicle   P.O. Box 5333, Orchard Lake, Michigan 48033
This magazine is published 10 times a year.

Doll Investment Newsletter   P.O. Box 1982, Centerville, Massachusetts 02632
This monthly newsletter reports on recent sales and auctions. It gives good, clear investing advice including suggestions of bargains, warnings of fakes, and repairs.

Doll Reader   900 Frederick Street, Cumberland, Maryland 21502   (301) 759-3770
This is a bimonthly magazine about dolls, miniatures, and related toys and ephemera. It runs about 70 pages and includes pictures, ads, and information for collectors.

Doll Shop Talk   Route 1, Box 100, Evanston, Indiana 47531   (812) 529-8561
This bimonthly pamphlet has about 30 pages of articles and ads.

Doll Talk   Kimport Dolls, P.O. Box 495, Independence, Missouri 63051   (816) 461-0757
This bimonthly 16-page pamphlet features articles about current and antique dolls.

Doll Times   P.O. Box 276, Montgomery, Illinois 60538   (312) 355-0033
This is a monthly newspaper of about 32 pages featuring auctions, shows, ads, clubs, and photographs.

The Dollmaker   P.O. Box 247, Washington, New Jersey 07882   (201) 689-7512
This bimonthly magazine has articles about how to make dolls and doll heads and features ads and show lists.

The Dollmasters   Auctions by Theriault, P.O. Box 151, Annapolis, Maryland 21404
(301) 269-0680
This newsletter is about recent auctions by Theriault and includes other doll market news. It is free to regular catalogue customers and available for a fee to others.

The Dolls of Sunnybrook   576 Greenlawn Avenue, Columbus, Ohio 43223
This is a bimonthly magazine about old dolls and paper dolls. It also features buy/sell ads and information about shows and sales.

International Toy and Doll Collector   P.O. Box 9, Halstead, Essex, Great Britain
This is a bimonthly magazine.

Midwest Paper Dolls & Toys Quarterly   P.O. Box 131, Galesburg, Kansas 66740   (316) 763-2247
This quarterly illustrated mimeographed publication of over 26 pages is filled with detailed information about paper dolls, ads, and a few notices of activities in the paper doll world.

P.D.Q. (Paper Doll & Paper Toy Quarterly Bulletin) 3135 Oakcrest Drive, Hollywood, California 90068 (213) 851-2772
This quarterly illustrated magazine carries articles and good information about paper dolls only.

Paperdoll Gazette Route #2, Box 52, Princeton, Indiana 47670 (812) 385-4080
This is a quarterly newsletter with over 30 pages of current news about paper dolls, drawings of paper dolls, and a few ads.

The Schoenhut Newsletter 45 Louis Avenue, West Seneca, New York 14224 (716) 674-6657
This mimeographed newsletter is filled with information and chatty comments about recent shows, prices, and other events of interest to Schoenhut collectors.

Swallowhill Newsletter P.O. Box 34, Midland, Ontario L4R 4K6 Canada (705) 526-4437
This monthly newsletter consists of 4 pages of chatty tips on making dolls.

Yesteryears Museum News Main & River Streets, Sandwich, Massachusetts 02563
(617) 563-6673 May to October, (617) 888-1711 November to April
This is a quarterly newsletter published by Yesteryears Doll Museum. It features some ads.

DECODING ADVERTISING COPY
Reading the ads for antiques and collectibles often takes special knowledge. Two collectors will speak a special language in the same way two doctors have a vocabulary known only to the profession. When looking up dolls it might help to know these terms and abbreviations.

Alex. Madame Alexander.
AM. Armand Marseille.
Amer Char. American character.
b. Back.
bj body. Ball-jointed body.
bk. Bent knees.
bl. Blue, blond, or blown.
br. Brown.
c. Circumference.
cell. Celluloid.
cl. Cloth or closed.
cl. m. Closed mouth.
comp. Composition.
d.h. Dollhouse.
dk. Dark.
EJ. Emile Jumeau.
ex. Excellent.
f. Front.

gc. Good condition.
gl. Glass.
h. High.
hd mk. Head mark.
hh. Human hair.
hp. Hard plastic.
IDMA. International Doll Makers Association.
incl. Included.
jcb. Jointed composition body.
JDK. Johannes Daniel Kestner.
jtb. Jointed.
K&R. Kammer and Reinhardt.
l. Long; luster, leather, or lower.
l.t. Lower teeth.
m. Mohair.
mib. Mint in box.
mk. Mark.
mld hair. Molded hair.

mtd. Mounted.

O.CL.M. or *o/c.* Open closed mouth (open lips parted but no opening in bisque).

ODACA. Original Doll Artist Council of America.

NIADA. National Institute of American Doll Artists.

oilcl. Oilcloth.

o.m. Open mouth.

orig. Original.

p. Pierced.

PD. Petit & Dumontier.

p.m. Papier-mâché.

pr. Pair.

pt. Paint or part.

ptd. Painted.

p.w. eyes. Paperweight eyes.

RD. Rabery & Delphieu.

redr. Redressed.

rep. Repair.

repl. Replacement.

rt. Right.

S&H. Simon & Halbig.

SFBJ. Société Française de Fabrication de Bébés et Jouets—a group of French dollmakers.

sh. pl. Shoulder plate.

sl. Sleeping.

stat. Stationary.

sw. n. Swivel neck.

syn. Synthetic.

t.c. Terra cotta.

UFDC. United Federation of Doll Clubs.

undr. Undressed.

u.t. Upper teeth.

vgc. Very good condition.

w. Wash.

BOOKS OF MARKS

Coleman, Dorothy S., Elizabeth A., and Evelyn J. *The Collector's Encyclopedia of Dolls.*
New York: Crown Publishers, 1968.

Shea, Ralph A. *Antique Doll Marks,* vols. 1–8.
Privately printed, 1980 (489 Oak Street, Ridgefield, New Jersey 07657).

White, Gwen. *Toys, Dolls, Automata: Marks and Labels.*
London: B. T. Batsford, 1975.

HOW-TO-FIX-IT BOOK

Doll Catalog, The, 2nd ed.
Cumberland, Maryland: Hobby House Press, 1981.

PARTS AND SUPPLIES

Antique Replica Dolls   2780 Mill Creek Road, Mentone, California 92359   (714) 794-2686
This firm handles parts for the repair and reproduction of dolls. The bodies are made of a latex product and the arms, legs, and heads are made of china and bisque. Catalogues are 50¢.

Bonnie-Lee Doll Makers   2005 George Washington Road, Vienna, Virginia 22180
(703) 893-7780
This firm's specialty is cotton muslin doll bodies for use only with an antique-type head and shoulder

combination that fastens over the top of the shoulder of the body. Assembled stuffed muslin bodies with earthenware arms and legs are also available. The feet of the assembled bodies are bare (no shoes are painted on). Send for a list.

Doll & Craft World, Inc.   125 8th Street, Brooklyn, New York 11215   (800) 221-6462
This firm carries replacement parts for dolls, including wigs, eyes, teeth, bodies, arms, legs, and hands, as well as tools and accessories. It also offers a large selection of patterns by Eleanor-Jean Carter, Betty James, Ella De Hart, Anna McQuilken, Mildred Seeley, and others. A catalogue is available.

The Doll Lady   P.O. Box 121-Z, Homecrest Station, Brooklyn, New York 11229   (212) 743-5219
The Doll Lady offers doll parts and doll kits. A catalogue is available.

The Doll Lady Doll Hospital   94 Pent Road, Branford, Connecticut 06405   (203) 488-6193
The Doll Lady Doll Hospital makes papier-mâché ball-jointed doll bodies and parts, bisque doll parts, and leather doll shoes. Its catalogue sells for $1.50.

The Doll Place   P.O. Box 536, Van Brunt Station, Brooklyn, New York 11215
Services include custom costuming and costume conservation. Send a self-addressed, stamped envelope with inquiries. An illustrated list of services is available for $1.00.

Doll Repair Parts, Inc.   9918 Lorain Avenue, Cleveland, Ohio 44102   (216) 961-3545
Doll hospital supplies—wigs, crowns, paint, books, elastic parts, etc.—are available. Bisque or china arms, legs, shoulders, Bye-Lo hands, and all bisque parts are offered as tie-on or wire-on. Ball-jointed parts, bodies, hands, repair kits, and tools are also carried. A catalogue is available for 50¢.

The Doll Shop   903 South A Street, Richmond, Indiana 47374   (317) 962-5365
The Doll Shop carries parts and supplies for dolls including arms, legs, wigs, clothing, stands, patterns for clothing, and books. A catalogue is available.

Dollspart Supply Company, Inc.   5-15 49th Avenue, Long Island City, New York 11101
(212) 361-0888
This company carries a complete line of supplies for the repair and restoration of dolls. Illustrated catalogues are $3.00.

M. Forster   5838 Huntington Avenue, Richmond, California 94804
Old, out-of-print crochet patterns for more than 100 doll costumes are offered. Illustrated catalogues are available for $1.00.

Hobby House Press, Inc.   900 Frederick Street, Cumberland, Maryland 21502   (301) 759-3770
Hobby House Press, Inc. has a large selection of books, patterns, and paper dolls.

L. Hulphers   3153 West 110th Street, Inglewood, California 90303   (213) 678-1957
L. Hulphers sells kid, cloth, composition, and bisque doll bodies in all sizes and shapes. A list is available for $1.00.

Leslie Designs   3702 Marwick Avenue, Long Beach, California 90808   (213) 425-6617
Leslie Designs carries costumes that have been adapted to preserve the authenticity of the originals. Oriental silks, satins, moire, cottons, and imported cotton velveteens are used along with fine laces and trims. Catalogues are available for $1.00, which is refundable with the first purchase.

Lyn's Doll House Patterns   P.O. Box 8341, Denver, Colorado 80201
Original dress, hat, and shoe patterns for antique or reproduction dolls are adapted from period fashion magazines. New patterns are developed regularly. An illustrated catalogue is available for $1.00.

Paradise Doll Part Supply   576 Roberts Road, Paradise, California 95969   (916) 877-1670
Porcelain arms, legs, and sawdust bodies for replacement of antique doll parts are offered. A brochure is available.

Pattern Lending Library   1938 South Edgemoor, Wichita, Kansas 67218
This library has 33 categories with over 27,000 patterns. Send a stamp and your name and address for details.

Schoepfer Eyes   138 West 31st Street, New York, New York 10001   (212) 736-6934 or 736-6939
This firm stocks practically all sizes of oval glass doll's eyes in brown and blue ready for immediate delivery. Call or write for prices.

Seeley's Ceramic Service, Inc.   9 River Street, Oneonta, New York 13820   (607) 432-3812
Seeley's offers a complete line of materials needed for the restoration of dolls. The illustrated catalogue is $2.00.

Standard Doll Company   23-83 31st Street, Long Island City, New York 11105
This firm has a catalogue, available for $2.00, offering doll parts, supplies, and accessories.

Sybil Wallender   3147 West 110th Street, Inglewood, California 90303   (213) 672-0284
Sybil Wallender offers many doll supplies including wigs, shoes, boots, stockings, straw hats, pates, eyes, bodies, bisque arms, and china arms and legs. For a list send 75¢ and a self-addressed, stamped envelope.

Yesteryears Museum   Main & River Streets, Sandwich, Massachusetts 02563   (617) 563-6673
May to October (617) 888-2088 November to April
The museum carries doll wigs and supplies. It also offers dollhouse miniatures through its quarterly newsletter.

REPAIR SERVICES
Local doll repair shops are often listed in the Yellow Pages of the phone book under "Doll, Repairing."

Antique Replica Dolls   2780 Mill Creek Road, Mentone, California 92359   (714) 794-2686
Doris R. Sheperd makes over 70 different jointed reproduction dolls, from bisque to composition. She also teaches dollmaking.

Berkley, Inc. 2011 Hermitage Avenue, Wheaton, Maryland 20902 (301) 933-4440
Berkley, Inc. does invisible repairs on bisque and porcelain dolls. For free information send a self-addressed, stamped envelope.

The Bric-A-Brac, Inc. 8120 Nelson Street, New Orleans, Louisiana 70118 (504) 861-8888
This firm offers restoration services and will answer questions by mail. It specializes in repairing or restoring antique porcelain including dolls.

Chili Doll Hospital & Victorian Doll Museum 4332 Buffalo Road (Route 33), North Chili, New York 14514 (10 miles west of Rochester) (716) 247-0130
This firm repairs antique and mama dolls in need of leather body repair; it does restringing; mending of broken heads, cloth bodies, fingers, teeth, glass eyes; replaces china and bisque hands, legs or arms, voice boxes, etc. For mail inquiries send a self-addressed, stamped envelope. Do not send any dolls.

The Doll Cellar Gloria McCarty, 2337 46th Avenue S.W., Seattle, Washington 98116 (206) 938-4446
Doll repairs are done by appointment.

The Doll Lady Doll Hospital 94 Pent Road, Branford, Connecticut 06405 (203) 488-6193
Repairs are done on all types of dolls.

The Doll Place P.O. Box 536, Van Brunt Station, Brooklyn, New York 11215
The Doll Place specializes in the restoration and conservation of bisque, china, wood, composition, rag, leather, hard plastic, and celluloid dolls. Eyes are reset, rewaxed, lashed, made to sleep. Also, eye weights and frames are made. Other services include restringing, cleaning, pates made and reset, wigs restored and made to order, teeth and tongues made and reset, missing parts rebuilt, custom costuming, and costume conservation. Send a stamped, self-addressed envelope with inquiries. An illustrated list is available for $1.00.

Doll Repair Parts 9918 Lorain Avenue, Cleveland, Ohio 44102 (216) 961-3545
This firm offers complete doll repair. Mail order business is welcome.

The Doll Shop 903 South A Street, Richmond, Indiana 47374 (317) 962-5365
This firm repairs antique and modern dolls.

Dolls, Inc. Route 3, Box 64C, Sandpoint, Idaho 83864
Dolls, Inc. is involved in invisible china, bisque, wax, wood, and composition repair. Mail the doll to Dolls, Inc. for an estimate.

Enchanted Valley Dolls 1412 Carver Road, Modesto, California 95350 (209) 522-9182
This firm repairs dolls made from composition, bisque, china, etc. and services the area of central California from Fresno to San Francisco, to Sacramento, via UPS and hand deliveries. It offers free estimates on all repairs, and if it can't repair the doll, the company will return it for just the cost of shipment/postage. For more information call or write.

International Antiques Repair Service, Inc.   8350 Hickman, Suite 14, Des Moines, Iowa 50322 (515) 278-2518 or 278-2515
Porcelain, pottery, and ceramic dolls are restored, missing parts replaced, hairline cracks, chips, and discoloration repaired. Repairs are made on porcelain and china doll heads. All work is invisible and blacklight proof and is guaranteed for 5 years. The firm does a large mail order business throughout the United States and surrounding countries. A brochure is available.

Kestner's Showcase   P.O. Box 186, Urbana, Illinois 61801   (217) 367-6216
This firm buys and sells antique and modern dolls, mechanical bears, carriages, books, accessories, and makes repairs.

MacDowell Doll Museum   "Oakwood," Aldie, Virginia 22001   (703) 777-6644
This firm does invisible china and bisque restoration. Hours are by appointment.

McKenzie Art Restoration Studio   2907 East Monte Vista Drive, Tucson, Arizona 85716 (602) 323-1466
This firm specializes in the restoration of bisque and china dolls. Prompt, personal attention is given to each restoration. Invisible mending is done without the use of acrylics. Shipments should be made parcel post insured. An estimate will be mailed to the customer and work begun upon receipt of payment. Missing pieces can be rebuilt and replaced.

Manhattan Doll Hospital   176 Ninth Avenue, New York, New York 10011   (212) 989-5220
The Manhattan Doll Hospital repairs and restores dolls.

New York Doll Hospital   787 Lexington Avenue, New York, New York 10021   (212) 838-7527
This is a third generation restorer of antique dolls. Dolls may be sent in for an estimate.

Vernal Restorations   Route 1, Box 152A, Waconia, Minnesota 55387
(612) 442-4984 or 475-9561
Donna Vernal restores dolls. She can copy any face and brushwork. She restores china and papier-mâché dolls. She also restores bisque dolls invisibly, even if smashed or without shoulder plates. Hours are by appointment only.

Sybil Wallender   3147 West 110th Street, Inglewood, California 90303   (213) 672-0284
Sybil Wallender offers restoration services for dolls. Call or write for more information.

Yesteryears Museum   Main & River Streets, Sandwich, Massachusetts 02563   (617) 563-6673 May to October and (617) 888-2088 November to April.
The museum repairs and restores dolls.

PRICE GUIDES
Doll Registry, The.
Annapolis, Maryland: Theriault's, 1981.

Foulke, Jan. *4th Blue Book of Dolls & Values.*
Cumberland, Maryland: Hobby House Press, 1980.

Glassmire, Carol Gast. *Price Guide to the Twentieth Century Doll Series.*
Des Moines: Wallace-Homestead, 1981.

Herron, R. Lane. *Herron's Price Guide to Dolls and Paper Dolls.*
Des Moines: Wallace-Homestead, 1982.

King, Constance Eileen. *The Price Guide to Dolls, Antique and Modern.*
Suffolk, England: Antique Collectors' Club (5 Church Steet, Clopton, Woodbridge, Suffolk
1P12 1BR England), 1977. Price revision, 1981, available.

Leuzzi, Marlene. *Antique Doll Price Guide,* 4th ed.
Privately printed, 1981 (P.O. Box 587, Corte Madera, California 94925).

McKeon, Barbara Jo. *Rare and Hard to Find Madame Alexander Collector's Dolls.*
Privately printed, 1981 (P.O. Box 1481, Brockton, Massachusetts 02402).

Marion, Frieda, and Werner, Norma. *The Collector's Encyclopedia of Half-Dolls.*
Paducah, Kentucky: Collector Books, 1979.

Miller, Robert W. *Price Guide to Dolls.*
Des Moines: Wallace-Homestead, 1979.

Miller, Susan. *Trolls, An Illustrated Price Guide.*
Paducah, Kentucky: Collector Books, 1981.

Robison, Joleen, and Sellers, Kay. *Advertising Dolls, Identification and Value Guide.*
Paducah, Kentucky: Collector Books, 1980.

Shoemaker, Rhoda. *Price Guide for Madame Alexander Dolls.*
Privately printed, 1980 (1141 Orange Avenue, Menlo Park, California 94025).

Smith, Patricia. *Patricia Smith's Doll Values, Antique to Modern.*
Paducah, Kentucky: Collector Books, 1979.

————. *Patricia Smith's Doll Values Antique to Modern,* Series 2.
Paducah, Kentucky: Collector Books, 1980.

————. *French Dolls.*
Paducah, Kentucky: Collector Books, 1979.

————. *French Dolls,* vol. II.
Paducah, Kentucky: Collector Books, 1981.

————. *German Dolls.*
Paducah, Kentucky: Collector Books, 1979.

————. *German Dolls, Character Children & Babies,* vol. II.
Paducah, Kentucky: Collector Books, 1980.

————. *Madame Alexander Collector's Dolls.*
Paducah, Kentucky: Collector Books, 1978. Revised price guide, 1981.

————. *Modern Collector's Dolls,* 4th ed.
Paducah, Kentucky: Collector Books, 1979.

————. *Oriental Dolls.*
Paducah, Kentucky: Collector Books, 1979.

————. *Price Guide for Madame Alexander Collector's Dolls.*
Paducah, Kentucky: Collector Books, 1982. (Updated price guide for *Madame Alexander Collector's Dolls,* 1978; and *Madame Alexander Collector's Dolls,* Second Series, 1981.)

————. *Price Guide for Shirley Temple Dolls and Collectibles,* Second Series.
Paducah, Kentucky: Collector Books, 1979. (Goes with *Shirley Temple Dolls and Collectibles,* Second Series, 1979.)

Standard Antique Doll Identification and Value Guide, The.
Paducah, Kentucky: Collector Books, 1979.

Standard Modern Doll, Identification and Value Guide, The.
Paducah, Kentucky: Collector Books, 1976. Values updated 1982.

Young, Mary. *A Collector's Guide to Paper Dolls.*
Paducah, Kentucky: Collector Books, 1980.

BUYING BY MAIL

Dolls can often be purchased by mail. Each of these firms has a catalogue or list available and there is a charge for some. For further information, see Part II, Chapter 90, Auctions by Mail, and Chapter 92, Buying by Mail. When writing for information, be sure to include a self-addressed, stamped envelope.

Antique Doll Reproductions   Box 103, Monterallo Road, Milo, Missouri 64767
Reproduction dolls and parts are offered.

The Doll Lady Doll Hospital   94 Pent Road, Branford, Connecticut 06405   (203) 488-6193
Dollhouse dolls and miniatures are available. Send 35¢ plus a stamped, self-addressed envelope for a list.

MacDowell Doll Museum   "Oakwood," Aldie, Virginia 22001   (703) 777-6644
This museum handles mail order dolls and accessories.

Merrily Supply Company   8542 Ranchito Avenue, Panorama City, California 91402
(213) 894-0637
This company sells dolls and teddy bears as well as hard-to-find supplies for repairing them, clothing, patterns, parts, tools, and books.

Yesteryears Museum   Main & River Streets, Sandwich, Massachusetts 02563   (617) 563-6673
May-October, (617) 888-2088 November-April
The museum carries doll wigs and supplies and will repair and restore dolls. It also offers dollhouse miniatures through its quarterly newsletter.

AUCTION HOUSES
Auctions by Theriault (dolls)   P.O. Box 151, Annapolis, Maryland 21404   (301) 269-0680
This is America's only auction house specializing solely in antique and collector dolls. A newsletter, *The Dollmasters,* is available.

The Magnificent Doll Brokerage Service   209 East 60th Street, New York, New York 10022
The new antique doll brokerage service will find the dolls you want at a 25 percent commission. It searches for the doll(s) you want at auctions, at doll shows, etc. You receive a copy of the actual auction bill or the doll show bill (the price the service paid), and pay that plus a 25 percent commission. For more information and a questionnaire send a self-addressed, stamped envelope.

Richard W. Withington, Inc.   Hillsboro, New Hampshire 03244   (603) 464-3232
Although this auction house sells a general line of antiques, it is well known for its special "dolls only" auctions. Catalogues are available but absentee bids are not accepted.

APPRAISERS
Auctions by Theriault   P.O. Box 151, Annapolis, Maryland 21404   (301) 269-0680
This auction firm, specializing solely in antique and collector dolls, holds appraisal clinics throughout the year and has designed a doll identification guide that allows you to learn about your doll through the mail. This opinion regarding the history and value of your doll is offered free of charge as a public service.

Chili Doll Hospital & Victorian Doll Museum   4332 Buffalo Road (Route 33), North Chili, New York 14514 (10 miles west of Rochester)   (716) 247-0130
This firm appraises dolls; however, it prefers to examine the doll personally for flaws, imperfections, hairline cracks, and so on, rather than use a photo. There is a $5.00 charge for appraisals, which are done on a regular appraisal form, dated, and signed by the shop's proprietor, Linda Greenfield.

MacDowell Doll Museum   "Oakwood," Aldie, Virginia 22001   (703) 777-6644
Hours are by appointment.

BOOKSELLERS
Mrs. Loraine Burdick   5 Court Place, Puyallup, Washington 98371

Doll Repair Parts, Inc.   9918 Lorain Avenue, Cleveland, Ohio 44102   (216) 961-3545
A list of books and their prices is included in this firm's catalogue for doll parts. Catalogues are 50¢.

Dollspart Supply Company, Inc.   5-15 49th Avenue, Long Island City, New York 11101
(212) 361-0888
This firm offers a selection of doll books with a 10 percent discount when you purchase 3 or more books. An illustrated catalogue is available for $3.00.

Edmonds Book Sales   P.O. Box 143, Ledbetter, Kentucky 42058   (502) 898-6716
This book list on antiques includes sections for dolls, paper dolls, and teddy bears. Payment should be made with the order or use VISA or MasterCard. Send a long self-addressed, stamped envelope for a free book list.

Hobby House Press, Inc.   900 Frederick Street, Cumberland, Maryland 21502   (301) 759-3770
Hobby House Press, Inc. has a large selection of books, patterns, and paper dolls. Its *Doll Book Catalog* is free upon request.

Kimport Dolls   P.O. Box 495, Independence, Missouri 64051   (816) 461-0757
This book list includes the following categories: price guides, dollhouses and furnishings, paper dolls, specific dolls and types, making, repair, dressing and costumes, encyclopedias, identification, and miscellaneous. Prices for the books are included.

Robert L. McCumber   201 Carriage Drive, Glastonbury, Connecticut 06033   (203) 633-4984

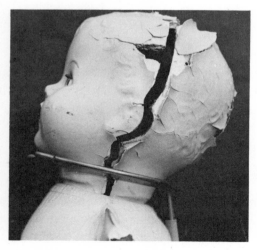 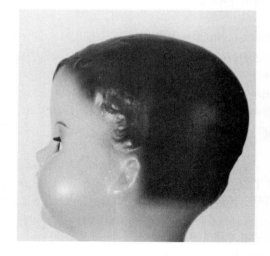

25. ENAMELWARE AND CLOISONNÉ

Once damaged, enamel and cloisonné are very difficult to repair. Dents and chipped enamel require the attention of an expert. Often the cost of the repair is more than the value of the piece. Radical changes in temperature will also crack enamel, so pieces should never be kept in a sunny window, over heat ducts, or washed in very hot or cold water.

CLUB

Cloisonné Collectors Club   1631 Mimulus Way, La Jolla, California 92037   (714) 454-0595
The Cloison is the club's newsletter.

BOOK OF MARKS

Fall, Frieda Kay. *Enamelled Objects.*
Skokie, Illinois: National Register Publishing (5201 Old Orchard Road, Skokie, Illinois 60077), n.d. Leaflet.

REPAIR SERVICES

Clifford Baron   Manhattan Art and Antique Center, Shop 26 (Street Floor), 1050 Second Avenue, New York, New York 10022   (212) 688-8510
This firm restores Russian enamels exclusively.

Just Enterprises   2790 Sherwin Avenue, Unit 10, Ventura, California 93003   (805) 644-5837
Just Enterprises restores Russian, French, and Chinese enamelware.

Richard George/George Studios   45-04 97th Place, Corona, New York 11368   (212) 271-2506
This firm does restoration and conservation of porcelain, lacquer, and enamel work, gold leafing, and ivory. Furniture, Coromandel screens, antique marble, and faux finishes are also restored. Call for an appointment or make arrangements for the delivery of the works to be restored. For restoration of large pieces of furniture, screens, fixed panels, or porcelain requiring on-location repairs, call or write for information.

Rosene Green Associates, Inc.   1622A Beacon Street, Brookline, Massachusetts 02146
(617) 277-8368
This firm specializes in the restoration of art objects: cloisonné, enamel on jewelry and clock faces, jade and ivory, tortoiseshell, alabaster, marble, tole and papier-mâché, and silver. It also restores Oriental lacquer, paintings, woodwork, glass, and porcelain.

26. FANS

Most of the organizations for fan collectors are interested in electric fans. Be sure to determine which kind of fan—the hand-held ladies' fan or the commercial electric fan—is the subject of the fan publications and clubs.

CLUB

East Bay Fan Guild   P.O. Box 1054, El Cerrito, California 94530
East Bay Fan Guild Newsletter is published 4 times a year and usually consists of 10 to 20 pages of information sent in by members. This club is concerned with collecting and studying men's and women's hand fans.

PUBLICATION

The Fan Collector Newsletter   4606 Travis Avenue, Dallas, Texas 75205   (214) 559-4440
This newsletter is about old electric fans and includes information on restoration.

REPAIRS, PARTS, AND SUPPLIES

The Fan Man   Kurt House, 4606 Travis Avenue, Dallas, Texas 75205   (214) 559-4440
This is a full service fan company—sales, service, installation, and parts. A catalogue of fan parts is available for $1.00.

27. FIREPLACE EQUIPMENT

An old fireplace had many pieces of equipment: a set of tools, a fireback, andirons, a coal basket, a fender, and such aids as bellows or match holders. All of these are considered collectibles and enjoy tremendous popularity.

CLUB

The Fire Mark Circle of the Americas   2859 Marlin Drive, Chamblee, Georgia 30341
(404) 451-2651
The Fire Mark Circle of the Americas Newsletter/Journal, published three times a year, contains club news, auction reports, and short articles about fire marks.

PARTS AND SUPPLIES

The Country Iron Foundry   P.O. Box 600, Paoli, Pennsylvania 19301   (215) 296-7122
Replica American and French firebacks and stove plates are handcast in iron using molds made from antique originals. Call or write for information. The showroom is located at 1792 East Lancaster Pike in Paoli, Pennsylvania. A catalogue is available for $1.00.

Jonathan Studios, Inc.   Architectural and Decorative Arts, 619 South Tenth Street, Minneapolis, Minnesota 55404   (612) 338-0213
Hand-carved wood mantels, ceramic tile mantels, incised stone mantels including Moorish motifs, decorative arts mantels, custom woodworking, stained glass, and hand-painted ceramic tiles are available. Send a self-addressed, stamped envelope for a brochure.

REPAIR SERVICES

Abercrombie & Company   8227 Fenton Street, Silver Spring, Maryland 20910   (301) 585-2385
This company repairs, polishes, buffs, and lacquers metal items including fireplace equipment.

A.E.S. Firebacks   27 Hewitt Road, Mystic, Connecticut 06355   (203) 536-0295 (after 6:00 P.M.)
This firm restores and reproduces early masonry and specializes in making solid cast iron firebacks taken from original designs. A brochure is available with a self-addressed, stamped envelope.

John N. Lewis   156 Scarboro Drive, York, Pennsylvania 17403   (717) 848-1080
Mr. Lewis repairs antique fireplace bellows.

28. FLOORCLOTHS

The eighteenth-century American home was more likely to have a heavy painted sailcloth rug called a floorcloth than any type of fabric covering used today. The floorcloths were painted with geometric borders, flowers, or patterns that resembled marble, carpet, or wooden floors. Although only small pieces of original canvas floorcloths have survived, it is possible to buy a modern reproduction of an old floorcloth.

PARTS AND SUPPLIES

Craftswomen   P.O. Box 715, Doylestown, Pennsylvania 18901   (215) 822-0721
Craftswomen can produce seamless painted floorcloths in any size up to 10 feet wide and in unlimited length. Colors are custom mixed to client's paint samples or swatches. Canvas floorcloths have a durable varnished surface and no special installation or padding is required. They are guaranteed for 10 years. Kits are also available for those who wish to stencil their own floorcloth. They come in 19 patterns and range from traditional eighteenth-century stenciled designs to the geometrics of Amish quilts. Each kit contains heavyweight cotton canvas cut to size, a complete and detailed stencil pattern, transparent Mylar plastic stencil sheets cut to size, marking pen, stencil brush, and instructions. Paint is not included but is available at local art supply stores. Floorcloth patterns with instructions may be ordered separately. A brochure is available.

Floorcloths Incorporated   P.O. Box 812, Severna Park, Maryland 21146   (301) 647-3328
Floorcloths Incorporated designs and manufactures custom floorcloths. Designs may be chosen from an assortment of documented patterns or may be custom designs. Its staff will work with the customer to create an original design. Floorcloths are made of specially milled canvas and painted with oil-based paints. They are available in hard-gloss or semi-gloss finish. Instructions for care and cleaning are included. A brochure and color chart are available.

Good Stenciling   P.O. Box 387, Dublin, New Hampshire 03444   (603) 563-8021
Stenciled floorcloths adapted from Early American floor coverings are available from this company. They are offered in 6 different designs and many sizes. The cloths are durable, made of heavy canvas, and finished with several coats of varnish. Custom colors are available, as are custom designs. A brochure and price list are available.

29. FOLK ART

There is an ongoing argument among the experts: what is folk art? For the purposes of this book, folk art is what is called folk art by some experts. It may be old or twentieth century. This is one collecting field with few hard and fast rules of quality and age. Beauty is in the eye of the beholder and what seems primitive to one is considered superior by another.

PUBLICATIONS

The Clarion   Museum of American Folk Art, 49 West 53rd Street, New York, New York 10019
This quarterly magazine is well illustrated and carries authoritative articles about folk art of museum quality. Events and exhibits of interest to folk art collectors are listed.

Folk Art Finder   Gallery Press, 98 North Main, Essex, Connecticut 06426   (203) 767–0313
This bimonthly newsletter includes book reviews, articles, and events.

PRICE GUIDE

Thuro, Catherine. *Primitives and Folk Art: Our Handmade Heritage.*
Paducah, Kentucky: Collector Books, 1979.

30. FURNITURE– GENERAL

Refinishing and restoring furniture is a subject that has been discussed in dozens of books. For exact information on what to do, how to do it, and what finishes are best, we suggest that you go to your local hardware, paint store, or library, and study the products, books, and methods. The general rule for refinishing an antique is: less is better. Never strip a piece that can be restored. Never remove a painted surface that can be saved. If you want furniture with a natural wood finish, don't buy an antique with an original finish that was painted.

Never use silicon polish or spray wax in your day-to-day care. Beeswax, lemon oil, and other waxes are more satisfactory. Dust regularly. A bit of soap and water will never hurt a dirty piece of furniture. Always be careful because too much water can affect the grain. Be a lazy housekeeper and don't polish every week. By polishing you are often only adding a layer of dirt-catching material. Some finishes require very special care. Lacquer and papier-mâché should only be cleaned or wiped with the appropriate creams.

Humidity and heat can damage the finish on old furniture. Always try to keep direct sunlight off the furniture to prevent fading. Never place a fragile piece in front of a heat duct or radiator. *See also* Chapter 9, Beds and Bed Hangings; Chapter 17, Chairs; Chapter 19, Clocks and Watches; Chapter 27, Fireplace Equipment; Chapter 36, Kitchenware; Chapter 51, Oriental Rugs; and Chapter 85, Wicker and Rattan.

CLUBS

The Historical Society of Early American Decoration, Inc.   19 Dove Street, Albany, New York 12210
The Decorator is published twice a year for members.

National Wood Carvers Association   7424 Miami Avenue, Cincinnati, Ohio 45243
(513) 561-9051
Chip Chats is a bimonthly magazine for members.

Roycrofters at Large Association   Erie City, East Aurora, New York 14052
The *Roycroft Campus Chronicle* is published occasionally and primarily concerns present-day Roycroft activities, but there is some mention of past history.

The Wooton Desk Owners' Society   P.O. Box 128, Bayside, New York 11361   (212) 767-9758
A quarterly newsletter comes with membership in the Society. Reprints of catalogues and Smithsonian booklets are also available.

PUBLICATIONS

Antique Furniture Newsletter   455 Bedford Center Road, Bedford Hills, New York 10507
(914) 234-9390
This bimonthly newsletter is illustrated with line drawings showing details of furniture. Much valuable information about fakes, restorations, and proper construction of period furniture is included.

Fine Woodworking   P.O. Box 355, Newtown, Connecticut 06470   (203) 426-8171
This quarterly magazine is about today's woodworking methods, tools, and products. It includes some articles about old furniture and some patterns for old pieces but is primarily for the modern woodworker.

The Shaker Messenger   P.O. Box 45, Holland, Michigan 49423
This slim magazine is filled with pictures and articles about the Shakers and their communities.

BOOKS OF MARKS AND IDENTIFICATION

Brodatz, Phil. *Wood and Wood Grains.*
New York: Dover Publications, 1971.

Haslam, Malcolm. *Marks and Monograms of the Modern Movement, 1875–1930.*
New York: Charles Scribner's Sons, 1977.

MacDonald-Taylor, Margaret, ed. *A Dictionary of Marks.*
New York: Hawthorn Books, 1962.

IDENTIFICATION

Center for Wood Anatomy Research   U. S. Forest Products Laboratory, Dr. Robert Koeppen, P.O. Box 5130, Madison, Wisconsin 53705
This is a free service of the U.S. Department of Agriculture. Take a sample of the wood with a sharp knife in the following manner: Cut across the grain to a depth of about 3/16 inch. Make two cuts like this about 1/2 inch apart, then pry up the piece of wood. Put the sample in an envelope and label the contents. Pack into another envelope to avoid breakage and mail to the above address. Remember, when checking antique furniture, often the interior woods are different from the surface woods.

Massachusetts Materials Research, Inc.   P.O. Box 326, 241 West Boylston Street, West Boylston, Massachusetts 01583   (617) 835-6262
This firm uses microscopy and chemical analysis to determine genuineness of paint on antique paintings and furniture. It can analyze material the size of a dot on an *i,* but larger pieces of material are preferred. For more information on using its services, contact Mr. Doug Shaw or Dr. David Krashes at the above telephone number.

Gordon K. Salter   2208 Lorelei Lane, Wilmington, Delaware 19810
For wood analysis: Using a sharp knife, take a small sample from the back of the piece, bottom of a drawer, or other inconspicuous place. The sample should be at least ¼ inch square. It will be returned to you. The fee for wood analysis is $25.00.

The Henry Francis duPont Winterthur Museum   Wood Analysis Laboratory, Michael Palmer, Winterthur, Delaware 19735
Write for instructions before sending a sample for analysis.

HOW-TO-FIX-IT BOOKS

Chambers, Donald L. *How to Gold-Leaf Antiques and Other Art Objects.*
New York: Crown Publishers, 1973.

Emerick, Carol and Robert. *A Guide to Furniture Restoration.*
Privately printed, 1979 (3201 Adams Avenue, San Diego, California 92116). Leaflet.

Furniture Restoration (Thames).
Ithaca: Cornell University, Media Services Distribution Center (7 Research Park, Ithaca, New York 14850), n.d. Leaflet.

Glazed Finish Over Enamel (Garner).
Ithaca: Cornell University, Media Services Distribution Center (7 Research Park, Ithaca, New York 14850), n.d. Leaflet.

Kovel, Ralph and Terry. *Magic Formula Refinishing*.
Des Moines: Register and Tribune Syndicate (715 Locust Street, Des Moines, Iowa 50304), 1972. Leaflet.

————. *Restoring and Refinishing Furniture*.
Des Moines: Register and Tribune Syndicate (715 Locust Street, Des Moines, Iowa 50304), 1972. Leaflet.

McGiffin, Robert F. *Basic Furniture Care*.
Privately printed, 1980 (Furniture Conservation Laboratory, Conservation and Collections Care Center, Peebles Island, Waterford, New York 12188). Leaflet.

Rodd, Hohn. *Repairing and Restoring Antique Furniture*.
New York: Van Nostrand Reinhold, 1981.

Technical Notes on the Care of Art Objects: Woodworm in Furniture, no. 2.
London: Victoria and Albert Museum, 1968.

Voss, Thomas M. *The Bargain Hunter's Guide to Used Furniture*.
New York: Dell Publishing, 1980.

PARTS AND SUPPLIES

Art Essentials of New York   P.O. Box 260, 28 West Maple Avenue, Monsey, New York 10952   (914) 356-0120 or 356-0130
Write or call Art Essentials of New York for a list of gold, silver, aluminum, and composition leaf supplies as well as a pamphlet, *How to Lay Gold Leaf Effectively.*

B. & L. Antiqurie   6217 South Lake Shore Road, Lexington, Michigan 48450   (313) 359-8623
This firm makes curved glass for china cabinets, custom cut to any size. It offers immediate delivery anywhere. For information call Tuesday through Saturday, 10:00 A.M. to 3:00 P.M.

Barap Specialties   835 Bellows, Frankfort, Michigan 49635
This firm carries decorative head nails in three sizes. The nails come in a hammered antique finish, a French natural (oxidized brass) finish, or nickel plated. Rubber cushion glides, monopoint glides,

platform rocker springs, chair swivel, and an assortment of upholstery tools are also offered. Catalogues are available for 50¢.

Richard Blaschke   670 Lake Avenue, Bristol, Connecticut 06010   (203) 584-2566
Curved china cabinet glass is for sale in 2 sizes for side panels and different sizes for doors. Call or write for more information.

Century Glass & Mirror Incorporated   1417 North Washington, Dallas, Texas 75204
(214) 823-7773
Services include custom beveling, sandblast etching, and glass molding. Send patterns for price quotes.

Connoisseur Studio Incorporated   P.O. Box 7187, Louisville, Kentucky 40207   (502) 426-6600
This firm offers "Treasure Gold," a one-step way to add a metallic finish to almost any surface. It is a nontarnishing wax that comes in 16 different colors. It can be used to highlight, stain, glaze, antique, stencil, or marbleize. It will not run off or fade and can be removed easily. Call or write for more information. A catalogue is available.

Albert Constantine and Son, Inc.   2050 Eastchester Road, Department A11, Bronx, New York
10461   (212) 792-1600
This firm specializes in exotic veneers, imported and domestic. There is a selection of over 100 different types of veneer including 16 varieties of Monarch veneers. Tools and materials needed for applying veneer (as well as upholstery) are also available. Veneer inlays and overlays are available in a large selection of designs and woods. A catalogue with 20 wood samples is available for $1.50 (the catalogue alone is $1.00), which is refundable with the first purchase.

Cyclo Sciences, Inc.   434 Bergen Boulevard, Palisades, New Jersey 07650
This firm sells Wood Dry, a nontoxic water-repellent preservative.

Darworth Company   Avon, Connecticut 06001
This firm offers Cuprinol, a water repellent wood preservative with fungicide and insecticide.

Furniture Revival and Company   P.O. Box 994, 580 Southwest Twin Oaks Circle, Corvallis,
Oregon 97330   (503) 754-6323
This company carries furniture and cabinet hardware including pulls, keyholes, knobs, hooks, hinges, kitchen and icebox hardware, casters and feet, trunk hardware, etc. It also offers cane webbing, reed spline, accessories, replacement chair seats, curved china cabinet glass, wood replacement parts, and finishing products. A catalogue is available for $2.00.

Keystone   P.O. Box 3292, San Diego, California 92103   (714) 280-1337
Keystone offers hardware and restoration products for period furniture. It carries wooden knobs of various shapes, sizes, and woods suitable for furniture and cabinets; hardwoods; veneer; pressed fiber seats; stripping fluid; and caning materials. Restoration services are available. A general price guide for its services, *Booklet on Antique Furniture Restoration,* is available for $2.50.

Bob Morgan Woodworking Supplies 1123 Bardstown Road, Louisville, Kentucky 40204 (502) 456-2545

A large selection of veneers, decorative inlays and borders, embossed wood moldings, and a new iron-on glue sheet for veneering are among the products offered. The *Veneer Craft Catalog* is available.

John Morgan 443 Metropolitan Avenue, Brooklyn, New York 11211

John Morgan offers bent glass replacement parts for curio cabinets, china closets, clocks, barometers, etc.

The Old-Fashioned Milk Paint Company P.O. Box 222, Groton, Massachusetts 01450 (617) 448-6336

This company makes paint in dry powder form using milk products, mineral fillers, and pigments. Literature and a color card are available for 60¢.

Old Hotel Antiques 68 Main Street, P.O. Box 94, Sutter Creek, California 95685 (209) 267-5901

This firm manufactures solid oak replacement trays, which are made to fit any type old oak high chair with 14 inches between arms. They are preassembled and sanded, ready to stain to match your high chair. Call or write for more information.

Shadovitz Bros. Inc. 1565 Bergen Street, Brooklyn, New York 11213 (212) 774-9100

This firm distributes a wide variety of glass, plastics, mirrors, and supplies, including bent glass for china cabinets and furniture.

Squaw Alley Incorporated 106 West Water Street, Naperville, Illinois 60540 (312) 357-0200

This firm cuts bent glass for china cabinets. A catalogue is available for $2.00.

Stulb Paint & Chemical Company, Inc. P.O. Box 297, 810 East Main Street, Norristown, Pennsylvania 19404 (215) 272-6660

This firm produces authentic eighteenth- and nineteenth-century paint colors for restoration and decorating in the Colonial, Federal, and Victorian periods. They can be used inside or outside and are sold through paint and hardware stores and antiques and gift shops. Customers will be furnished with the name of the nearest dealer, or a mail order form can be requested. A set of color cards is available for $1.00.

Sunwood Veneers 2110 North Dragoon, Tucson, Arizona 85705 (602) 623-0636

A wide variety of veneers are available featuring common and exotic woods. Premium hardwood, fiber-backed, can be special ordered up to 4 by 12 feet. Chevron, butcher block, and regular match are offered. Price lists and samples are available.

Tuxedo Carvings Tuxedo, New York 10987 (914) 351-4544

Here is a source for solid oak carvings suitable for antique or reproduction furniture. These hand carved items include rolltop pulls, handles, and carvings for china closets, bookcases, clock shelves, etc.

Weird Wood   P.O. Box 190SB, Chester, Vermont 05143   (802) 875-2163
This company is a supplier of native American woods—cherry, maple, pine, butternut—and some Central American woods for cabinetwork and crafts. Send 50¢ for a brochure and price list.

Wood & Leather Craft   Star Route, Callicoon, New York 12723   (914) 887-4195
Leather tabletops with gold-tooled, period designs are made up to fit your secretary, desk, etc. Antique black, brown, red, or green mellow finishes are available. Send measurements or a paper pattern. Easy gluing directions are given.

The Woodworkers' Store   21801 Industrial Boulevard, Rogers, Minnesota 55374 (612) 428-4101
The Woodworkers' Store carries over 3,000 useful products for the woodworker including flexible veneers, furniture trim, specialty hardware, tools, a wide variety of wood products, and books. Items for inlay, veneer, and turned wood are also offered. A catalogue is available for $1.00.

REPAIR & RESTORATION SERVICES

Abend Metal Repair   Delavan Center, 501 West Fayette Street, Syracuse, New York 13204 (315) 478-2749
This firm repairs and restores metal furniture.

Alexandria Wood Joinery   George and Judy Whittaker, Plumer Hill Road, Alexandria, New Hampshire 03222   (603) 744-8243
Services include furniture stripping, refinishing, and repair of antique furniture. Chair seats, cane, splint, rush, and Shaker tape are also available. All work is done on a custom basis and no price list is offered.

All-Tek Finishing Company   355 Bernard Street, Trenton, New Jersey 08618   (609) 695-3644
Furniture stripping and finishing, mirror resilvering, glass beveling, and gold leafing are among the services offered by this firm.

Antique Furniture Workroom, Inc.   225 East 24th Street, New York, New York 10010 (212) 683-0551
This firm specializes in restoration of antique furniture.

Barnstead Antiques, Jim Riggs   Morvale & Wottrings Mill Road, Easton, Pennsylvania 18042 (215) 258-9615
Mr. Riggs restores furniture.

J. W. Berry & Son   222 West Read Street, Baltimore, Maryland 21201   (301) 727-4687
Services include the appraisal and restoration of antique furniture only. Questions will be answered by mail.

Carriage Trade Antiques   C. Gentry Trimble, 406 West Lenoir Avenue, Kinston, North Carolina 28501   (919) 523-2946
Refinishing and restoration are done. Estimates, pickup, and delivery are available. For further information please write or call.

The Copper Horse   81 Racine Street, Menasha, Wisconsin 54952   (414) 725-3756 or 725-4880
The Copper Horse refinishes furniture entirely by hand. A full line of other services are available including repair and replacement of damaged parts, caning (including splint and rush), regluing, and whatever else is needed.

Couret & Son   1027 Richard Street, New Orleans, Louisiana 70130   (504) 524-4145
Couret & Son repairs all types of furniture: American, Oriental, English, and French. It specializes in the restoration of the fine pieces that are almost beyond repair. Services include replacement of veneer, marquetry, hand carving, wood turning, faux-bois, lacquering, etc.

Dante's   755 South 3rd Street, Philadelphia, Pennsylvania 19147   (215) 922-5118 or 922-8316
All restoration and refinishing is done by hand. The company's work has included painting of Chinese figures and screens as well as replacing inlay work and broken or missing parts. The range of work restored includes sixteenth-century to contemporary items.

Dan Diehl   6374 Waterloo Road, Atwater, Ohio 44201   (216) 947-3385
Dan Diehl specializes in Victorian interior restoration and cabinetry. A brochure is available.

Ed's Antiques, Inc.   422 South Street, Philadelphia, Pennsylvania 19147   (215) 923-4120
Services include refinishing and repairing antique furniture and caning.

Froelich Leather Craft Company, Inc.   18 West 18th Street, New York, New York 10011   (212) 243-1585
Restoration services are available to the public. Questions are answered by mail.

Thom Gentle   74 Elmwood Place, Oberlin, Ohio 44074   (216) 775-7335
Thom Gentle is a conservator of furniture and wooden objects. His services are available to anyone in the U.S. and he will answer questions by mail. Fees are hourly or by the day.

Richard George/George Studios   45-04 97th Place, Corona, New York 11368   (212) 271-2506
Services include restoration and conservation of furniture, gold leafing, Coromandel screens, and antique marble and faux finishes. For the restoration of large pieces of furniture, screens, or fixed panels requiring on-location repairs, call or write for information.

The Guild   2749 East Anaheim Street, Long Beach, California 90804   (213) 434-1255
The Guild restores fine antique furniture. Call or write for further information.

R. Bruce Hamilton   Furniture Restoration, 551 Main Street, P.O. Box 587, West Newbury, Massachusetts 01985   (617) 363-2638 or 729-1569
General restoration is done by appointment.

Robert H. Harris   120 East Main Street, Falconer, New York 14733
Missing or broken wooden parts are replaced with hand carved replicas.

Wade Holtzman   259 Pond Street, Winchester, Massachusetts 01890   (617) 729-2351
Services include furniture restoration, repair and refinishing of period antique pieces, repair of inlay and marquetry, Boulle work, gilding, lacquer and japanning work, and French polish finish.

Kenneth R. Hopkins   3001 Monta Vista, Olympia, Washington 98501   (206) 943-1118
Mr. Hopkins's services include appraisal and restoration of furniture, stenciling, decoration, distressing, and making rawhide seats for chairs. He will answer questions by mail.

Bronislaus F. Janulis   6253 North Troy, Chicago, Illinois 60659   (312) 743-7868
Services include gilding, hand carving, and wood leafing.

Thomas Johnson, Antique Restoration,   5 Bridge Street, Watertown, Massachusetts 02172 (617) 924-0075
Mr. Johnson repairs and restores antique furniture. He will reproduce missing parts, repair veneer, and do invisible repairs.

Just Enterprises   2790 Sherwin Avenue, Unit 10, Ventura, California 93003   (805) 644-5837
Services include furniture restoration and repair, structural stabilization, refinishing, and inlay repair of brass, wood, ivory, and mother-of-pearl.

Keystone   P.O. Box 3292, San Diego, California 92103   (714) 280-1337
Keystone carries hardware and restoration products for period furniture. Its restoration services include turning spindles, reproducing wood parts, gluing, veneering, gold leafing, caning, glass bending and beveling, and mirror resilvering. A general price guide for its services, *Booklet on Antique Furniture Restoration,* is available for $2.50.

Jos. Kilgridge Antiques of Early America   Main Street (Route 119), Groton, Massachusetts 01450   (617) 448-3330
Services include furniture restoration, structural work, surface finishing (including traditional French polishes), veneering, replacement of missing or broken parts from an extensive stock of aged wood, old paint touch-up, fitting of reproduction brasses, hinges, etc. For estimates or consultation ask for Jon Vanderhorst.

Lacquercraft, Inc.   175 East 87th Street, New York, New York 10028   (212) 427-1652
Services include restoration of antique furniture, screens, and objets d'art, and lacquer work.

Len's Country Barn Antiques, Inc.   9929 Rhode Island Avenue, College Park, Maryland 20740
(301) 441-2546
This firm specializes in repairs, refinishing, and supplies. It offers a complete line of refinishing supplies including paint removers, brass hardware, chair cane, solvents, dowels, locks, and hard-to-find items.

Levine's Restorations   4801 7th Street North, Arlington, Virginia 22203   (703) 525-4009
This firm repairs and restores furniture of all woods, finishes, periods, and styles of American and European design. Mail orders and phone calls are encouraged and there is a pick up and delivery service within a 100-mile radius of their location. Estimates are given and a catalogue is available.

Allen & Ina Brosseau Marx   15 Shadow Lane, Great Neck, New York 11021   (516) 466-4759
Allen and Ina Brosseau Marx specialize in painted and gilded surfaces with emphasis on the conservation of Oriental lacquer. Their work includes restoration of decorative painting, graining, marbleizing and all faux, verre églomisé, papier-mâché, marquetry, coquillage, Art Deco lacquer, eggshell inlay, and seventeenth- to nineteenth-century inlaid, incised, carved lacquer on porcelain. They will travel and will answer questions by mail for a fee. A brochure is available.

Robert F. McGiffin   Division for Historic Preservation, Peebles Island, Waterford, New York
12188   (518) 237-8090
Mr. McGiffin has a private practice but may be contacted at the above facility. He will restore furniture, give an opinion on conservation, and answer questions by mail. There is a fee for all services.

John W. Melody, Conservator of Furniture   Winterthur Museum, Winterthur, Delaware 19735
(302) 656-8591, Ext. 329
Mr. Melody will restore furniture and wooden art objects and give advice on their conservation. He will answer questions by mail and does collection surveys to determine problems and offer advice. He charges an hourly rate plus expenses.

Rosene Green Associates, Inc.   1622A Beacon Street, Brookline, Massachusetts 02146
(617) 277-8368
Decorative borders and inlays are restored. Missing areas are hand carved to match the original. Oriental lacquered furniture, caddies, Coromandel screens, and cracked or blistering pieces are restored.

William Therry   Furniture Conservation Laboratory, Unionville, Pennsylvania 19375
(215) 347-1684
Conservation of period furniture, combining traditional and state-of-the-art skills in carving, inlay, turning, finish rejuvenation, and all areas of cabinetmaking are handled at the laboratory. An object examination and verbal conservation estimate at the Unionville lab is free. Written estimates are $50.00. In situ (museums, institutions, dealers, private collections) the fee is $100.00 per day plus expenses. Questions are answered by mail and an appointment is necessary to visit the laboratory.

Brian J. Tuck   18 Elm Street, Newport, Rhode Island 02840   (401) 847-0310
Mr. Tuck restores marquetry, japanning, lacquer, veneer, and carving and gilding on furniture.

Van Parys Studio   6338 Germantown Avenue, Philadelphia, Pennsylvania 19144   (215) 844-1930
This firm does raised lacquer painting on furniture and wall plaques.

Robert G. Walker   Museum of Fine Arts, Boston, Massachusetts 02215   (617) 267-9300, Ext. 343
Furniture restoration and conservation services are available to anyone in the U.S. Mr. Walker will answer questions if a self-addressed, stamped envelope is enclosed. Sometimes there is a fee.

Robert Whitley, Master Craftsman, Conservator   Laurel Road, Bucks County, Solebury, Pennsylvania 18963   (215) 297-8452
Mr. Whitley restores furniture. A brochure is available.

George G. Whitmore Company, Inc.   311 Farm Hill Road, Middletown, Connecticut 06457
(203) 346-3492
This company does restoration and appraisals, primarily dealing with wood. It does some restoration of Oriental lacquered items. Services are available to anyone in the U.S. Questions are answered by mail.

Wood Work Arts   4808 Lawrence Street, Hyattsville, Maryland 20781   (301) 779-7911
Wood Work Arts repairs and restores fine cabinetry, carving, and delicate antique furniture. It replaces missing carved pieces, turned pieces, veneers, and inlays. It handles not only American and European, but also Chinese furniture.

Y and J Furniture Company   P.O. Box 1361, 1612 East Geer Street, Durham, North Carolina 27702   (919) 682-6131
This firm does restoration of furniture only. No examinations or deliveries over 100 miles are accepted. Questions are answered by mail.

The Yankee Drummer Antiques   Antique Clock Refurbishment/Restoration, 23 Burnham Road (Route 111), Hudson, New Hampshire 03051
(603) 889-1415
This firm does custom restoration and refinishing of furniture including the duplication of any parts of the furniture that require replacement due to loss or damage (wood carving included).

PRICE GUIDES

Andrews, John. *The Price Guide to Antique Furniture.*
Suffolk, England: Antique Collectors' Club (5 Church Street, Clopton, Woodbridge, Suffolk 1P12 1BR England), 1969. Price revision 1981.

————. *The Price Guide to Victorian, Edwardian and 1920s Furniture.*
Suffolk, England: Antique Collectors' Club (5 Church Street, Clopton, Woodbridge, Suffolk 1P12 1BR England), 1981.

Blundell, Peter S. *The Marketplace Guide to Oak Furniture: Styles and Values.*
Paducah, Kentucky: Collector Books, 1980.

Curtis, Anthony, comp. *The Lyle Antiques and Their Values: Furniture.*
New York: Coward, McCann & Geoghegan, 1982.

Grotz, George. *The Current Antique Furniture Style & Price Guide.*
New York: Doubleday, 1981.

Shirley, G. E. *Great Grandmother's Wicker Furniture, 1880s–1920s.*
Privately printed, 1979 (900 North 6th Street, Burlington, Iowa 52601).

Swedberg, Robert and Harriett. *Country Pine Furniture Styles & Prices.*
Des Moines: Wallace-Homestead, 1980.

————. *Victorian Furniture: Styles and Prices,* Book I Revised.
Des Moines: Wallace-Homestead, 1981.

————. *Victorian Furniture, Styles and Prices,* Book II.
Des Moines: Wallace-Homestead, 1981.

Voss, Thomas M. *The Bargain Hunter's Guide to Used Furniture.*
New York: Dell Publishing, 1980.

Weiss, Jeffrey. *Cornerstone Collector's Guide to Wicker.*
New York: Simon & Schuster, 1981.

BUYING BY MAIL

Hundreds of dealers sell furniture by mail in the United States and Canada. Many advertise in the general antiques publications in the furniture section. (See Chapter 99, General Publications.)

APPRAISERS

J. W. Berry & Son   222 West Read Street, Baltimore, Maryland 21201   (301) 727-4687
This firm does appraisal of antique furniture only. It will answer questions by mail.

Kenneth R. Hopkins   3001 Monta Vista, Olympia, Washington 98501   (206) 943-1118
Mr. Hopkins appraises furniture and answers questions by mail.

George G. Whitmore Company, Inc.   311 Farm Hill Road, Middletown, Connecticut 06457
(203) 346-3492
This company does appraisals, primarily dealing with wood. Services are available to anyone in the
U.S. by mail.

BOOKSELLERS

Books about woodworking can be found in every good bookstore or library. Most stores will special
order the books for you. Books are also available through the mail order antiques book dealers listed in
Chapter 91, Booksellers. If you cannot find the books, or if they are privately printed, write to the
address listed to buy a copy.

Bark Service Company   P.O. Box 637, Troutman, North Carolina 28166
This company offers a selection of books pertaining to woodworking. Included are books on boats,
carpentry, carving, furniture design and construction, furniture restoration, home building, veneering,
upholstering, tools, and more. A catalogue is available.

R. Sorsky, Bookseller   3845 North Blackstone, Fresno, California 93726
R. Sorsky carries new and out-of-print books on woodworking exclusively. Frequently updated
catalogues are available for $1.50.

31. GLASS

Glass collecting covers a wide range of glass types including stained glass, bottles, paperweights, cameo glass, art glass, Carnival glass, and the twentieth-century wares such as Heisey, Fenton, Paden City, Tiffin, Depression glass, and many more. There is a new collecting area called "modern collectibles" in glass that includes the new pieces such as Pairpoint cup plates. Also included in this chapter are the many glass replacement parts for doors and windows. Reproductions are to be found in any of the glass products, so be cautious when you buy. The publications and price guides often list the well-known reproductions. Fake glass marks are often seen, as it is simple to acid stamp, etch, or sandblast a name on a less desirable piece of glass that will raise the value of it for the unsuspecting.

Glass should never be kept in a sunny window. Old glass (made before 1900) was made of a slightly different mixture and may turn colors. New glass could magnify the sun and cause scorch marks on furniture or carpets, or even start a fire.

Chipped glass can be ground down. There is often a local glass repair shop that can be located through the Yellow Pages of the telephone book. New epoxy mixtures can be used to make repairs on glass that are almost impossible to detect without the use of a black light. This type of repair is very expensive and there are only a few restorers who currently offer the service. Any glass can be polished, including the insides of small-neck bottles. There is a danger and it is a very specialized job.

See also Chapter 100, Matching Services.

CLUBS

Air Capital Carnival Glass Club   Donald Kime, Secretary-Editor, 1202 West 4th Street, Haysville, Kansas 67060
This is a local club.

American Carnival Glass Association   Emma Tilton, Secretary, P.O. Box 273, Gnadenhutten, Ohio 44629   (614) 254-9446
American Carnival Glass News is a newsletter listing club activities, recent auction prices, and information about new discoveries.

American Custard Glass Collectors   P.O. Box 5421, Kansas City, Missouri 64131
This club has a mimeographed newsletter, *Partyline*, listing prices, sales, and news about rarities and the custard glass market.

American Cut Glass Association   P.O. Box 7095, Shreveport, Louisiana 71107
Hobstar, issued monthly, is a newsletter filled with information about old cut glass, shows, and sales.

Fenton Art Glass Collectors of America, Inc.   P.O. Box 2441, Appleton, Wisconsin 54911
Butterfly Net is a mimeographed newsletter with information about club activities and discoveries in Fenton glass.

Fostoria Glass Society of America, Inc.   P.O. Box 826, Moundsville, West Virginia 26041
Facets of Fostoria is a 12-page newsletter featuring articles and ads.

Glass Art Society   c/o Tom McGlauchlin, Toledo Museum of Art, Toledo, Ohio 43609
The *Glass Art Society Newsletter* is sent to all members who pay dues. There is also an annual magazine.

Happy Hunters Carnival Glass Club   Bernice Allen, Secretary, 3316 Boston Street, Hopewell, Virginia 23860

Heart of America Carnival Glass Association   3048 Tamarak Drive, Manhattan, Kansas 66502
(913) 539-1933
H.O.A.C.G.A. Bulletin is a monthly newsletter with a few articles about Carnival glass and a lot of information about shows, members, etc.

Heisey Collectors of America, Inc.   P.O. Box 27, Newark, Ohio 43055
The *Heisey News* is a newsletter filled with pictures, information on patterns, history of Heisey, and advertisements offering glass for sale. This is an important research source for the serious collector.

Imperial Glass Collectors' Society   P.O. Box 4012, Silver Spring, Maryland 20904
The *Imperial Collectors Glasszette* is a quarterly newsletter.

International Carnival Glass Association   R.R. #1, Mentone, Indiana 46539   (219) 353-7678
Carnival Town Pump is the association's newsletter.

Land of Lincoln Carnival Glass Association   Jean Spierling, Secretary, 5113 North Nordica, Chicago, Illinois 60656

National Cambridge Collectors, Inc.   P.O. Box 416, Cambridge, Ohio 43725
The *Cambridge Crystal Ball* is a monthly newsletter filled with information about Cambridge glass patterns, factory history, and other valuable facts for collectors.

National Depression Glass Association, Inc.   8337 Santa Fe Lane, Shawnee Mission, Kansas 66212   (913) 383-1921
News & Views is a monthly newsletter reporting club business and meetings. A few articles, ads for shows, and dealer names are included.

The National Duncan Glass Society   P.O. Box 965, Washington, Pennsylvania 15301
The *National Duncan Glass Journal* is a newsletter including over 20 pages of reprints of early ads for Duncan glass, articles, and club news.

The National Early American Glass Club   c/o Mrs. Shirley Pope, 9 Commonwealth Avenue, Apt. 4A, Boston, Massachusetts 02116
The Glass Club Bulletin carries valuable articles about old glass. *The National Early American Glass Club Newsletter* lists events.

National Greentown Glass Association   1807 West Madison, Kokomo, Indiana 46901 (317) 628-3344
The *N.G.G.A. Newsletter* is a quarterly publication.

Northern California Carnival Glass Club   Charlotte Williams, Secretary-Editor, 630 North Lower Sacramento Road, Lodi, California 95240

Ohio Candlewick Collectors' Club   613 South Patterson Street, Gibsonburg, Ohio 43431 (419) 637-2695

Pacific Northwest Carnival Glass Club   Madonna Woodward, President, 48900 Middle Fork Road, North Bend, Washington 98045

Pairpoint Cup Plate Collectors of America, Inc.   9308 Brandywine Road, Clinton, Maryland 20735   (301) 868-4331
The Thistle is an attractive newsletter issued 4 times a year. It features illustrations, news about members, meetings, and cup plates, and a few articles about old glass.

Stained Glass Association of America   1125 Wilmington Avenue, St. Louis, Missouri 63111
Stained Glass Magazine is a quarterly publication.

Texas Carnival Glass Club   Mrs. Chester Herring, Secretary, 101 East Evans Avenue, Bonham, Texas 75418

PUBLICATIONS

Carnival Glass News and Views   P.O. Box 5421, Kansas City, Missouri 64131   (816) 444-8220
This newsletter is published 6 to 9 times a year and is a mimeographed report on auctions, collectors, and Carnival glass.

Carnival Glass Tumbler and Mug News   P.O. Box 5421, Kansas City, Missouri 64131
(816) 444-8220
This publication consists of 8 mimeographed pages of line drawings and information about patterns and new discoveries. It is especially informative for the serious collector.

Depression Glass Daze   P.O. Box 57, Otisville, Michigan 48463
This monthly newspaper is filled with articles, ads, and pictures. It is an important publication for the Depression glass collector.

Encore   Dorothy Taylor, Editor, P.O. Box 11734, Kansas City, Missouri 64138
This is a bimonthly magazine for new Carnival glass collectors.

The Glass Collector   P.O. Box 27037, Columbus, Ohio 43227   (614) 863-5400
This is an illustrated quarterly magazine about late nineteenth- and twentieth-century American glassware and related glass production.

Glass Review   P.O. Box 542, Marietta, Ohio 45750   (614) 374-2719
This monthly magazine is filled with articles about old and new glass of the twentieth century and also features dealer ads, pictures, and other good information.

Heisey Glass Newscaster   P.O. Box 102, Plymouth, Ohio 44865
This quarterly pamphlet by Clarence Vogel (a well-known authority on Heisey glass) includes pictures, tips on identifying Heisey, and valuable research information.

The Paden City Partyline   13325 Danvers Way, Westminster, California 92683   (714) 892-2278
This is a quarterly newsletter of about 8 pages featuring newly discovered information about Paden glass and recent price listings.

DECODING ADVERTISING COPY

Reading the ads for antique and collectible glassware often takes special knowledge. Two collectors will speak a special language in the same way two doctors have a vocabulary known only to the profession. When looking up glass it might help to know the terms and abbreviations. There is a general book, *An Illustrated Dictionary of Glass* by Harold Newman (London: Thames and Hudson, 1977) that defines most of the terms. *The History and Art of Glass, Index of Periodical Literature, 1956–1979* by the Corning Museum of Glass (Corning, New York, 1981) lists magazine articles about glass.

Candy container and glass bank collectors often use numbers that refer to special books. Eikelberner numbers refer to the two books by George Eikelberner and Serge Agadjanian, *American Glass Candy Containers* and *More American Glass Candy Containers*, both privately printed, 1967 and 1970 respec-

tively (River Road, Belle Mead, New Jersey 08502). Stanley numbers are from the book *A Century of Glass Toys* by Mary Louise Stanley, privately printed, 1972 (71 Chapin Parkway, Buffalo, New York 14209).

Milk glass collectors use Belknap numbers from the book *Milk Glass* by E. McCamly Belknap (New York, Crown Publishers: 1959), and the Ferson numbers from *Yesterday's Milk Glass Today* by Regis and Mary Ferson, privately printed, 1981 (122 Arden Road, Pittsburgh, Pennsylvania 15216).

Some advertisements refer to Weatherman reference numbers (W#). These are based on two books by Hazel Marie Weatherman, W1—*Colored Glassware of the Depression Era*, and W2—*Colored Glassware of the Depression Era 2*, privately printed, 1970 and 1974 respectively (P.O. Box 4444, Springfield, Missouri 65804). Mentions of the Stout books refer to *Depression Glass in Color, Depression Glass Number Two,* and *Depression Glass III,* all by Sandra McPhee Stout (Des Moines: Wallace-Homestead, 1970, 1971, and 1976 respectively).

Pressed or pattern glass collectors use a variety of books to identify patterns. Each is called by the author's last name. These include: *Kamm Pattern Glass Books,* vols. 1 to 8, by Minnie Watson Kamm, privately printed 1939–1954, available in reprint (Box 36332, Grosse Pointe Farms, Michigan 48236); *Early American Pressed Glass* and *Sandwich Glass* by Ruth Webb Lee (Wellesley Hills, Massachusetts: 1966); *American Historical Glass* by Bessie M. Lindsey (Rutland, Vermont: Charles E. Tuttle, 1967); *Early American Pattern Glass* and *Much More Early American Pattern Glass* by Alice Hulett Metz, privately printed in 1958 and 1965 respectively (Heritage Antiques, Box 336, South Orleans, Massachusetts 02662); *American and Canadian Goblets,* vols. 1 and 2 by Doris and Peter Unitt (Peterborough, Ontario: Clock House, 1974); and *American Pressed Glass and Figure Bottles* by A. Christian Revi (New York: Thomas Nelson & Sons, 1964).

These terms and abbreviations are often encountered in mail order advertisements for glassware:

Amb. Amber.	*Fl.* Flashed, flint or fluted.	*Ped.* Pedestal.
AOP. All over pattern.	*Flr.* Flower.	*Per.* Perfect.
B/B. Bread and butter.	*Ftd.* Footed.	*Pit.* Pitcher.
Bl. Blue.	*Gd.* Gold decorated.	*Pk.* Pink.
Cg. Cut Glass.	*Gr.* Green.	*R.* or *rnd.* Round.
C/s. Cup and saucer.	*Hdld.* Handled.	*SB.* Scalloped base.
Cam.. Cambridge glass.	*Hex.* Hexagonal.	*S-p.* Salt and pepper.
Carn. Carnival glass.	*Irid.* Iridescent.	*Sq. b.* Square base.
Cl. Clear.	*Jug.* Same as pitcher.	*Tpk.* Toothpick holder.
Cndl. hldrs. Candleholders.	*Lg.* Large.	*Tumb.* Tumbler.
Cov'd. Covered.	*Mk.* Marked.	*Turq.* Turquoise.
Cr. Creamer.	*M.* or *Mar.* Marigold.	*Veg.* Vegetable.
Cry. Crystal.	*M.g.* Milk glass.	*V.n.m.* Very near mint.
D. or *dia.* Diameter.	*Op.* or *Open.* No cover or opalescent.	*Water pitcher.* Pitcher with lip
Dec. Decoration.	*PAT.* Pattern around	bent to hold back ice.
DG. Depression glass.	top only.	*W/Plat.* With platinum.
Dia. or *diam.* Diamond.	*Pat.* Pattern or patent.	*Yel.* Yellow.
Dq. Diamond quilted.	*Pc.* Pieces	

BOOKS OF MARKS

Arwas, Victor. *Glass: Art Nouveau to Art Deco.*
New York: Rizzoli, 1977.

Haslam, Malcolm. *Marks and Monograms of the Modern Movement, 1875–1930.*
New York: Charles Scribner's Sons, 1977.

Kovel, Ralph and Terry. *Kovels' Know Your Antiques,* rev. and updated.
New York: Crown Publishers, 1981.

————. *Kovels' Know Your Collectibles.*
New York: Crown Publishers, 1981.

Peterson, Arthur G. *400 Trademarks on Glass.* Takoma Park, Maryland: Washington College Press, 1968.

HOW-TO-FIX-IT BOOKS

Hinds, Maxine. *Smashed Glass Reclaimed and Restored.*
Privately printed, 1972 (Route 2, P.O. Box 540, Galt, California 95632).

Klein, William Karl. *Repairing and Restoring China and Glass.*
New York: Harper & Row, 1962.

Malone, Laurence Adams. *How to Mend Your Treasures: Porcelain—(China)—Pottery—Glass.*
New York: Phaedra Publishers, 1972.

PARTS AND SUPPLIES

Abercrombie & Company   8227 Fenton Street, Silver Spring, Maryland 20910   (301) 585-2385
This firm supplies metal tops for shakers and bottles.

B. & L. Antiqurie   6217 South Lake Shore Road, Lexington, Michigan 48450   (313) 359-8623
Curved glass for china cabinets, picture frame glass, and clock glass are custom cut and delivered anywhere. For information call Tuesday through Saturday 10:00 A.M. to 3:00 P.M.

Blenko Glass Company, Inc.   Milton, West Virginia 25541   (304) 743-9081
This company supplies hand-blown sheet glass, also referred to as "antique glass," and dalles, or slab glass. Both are used to make stained glass windows. Catalogues and price lists are available. Call weekdays 8:00 A.M. to 4:00 P.M.

Century Glass & Mirror, Inc.   1417 North Washington, Dallas, Texas 75204   (214) 823-7773
This firm offers custom beveling for tabletops, clock glass, barometers, and wall mirrors. Send patterns for quotes. Sandblast etching and glass molding are also done.

Cherry Creek Enterprises   937 Santa Fe Drive, Denver, Colorado 80204   (303) 892-1819
This firm offers wheel engraved bevels, straight-line beveled glass, modular bevels, beveled glue chip, mirrored glass, and colored plate. A catalogue is available.

Crystal Mountain Prisms   P.O. Box 31, Westfield, New York 14787   (716) 326-3676
Prisms, pendants, bobeches, chains, pendeloques, plug drops, kite pendants, and prism pins are some of the items offered by this company. Send a self-addressed, stamped envelope for a complete list of sizes, shapes, colors, and prices.

Dexter Sunberg   15140 Washington Street, Riverside, California 92506
Dexter's Stain Remover takes stains, cloudiness, rust, and mineral and calcium deposits from glass. It will also remove water stains, rust lines, and any type of mineral deposits from pottery, porcelain, frosted glass, anything made from sand, quartz, etc. This cleaner can be used repeatedly but requires special precautions. Write for more information.

Electric Glass Company   One East Mellen Street, Hampton, Virginia 23663   (804) 722-6200
Electric Glass Company offers leaded and fully beveled panel inserts for doors, windows, tables, and architectural accents. Replacement pieces for old beveled windows can be made from a template or from exact measurements. New and old art glass, stained glass windows, and new Tiffany-type lampshades are also manufactured. Call or write for more information. A brochure is available for $3.00.

Furniture Revival and Company   P.O. Box 994, 580 Southwest Twin Oaks Circle, Corvallis, Oregon 97330   (503) 754-6323
This company offers curved china cabinet glass. A catalogue is available for $2.00.

Glassmasters Guild   621 Avenue of Americas, New York, New York 10011   (212) 924-2868
The Glassmasters Guild is known as "The Art Glass Department Store." It offers books, glass, lamp molds and bases, supplies, and tools. A catalogue is available.

Hand Blown Glass   Michael Kraatz, Susan Russell Kraatz, R.F.D. 2, Canaan, New Hampshire 03741   (603) 523-4289
This firm makes bull's-eye windowpanes suitable for sidelights and transoms. Each pane is hand blown, has the pontil mark in the center, and is cut to customer specifications. Call weekdays noon to 1:00 P.M. or 5:00 P.M. to 9:00 P.M., or write for further information.

Jonathan Studios, Inc.   Architectural and Decorative Arts, 619 South Tenth Street, Minneapolis, Minnesota 55404   (612) 338-0213
This firm offers stained, carved, etched, and leaded glass. Brochures are available.

The Lid Lady   Virginia Bodiker, 7790 East Ross Road, New Carlisle, Ohio 45344
A variety of lids and covers for a number of ceramic and glass vessels and containers are offered. There is a selection of over 10,000 lids.

John Morgan   443 Metropolitan Avenue, Brooklyn, New York 11211
Mr. Morgan offers bent glass replacement parts for Tiffany-type lampshades, curio cabinets, china closets, clocks, barometers, etc.

Pat's Etcetera Company, Inc. (PECO)   810 East First Street, Smithville, Texas 78957
(512) 237-3600
This company offers curved china cabinet glass and beveled glass panels for doors and windows. Send a stamped, self-addressed envelope for details. A catalogue is available for $3.00.

Raytech Industries, Inc.   P.O. Box 6, Stafford Springs, Connecticut 06076   (203) 684-4273
Raytech manufactures a machine that will restore chipped glasses, dishes, plates, etc. It grinds, bevels, and polishes. The machine comes with a goblet finishing cone and papers to restore difficult-to-finish glasses with turned-in rims. A brochure is available.

The Ross's Antiques   Apple Valley Village, Route 6, Milford, Pennsylvania 18337
The Ross's Antiques offers heavy tinplate shaker tops made from the original dies as used by old glasshouses between 1878 and 1926. Also, silver plated tops for cut glass and crystal shakers, castor bottle tops, Pairpoint shaker tops, lead pewter spouts for bottles, glass stoppers for castor bottles and cruets, and antique syrup jug lids are available. Do not send shakers or tops through the mail to be fitted. If the size is in doubt, invert the shaker, rub its glass top on a stamp pad, and send a print of its actual size. A brochure is available.

Shadovitz Bros., Inc.   1565 Bergen Street, Brooklyn, New York 11213   (212) 774-9100
This company distributes a wide variety of glass, plastics, mirrors, and supplies. Bent glass for china cabinets and furniture is also offered.

REPAIR AND RESTORATION SERVICES

All-Tek Finishing Company   355 Bernard Street, Trenton, New Jersey 08618   (609) 695-3644
Mirror resilvering, glass beveling, gold leafing, lamp and chandelier rewiring, and glass drilling are available through this company.

Asylum Glass Studio   Grove Street, Newport, Maine 04953   (207) 368-5340
This firm restores stained, leaded, painted, and sandblasted glass and windows. It also offers contemporary and traditional bent panel shades and custom windows. Write for a free brochure.

Atlas Minerals & Chemicals, Inc.   Farmington Road, Mertztown, Pennsylvania 19539
(215) 682-7171
This firm offers a master mending kit for china and glass. It includes all the materials you need to restore or mend china, porcelain, pottery, glass, and other treasures as well as step-by-step instructions. There are four basic systems: (1) porcelainate for mending china and porcelain, (2) epoxyglass for mending glass, (3) porcelainizing finish with tints—no firing necessary, and (4) new gloss glaze for restoring glaze without firing. A brochure is available.

Paul Baron Company   Baron-Rolen Jewelers, 2825 East College Avenue, Decatur, Georgia 30030 (404) 299-1400
Pack your pieces to be repaired and ship to the company for an estimate.

The Boulder Art Glass Company   1920 Arapahoe Avenue, Boulder, Colorado 80302 (303) 449-9030
The Boulder Art Glass Company is comprised of several divisions working with different aspects of the art glass industry. Sandblasting, sand carving, glue-chipping, and acid-etching facilities are a major part of its business in restoration and commissioned work. Matching painted glass is a specialty. Duplication of replacement panels, bent panels (slumps) for replacement in curved panel lampshades, and beveling to match broken beveled pieces are other services offered.

Sandra Brauer/Stained Glass   235 Dean Street, Brooklyn, New York 11217   (212) 855-0656
Services include custom work and expert repair of stained glass windows and lampshades. Call or write for information or an appointment.

Butterfly Shoppe   637 Livernois, Ferndale, Michigan 48220   (313) 541-2858
This firm repairs crystal, china, silver, and other items (no wood). Estimates are given before repairing. Pieces to be repaired should be packed carefully and shipped UPS. The shop is open Monday through Wednesday 10:30 A.M. to 4:00 P.M. and Thursdays until 7:00 P.M.

David Lee Colglazier   Old Sturbridge Village, Sturbridge, Massachusetts 01566   (617) 347-3362
Private conservation is done on a fee basis. Mr. Colglazier will answer questions by mail.

The Condon Studios, Stained Glass   33 Richdale Avenue (Porter Square), Cambridge, Massachusetts 02140   (617) 661-5776
This firm specializes in the restoration and repair of stained glass windows, lamps (both bent and flat), and other items. Structural resupporting, protective glazing, and framing are among the services offered. A brochure is available.

Crown Glass Company   1418 16th Street, Denver, Colorado 80202   (303) 571-4333
This company restores stained glass. It has a large stock of colored glass on hand for its work, and many tints and thicknesses of old plate glass are used to duplicate bevel work. It can also match engraving, notching, marvering, and crosshatching.

The Crystal Workshop   P.O. Box 475, 883 Sandwich Road, Sagamore, Massachusetts 02561 (617) 888-1621
The Crystal Workshop offers restoration of antique glass paperweights, art glass, and cut glass. Other services include replacement of engraved window panels, fitting stoppers, drilling, and engraving. Hours by appointment. Call or write for further information.

Fred & Nancy Dikeman   42-66 Phlox Place, Flushing, New York 11355   (212) 358-1571
The Dikemans restore Tiffany lamps. All work is done with original tools, patterns, blocks, foil, and glass from Tiffany Studios.

Harry A. Eberhardt & Son Inc. 2010 Walnut Street, Philadelphia, Pennsylvania 19103
(215) 568-4144
This company specializes in the repair of porcelains, glass, ivory, jade, etc. They will answer questions by mail. There is no fee for estimates.

Ed's Antiques, Inc. 422 South Street, Philadelphia, Pennsylvania 19147   (215) 923-4120
Stained glass is repaired, reframed, and bought and sold.

Raymond F. Errett Corning Museum of Glass, P.O. Box 1332, Corning, New York 14830
(607) 937-5371
Mr. Errett does restorations and will answer questions by mail.

Ferguson's Cut Glass Works 4292 Pearl Road, Cleveland, Ohio 44109   (216) 459-2929
Services include cutting, beveling, and repairing of glass.

Gem Monogram & Cut Glass Corporation 623 Broadway, New York, New York 10012
(212) 674-8960
This firm offers extensive service in glass replacement and repair. Write before sending pieces. Replacement parts include blue glass liners for salts, mustards, bowls, and baskets, but its specialty is parts for chandeliers, including bobeches. Give accurate details, a penciled outline of the container, and a photo or sketch of the piece to be matched. For best results send the silver piece to be fitted with a liner.

Rosene Green Associates, Inc. 1622A Beacon Street, Brookline, Massachusetts 02146
(617) 277-8368
Venetian glass, crystal chandeliers, cut glass, etc. are restored. Shattered or missing pieces are duplicated in a high technology polymer with a refractive index that matches glass.

Hess Repairs 200 Park Avenue South, New York, New York 10003   (212) 741-0410
This firm restores glass. It will grind chips off glasses and its specialty is blue glass liners for silver salt, condiment, and sugar holders.

Howard's Stained Glass 2602 South 11th Street, Gadsden, Alabama 35901   (205) 543-2969
This firm repairs and restores Tiffany as well as other stained and leaded glass.

International Antique Repair Service, Inc. 8350 Hickman, Suite 14, Des Moines, Iowa 50322
(515) 278-2518 or 278-2515
Services include removal of chips, scratches, and stains, understaking of etchings, replacement of missing sections or pieces of clear glass (including high quality crystal), restoration of stained glass and paneled lampshades, and invisible repairs on Tiffany Favrile, Steuben Aurene, and any iridescent glass including Carnival glass. All the firm's work is invisible, blacklight proof, and guaranteed for 5 years. Ninety percent of its work is done through mail order. A brochure is available.

Iorio Glass Shops   South Main Street, Flemington, New Jersey 08822   (201) 782-5311
This firm specializes in the restoration of fine glass pieces. Edges are ground and finished by hand. Inquire first, enclosing a self-addressed, stamped envelope along with a description of your problem.

Ross E. Jasper   2213 West 2nd Street, Davenport, Iowa 52802   (319) 323-0661
Mr. Jasper will grind and buff chips from glassware and crystal, make goblets into bells, remove and fit stoppers, and apply new glass bases on goblets and compotes with heat epoxy. Prices are quoted upon receipt of material. For a free brochure send a self-addressed, stamped envelope.

Julie's Handcut Crystal   1851 A West Vista Way, Vista, California 92083   (714) 724-6381
This firm offers crystal repair. Chips are removed, beveled, and polished from goblets, pitchers, or vases. Written estimates are provided after receipt of the piece to be repaired. It also does hand-cut designs and monogramming on wind-wings for old or new classic cars.

Keystone   P.O. Box 3292, San Diego, California 92103   (714) 280-1337
Glass bending, beveling, etching, and mirror resilvering are among its services.

H. W. Kopp, Glass Grinding   26 State Street, Skaneateles, New York 13152   (315) 685-5073
H. W. Kopp restores damaged pieces of fine crystal by grinding down below chips and polishing them to the original finish. The firm does not mend cracks or breaks.

Betsy Labar   105 Plantation Lane, Stafford, Virginia 22554   (703) 752-9601
Betsy Labar is a crystal cutter and repairer. Chips are professionally removed, beveled, and polished from goblets, vases, or pitchers. Holes are drilled and stoppers repaired.

Robert Lehmann   P.O. Box 438, Lahaska, Pennsylvania 18931   (215) 794-5577
Mr. Lehmann does glass cutting and engraving as well as repairs (except for cracks). Write for an estimate, describing all the damage in detail.

Louisville Art Glass Studio   P.O. Box 4665, 1110 Baxter Avenue, Louisville, Kentucky 40204 (502) 585-5421
This firm restores old windows, including stained glass, transoms, sidelights, beveled glass, and sashes and frames.

Laurence A. Malone   The 1749 House, Route 63, Goshen, Connecticut 06756   (203) 491-2141
Mr. Malone mends and restores glass and china. Missing parts are restored. All work is guaranteed and boilproof.

Michael Glassworks   21427 Dexter, Warren, Michigan 48089   (313) 775-5338
This firm specializes in the repair and restoration of Tiffany and Tiffany-type lampshades, using only old glass.

Newburyport Stained Glass Studio   P.O. Box 683, 2 A Whites Court, Newburyport, Massachusetts 01950   (617) 465-2989
This firm specializes in repair and restoration of stained glass. It does anything from minor repairs to

major restoration of windows, skylights, and lamps. Services also include sash repairs and installation of polycarbonate protective covers. A brochure is available.

Old Hickory Stained Glass Studio   221 South 3rd Street, LaCrosse, Wisconsin 54601 (608) 784-6463
This firm does lampshade and window repair and restoration. Contact can be made by mail or visit.

Pairpoint Glass Works   851 Sandwich Road (Route 6A), Sagamore, Massachusetts 02561 (617) 888-2344
This firm restores clear antique glass and crystal. Such work often includes making new parts or pieces which must be hand blown. The firm is also a source for matching chandelier parts. Send broken pieces or a well-packed sample with complete details and photographs. Work is done on clear glass only.

Pompei Stained Glass   455 High Street (Route 60), West Medford, Massachusetts 02155 (617) 395-8867
Repairs and restorations on beveled glass, sandblasted glass, glass slumping, etching, and antique glass are available.

R & K Weenike Antiques   Box 140, Route 7, Ottumwa, Iowa 52501   (515) 934-5427
This firm repairs antiques, especially glass. Services include cleaning of cloudy vases and cruets.

Santa Fe Glass & Mirror Company, Inc.   P.O. Box 2002, Santa Fe, New Mexico 87501 (505) 982-3828
This company repairs and restores stained leaded glass windows, beveled leaded glass windows, and Tiffany-style and other lamps. It also offers beveled glass replacements for antique clocks, barometers, and other instruments. If necessary, it will custom form curved or convex glass. Submit a detailed description of the work needed or ship the article needing repair to the company for an accurate price estimate.

Such Happiness, Inc.   The Glass Works, New Ipswich, New Hampshire 03071   (603) 878-1031
Stained glass and old windows are repaired and restored.

Sunburst Stained Glass Company   825 Church, New Harmony, Indiana 47631   (812) 682-4065
This company restores stained glass, specializing in exact reproduction of the original work. It will make on-site inspections to prepare estimates where needed.

Lawrence Tschopp   Tschopp Stained Glass, 312 Bryant, Buffalo, New York 14222 (716) 881-1019
Mr. Tschopp specializes in restoration of Tiffany, curved panel lamps, and leaded glass windows. He will answer questions by mail without a fee if a self-addressed, stamped envelope is enclosed. His services are available to anyone in the U.S.

Unique Art Glass Company   5060 Arsenal, St. Louis, Missouri 63139   (314) 771-4840
This company repairs art glass and will do extensive repairs of any type, including delicate rematching of painted and stained art glass pieces. It also makes leaded glass shades.

Arthur Wilk   7261 Clinton Street, Elma, New York 14059   (716) 684-4389
Mr. Wilk specializes in the repair of Brilliant Period American cut glass. Write or call for more information.

H. Weber Wilson, Antiquarian   9701 Liberty Road, Frederick, Maryland 21701   (301) 898-9565
Stained glass windows are repaired.

FACTORY ADDRESSES

Most companies manufacturing crystal in the United States can be found listed in Giftware News magazine's 1981 *Buyers' Guide and Tableware Directory*, available at many large libraries or from the magazine. Listed here are some of the companies that have been making glass for many years. They may be able to help you fill in one of their sets.

Baccarat Inc.   55 East 57th Street, New York, New York 10022   (212) 826-4100

Blenko Glass Company, Inc.   P.O. Box 67, Milton, West Virginia 25541   (304) 743-9081

The Fenton Art Glass Company   704 Elizabeth Street, Williamstown, West Virginia 26187
(304) 375-6122

Fostoria Glass Company   1200 First Street, Moundsville, West Virginia 26041   (304) 845-1050

Gorham   333 Adelaide Avenue, Providence, Rhode Island 02907   (401) 785-9800

Libbey Glass   P.O. Box 919, Toledo, Ohio 43693   (419) 247-5000

Viking Glass   P.O. Box 29, New Martinsville, West Virginia 26155   (304) 455-2900

Waterford Glass, Inc.   225 Fifth Avenue, New York, New York 10010   (212) 481-1978

PRICE GUIDES

Bickenheuser, Fred. *Tiffin Glassmasters,* Books I and II.
Grove City, Ohio: Glassmasters Publications, 1979, 1981.

Brady, Ann. *1979 Western Depression Glass Price Guide.*
Privately printed, 1979 (4413 N. E. Fremont, Portland, Oregon 97213).

Curtis, Anthony, comp. *The Lyle Antiques and Their Values: Glass.*
New York: Coward, McCann & Geoghegan, 1982.

Duncan, Alastair. *Tiffany at Auction.*
New York: Rizzoli, 1982.

Edwards, Bill. *Fenton Carnival Glass: The Early Years.*
Paducah, Kentucky: Collector Books, 1981.

Evers, Jo. *The Standard Cut Glass Value Guide,* values updated 1981–1982.
Paducah, Kentucky: Collector Books, 1981.

Ferson, Regis and Mary. *Yesterday's Milk Glass Today.*
Privately printed, 1981 (122 Arden Road, Pittsburgh, Pennsylvania 15216).

Florence, Gene. *The Collector's Encyclopedia of Depression Glass,* 5th ed.
Paducah, Kentucky: Collector Books, 1982.

————. *Kitchen Glassware of the Depression Years.*
Paducah, Kentucky: Collector Books, 1981.

Fountain, Mel. *Swankyswigs with Price Guide.*
Privately printed, 1979 (201 Alvena, Wichita, Kansas 67203).

Hand, Sherman, and Williams, Charlotte. *Price Guide to Carnival Glass,* No. 9.
Privately printed, 1981 (127 Olympic Circle, Vacaville, California 95688).

Heacock, William. *Fenton Glass: The Second Twenty-Five Years.*
Marietta, Ohio: O-Val Advertising (P.O. Box 663, Marietta, Ohio 45750), 1980.

————. *Victorian Colored Glass 2: Patterns and Prices.*
Marietta, Ohio: Antique Publications, 1980.

James, Margaret. *Black Glass, An Illustrated Price Guide.*
Paducah, Kentucky: Collector Books, 1981.

Kovel, Ralph and Terry. *The Kovels' Illustrated Price Guide to Depression Glass and American Dinnerware.*
New York: Crown Publishers, 1980.

McCain, Mollie Helen. *Pattern Glass Primer.*
Leon, Iowa: Lamplighter Books, 1979.

McGrain, Pat. *1982 Price Survey* (Depression Glass).
Frederick, Maryland: McGrain Publications, 1981.

Selman, L. H. *Collector's Paperweights: Price Guide and Catalog.*
Santa Cruz, California: L. H. Selman, Ltd., 1979.

Shuman, John A., III. *Art Glass Sampler.*
Des Moines: Wallace-Homestead, 1978.

Smith, Allan B. and Helen B. *840 Individual Open Salts Illustrated, The Seventh Book.*
Topsham, Maine: The Country House, 1980.

Turnbull, George, and Herron, Anthony. *The Price Guide to English 18th Century Drinking Glasses.*
Suffolk, England: Antique Collectors' Club (5 Church Street, Clopton, Woodbridge, Suffolk,
1P12 1BR England), 1970. Price revision 1981.

Upton, Charles and Mary Alice. *1979 Price Guide to The Cambridge Glass Book.*
Privately printed, 1979 (68764 Eighth Street, Cambridge, Ohio 43725). (*The Cambridge Glass Book* by
Harold and Judy Bennett [Des Moines: Wallace-Homestead, 1970] is required in order to use this
book.)

Weatherman, Hazel Marie. *The 2nd Price Watch to Fostoria.*
Springfield, Missouri: Weatherman Glassbooks (P.O. Box 4444, Springfield, Missouri 65804), 1977.

————. *Price Guide to the Decorated Tumbler.*
Springfield, Missouri: Weatherman Glassbooks (P.O. Box 4444, Springfield, Missouri 65804), 1979.

Weiss, Jeffrey. *Cornerstone Collector's Guide to Glass.*
New York: Simon & Schuster, 1981.

Wetzel, Mary M. *Candlewick: The Jewel of Imperial Glassware.*
Privately printed, 1981 (2817 Appletree Lane, South Bend, Indiana 46615).

BUYING BY MAIL

Hundreds of dealers sell glass by mail in the United States and Canada. Many advertise in the general
antiques publications in the section about glass (see Chapter 99, General Publications) or in the
specialized publications for glass collectors.

AUCTION HOUSE

Woody Auction Company   P.O. Box 618, Douglass, Kansas 67039   (316) 746-2694
This general auction company specializes in Carnival glass.

APPRAISERS

The Condon Studio, Stained Glass   33 Richdale Avenue (Porter Square), Cambridge, Massachusetts 02140   (617) 661-5776
This firm offers appraising and locating services.

Harry A. Eberhardt & Son Inc.   2010 Walnut Street, Philadelphia, Pennsylvania 19103
(215) 568-4144
This company does appraisals of porcelains, glass, ivory, jade, etc. It will answer questions by mail.

Roundhill's Patterns Unlimited International   P.O. Box 15238, Seattle, Washington 98115
(206) 523-9710
An appraisal service for evaluating discontinued patterns of crystal is offered. Cost is $30.00 per pattern,
with no limit on the number of pieces.

Lawrence Tschopp   Tschopp Stained Glass, 312 Bryant, Buffalo, New York 14222
(716) 881-1019
Mr. Tschopp appraises Tiffany, curved panel lamps, and leaded glass windows. His services are available to anyone in the U.S. Include a self-addressed, stamped envelope for responses to questions.

Arthur Wilk   7261 Clinton Street, Elma, New York 14059
Mr. Wilk appraises Brilliant Period American cut glass. Call or write for more information.

BOOKSELLERS

The Book Exchange   90 West Market Street, Corning, New York 14830   (607) 936-8536
The Book Exchange specializes in books about glass. Most of the titles are out of print and unavailable
through the publishers. It offers a search service for out-of-print books on glass as well as other books.
Send title, author, and as much information as possible, or the name of the specific company or process
of glass production you are interested in. The Book Exchange issues 2 or 3 catalogues per year and may
be contacted by phone or mail.

V. R. Desmond   P.O. Box 36332, Grosse Pointe, Michigan 48236
This is a source for *Kamm Pattern Glass Books.*

National Cambridge Collectors, Inc.   P.O. Box 416, Cambridge, Ohio 43725
The National Cambridge Collectors club offers a list of books relating to Cambridge glass that can be
ordered directly through them. A price list is available.

32. HARDWARE

Some collectors want old doorknobs or iron latches as part of a collection but most people want to use the old hardware. Hardware for old furniture is difficult to match but relatively easy to replace. When possible, match any existing hardware—some designs are still being made. A few companies will make a copy of your hardware from a sample you submit. If the hardware is not original or can't be matched, replace it with either old hardware purchased for the piece or new hardware. Be sure to get hardware of the correct style and period.

When replacing hardware, try to buy pieces that will cover the old screw holes. Special hardware for old refrigerators, trunks, and, of course, doors and windows can also be found.

CLUBS

American Lock Collectors Association   14010 Cardwell, Livonia, Michigan 48154 (313) 522-0920
This club publishes a bimonthly newsletter with information about members, activities, and the history of locks.

Antique Doorknob Collectors of America   c/o Marjorie H. Weimer, P.O. Box 3088, Sedona, Arizona 86340-3088
Established in 1981, this group has a quarterly newsletter, *The Doorknob Collector,* with articles for and by members.

Key Collectors International   P.O. Box 9397, Phoenix, Arizona 85068   (602) 997-2266
Key Collectors Journal consists of mimeographed pages of lock and key information made to keep in a notebook.

PARTS AND SUPPLIES

Anglo-American Brass Company   Box 9792, 4146 Mitzi Drive, San Jose, California 95157 (408) 246-0203
This firm offers solid brass reproduction antique-style hardware and locks for restoration. All products are solid brass and made in the traditional way of hand casting and finishing. Order forms are supplied with every catalogue for mail order service, or local people may call in person. Catalogue 113R is available for $1.00.

Antique Hardware Company   P.O. Box 877, Redondo Beach, California 90277   (213) 378-5990
This company makes exact replicas of carefully selected antique furniture hardware. The authentic

appearance is achieved by using the old methods of handcrafting. A selection of knobs, escutcheons, keyholes, bin teardrop and armoire pulls, balls and trim plates, drawer pull units, and hall tree hooks are carried. A catalogue is available.

Architectural Antiques and Reproductions, Inc. 1327 9th Street, N.W., Washington, D.C. 20001 (202) 232-2772
Anything that might be needed to restore a Victorian house is offered. The policy is to find or make whatever is required. It has brass hardware, doorknobs, newel posts, Victorian lighting, etc. Write or call Barry S. Levy. The shop is open Friday, Saturday, and Sunday from noon to 5:00 P.M.

Artifacts, Inc. 702 Mount Vernon Avenue, Alexandria, Virginia 22301 (703) 548-6555
"Rescued" architectural features (among which are certain hardware items) are the specialty of this firm. Because of rapid business turnover, no list is issued, but the firm will answer all inquiries for particular items. Include a self-addressed, stamped envelope with each request.

George & Ione Baker 921 Gravel Road, Webster, New York 14580 (716) 671-7765
Antique hardware for furniture and home restoration is this firm's specialty. Approximately 250,000 pieces are now in stock. By appointment only.

Baldwin Hardware Manufacturing Corporation 841 Wyomissing Boulevard, Reading, Pennsylvania 19603 (215) 777-7811
Authentic reproductions of early brasses used in Colonial America are offered by this company. Locks, latches, decorative handles, knobs, and trim are included in its selection. Four brochures are available for 75¢ each: *Eighteenth Century Colonial Lock Makers, Quality Mortise Locks and Latches, Narrow Backset Mortise Locks,* and *Authentic Colonial Brass Reproductions.*

Ball and Ball 463 West Lincoln Highway, Exton, Pennsylvania 19341 (215) 363-7330
This firm sells reproductions of furniture and house hardware including pulls, knobs, locks, hinges, keys, keepers, etc. It can make copies of your originals or try to match your sample. Literature is available.

Barap Specialties 835 Bellows, Frankfort, Michigan 49635
This firm offers authentic reproductions of English antique hardware for Colonial period furniture and cabinets are available in solid brass and steel with English antique finish. A catalogue is available for 50¢.

Bona Decorative Hardware 2227 Beechmont, Cincinnati, Ohio 45230 (513) 232-4300
Reproduction hardware for bathrooms, doors and cabinets, furniture, decorative hooks, and mail slots and boxes is available. Call or write for more information or send $5.00 for a catalogue.

James W. Broaddus 1635 South 4th Street, Terre Haute, Indiana 47802
Mr. Broaddus makes cherry, walnut, and oak drawer knobs which are hand turned from the wood of old tabletops, chests of drawers, etc. New wood will not match the color and texture of old wood. The

knobs come in different styles (mushroom, Empire, country, and Victorian) and sizes. Duplicates of turned cherry or walnut drawer knobs also can be made. For literature send a self-addressed, stamped envelope.

Bygone Era   4783 Peachtree Road, Atlanta, Georgia 30341   (404) 458-3016 or 458-6883
Thousands of knobs, plates, hinges, and letter slots are offered. A listing of these items is available.

Colonial Lock Company   172 Main Street, Terryville, Connecticut 06786   (203) 584-0311
This company offers wood-covered stock locks and wood-covered wrought-iron plate locks with solid maple covers available in dark Colonial stain, antique black, or unfinished (so that they can be matched to the door). It also features a 1½-inch-wide hardened laminated steel dead bolt with a 1-inch throw. The bolt is mounted to a steel backplate and engages a flat strike that is mounted with three screws to the doorjamb. The lock is operated by a knob inside and a 5-pin tumbler outside. It is easy to install, requiring only one drilled hole in the door.

Albert Constantine and Son, Inc.   2050 Eastchester Road, Department A11, Bronx, New York 10461   (212) 792-1600
A diversified group of decorative furniture hardware in both period and modern styles is available from this firm. Most are copies of fine old originals in museums or private collections. Included in this selection is hardware for small boxes. A catalogue is available for $1.00.

Custom House   South Shore Drive, Owl's Head, Maine 04854   (207) 594-9281
This is a custom casting foundry offering brass or bronze decorative pieces for furniture, antique stove replacement parts, designs for fireplace fronts, frieze work, and cornice ornaments. Catalogue sheets are available.

The Decorative Hardware Studio   160 King Street, Chappaqua, New York 10514
(914) 238-5220 or 238-5251
This firm sells a wide selection of hardware trim and accessories: knobs, pulls, hinges, escutcheons, cabinet locks, etc. A brochure is available.

18th Century Hardware Company, Inc.   131 East 3rd Street, Derry, Pennsylvania 15627
(412) 694-8421
Brass and iron hardware are made by this company. All brass hardware is supplied in two standard finishes: antique and bright. Some types of hardware have a special finish. The hardware includes fittings, casters, escutcheons, hinges, hooks, door knockers, furniture locks, clock parts, bed hardware, cabinet hardware, and much more. Various styles of drawer pulls are available including William and Mary, Chippendale, Hepplewhite, and Victorian. A catalogue and price list are available.

Faneuil Furniture Hardware   94-100 Peterborough Street, Boston, Massachusetts 02215
(617) 262-7516
This firm offers an extensive selection of furniture hardware. Many items have been reproduced from eighteenth-century originals. To get its 138-page catalogue send $2.00 or call.

Finishing Products and Supply Company, Inc.   4611 Macklind Avenue, St. Louis, Missouri 63109
(314) 481-0700
Stamped and cast brass reproduction hardware including pulls, keyhole covers, and cabinet hinges are made by this company. A catalogue is available for $2.00.

Folger Adam Company   P.O. Box 688, Joliet, Illinois 60434   (815) 723-3438
"Williamsburg" brass rim locks are manufactured with careful attention to detail. The reproductions are so authentic that they are used along with genuine antique locks in the restored houses and exhibition buildings in the Colonial village of Williamsburg. These lock reproductions are made of heavy, special-formula brass, hand-fitted and polished. They are available in three sizes: No. 1 (large) is used on larger and more formal doors of homes and public buildings; No. 2 (medium) is the most popular size for interior and exterior doors; and No. 3 (small) is most suitable for interior doors. A brochure is available.

Furniture Revival and Company   P.O. Box 994, 580 Southwest Twin Oaks Circle, Corvallis, Oregon 97330   (503) 754-6323
This company offers furniture and cabinet hardware, including pulls, keyholes, knobs, hooks, hinges, kitchen and icebox hardware, casters and feet, trunk hardware, etc. A catalogue is available for $2.00.

Gaston Wood Finishes, Inc.   P.O. Box 1246, 3630 East 10th Street, Bloomington, Indiana 47402
(812) 339-9111
This firm carries a large selection of hardware items, mainly reproduction hardware for antiques. It also offers many related items for use in restoring antique furniture. A catalogue is available.

The Guild   2749 East Anaheim Street, Long Beach, California 90804   (213) 434-1255
This company offers a rolltop desk lock. Each lock bears a brass front plate on the casing and a brass, spring-loaded strike plate. Accompanying every lock is a set of nickeled keys. Write for further information.

Heirloom Brass Company   P.O. Box 146, Dundas, Minnesota 55019   (507) 645-9341; out of state
(800) 533-2014
This company manaufactures antique replacement hardware. Choose from a large selection of Victorian, Eastlake, and turn-of-the-century hardware. All items are made from solid brass. Send for a free catalogue.

Horton Brasses   Box 95, Nooks Hill Road, Cromwell, Connecticut 06416   (203) 635-4400
This firm offers more than 450 authentic copies of old pieces (1680–1920) made in the same manner as the originals. If yours does not match any of the hardware in stock, a price can be quoted for a custom-made copy from your sample. The firm will advise if broken or damaged hardware can be repaired. Do not ship any hardware for repair or duplication without prior approval. Enclose a self-addressed, stamped envelope when asking for special information. Catalogues are available for $1.50 from P.O. Box 120-K, Cromwell, Connecticut 06416.

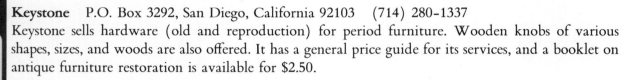

Steve Kayne Hand Forged Hardware   17 Harmon Place, Smithtown, New York 11788
(516) 724-3669
Creating custom Colonial and Early American ironwork for the home is a specialty of this firm. Work is done to the customer's requirements. Locks are repaired, keys made/warded. Drawings, photos, and correspondence will receive a quote and reply. Three catalogues are available: *Hand Forged Hardware* (forgings—Colonial and Early American), *Colonial Hardware—Solid Cast Brass and Bronze,* and *Designs at the Forge.* Each costs $1.00.

Keystone   P.O. Box 3292, San Diego, California 92103   (714) 280-1337
Keystone sells hardware (old and reproduction) for period furniture. Wooden knobs of various shapes, sizes, and woods are also offered. It has a general price guide for its services, and a booklet on antique furniture restoration is available for $2.50.

Cloyd Laibe   P.O. Box 1057, Newport Beach, California 92663   (714) 962-3265
Cloyd Laibe offers reproduction hardware for American and some turn-of-the-century furniture: bails, bail pulls, knobs, keyhole covers, coat hooks, hall seat hooks, etc. are available. For information send a self-addressed, stamped envelope.

Litchfield House   Pocket Knife Square, Lakeville, Connecticut 06039   (203) 364-0236
Litchfield House offers English porcelain door finishings including porcelain doorknobs, keyhole covers, and pushplates. They are available in 5 authentic eighteenth-century English garden patterns, and black or ivory with gilt trim. Doorknob assemblies fit any standard door closure device in use in the United States on doors up to 1¾ inches in thickness—with the exception of lock-in devices. Pushplates are packaged singly with brass screws for flush mounting. A free catalogue and price list are available upon request.

Monroe Coldren Antiques   723 East Virginia Avenue, Westchester, Pennsylvania 19380
(215) 692-5651
This firm supplies old and original hardware for restoring early furniture and houses.

19th Century Company   P.O. Box 1455, Upland, California 91786
Turn-of-the-century hardware is reproduced in solid cast brass. All items are like the originals that were common to American oak and other furniture of this era. Other items include Victorian hardware, cast brass reproductions of 1860s vintage hardware, and reproductions of antique icebox hardware. A catalogue is available for $1.00.

Ole Timey Furniture Supply Company   P.O. Box 1165, Smithfield, North Carolina 27577
(919) 965-6555
This company offers an assortment of hardware for furniture repair or restoration. A flyer is available.

Paxton Hardware Company   Upper Falls, Maryland 21156   (301) 592-8505
This company offers Chippendale, Hepplewhite, Queen Anne, Rosette, Spanish, French, and Victorian hardware including pulls, knobs, escutcheons, hooks, etc. Among these items are also casters and sockets, bed hardware, table hardware, lid and fall supports, hinges, latches, catches, icebox hardware, furniture locks, case and box hardware, bail handles, and posts. A catalogue is available for $1.50.

H. Pfanstiel Hardware Company, Inc.   Jeffersonville, New York 12748   (914) 482-4445
Hardware available includes the more common pieces: door plates, levers, knobs, pulls, etc., as well as those that are more difficult to find: 8 different styles of solid brass grilles, sprays, rail posts, flushcups, thumbturns, and so on. A catalogue is available for $5.00, refundable with the first purchase.

The Renovator's Supply   149 Northfield Road, Millers Falls, Maryland 01349   (413) 659-3152
This firm offers old-style hardware, lighting and plumbing fixtures, decorative accessories, and other hard-to-find products. They manufacture pieces from the Colonial era through the nineteenth century in solid brass, wrought iron, porcelain, pewter, and oak. All items are newly manufactured and many are authentic reproductions of period pieces. A catalogue is available for $2.00, refundable with the first purchase.

Restoration Hardware   438 Second Street, Eureka, California 95501   (707) 443-3152
Restoration Hardware is a retail and mail order concern specializing in Period and Victorian hardware, lighting, millwork, and plumbing fittings. A catalogue is available for $3.00, refundable with the first purchase.

Restoration Works, Inc.   412½ Virginia Street, Buffalo, New York 14201   (716) 881-1159
This firm carries furniture and builders' hardware, Victorian and Colonial reproductions, and brass and iron. It also offers specialty moldings, tools, cleaners, etc. for restoring older homes. A catalogue is available for $2.00.

Ritter and Son Hardware   Gualala, California 95445   (800) 358-9120; California (800) 862-4948
Ritter and Son Hardware offers solid brass antique replica hardware including bail sets, icebox hardware, cast and stamped dresser pulls, keyholes, knobs, knob backplates, hat hooks, bin pulls, file cabinet pulls, cardholder pulls, and matching cup pulls. Call or write for a catalogue.

San Francisco Victoriana   2245 Palou Avenue, San Francisco, California 94124   (415) 648-0313
This company has concentrated on the Victorian and Edwardian periods for its selection of hardware. The hardware is hand-cast in solid bronze, using the lost wax casting method. The hardware is provided unlacquered with screws. A catalogue is available.

Sign of the Crab   8101 Elder Creek Road, Sacramento, California 95824   (916) 383-2722
This company's line of brass hardware includes hooks, faucets, hinges, latches, locks, plates, doorknob sets, pulls, icebox labels, hinges, latches, and more. A catalogue is available.

The Smithy   Wolcott, Vermont 05680   (802) 472-6508
The Smithy specializes in hand-forged iron executed in the centuries-old manner with forge, hammer, and anvil. Most production consists of hardware and other ironwork necessary in the restoration of old buildings and in the construction of new reproduction homes. Duplications can also be made from most of the work shown in A. H. Sonn's *Early American Wrought Iron* (New York: Bonanza Books, 1979) and Wallace Nutting's *Furniture Treasury* (New York: Macmillan, 1961), as well as work from other photos or drawings.

Specialized Repair Service   2406 West Bryn Mawr Avenue, Chicago, Illinois 60659
(312) 784-2800
Missing hardware and castings in yellow brass and red brass or bronze are made to match existing hardware. Other services include welding, machining, refinishing, and silver brazing.

Squaw Alley Incorporated   106 West Water Street, Naperville, Illinois 60540   (312) 357-0200
Both antique and reproduction hardware can be found here. Squaw Alley's selection includes items such as Hoosier cabinet hardware, icebox hardware, trunk hardware, pulls, knobs, hooks, etc. A catalogue is available for $2.00.

Tremont Nail Company   P.O. Box 111, Wareham, Massachusetts 02571   (617) 295-0038
Old-fashioned cut nails are manufactured according to old patterns, which include the rose, oval-bung head, and a special nineteenth-century wrought-head nail. This hardware is ideal for restorations, furniture repair, cabinetwork, and flooring where authenticity is important to the project. Write for free literature.

Tuxedo Carvings   Tuxedo, New York 10987   (914) 351-4544
This firm offers a selection of carvings made of solid oak, suitable for antique or reproduction furniture. Although only oak carvings are stocked, orders in other wood are welcomed. Price will be determined by cost of wood and number of pieces ordered. Custom orders are also handled. For a price quote, send a sample of a detailed design as well as the required number of pieces.

Victorian Reproductions, Inc.   1601 Park Avenue South, Minneapolis, Minnesota 55404
(612) 338-3636
Brass hardware and plumbing fixtures are offered by this firm. A catalogue is available for $5.00.

The Waymar Company   1165 First Capitol Drive, Saint Charles, Missouri 63301   (314) 946-5811
This company has a wide assortment of hardware for antiques and reproductions. Among its cast and stamped brass hardware are drawer pulls, keyhole covers, knobs, pulls, hooks, and hinges. Icebox and trunk hardware are also offered. A catalogue is available.

Williamsburg Blacksmiths, Inc.   Goshen Road, Williamsburg, Massachusetts 01096
Authentic reproductions of Early American wrought-iron hardware are forged by the same methods used early in the craft of blacksmithing. All products are "Parkerized" for protection against rust. The hardware is finished with pyramid-head screws simulating antique nails with deeply cut screwdriver slots. Its assortment includes thumb latches, bar sets, locking devices, mortise lock sets, collars, slide bolts, hinges, door knockers, and more. A catalogue is available for $2.50.

The Woodworkers' Store   21801 Industrial Boulevard, Rogers, Minnesota 55374
(612) 428-4101
The Woodworkers' Store carries over 3,000 useful products for the woodworker, including specialty hardware, furniture hardware, tools, and books. A catalogue is available for $1.00.

33. HORSE-DRAWN CARRIAGES

Horse-drawn vehicles, like carriages and sleds, are collected by a small, earnest group with space and probably with horses. To learn more about horse-drawn vehicles, read the special publications on the subject. Meets, restoration problems, and history are discussed.

CLUBS

American Driving Society   79 Southgate Avenue, Hastings-on-Hudson, New York 10706 (914) 478-4045
The Whip is a newsletter published 10 times a year, featuring events and articles.

The Carriage Association   P.O. Box 3788, Portland, Maine 04104   (207) 773-8989
The Carriage Journal is a quarterly magazine containing articles, history, restoration tips, color photos, and ads.

REPAIR SERVICES

Chimney Farm Carriages   Charles C. Bent II, R.F.D. 2, North Canaan, New Hampshire 03741 (603) 523-4259
This firm offers complete restoration of horse-drawn vehicles. It will locate specific vehicles for collectors.

Kromer's Carriage Shop   Box 115, R.R. 4, Hodgenville, Kentucky 42748   (502) 358-3912
Kromer's Carriage Shop builds and restores horse-drawn wheeled vehicles and wheels and repairs harnesses.

AUCTION HOUSE

Martin Auctioneers, Inc.   P.O. Box 71, Blue Ball, Pennsylvania 17506   (717) 354-7006
Martin Auctioneers, Inc. specializes in horse-drawn carriages and sleighs. Catalogues are available and list vehicles by picture and description. Single copies are $6.00.

34. IVORY

Ivory requires special care and cleaning. Never make the mistake that we made many years ago when we carefully washed our first ivory carving, leaving it an undesirable white color. It has been 25 years since we erred and the carving has still not regained the yellow-brown tint or patina preferred by collectors. It is possible to color ivory with a solution of tea, but there is always the fear of doing more damage. If a carving is handled as much as possible, the body oils and moisture will eventually help to age it, but that would take more than one lifetime. Do not *ever* wash old ivory.

Ivory can be repaired by experts. Minor breaks can be mended by using a good commercial glue. Thin slices of ivory for inlay replacement are available.

HOW-TO-FIX-IT BOOK
Technical Notes on the Care of Art Objects: The Care of Ivory, No. 6.
London: Victoria and Albert Museum, 1971. Booklet.

PARTS AND SUPPLIES
Ken's   P.O. Box 706, Hayden Lake, Iowa 83835   (208) 772-7452
Ken's supplies several different kinds of ivory, including African elephant, hippopotamus, fossil (mammoth, mastodon, and walrus), warthog, and vegetable ivory (commonly called "ivory nuts," these are the fruit of tropical palm). A brochure and price list are available.

REPAIR SERVICES
David Lee Colglazier   Old Sturbridge Village, Sturbridge, Massachusetts 01566   (617) 347-3362
Private conservation of ivory is done on a fee basis. He will answer questions by mail.

Joseph DeVoren, Silversmiths   6350 Germantown Avenue, Philadelphia, Pennsylvania 19144
(215) 844-7577
Mr. DeVoren restores or replaces ivory insulators for pots and ivory knobs for urns. Send for a price list.

Harry A. Eberhardt & Son, Inc.   2010 Walnut Street, Philadelphia, Pennsylvania 19103
(215) 568-4144
Harry A. Eberhardt & Son, Inc. repairs ivory. Questions are answered by mail and there is no fee for an estimate.

Richard George/George Studios   45-04 97th Place, Corona, New York 11368   (212) 271-2506
Restoration and conservation of ivory are done at this studio. Call for an appointment or make arrangements for the delivery of the works to be restored. For restoration of large pieces of furniture, screens, fixed panels, or porcelain requiring on location repairs, call or write for information.

Rosene Green Associates, Inc.   1622A Beacon Street, Brookline, Massachusetts 02146
(617) 277-8368
This firm restores ivory art objects.

Hiles Plating Company, Inc.   2028 Broadway, Kansas City, Missouri 64108   (816) 421-6450
This company repairs ivory insulators in teapots as well as ivory, ebony, and boxwood knobs. An opinion and/or estimate will be sent upon receipt of pieces to be restored.

Mort Jacobs Restorations   Jackson-Green Building, 231 South Green Street, Chicago, Illinois 60607   (312) 648-0009
This is a nationwide restoration business. There is no charge for estimates. Printed packing and shipping instructions are available for out-of-state inquiries. Business hours are weekdays 9:00 A.M. to 3:30 P.M.

Michael Leon & John Hegnauer   18 Elm Street, Newport, Rhode Island 02840   (401) 849-3476
or 849-6178
This firm does ivory carving repairs and inlay.

REPRODUCTIONS
Artek, Inc.   Elm Avenue, Antrim, New Hampshire 03440   (603) 588-6825
Artek, Inc. sells reproductions of sperm whale teeth, blanks for carving, and scrimshaw kits. All their reproductions are clearly labeled. A catalogue is available.

APPRAISERS
Harry A. Eberhardt & Son, Inc.   2010 Walnut Street, Philadelphia, Pennsylvania 19103
(215) 568-4144
These appraisers will answer questions by mail. There is no fee for an estimate.

Betty Parker Simpson   33112 Lake Road, Avon Lake, Ohio 44012   (216) 933-6553
Jade and Oriental pieces are her specialty.

35. JEWELRY

Antique jewelry has become very popular during the past few years, particularly Georgian, Victorian, Art Nouveau, Art Deco, and Indian jewelry. Always be sure when buying old jewelry that you get an all original piece. Many are changed, "married" (mismatched), or modern copies.

Repairing old jewelry requires the greatest concern, because repairing or remodeling can destroy the antique value. Repairs should be made in the spirit of the original jewelry. Replace old gems or stones with old stones; if you put a modern cut diamond in a piece with old mine-cut diamonds, the new one will look out of place. At the same time, replacing earring backs, safety catches, modern pin backs, or restringing beads does not harm the value of most old jewelry and it will definitely help to prevent loss.

Some local jewelers know how to appraise and repair old jewelry, but many consider old jewelry "scrap" and figure the value based on the melt-down of the elements. Be sure to go to someone who understands the problems of old pieces, old methods, and old stones.

Jewelry can and should be cleaned at home. Be particularly careful of pieces with pearls or opals. These can be damaged with incorrect care, oil, and temperature changes.

CLUBS

The Bead Society   P.O. Box 605, Venice, California 90291
The Bead Society Newsletter is published every 2 months. It is
a mimeographed pamphlet with chatty news for members and
a few articles.

International Club for Collectors of Hatpins and Hatpin Holders
15237 Chanera Avenue, Gardena, California 90249   (213) 329-2619
Points is a monthly newsletter for members and *Hatpins and Hatpin
Holders Pictorial Journal* is a semiannual publication.

PUBLICATIONS

The Jade Collector   33112 Lake Road, Avon Lake, Ohio 44012   (216) 933-6553
This newsletter is published 10 times a year.

Ornament, A Quarterly of Jewelry & Personal Adornment   P.O. Box 35029, Los Angeles, California 90035-0029   (213) 652-9914

This is a quarterly magazine with articles, pictures, and ads about antique and modern jewelry.

BOOKS OF MARKS

Haslam, Malcolm. *Marks and Monograms of the Modern Movement, 1875–1930.* New York: Charles Scribner's Sons, 1977.

Kovel, Ralph and Terry. *Kovels' Know Your Collectibles.* New York: Crown Publishers, 1981.

PARTS AND SUPPLIES

Aiku Amber Center   760 Market Street, No. 617, San Francisco, California 94102   (415) 986-1286
This firm offers bead- and pearl-stringing silk (100 percent net silk from Germany with attached needle for easy stringing) in many weights and gem colors. It also has a large supply of amber. A catalogue is available.

The Carol Company   612 South Hawley Road, Milwaukee, Wisconsin 53214   (414) 771-0342
The Carol Company developed, manufactures, and distributes a gold, silver, and diamond test kit that contains 3 separate tests, each of which can be used for numerous tests. This test kit is easy to use and does not contain dangerous acids. Call or write for more information.

D. A. Culpepper   Mother of Pearl Company, Box 966, Route 9, Franklin, North Carolina 28734
D.A. Culpepper supplies pearls for jewelry.

Estes-Simmons Silverplating Ltd.   1168 Howell Mill Road, N.W., Atlanta, Georgia 30318 (404) 875-9581
This firm restores, replates, polishes, and repairs silver, gold, brass, copper, nickel, and pewter. It also replaces missing parts, relines jewel boxes with plush velvet, and removes engraving. A brochure is available.

Grey Owl Indian Craft Company, Inc.   113-15 Springfield Boulevard, Queens Village, New York 11429   (212) 464-9300
Indian craft supplies, jewelry findings, and books on Indians and Indian crafts are available. The company has an illustrated catalogue for $1.00.

S. LaRose, Inc.   234 Commerce Place, Greensboro, North Carolina 27420   (919) 275-0462
This firm carries ring shanks, heads, Fuller findings, and equipment to make or repair jewelry. Catalogues are published every 60 days.

Nasco   901 Janesville Avenue, Fort Atkinson, Wisconsin 53538   (414) 563-2446; free phone order service (800) 558-9595
Nasco carries an extensive line of supplies for arts and crafts. Included in their jewelry supplies are wire, clasps, beads, findings, cords, chains, and tools. Nasco also has a division in Modesto, California. Send for the *Nasco Arts & Crafts Catalogue* for more information.

Myron Toback, Inc.   23 West 47th Street, New York, New York 10036   (212) 247-4750
This firm sells beads, roundels for spacers, clasp shorteners, cloisonné wire, spring rings, ring guards, tubing, ear wires, locks and clasps, bezels, solder, diamond friction items, etc. Catalogues are available.

Williamson International, Inc.   P.O. Box 6778, Reno, Nevada 89503   (702) 747-7005
Barrel clasps, surgical steel kidney ear wires, spring rings, jump rings, crimping beads for necklace ends, chains, nuggets, beads, charms, etc. are available. Items are shipped COD, usually the same day as the order is received. A catalogue is available.

REPAIR SERVICES

The Arizona Turquoise and Silver Company Ltd.   7086 Fifth Avenue, Scottsdale, Arizona 85251   (602) 945-2118 or 947-8610
This company offers full service repair and custom jewelry production. It specializes in Indian goods.

The Clock Shop   806 Main Street, Lake Geneva, Wisconsin 53147   (414) 248-3736
The Clock Shop repairs antique jewelry.

"The Consortium"   5 South Wabash, Suite 1210, Chicago, Illinois 60603   (312) 346-6488 or 677-5070
"The Consortium" repairs antique jewelry, much of it by mail. Two lists are available, one for repairs and one for findings.

Diamonds By Terry   P.O. Box 922, Burnsville, Minnesota 55337   (612) 432-3557
This firm will repair any type of gold or platinum antique jewelry. It carries a complete line of replacement stones, many cut over 80 years ago. Unusual shapes are not a problem, as it employs a stonecutter. Send the item to be repaired by registered mail with your name, address, and phone number enclosed, and a description of the work you want to have done. The firm will make an estimate of the cost of repair and call you for approval before proceeding with the work.

Rosene Green Associates, Inc.   1622A Beacon Street, Brookline, Massachusetts 02146
(617) 277-8368
This firm restores enamel on jewelry and jade.

International Antique Repair Service, Inc.   8350 Hickman, Suite 14, Des Moines, Iowa 50322
(515) 278-2518 or (515) 278-2515
This company repairs rings, brooches, chains, and other jewelry and replaces missing pieces including stones. It is also able to construct matching pieces, such as a single earring or a brooch. It specializes in Victorian, Edwardian, and American jewelry in solid gold, silver, or fashion jewelry. All work is guaranteed for 5 years. A brochure is available.

Just Enterprises   2790 Sherwin Avenue, Unit 10, Ventura, California 93003   (805) 644-5837
This firm restores jewelry: metal, ivory, mother-of-pearl, and semiprecious stones.

Silver Ray   7000 Zuni S.E., Albuquerque, New Mexico 87108   (505) 265-0444

Silver Ray features custom-made jewelry and complete jewelry repair work. Flyers are available upon request.

Thompsons Studio, Inc.   Back Meadow Road, Damariscotta, Maine 04543   (207) 563-5280
This firm restores jewelry of any period. Hours are weekdays 10:00 A.M. to 5:00 P.M. and Saturdays 9:00 A.M. to noon. A brochure is available for $1.00.

The Trail Blazer   210 West Hill, Gallup, New Mexico 87301   (505) 722-5051
The Trail Blazer repairs Indian jewelry. Other services include ring sizing, stone replacement, restringing, and soldering broken jewelry. Send for a free repair price list.

Mr. William and Company   14 Garfield Place, Cincinnati, Ohio 45202   (513) 421-6898
This firm repairs fine jewelry and will make replacement parts if necessary.

PRICE GUIDES

Baker, Lillian. *Art Nouveau and Art Deco Jewelry: An Identification and Value Guide.*
Paducah, Kentucky: Collector Books, 1981.

Bell, Jeanenne. *Answers to Questions About Old Jewelry, 1840–1950.*
New York: Crown Publishers, 1982.

Kaplan, Arthur Guy. *Official 1982 Price Guide to Antique Jewelry.*
Orlando, Florida: House of Collectibles, 1981.

Poynder, Michael. *Price Guide to Jewelry 3,000* B.C.–*1950* A.D.
Suffolk, England: Antique Collectors' Club (5 Church Street, Clopton, Woodbridge, Suffolk 1P12 1BR, England).

Sallee, Lynn. *Old Costume Jewelry 1870–1945.*
Florence, Alabama: Books Americana, 1979.

APPRAISERS

Diamonds By Terry   P.O. Box 922, Burnsville, Minnesota 55337   (612) 432-3557
These are certified appraisals by a graduate gemologist.

Betty Parker Simpson   33112 Lake Road, Avon Lake, Ohio 44012   (216) 933-6553
Jade and Oriental pieces are her specialty.

36. KITCHENWARE

Anything that was used in an old kitchen, from the cookstove to the eggbeater, is in demand. Collectors should remember that while old items are fine for decorations, they are sometimes not safe to use for food preparation. Some types of pottery had a lead glaze that is dangerous. Copper molds and pots should never be used unless the tin lining is flawless. Chipped graniteware could add bits of crushed glass to your food. Woodenwares should only be treated with edible oils and not linseed oil.

Directions and supplies for the care of ceramic, tin, glass, and metal wares are listed in the proper chapters.

CLUBS

American Graniteware Association   P.O. Box 605, Downers Grove, Illinois 60515
The Granitegram is a newsletter for collectors of enameled cooking wares called graniteware or agateware. It includes a shop and swap column and short histories.

Cookie Cutter Collectors Club   5426 27th Street, N.W., Washington, D.C. 20015
(202) 966-1766
Cookie Cutter Collectors Club Newsletter is issued 6 times a year.

National Reamer Collectors Association   277 Highland Avenue, Wadsworth, Ohio 44281
National Reamer Collectors Association Quarterly Review is this group's publication.

PARTS AND SUPPLIES

Barap Specialties   835 Bellows, Frankfort, Michigan 49635
This firm offers genuine coffee mill mechanisms of heavy cast iron with 6-inch-square top plates. It supplies the complete mechanism and plans for construction of the box. A catalogue is available for 50¢.

Clark Manufacturing Company   Route 2, Raymore, Missouri 64083   (816) 331-6851
This firm manufactures pierced tins for replacement in pie safes and other uses. Standard size is 14 by 10 inches but they can be custom made. Items of brushed antique pewter are also available.

The Collectors' Store   P.O. Box 22200, Beachwood, Ohio 44122
Kitchen Wood Preserver is a product made especially to treat rolling pins, chopping bowls, and other kitchen items. It preserves and protects the wood.

Country Store Antiques   Win and Gin Dahlquist, 618 49th Avenue N.W., Puyallup, Washington 98371   (206) 952-6160
Country Store Antiques carries new flour sifters and sugars for Hoosiers and Kitchen Queens. Write for prices and information.

Furniture Revival and Company   P.O. Box 994, 580 Southwest Twin Oaks Circle, Corvallis, Oregon 97330   (503) 754-6323
This company sells furniture and cabinet hardware, including pulls, keyholes, knobs, hooks, hinges, kitchen and icebox hardware, casters, and feet. A catalogue is available for $2.00.

REPAIR SERVICES

Bernard Plating Works   660 Riverside Drive, Florence, Massachusetts 01060   (413) 584-0659
This firm does re-tinning of copper and brass cookware, excluding teakettles. Free estimates are given.

Gary Bradley   Box 606, Route 3, Corvallis, Oregon 97330   (503) 753-8896
Mr. Bradley sells completely restored sadiron handles. Call or write for more information.

Hormel Corporation   Box 218, 15 Alabama Avenue, Island Park, New York 11558 (516) 889-2244
This company repairs and relines old thermos bottles and ice buckets. Contact for further information.

PRICE GUIDES

Bremseth, Hattie. *Washboards Identification and Values.*
Privately printed, 1980 (Grand Meadow, Minnesota 55936).

————. *Washboards, Book II, Identification and Values.*
Privately printed, 1981 (Grand Meadow, Minnesota 55936).

Bunn, Eleanore. *Metal Molds.*
Paducah, Kentucky: Collector Books, 1981.

Franklin, Linda Campbell. *300 Years of Kitchen Collectibles.*
Florence, Alabama: Books Americana, 1981.

Vogelzang, Vernagene, and Welch, Evelyn. *Graniteware: Collectors' Guide with Prices.*
Des Moines: Wallace-Homestead, 1981.

Walker, Mary. *Reamers 200 Years.*
Sherman Oaks, California: Muski Publishers, 1980.

37. KNIVES

Knife collecting includes everything from penknives to daggers, regardless of their age. Some of these items are listed in Chapter 43, Metal Antiques and Collectibles, and Chapter 44, Military Memorabilia.

CLUBS

American Blade Collectors   112 Lee Parkway Drive, Stonewall Building, Suite 104, Chattanooga, Tennessee 37421   (615) 894-0339
Edges is a newspaper on knives and knife clubs.

The Ka-Bar Knife Collectors Club   434 North Ninth Street, Olean, New York 14760
(716) 372-5611
The Collector is a booklet about new and old Ka-Bar knives.

The National Knife Collectors Association   P.O. Box 21070, 7201 Shallowford Road, Chattanooga, Tennessee 37421   (615) 892-5007
The National Knife Collector is a monthly magazine for members. It features buy and sell ads and information about local clubs and shows. Although primarily interested in new knives, it does discuss some older examples and factory history.

PUBLICATIONS

The American Blade   112 Lee Parkway Drive, Stonewall Building, Suite 104, Chattanooga, Tennessee 37421   (615) 894-0339
This magazine covers all aspects of the knife-making industry. It features illustrations, informative articles, and ads.

The Blue Mill Blade 203 East Mineral Street, Newport, Tennessee 37821
This is a monthly newsletter.

Knife World P.O. Box 3395, Knoxville, Tennessee 37917
This newspaper contains articles, events, price guide information, and buy and sell ads.

REPAIR SERVICES

Abercrombie & Company 8227 Fenton Street, Silver Spring, Maryland 20910 (301) 585-2385
This company repairs metal items. It replaces knife blades and polishes, buffs, and lacquers metal, including gold, silver, nickel, copper, brass, and tin.

Bernard Plating Works 660 Riverside Drive, Florence, Massachusetts 01060 (413) 584-0659
Knife and serving blades are replaced with stainless steel blades. Free estimates are given.

New England Country Silver, Inc. Smith Road, East Haddam, Connecticut 06423
(203) 873-1314
This firm replaces knife blades with stainless steel from Sheffield, England. Send your piece for a free estimate and the firm will pay the return postage. A brochure is available.

Peninsula Plating Works, Inc. 232 Homer Avenue, Palo Alto, California 94301 (415) 326-7825
Restoration of knife blades, pearl handles, and any metal item found in the home or office is done by this company. A brochure is available.

PRICE GUIDES

Doyle, Robert A. *Straight Razor Collecting.*
Paducah, Kentucky: Collector Books, 1980.

Parker, James F., and Voyles, Bruce. *The Official Price Guide to Collector Pocket Knives.*
Orlando, Florida: House of Collectibles, 1979.

Sargent, Jim, and Schleyer, Jim. *1982 Pocket Price Guide, W.R. Case And Sons Cutlery.*
Privately printed, 1981 (Knife Nook, P.O. Box 243, Burke, Virginia 22015).

BOOKSELLER

Books about knives can be found in most major bookstores and libraries. Most stores will special order the books for you. These books are also available through the mail order antiques book dealers listed in Chapter 91. The dealer listed here specializes in books about knives.

American Blade Books 112 Lee Parkway Drive, Stonewall Building, Suite 104, Chattanooga, Tennessee 37421 (615) 894-0339
This company publishes several titles related to knives.

38. LAMPS AND LIGHTING DEVICES

Lamps and lighting devices are collected for many reasons, the most obvious being that they can light a room. If you are using old lamps in your home, be sure they are restored so they can be used safely. Oil and kerosene lamps have well-known hazards. Always check to be sure that all of the parts are working. Most early lamps can be converted to electric with the addition of a simple part. The original burner can be replaced with a new electric socket and cord. The unit will fit into the available space of the old lamp and can be removed or added with no damage to the antique value of the lamp. If you do electrify an old lamp, be sure to keep the old parts. The next owner may want an all original lamp.

The light bulb was invented in 1879. That means that some electric lamps can be over 100 years old. If you are using any electric lamp that is more than 25 years old, be sure it is safe. The cord should be unfrayed, and if it is the old-style silk-wrapped cord or a stiff rubber cord it should be totally replaced. Local lamp shops can rewire any lamp. Look for these in the Yellow Pages of the telephone book under "Lamps—Mounting & Repairing." If the sockets or pull chains need repairing, ask the shop to use as many of the old pieces as possible. Old sockets were made of solid brass and now most of them are plated. A serious collector will always want the original chain (some pay extra to get old ones with the acorn-tipped pull chain).

Reproductions of almost all parts of old lamps are available: glass shades, lamp chimneys, sockets, hangers for chandeliers, and much, much more. Old metal lamps can be cleaned or replaced. Leaded shades can be repaired. Art glass shades are being reproduced or can be repaired.

The lampshade and lamp finial can often make the difference between an attractive period-look lamp and an unattractive hodgepodge. Finials with old pieces of jade or porcelain are again being offered by the better decorating services and mail order houses. *See also* Chapter 31, Glass, and Chapter 43, Metal Antiques and Collectibles.

CLUB

Aladdin Knight   Route 1, Simpson, Illinois 62985
The Mystic Light of the Aladdin Knights is a newsletter with detailed information about the Aladdin lamps.

PUBLICATIONS

The Coleman Lite   The Coleman Company Inc., History Department, P.O. Box 1762, Wichita, Kansas 67201
The Coleman Lite is published now and then for collectors of early-day Coleman pressure lamps, lanterns, irons, and related products.

Font & Flue   P.O. Box 68, Pattonsburg, Missouri 64670   (816) 367-2215 or 367-2201
This is a bimonthly newsletter about flat wick kerosene lamps. It features ads and articles.

DECODING ADVERTISING COPY

Reading the ads for antiques and collectibles often takes special knowledge. Two collectors will speak a special language in the same way two doctors have a vocabulary known only to their profession. When looking up lamps it is helpful to know that a few types of lamps are referred to by number. Miniature lamps are identified with the Smith numbers from the book *Miniature Lamps* by Frank and Ruth Smith, Thomas Nelson & Sons, 1968. Aladdin lamps are often identified by number but these are the original numbers used by the factory. Many of these numbers can be matched with the proper lamps with the book *Aladdin, the Magic Name in Lamps* by J. W. Courter, Wallace-Homestead, 1971.

BOOK OF MARKS

Kovel, Ralph and Terry. *Kovels' Know Your Collectibles.*
New York: Crown Publishers, 1981.

HOW-TO-FIX-IT BOOKS

Martens, Rachel. *The How-to Book of Repairing, Rewiring, and Restoring Lamps and Lighting Fixtures.*
Garden City, New York: Doubleday, 1979.

Smart, William Silver. *Kerosene Lamps: The Confessions of an Oil Lamp Addict.*
Privately printed, 1980 (440 9W, Newburgh, New York 12550).

SHADES

These firms specialize in hard-to-find lampshades. For other companies, see Parts and Supplies and Repair Services.

Burdoch Silk Lampshade Company   3283 Loma Riviera Drive, San Diego, California 92110 (714) 223-5834
Embroidered, hand-sewn fabric shades are available in 6 different styles. A free color brochure and price list are available.

Campbell Lamps   1108 Pottstown Pike, West Chester, Pennsylvania 19380   (215) 696-8070
This firm sells a large selection of shades for gas and electric lamps, including Emeralite lamps. A catalogue is available for $1.00.

Paul Crist Studios   14903 Marquardt Avenue, Santa Fe Springs, California 90670   (213) 921-0101
This firm offers Tiffany replacement shades.

Custom House   South Shore Drive, Owl's Head, Maine 04854   (207) 594-9281
Reproduction Victorian stenciled lampshades can be found here, as well as reproduction brass bases. Catalogue sheets are available.

Irvin's Craft Shop   P.O. Box 45, R.D. 1, Mount Pleasant, Pennsylvania 17853   (717) 539-8200
This shop carries pierced tin and copper lampshades. A catalogue is available.

Lundberg Studios   P.O. Box 26, 131 Marine Avenue, Davenport, California 95017 (408) 423-2532
This firm designs art lamps and shades that imitate Tiffany and Steuben shades. They are heat and shock resistant, which allows for the use of high-wattage bulbs. The firm recommends a 75-watt bulb. It is within its capabilities to fill any special requests including engraved or cameo shades.

The Old Lamplighter Shop   Route 12-B, Deansboro, New York 13328   (315) 841-8774
Custom-painted china shades are sold by this shop. Prices depend on size, style, pattern, and colors. Satisfaction is guaranteed. Call or write for more information.

Rumplestiltskin Designs   P.O. Box 84109, Los Angeles, California 90073   (213) 839-4747
This firm offers hand-beaded lampshade fringe for your lamp. Different patterns and colors are available. For a brochure send $1.00 and a self-addressed, stamped envelope. All deliveries are COD.

Schutte's Lamp Supply   503 West Spring Street, Lima, Ohio 45801   (419) 223-7406
Hundreds of shades of all sizes and colors are available from this company. Call or write for prices and shipping instructions.

Shades of the Past   P.O. Box 502, Corte Madera, California 94925   (415) 459-6999
All lampshades are hand sewn using antique fabrics imported from mainland China, Japan, and France. The hand-strung beaded fringe is from Italy. A range of styles are available. Write for more information.

Shirna Lampshades   166 Allied Street, Manchester, New Hampshire 03103   (603) 669-1615
This firm offers lampshades made of fine quality paper, cut and pierced. Over 250 printed patterns and

30 colors are available. All orders are custom made and cost from $12.50 to $45.00. Send the exact size needed and the color desired and the company will quote a price. It also sells tools, supplies for making shades, and electrical supplies for wiring or rewiring lamps. Send for a price list.

Van Parys Studio   6338 Germantown Avenue, Philadelphia, Pennsylvania 19144   (215) 844-1930
Custom designed shades are made of "everything and anything": parchments, laminated fabrics, wallpaper, foils, silks, cottons, linens, laces, brocades, etc. The shades may be hand painted with transparent colors so that when they are lit the colors are still pure. The wire frames for the shades are also custom made.

Victorian D'Light   533 West Windsor Road, Glendale, California 91204   (213) 956-5656
This firm offers turn-of-the-century reproduction lighting and shades, including shades for Emeralite lamps. A brochure is available for $3.00.

PARTS AND SUPPLIES
For other companies that sell parts and supplies see the sections on Shades, and Repair Services.

Alcon Lightcraft Company   1424 West Alabama, Houston, Texas 77006   (713) 526-0680
Alcon Lightcraft maintains a large inventory of lamps and parts. A brochure is available.

Angelo Brothers Company   10981 Decatur Road, Philadelphia, Pennsylvania 19154
(215) 632-9600
This company offers lamp parts: chimneys, glass shades, candle covers, crystal prisms, etc. Minimum order is $50.00. Catalogues are available.

Barap Specialties   835 Bellows, Frankfort, Michigan 49635
Choose from a wide variety of lamp parts: brass finials, harps, sockets, bases, spindles, cords, switches, glass chimneys, chimney holders, oil lamp converters, and more. Catalogues are available for 50¢.

The Boulder Art Glass Company   1920 Arapahoe Avenue, Boulder, Colorado 80302
(303) 449-9030
This company offers bent panel (slumps) for replacement in curved panel lampshades.

Bradford Consultants   16 East Homestead Avenue, Collingswood, New Jersey 08108
(609) 854-1404
The Bradford Consultants offer the "Phoenix" carbon light bulb, a reproduction of the bulb used from 1880 to the early years of the twentieth century.

Campbell Lamps   1108 Pottstown Pike, West Chester, Pennsylvania 19380   (215) 696-8070
This firm offers shades for gas and electric lamps, including Emeralite lamps. A catalogue is available for $1.00.

Chandelier Warehouse   1059 Third Avenue, New York, New York 10021   (212) 753-2507
Chandelier Warehouse offers a variety of prisms, drops, and pendeloques. A catalogue is available

The Collectors' Store   P.O. Box 22200, Beachwood, Ohio 44122

The Collectors' Store carries stickum to hold your candles securely in the candleholder. It never hardens, is safe for silver, and is transparent. A catalogue is available.

Albert Constantine and Son, Inc.   2050 Eastchester Road, Department A11, Bronx, New York 10461   (212) 792-1600

This firm sells parts and fixtures needed for all styles of lamps: filigree bases, cluster assemblies, swivel heads, pipe, finials, flexible arms, reducers, oil lamp converters, jug and bottle fittings, harps, bulb adapters, and more. A catalogue is available for $1.00.

Paul Crist Studios   14903 Marquardt Avenue, Santa Fe Springs, California 90670   (213) 921-0101

Paul Crist Studios carries replacement hardware, bases, and shades for Tiffany type lamps. Bases and hardware are brass or bronze.

Crystal Mountain Prisms   P.O. Box 31, Westfield, New York 14787   (716) 326-3676

Prisms, pendants, bobeches, chains, pendeloques, plug drops, kite pendants, and prism pins are some of the items offered by this company. Send a self-addressed, stamped envelope for a complete list of sizes, shapes, and colors.

Electric Candle Manufacturing Company   60 Chelmsford Street, Chelmsford, Massachusetts 01824   (617) 256-6555 or 256-9972

This company offers electric wax candles. They are made like real candles and then hand dripped to give the effect of a burning candle. The Morelite candle is also offered and uses conventional voltage and regular candelabra base bulbs. Instructions on how to wire and adapt the electric wax candles for holders and fixtures accompany each order.

The Elements Pottery   Linda and André Brousseay, 629 North Third Street, Danville, Kentucky 40422

The Elements Pottery makes rolled beeswax candles in several different colors. Two price lists are available free of charge with a self-addressed, stamped envelope, one for retail stores and one for individuals. Please specify.

Faire Harbour Ltd.   44 Captain Peirce Road, Scituate, Massachusetts 02066   (617) 545-2465

Parts and supplies for kerosene mantle lamps are available from this company. These include mantles, chimneys, burners and converters, wicks, tripods (shade holders), shades, lamp bowls, brackets and hangers, and some miscellaneous parts. Catalogues are available for $1.00, refundable with the first purchase.

Gem Monogram & Cut Glass Corporation   623 Broadway, New York, New York 10012   (212) 674-8960

This firm's specialty is chandelier parts including bobeches.

"Good Ole Stuff" Antiques and Lamp Supply   610 North Meridian Street, Lebanon, Indiana 46052   (317) 482-3142

Parts for kerosene lamps including hand-painted glass shades, chimneys, burners, wicks, and both old and new parts are available. Write or call for a price list.

W. J. Hagerty & Sons Ltd., Inc.   P.O. Box 1496, South Bend, Indiana 46624   (219) 623-2923
This firm carries "Chanda Clean," a product that allows you to "drip dry" your chandelier. Catalogues are available.

Irvin's Craft Shop   P.O. Box 45, R.D. 1, Mount Pleasant Mills, Pennsylvania 17853
(717) 539-8200
Sconces, ceiling plates, and other items are handcrafted from tin, copper, and brass. A catalogue is available.

Jefferson Brothers Art Lighting   4371 Lima Center Road, Ann Arbor, Michigan 48103
(313) 996-0011 or 428-7361
This firm specializes in custom lighting and carries lamp components such as bases and wall sconces in bronze. Ornaments include cast china components of variegated colors in conjunction with cast china intaglio "lithophane" jewels, panels, globes, and shades. A catalogue of over 3,300 items is available.

Luigi Crystal   7332 Frankford Avenue, Philadelphia, Pennsylvania 19136
Luigi Crystal offers a selection of imported hand-cut crystal pieces, marble, and exotic metals. Individual pieces are made to your specifications. Bobeches, prisms, pendeloques, and bulbs for lamps and chandeliers are available. Send for a catalogue.

Nowell's, Inc.   P.O. Box 164, 490 Gate 5 Road, Sausalito, California 94965   (415) 332-4933
Nowell's has a full line of oil lamp parts. Burners and fittings, shade holders (both student and ball), clear and frosted glass chimneys, collars, and wicks are offered. A catalogue is available.

Pairpoint Glass Works   851 Sandwich Road, Sagamore, Massachusetts 02561   (617) 888-2344
This firm is a source for missing chandelier parts. Call or write for information.

Paxton Hardware Company   Upper Falls, Maryland 21156   (301) 592-8505
This company offers a complete line of lamp parts including parts for Aladdin oil, wall, and hanging lamps. Opal glass lampshades and glass chimneys, decorative light bulbs, glass prisms, and so forth are also carried. A catalogue is available for $1.50.

E. W. Pyfer   218 North Foley Avenue, Freeport, Illinois 61032   (815) 232-8968
E. W. Pyfer carries parts for old and new lamps. Chimneys and glass globes and shades are available. Please write and state your needs.

Rejuvenation House Parts Company   4543 North Albina Avenue, Portland, Oregon 97217
(503) 282-3019
This company carries gas and electric shades, shade holders, brass canopy and turnkey sockets. A catalogue is available for $2.00.

Restoration Hardware   438 Second Street, Eureka, California 95501   (707) 443-3152
Restoration Hardware carries fringed lace shades, available in white or beige. It also offers a light kit with a ceramic fixture, cord, plug, and switch; and reproduction lighting fixtures. A catalogue is available for $3.00, refundable with the first purchase.

St. Louis Antique Lighting Company   P.O. Box 8146, St. Louis, Missouri 63156   (314) 535-2770
This company carries antique lighting fixtures. All are solid brass, polished and lacquered, fully electrified with U.L. approved electrical components. Glass shades are also available. Send for a catalogue.

Schutte's Lamp Supply   503 West Spring Street, Lima, Ohio 45801   (419) 223-7406
A complete line of lamp parts and chimneys is available from Schutte's. Call or write for further information.

Skaron Narrow Fabric, Inc.   P.O. Box 315, 99 West Hawthorne Avenue, Valley Stream, New York 11580   (516) 825-1525
This firm carries wide wicks for the old-type chafing dishes and tubular wicks for Rayo lamps. Send the length and thickness required.

Squaw Alley Incorporated   106 West Water Street, Naperville, Illinois 60540   (312) 357-0200
This firm has a complete selection of lamp repair parts, shades, and chimneys. A catalogue is available for $2.00.

Williams Lamp Supply and Antiques   Fifth and Main, Albion, Illinois 62806   (618) 445-3224 or 445-3353
This firm supplies authentic Aladdin kerosene lamp replacement parts. It also carries a line of parts for electric lamps, as well as a large selection of glass shades and chimneys. Prisms or pendeloques come complete with glass top bead and hanging wire. A catalogue is available.

REPAIR SERVICES

Abend Metal Repair   Delavan Center, 501 West Fayette Street, Syracuse, New York 13204
(315) 478-2749
This firm repairs and restores metal lamps.

Abercrombie & Company   8227 Fenton Street, Silver Spring, Maryland 20910   (301) 585-2385
Metal items including lamps are rewired.

Al Bar Wilmette Platers   127 Green Bay Road, Wilmette, Illinois 60091   (312) 251-0187
This firm does complete metal restoration. Lamps are repaired and rewired. Missing pieces are reproduced. Hours are Monday through Friday 8:00 A.M. to 4:30 P.M., Saturday 8:00 A.M. to noon.

All-Tek Finishing Company   355 Bernard Street, Trenton, New Jersey 08618   (609) 695-3644
This company does lamp and chandelier rewiring and glass drilling.

Ball and Ball   463 West Lincoln Highway, Exton, Pennsylvania 19341
(215) 363-7330   Restoration services offered for lighting fixtures include polishing,
wiring (or rewiring), repairing, and duplication of almost any fixture from the
eighteenth or nineteenth century.

Bernard Plating Works   660 Riverside Drive, Florence, Massachusetts 01060   (413) 584-0659
Free estimates are given for rewiring lamps.

Sandra Brauer/Stained Glass   235 Dean Street, Brooklyn, New York 11217   (212) 855-0656
Custom work and expert repair of stained glass lampshades are available. Contact by mail or phone for
information or an appointment.

Chandelier Warehouse   1059 Third Avenue, New York, New York 10021   (212) 753-2507
This firm restores antique lighting. Call or write for more information.

The Condon Studios, Stained Glass   33 Richdale Avenue (Porter Square), Cambridge, Massachusetts 02140   (617) 661-5776
This firm does restoration and repair of lamps, both bent and flat. Glass bending (slumping) to match
antique curved panel lamps is also offered. A brochure is available.

Country Fare   Route 188 S, Southbury, Connecticut 06488   (203) 264-7517
Country Fare restores old light fixtures. It handcrafts pierced or painted lampshades, recovers old
frames, polishes and lacquers fine brass, and does just about everything with lighting old and new. It
will attempt to answer any request via mail or telephone.

Paul Crist Studios   14903 Marquardt Avenue, Santa Fe Springs, California 90670   (213) 921-0101
This firm restores and reproduces Tiffany lamps and lampshades.

Joseph DeVoren, Silversmiths   6350 Germantown Avenue, Philadelphia, Pennsylvania 19144
(215) 844-7577
Lamps are restored, rewired, and refinished.

Fred & Nancy Dikeman   42-66 Phlox Place, Flushing, New York 11355   (212) 358-1571
Tiffany lamps are repaired and restored using only the original glass from Tiffany Studios. All work is
done with original tools, patterns, blocks, foil, etc.

Ed's Antiques, Inc.   422 South Street, Philadelphia, Pennsylvania 19147   (215) 923-4120
Antique lighting fixtures are rewired and repaired.

Estes-Simmons Silverplating Ltd.   1168 Howell Mill Road, N.W., Atlanta, Georgia 30318
(404) 875-9581
This firm rewires and restores lamps. It constructs lamps from practically any object. A brochure is
available.

"Good Ole Stuff" Antiques and Lamp Supply   610 North Meridian Street, Lebanon, Indiana 46052   (317) 482-3142

This firm offers repair service for kerosene lamps including restoration, electrification, and metal stripping.

Jefferson Brothers Art Lighting   4371 Lima Center Road, Ann Arbor, Michigan 48103 (313) 996-0011 or 428-7361

This company restores antique lighting. It requests that interested parties contact the firm directly, at which time it will consider your individual needs and respond accordingly. A catalogue of over 3,300 items is available.

Steve Kayne Hand Forged Hardware   17 Harmon Place, Smithtown, New York 11788 (516) 724-3669

This firm repairs, restores, and reproduces items of iron, brass, bronze, copper, and tin. Lighting devices are refurbished and wired. Write or call for more information.

McAvoy Antique Lighting   Historical Lafayette Square, St. Louis, Missouri 63104 (314) 773-9136

McAvoy Antique Lighting restores antique light fixtures. It specializes in historic restoration and can provide lights for any restoration. Although it doesn't operate a retail establishment, you can visit its workshop by calling for an appointment.

Michael Glassworks   21427 Dexter, Warren, Michigan 48089   (313) 775-5338

Michael Glassworks specializes in the repair and restoration of Tiffany and Tiffany-type lampshades, using only old glass.

John Morgan   443 Metropolitan Avenue, Brooklyn, New York 11211

John Morgan offers bent glass replacement parts for Tiffany-style lamps.

Nowell's, Inc.   P.O. Box 164, 490 Gate 5 Road, Sausalito, California 94965   (415) 332-4933

Nowell's repairs and restores old fixtures.

Old Hickory Stained Glass Studio   221 South 3rd, LaCrosse, Wisconsin 54601   (608) 784-6463

This firm repairs and restores stained glass lampshades. Contact can be made by mail or by stopping by the studio.

The Old Lamplighter Shop   Route 12-B, Deansboro, New York 13328   (315) 841-8774

This shop restores old lamps. Slag glass lamps are repaired and colored glass bent and installed. Prices depend on the number of bends and the size. If you have an old lamp with parts missing, the shop generally can supply you with old or replacement parts.

Peninsula Plating Works, Inc.   232 Homer Avenue, Palo Alto, California 94301   (415) 326-7825

This firm polishes, plates, and repairs metal and refinishes lamps. A brochure is available.

E. W. Pyfer 218 North Foley Avenue, Freeport, Illinois 61032 (815) 232-8968
E. W. Pyfer repairs and wires lamps, replacing all missing parts. Old chandeliers are restored and oil and gas lamps are converted to electric. Please write stating your needs.

Roy Electric Company, Inc. 1054 Coney Island Avenue, Brooklyn, New York 11230 (212) 339-6311 or 761-7905
This company restores antique lighting fixtures. Each piece is completely disassembled, polished, lacquer-dipped, and rewired. Call or write for more information. A catalogue is available for $2.00.

Schutte's Lamp Supply 503 West Spring Street, Lima, Ohio 45801 (419) 223-7406
This firm will strip, polish, and lacquer any brass or copper item, such as Rayo-type lamps, chandeliers, fire extinguishers, candlesticks, etc. Restoration of antique lamps, shades in all sizes and colors, and a complete line of hardware are available. Call or write for prices and shipping instructions.

Specialized Repair Service 2406 West Bryn Mawr Avenue, Chicago, Illinois 60659 (312) 784-2800
This firm repairs brass, pewter, copper, steel, and white metal (zinc die casting or spelter,) Missing hardware and castings in yellow and red brass or bronze are made to match. Other services include welding, machining, refinishing, and silver brazing.

Squaw Alley Incorporated 106 West Water Street, Naperville, Illinois 60540 (312) 357-0200
Antique lamps are restored and/or rewired. A catalogue is available for $2.00.

Such Happiness, Inc. The Glass Works, New Ipswich, New Hampshire 03071 (603) 878-1031
This firm restores Tiffany-style lamps and stained glass.

Theiss Plating Corporation 9314 Manchester, St. Louis, Missouri 63119 (314) 961-0600
This firm rewires and repairs crystal or metal chandeliers and lamps.

Universal Electro-Plating Company, Inc. 1804 Wisconsin Avenue, N.W., Washington, D.C. 20007 (202) 333-2460
This company restores, rewires, repairs, and redesigns wall sconces, coach lamps, and other lamps. A brochure is available.

Van Parys Studio 6338 Germantown Avenue, Philadelphia, Pennsylvania 19144 (215) 844-1930
This firm does complete restoration of lamps from the base to the shade. Missing parts are replaced and painted if necessary, brass and bronze are repaired.

Yankee Craftsman 357 Commonwealth Road, Wayland, Massachusetts 01778 (617) 653-0031
The Yankee Craftsman restores Victorian period lighting by using existing holes and openings to wire a lamp and make it functional without destroying the way in which it was originally used. Call or write for more information.

ANTIQUE AND REPRODUCTION LIGHTING

Architectural Antiques and Reproductions, Inc.   1327 9th Street, N.W., Washington, D.C. 20001   (202) 232-2772

This firm carries a collection of gas and gas-electric lighting. Write or phone Barry S. Levy. The shop is open Fridays, Saturdays, and Sundays from noon to 5:00 P.M.

Authentic Designs   330 East 75th Street, New York, New York 10021   (212) 535-9590

Authentic Designs offers handcrafted re-creations and adaptations of Early American lighting fixtures. Solid brass, real pewter plating, and clear maple are used in the construction of chandeliers and sconces. Fixtures are produced when ordered so size adjustments can be made to fit any special situation. A catalogue is available for $2.00.

Authentic Reproduction Lighting Company   P.O. Box 218, Avon, Connecticut 06001 (203) 673-5736

This firm offers handmade Colonial lighting fixtures in either candle or electric models. Any chandelier can be reproduced if a picture or drawing with dimensions is sent to the company. A catalogue is available for $2.75.

Brasslight, Inc.   90 Main Street, Nyack, New York 10960   (914) 353-0567

This firm sells lamps and fixtures of brass, polished and lacquered. It offers one-of-a-kind fixtures and a small line of its most popular styles. Literature is available.

Chandelier Warehouse   1059 Third Avenue, New York, New York 10021   (212) 753-2507

This firm offers a complete selection of lighting from many parts of the world. Crystal, brass, pewter, and wood chandeliers, and sconces in contemporary, traditional, provincial, and transitional styles are carried. A catalogue is available.

City Lights   2226 Massachusetts Avenue, Cambridge, Massachusetts 02140   (617) 547-1490

City Lights deals in antique lighting 1880–1930. Its stock includes only fully restored antique lighting. Restoration to this company means repair, polishing, lacquering, reassembly, electrification, and outfitting the fixture with original period glass shades. One may choose from ceiling fixtures, wall lights and sconces, table lamps, and floor lamps. A photo sheet of typical fixtures is available for $1.50.

The Classic Illumination   431 Grove Street, Oakland, California 94607   (415) 465-7786

This firm offers reproduction Victorian lighting. Chandeliers, wall sconces, and table lamps are available. All fixtures are solid brass and unlacquered. A catalogue is available.

Colonial Metalcrafters   P.O. Box 1135, Tyler, Texas 75710   (214) 561-1111

This firm manufactures seventeenth- and eighteenth-century-style brass chandeliers, sconces, and accessories. A catalogue is available for $3.00.

Faire Harbour Ltd.   44 Captain Peirce Road, Scituate, Massachusetts 02066   (617) 545-2465

Oil incandescent lamps are offered in several styles. Every model features an incandescent mantle and burner assembly that produces a white light and is adjustable in intensity up to the equivalent of a 60-watt bulb. It requires no pumping. Optional electric converters are available. The lamps are made of solid brass and topped with a hand-blown and, if desired, hand-painted glass shade. Also available is the Lincoln Drape lamp base design reproduced in amber, ruby red, or clear glass. A catalogue is available for $1.00, refundable with the first purchase.

"Good Ole Stuff" Antiques and Lamp Supply   610 North Meridian, Lebanon, Indiana 46052
(317) 482-3142
This firm offers a selection of antique lighting fixtures. Call or write for a list of fixtures in stock.

Greg's Antique Lighting   12005 Wilshire Boulevard, Los Angeles, California 90025
(213) 478-5475
Greg offers authentic fixtures that are rewired and restored to their original beauty. His fixtures date from 1840 to 1930. You will find chandeliers, wall sconces, floor and table lamps.

Irvin's Craft Shop   P.O. Box 45, R.D. 1, Mount Pleasant Mills, Pennsylvania 17853
(717) 539-8200
Irvin's Craft Shop offers handcrafted tin, copper, and brass Early American reproduction lighting. Lanterns, lamps, sconces, and chandeliers are available as well as candleholders and chambersticks. A catalogue is available.

Jefferson Brothers Art Lighting   4371 Lima Center Road, Ann Arbor, Michigan 48103
(313) 996-0011 or 428-7361
This company manaufactures reproduction lighting. A catalogue of over 3,300 items is available.

JO-EL Shop   7120 Hawkins Creamery Road, Laytonsville, Maryland 20760   (301) 972-4100
JO-EL Shop offers restored light fixtures from early 1890 through the 1930s. Most are made of brass and some are of pewter-type alloys and other metals. There are hanging fixtures, floor lamps, wall-mounted fixtures, and table lamps. Almost all are electric, though there are a few electrified gas fixtures. Many of the shades are of irreplaceable cut glass, milk glass, and Carnival glass and some are hand painted. A catalogue is available for $2.00.

King's Chandelier Company   Highway 14, Eden (Leaksville), North Carolina 27288
(919) 623-6188
This company offers one-of-a-kind, custom-designed, and imported chandeliers and sconces. The metal parts are made in the USA and the crystal parts are made in Europe. Choose from a large selection. A catalogue is available for $1.50.

The London Ventures Company   Two Dock Square, Rockport, Massachusetts 01966
This company carries early light fixtures, most wired and ready to hang. There are over 100 different fixtures in solid brass, polished and lacquered. Its catalogue represents the fixtures that it presently has in stock, but does not cover all the different types of fixtures that the company gets yearly. If you have a specific fixture that you want, let the company know; it may be able to help you.

Kenneth Lynch & Sons   The Craft Center Buildings, 78 Danbury Road, Wilton, Connecticut 06897   (203) 762-8363
This firm offers chandeliers and brackets of wrought iron and/or wood. Exterior post lanterns, posts, and Japanese stone lanterns are also offered. A hardcover catalogue is available for $5.00.

Newstamp Lighting Company   227 Bay Road, North Easton, Massachusetts 02356 (617) 238-7071
This company manufactures handmade Early American and Colonial lighting fixtures from solid copper and brass. A catalogue is available for $2.00.

Nowell's, Inc.   P.O. Box 164, 490 Gate 5 Road, Sausalito, California 94965   (415) 332-4933
Nowell's offers authentic handmade reproductions of Victorian light fixtures. If you don't see exactly what you want in the catalogue, ask, send some specifications, or show them a picture.

The Old Lamplighter Shop   Route 12-B, Deansboro, New York 13328   (315) 841-8774
This shop offers a selection of restored antique lighting fixtures including table models, hanging lamps, wall sconces, and brackets that range from oil and kerosene to gas and early electric.

Old Tavern Lighting   R.F.D. #1, Dutton Road, Wilton, New Hampshire 03086 (603) 654-2002
This firm produces Early American lighting fixtures each individually handcrafted with a "distressed" tin finish. Both chandeliers and sconces are available. Send for its catalogue.

Rejuvenation House Parts   4543 North Albina Avenue, Portland, Oregon 97217   (503) 282-3019
This firm offers a line of authentic turn-of-the-century lighting handcrafted in the same manner and of the same materials as the originals. Fixtures are solid brass and brightly polished. Custom orders are welcomed. Catalogues are available for $2.00.

Restoration Hardware   438 Second Street, Eureka, California 95501   (707) 443-3152
Restoration Hardware is a retail and mail order concern which carries Period and Victorian lighting. Catalogues are available for $3.00, refundable with the first purchase.

Roy Electric Company, Inc.   1054 Coney Island Avenue, Brooklyn, New York 11230 (212) 339-6311 or 761-7905
Roy Electric Company sells antique Victorian and turn-of-the-century lighting fixtures. It has accumulated gas, oil, and early electric fixtures along with sconces, brackets, table lamps, floor reading lamps, and many unusual pieces of fixture art. A catalogue is available for $2.00.

San Francisco Victoriana   2245 Palou Avenue, San Francisco, California 94124   (415) 648-0313
This firm offers reproductions of Victorian lighting fixtures used in late nineteenth-century America and typical of those found in San Francisco. A catalogue is available.

Squaw Alley Incorporated   106 West Water Street, Naperville, Illinois 60540   (312) 357-0200
This firm sells antique lighting fixtures. A catalogue is available for $2.00.

Stansfield's Lamp Shop   P.O. Box 332, Slate Hill, New York 10973   (914) 355-1300
This shop offers a line of reproduction Victorian lighting. All fixtures are of solid brass and U.L. listed. The fixtures are soldered and assembled by hand, then polished and lacquered (if desired). Catalogues are available for $2.00.

L. D. Stevens Colonial Lighting Fixtures   2423 East Norris Street, Philadelphia, Pennsylvania 19125   (215) 425-5947
This firm offers handcrafted Colonial lighting fixtures. The wood spindles can be finished in black walnut (no grain shows); regular walnut (grain is visible); old pine; fruitwood (natural finish); or historic red, blue, green, or mustard. The arms are hand formed from steel tubing and can be pulled out for more diameter or pushed in for less. The arms, metal candle cups, bottom cone, and top cap are finished in (old iron) black-brown. All lighting fixtures are wired complete with canopy and 2½ feet of chain (more chain is available upon request). A catalogue is available.

Victorian D'Light   533 West Windsor Road, Glendale, California 91204   (213) 956-5656
Victorian D'Light offers turn-of-the-century reproduction lighting. All lamps are solid brass and U.L. listed. Each lamp is hand assembled and then hand polished. A catalogue is available for $3.00.

Victorian Reproductions, Inc.   1601 Park Avenue South, Minneapolis, Minnesota 55404 (612) 338-3636
This firm offers reproduction lighting fixtures, lamps, glass shades, and globes. A catalogue is available for $5.00.

The Village Forge   P.O. Box 1148, Smithfield, North Carolina 27577   (919) 934-2581
The Village Forge offers Early American lighting fixtures. All lamps are handcrafted from heavy iron. Turnings and spinnings are solid brass; standard finish is dull black. Lamps and lighting are wired with approved electrical components. A catalogue is available.

PRICE GUIDES

Battersby, Dorla. *Price Guide for Miniature Oil Lamps "According to Battersby,"* rev. ed.
Privately printed, 1978 (651 Shahar Avenue, Lone Pine, California 93545).

Brown, Eugene H. *Guide for Antique Bulb Collecting.*
Privately printed, 1979 (P.O. Box 477, Dodge City, Kansas 67801).

Courter, J. W. *Aladdin Collectors Manual and Price Guide Eight.*
Privately printed, 1981 (Route 1, Simpson, Illinois 62985).

Duncan, Alastair. *Tiffany at Auction*
New York: Rizzoli International, 1982.

Kell, C. M., Jr. *Railroad Lanterns, An Easy to Use Buying Guide with Price References.*
Privately printed, 1981 (Mabius Marketing Systems, P.O. Box 168, Marietta, Pennsylvania 17547).

Thomas, Jo Ann. *Early Twentieth Century Lighting Fixtures.*
Paducah, Kentucky: Collector Books, 1980.

BOOKSELLERS
Books about lighting can be found in every good bookstore or library. Most stores will special order the books for you. Many of these books are available through the mail order antiques book dealers listed in Chapter 91, Booksellers.

39. LEATHER GOODS

Leather requires special care. Use only accepted leather cleaners and preservatives. Never use general purpose waxes and polishes. Most department, furniture, and hardware stores sell suitable leather cleaners. There are products such as neat's-foot oil and mink oil sold in shoe stores, leather shops, and shoe repair shops that are made especially for use on leather. *See also* Chapter 12, Books and Bookplates, and Chapter 17, Chairs.

HOW-TO-FIX-IT BOOKS
Guldbeck, Per E. *Leather: Its Understanding and Care.*
Nashville, Tennessee: American Association for State and Local History (708 Berry Road, Nashville, Tennessee 37204), 1969. Leaflet.

Horton, Carolyn. *Cleaning and Preserving Bindings and Related Materials.*
Chicago: American Library Association, 1967.

Middleton, B. C. *The Restoration of Leather Bindings.*
Chicago: American Library Association, 1972.

Rogers, J. S., and Beebe, C.W. *Leather Bookbindings: How to Preserve Them.*
Washington, D.C.: U.S. Department of Agriculture, 1956.

Waterer, J. W. *Conservation and Restoration of Leather.*
New York: Drake Publishers, 1972.

PARTS AND SUPPLIES

Graco Sales Company   8152 Highway 70, Arlington, Tennessee 38002   (901) 386-3043
This firm supplies Kotten Klenser, a cleaner for tanned leather.

The Lexol Division   Corona Products Company, P.O. Box 1214, Atlanta, Georgia 30301
(404) 524-5434
This firm makes Lexol emulsion for softening stiff leather.

McCune, Inc.   425 Jackson Square, San Francisco, California 94111   (415) 956-3300
McCune distributes Renaissance leather polish.

Timothy J. Somers Leathers   Illuminations in Leather, 1340 West School Street, Chicago, Illinois
60657   (312) 549-6996
Hand-tooled leather wall panels, chair seats, table tops, etc. are custom designed in natural browns or
color, with or without gold leaf. Please write for more information.

Technical Library Service   261 Broadway, New York, New York 10007   (212) 675-0718
This company provides leather dressing.

Triple X Chemical Company   841 Skokie Highway, Lake Bluff, Illinois 60044   (312) 689-0522
Triple X makes Leather Sof, a softener and preservative.

Utrecht Linens, Inc.   33 35th Street, Brooklyn, New York 11232   (212) 768-2525
Linen for backing stiff or broken pieces of leather is available.

REPAIR SERVICE

Brandywine Battlefield National Museum, Inc.   P.O. Box 265, Route 1, Chadds Ford, Pennsylvania 19317   (215) 388-1134
The museum offers restoration and appraisal services for leather goods including letters of identification, authentication, and appraisal.

40. LIMITED EDITIONS

Limited editions include many types of the newer collectibles. The name "limited edition" first became
popular during the 1960s, even though the first limited edition plate was the Bing & Grondahl

Christmas plate of 1895. Many types of porcelains and silver were made in limited quantities but the idea of stating the limits before offering the collectible was new. Some pieces are limited to an announced number; some to the number made before a special date. Limited editions can include plates, figurines, eggs, bells, forks, spoons, plaques, boxes, steins, mugs, urns, Christmas ornaments, paperweights, bottles, thimbles, and other items.

Repairs to limited editions are almost useless, if you are concerned with its value. The slightest chip, crack, or imperfection lowers the value considerably and almost any repair will cost more than the value of the repaired piece. The only exception might be for very rare figurines. When reselling a limited piece it is best to have the original box and certifying papers. Because of the demand for the original box, some dealers will gladly pay for a rare empty box. There are many limited edition dealers in gift shops throughout the country. They buy and sell the pieces. Many deal through the mail and through ads in various publications. *See also* Chapter 61, Pottery and Porcelain.

CLUBS

Collectible Resource Group, Inc.   6700 Griffin Road, Fort Lauderdale, Florida 33314 (305) 791-1264
CRGram is a monthly newsletter for limited edition dealers.

The Franklin Mint Collectors Society   Franklin Center, Pennsylvania 19091
The Franklin Mint Almanac is a colorful magazine with articles of interest to collectors of Franklin Mint limited editions.

The International Plate Collectors Guild   c/o Mrs. Anita Smith, 5581 Sandoval Avenue, Riverside, California 92509
This organization publishes *International Plate Collectors Guild Newsletter*.

Norman Rockwell Memorial Society   P.O. Box 270328, Tampa, Florida 33688   (813) 961-8834
There is a newsletter for members listing new Rockwell items and for-sale ads.

Plate Insider's Club   P.O. Box 981, Kermit, Texas 79745   (915) 586-2571
Plate Market Insider, the club's newspaper, comes out every other week and lists the latest releases and prices.

PUBLICATIONS

The Plate Collector   P.O. Box 1041, Kermit, Texas 79745   (915) 586-2571
This semimonthly magazine contains articles and many full-color advertisements for all types of limited editions.

Plate Newsletter   P.O. Drawer C, Kermit, Texas 79745
This newsletter is for the very serious collector or dealer.

Plate-O-Holic   The Plate Collector's Stock Exchange, 478 Ward Street Extension, Wallingford, Connecticut 06492   (203) 265-1722
This chatty bimonthly newsletter is from a dealer and includes suggestions about which items are going to be popular, what is going down in price, etc.

Plate World   6054 West Touhy Avenue, Chicago, Illinois 60648
This bimonthly magazine is about limited edition plates. It is in full color and contains many articles and advertisements. It is published by an affiliate of Bradford Galleries, a plate-selling organization.

Rockwell Society News   P.O. Box BE, Stony Brook, New York 11790
This is a quarterly newsletter.

PRICE GUIDES

Bradford Exchange. *The Bradford Book of Collector Plates 1981.*
Chicago: Rand McNally, 1981.

The Charlton Standard Catalogue of Royal Doulton Figurines. Toronto: The Charlton Press (299 Queen Street West, Toronto, Ontario, M5V, 1Z9 Canada). 1982

Hotchkiss, John F. *Hummel Art Price Guide and Supplements.*
Des Moines: Wallace-Homestead, 1980.

Kovel, Ralph and Terry. *The Kovels' Illustrated Price Guide to Royal Doulton.*
New York: Crown Publishers, 1980.

————. *The Kovels' Price Guide for Collector Plates, Figurines, Paperweights, and Other Limited Editions.*
New York: Crown Publishers, 1978.

Krause, Chester L. *Guidebook of Franklin Mint Issues,* 1982 ed.
Iola, Wisconsin: Krause Publications, 1981.

Luckey, Carl F. *Hummel Figurines and Plates,* 4th ed.
Florence, Alabama: Books Americana, 1980.

————. *Norman Rockwell Art and Collectibles.*
Florence, Alabama: Books Americana, 1981.

Lynch, Rebecca and Robert. *A Price Guide to Royal Doulton Figurines.*
Privately printed, 1979 (P.O. Box 18233, East Hartford, Connecticut 06118).

Moline, Mary. *Norman Rockwell Collectibles Value Guide,* 4th ed.
San Francisco: Rumbleseat Press, 1982.

Yeager, Mary Lou. *The Price Guide to the Complete Royal Doulton Figurine Collection.*
Privately printed (P.O. Box 1042, Williamsburg, Virginia 23185). 1978, Supplement 1979.

BUYING BY MAIL

Hundreds of dealers sell limited editions by mail. Many advertise in general antiques publications (see Chapter 99, General Publications) or in the specialized publications. Some have price lists or catalogues available at a minimal fee.

APPRAISERS

The Bradford Exchange P.O. Box 48204, Chicago, Illinois 60648
A monthly price list is available giving current values of limited edition plates.

The Plate Collector's Stock Exchange Adam, Terry, and Tiffany Selesh, 478 Ward Street Extension, Wallingford, Connecticut 06492 (203) 265-1722
Appraisals of Hummel figurines and limited editions are done by mail. There is a discount to members.

41. MARBLE RESTORATION

The major concern regarding marble is its care and upkeep. Marble should be kept clean. Wipe up any spills as soon as possible or the marble may become etched. If the stain is stubborn, use some soap and lukewarm water. Marble should be dusted with a damp cloth and washed with a mild detergent and water about twice a year. You can wax marble with a colorless paste wax but white marble may appear yellow if waxed.

Minor breaks can be mended with instant epoxy glue. Most marble cutters, cemetery monument makers, or windowsill installers have this product. Stains can be removed, but it takes time and requires more information. Check your library or contact a marble worker in your area.

HOW-TO-FIX-IT BOOKS

Care and Cleaning of Interior Marble Surfaces.
Center Rutland, Vermont: Gawet Marble & Granite (Route 4, Center Rutland, Vermont 05736), n.d. Brochure.

How to Keep Your Marble Beautiful.
Washington, D.C.: Marble Institute of America, n.d. Booklet.

Technical Notes on the Care of Art Objects: The Care of Marble Sculptures, No. 7.
London: Victoria and Albert Museum, 1972. Booklet.

PARTS AND SUPPLIES

Gawet Marble & Granite, Inc.   Route 4, Center Rutland, Vermont 05736
Products needed for the care and cleaning of marble are available through this company.

Graco Sales Company   8152 Highway 70, Arlington, Tennessee 38002   (901) 386-3043
The Kotton Klenser products offered by Graco Sales Company can be used to clean marble and
alabaster. A brochure is available.

The F. A. Seeds Company   113 Walton Avenue, Lexington, Kentucky 40508   (606) 254-7263
Seeds' Merit Wax Polish is for hard-finished furniture and marble.

Vermarco Supply Company   (Division of Vermont Marble Company)61 Main Street, Proctor,
Vermont 05765
A marble care kit can be purchased. This kit includes marble cleaner, polishing powder, a buffing pad,
and Tri-Seal, the marble sealer. Items can be bought separately and a brochure is available.

REPAIR SERVICES

Alexander's Sculptural Service   117 East 39th Street, New York, New York 10016
(212) 867-8866
This firm specializes in restoration of marble sculpture, limiting its service to works of art museum
quality. They will travel for on-site restoration. Telephone or write with inquiries.

Richard George/George Studios   45-04 97th Place, Corona, New York 11368   (212) 271-2506
This firm conserves and restores antique marble. Call for an appointment or make arrangements for
the delivery of the works to be restored. For restoration of large pieces requiring on-location repairs,
call or write for information.

Rosene Green Associates, Inc.   1622A Beacon Street, Brookline, Massachusetts 02146
(617) 277-8368
This firm restores marble.

Jack T. Irwin, Inc.   601 East Gude Drive, Rockville, Maryland 20852   (301) 762-5800
Marble is cut to order for tabletops, vanities, fireplace facings and mantels. Tabletops, both antique and
new, are repaired.

New York Marble Works, Inc.   1399 Park Avenue, New York, New York 10029
(212) 534-2242 or 534-2243
This firm restores, replaces, and supplies marble, both domestic and imported. It can be cut to order for
tabletops or bases, whole dining tables, fireplaces, or sink tops. Telephone or write with inquiries.

42. MARITIME MEMORABILIA

The lure of the sea remains as romantic today as it has for centuries. Many collectors search for memorabilia about whaling, steamships, famous sinkings, sailboats, fishing, and other specialties. All these are included in maritime antiques. *See also* Chapter 34, Ivory (for scrimshaw).

CLUBS

The Antique and Classic Boat Society, Inc.   P.O. Box 831, Lake George, New York 12845
Rusty Rudder is a quarterly newsletter for members, containing articles, events, and buy/sell ads.

National Maritime Historical Society   2 Fulton Street, Brooklyn, New York 11201
(212) 858-1348
Sea History is a quarterly magazine with articles and color pictures.

Oceanic Navigation Research Society, Inc. (Ocean Liners, 1840–1940)   P.O. Box 8005, Studio City, California 91608   (213) 985-1345
Ship to Shore is a quarterly journal.

Steamship Historical Society of America, Inc.   345 Blackstone Boulevard, H.C. Hall Building, Providence, Rhode Island 02906
Steamboat Bill is a quarterly journal for members.

Titanic Historical Society, Inc.   P.O. Box 53, Indian Orchard, Massachusetts 01151-0053
(413) 543-1891
The Titanic Commutator is a quarterly magazine with articles about the *Titanic,* her sister ship the *Britannic,* and the White Star Line.

PUBLICATION

Nautical Brass   P.O. Box 744, Montrose, California 91020   (213) 248-2616
This is a bimonthly newsletter for the nautical collector. It contains excellent technical articles about all sorts of items from scrimshaw to helmets.

REPAIR SERVICE

New York Nautical Instrument and Service Corporation   140 West Broadway, New York, New York 10012   (212) 962-4522

Marine clocks, compasses, sextants, barometers, barographs, stick barometers, and chronometers are repaired. Although most of its work is done for commercial vessels, the company will do repairs for collectors. Call or write for more information.

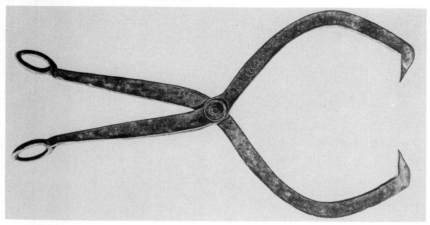

43. METAL ANTIQUES AND COLLECTIBLES

Each type of metal requires particular cleaning care. Copper, bronze, and some brass should be kept polished. Bronze should never be cleaned in any way that might affect the patina. Soap, water, dusting, and even a light waxing are safe for most metal items. There are several tarnish preventative silicon-based polishes that are safe for some metals. Never use harsh abrasives like scouring powder or steel wool on any metal if it can be avoided. Always wash all strong polishes off completely. Many polishes are made with acids that continue to "eat" the metal after it has been polished.

Do not keep bronzes in a room that is being cleaned with bleaching powders, disinfectants, or floor-washing products with chlorine. They can harm the bronze. Never store bronzes near rubber mats.

Iron cooking utensils should be seasoned. Coat an iron pot with edible cooking oil and bake it at 300° for about two hours. There is special dull black and rust-resistant paint if you want to repaint iron. This cannot be used on utensils that will hold food.

Never wrap metals in plastic or nonventilated materials. Some moisture can collect under the wrap or the plastic may melt and cause serious damage.

Check in the Yellow Pages of the telephone book under Plating to find shops that replate, polish, and restore metal items. *See also* Chapter 56, Pewter, and Chapter 70, Silver and Silver Plate.

BOOKS OF MARKS

Haslam, Malcolm. *Marks and Monograms of the Modern Movement, 1875–1930.*
New York: Charles Scribner's Sons, 1977.

Kovel, Ralph and Terry. *Know Your Collectibles.*
New York: Crown Publishers, 1981.

MacDonald-Taylor, Margaret, ed. *A Dictionary of Marks.*
New York: Hawthorn Books, 1962.

HOW-TO-FIX-IT BOOK

Conservation of Metals.
Nashville: American Association for State and Local History (708 Berry Road, Nashville, Tennessee 37204), n.d. Leaflet.

PARTS AND SUPPLIES

There are many commercial metal polishes available through grocery and hardware stores. If you cannot find any locally, these may be bought from the sources listed.

Antiquax, U.S.A.   713 South Main Street, Mansfield, Ohio 44907   (419) 756-3814
Antiquax has a full line of cleaners and polishes for silver, copper, and brass.

F. A. Seeds Company   113 Walton Avenue, Lexington, Kentucky 40508   (606) 254-7263
They have a full line of metal polishes.

Graco Sales Company   8152 Highway 70, Arlington, Tennessee 38002   (901) 386-3043
Kotton Klenser cleans copper, brass, stainless, chrome, pewter, silver, and silver plate.

W. J. Hagerty & Sons Ltd., Inc.   P.O. Box 1496, South Bend, Indiana 46624   (219) 623-2923
Hagerty has polishes for pewter, copper, or silver.

The Magazine Silver   P.O. Box 2217, Milwaukee, Oregon 97222   (503) 654-4155
Duraglit Wadding Silver Polish is available.

Triple X Chemical Company   841 Skokie Highway, Lake Bluff, Illinois 60044   (312) 689-0522
Metal Aid is a general purpose metal polish and stove polish for stoves or cast iron.

REPAIR SERVICES

Abend Metal Repair   Delavan Center, 501 West Fayette Street, Syracuse, New York 13204
(315) 478-2749

This firm repairs and restores bronze, brass, cast iron, or steel. It also repairs metal furniture, lamps, and sculpture. Work is done by a professional welder and sculptor. Estimates are given.

Abercrombie & Company   8227 Fenton Street, Silver Spring, Maryland 20910   (301) 585-2385
Metal items including weighted silver candlesticks and compotes, brass beds, fireplace equipment, and lamps are repaired by this firm. It replaces knife blades, brushes, and hardware for dresser sets; removes dents from pewter; and supplies metal tops for shakers and bottles. It also polishes, buffs, and lacquers metal, including gold, silver, nickel, copper, brass, and tin.

Al Bar Wilmette Platers   127 Green Bay Road, Wilmette, Illinois 60091   (312) 251-0187
This firm restores, plates, polishes, lacquers, and repairs gold, silver, brass, copper, pewter, chrome, and bronze. It also repairs and rewires lamps and reproduces missing parts. Hours are weekdays 8:00 A.M. to 4:30 P.M. and Saturdays 8:00 A.M. to noon.

All-Tek Finishing Company   355 Bernard Street, Trenton, New Jersey 08618   (609) 695-3644
This firm polishes and plates metal.

Bernard Plating Works   660 Riverside Drive, Florence, Massachusetts 01060   (413) 584-0659
Although this firm specializes in silver, it also refinishes and repairs gold, copper, brass, and pewter. It does plating with nickel, gold, silver, and copper and hand-wiped tinning on copper and brass cookware, excluding teakettles. Copper and brass are also cleaned, polished, and lacquered. Knife and serving blades can be replaced.

Joseph DeVoren, Silversmiths   6350 Germantown Avenue, Philadelphia, Pennsylvania 19144 (215) 844-7577
Services include refinishing, repairing, replating, lacquering, and Perma-shielding pewter, brass, copper, gold, and nickel. Brass beds, tea services, and flatware are also restored. A price list is available.

Michael J. Dotzel & Son   402 East 63rd Street, New York, New York 10021   (212) 838-2890
Services include refinishing, repairing, replating, lacquering, and Perma-shielding pewter, brass, copper, gold and nickel; restoration of brass beds, tea services, flatware, chandeliers, and lighting fixtures; replacement of Thermos ice bucket liners, bristles for hair and clothes brushes, shell combs for silver mounts, mirror glasses for hand mirrors, ivory insulators for pots, ivory knobs for urns, handles for pots, nail files, shoe horns, bottle openers, wooden salad forks or spoons, picture frame backs, wicker handles on hot milk pots, etc. Send a self-addressed, stamped envelope and description of the problem for an estimate.

Estes-Simmons Silverplating, Ltd.   1168 Howell Mill Road, N.W., Atlanta, Georgia 30318 (404) 875-9581
This firm restores, replates, polishes, and repairs silver, gold, brass, copper, nickel, and pewter. It also replaces missing parts, repairs brushes, combs, mirrors, blades, and sterling handles, relines jewelry boxes with plush velvet, and removes engraving. A brochure is available.

Forgecraft Manufacturing Company   P.O. Box 156, Route 1, Highway 99W, McMinnville, Oregon 97128   (503) 835-7754

This company restores antique ironwork including chandeliers, gates, armor suits, etc. Other services include smithing of lighting fixtures, fireplace tools, family coats of arms or crests, and architectural ironwork. Write for further information.

Hiles Plating Company, Inc.   2028 Broadway, Kansas City, Missouri 64108   (816) 421-6450

Metal restoration of all kinds is done by this firm. It specializes in replating of silver flatware and hollow ware and repairs damaged flatware, handles, and spouts and replaces stainless steel knife blades, ivory insulators in teapots, ivory, and ebony or boxwood knobs. Lost lids or feet can be replaced. An opinion and/or estimate will be sent upon receipt of pieces to be restored.

Mort Jacobs Restorations   Jackson-Green Building, 231 South Green Street, Chicago, Illinois 60607   (312) 648-0009

This is a nationwide restoration business. They repair bronze and spelter (pot metal, white metal), replace lost patination, refinish, and replace missing parts. There is no charge for estimates. Packing and shipping instructions are available for out-of-state inquiries. Business hours are 9:00 to 3:30 Monday through Friday.

Just Enterprises   2790 Sherwin Avenue, Unit 10, Ventura, California 93003   (805) 644-5837

This firm does metal surface finishing, electroplating, buffing, silver soldering, and smithing of gold, silver, brass, copper, pewter, etc.

Steve Kayne Hand Forged Hardware   17 Harmon Place, Smithtown, New York 11788 (516) 724-3669

This firm repairs and restores iron, brass, bronze, copper, and tin. Write for more information.

M & V Electroplating Corporation   5 Greenleaf Street, Newburyport, Massachusetts 01950 (617) 462-6646 or 462-6619

The Consumer Products Division will strip, polish, plate, buff, and color anything from silver tea services to motorcycle fenders, jewelry to wood stoves, etc. It will plate items using copper, nickel, chromium, cadmium, zinc, tin, tin-lead, gold, silver, platinum, and rhodium. Other services include chromic and sulfuric anodizing, color dyeing, etching and electroplating on aluminum, and passivating and electropolishing stainless steel. On most metals the company can clean, degrease, vapor blast, sandblast, grind, polish, buff, grain, strip, pickle, phosphate, and chromate. A brochure and price list are available.

Midwest Burnishing   208 East Main Street, Round Lake Park, Illinois 60073   (312) 546-2200

This firm does antique metal polishing, specializing in all metals including brass, silver, pewter, steel, bronze, and copper. It also custom makes any needed items. A leaflet is available.

New England Country Silver, Inc.   Smith Road, East Haddam, Connecticut 06423 (203) 873-1314

This firm repairs, refinishes, and replates old silver and other metals including copper, brass, pewter, or metals plated with silver or gold. It replaces knife blades with stainless steel. Repairs also include removing dents, soldering parts, sealing leaks, or making new parts, as well as buffing, polishing, and plating. Send your piece for a free estimate and the company will pay return postage. A brochure is available.

Peninsula Plating Works, Inc.   232 Homer Avenue, Palo Alto, California 94301   (415) 326-7825
This firm polishes, plates, and repairs silver, steel, iron, brass, nickel-silver, copper, bronze, pewter, white metal, lead, and zinc. Services include soldering, gas welding, replacement of combs, brushes, knife blades, salad servers, and restoration of sterling, silver plate, and pewter, brass, and copper items. Tarnish-proof silver containers are offered. A brochure is available.

Peter M. Pflock   18 Elm Street, Newport, Rhode Island 02840   (401) 847-6758
Complete restoration service for most metals and fixtures—silver, brass, copper, tin, pewter—is available.

Retinning & Copper Repair, Inc.   525 West 26th Street, New York, New York 10001
This firm re-tins and repairs copper cooking pots. It will polish and reshape copper, brass, and iron antiques.

Schutte's Lamp Supply   503 West Spring Street, Lima, Ohio 45801   (419) 223-7406
Schutte's will strip, polish, and lacquer any brass or copper item. Call or write for prices and shipping instructions.

Specialized Repair Service   2406 West Bryn Mawr Avenue, Chicago, Illinois 60659
(312) 784-2800
This firm repairs metal, brass, pewter, copper, steel, white metal (zinc die casting or spelter). Missing hardware and castings in yellow and red brass or bronze are made to match. Other services include welding, machining, refinishing, silver brazing.

Studio Foundry   1001 Old River Road, Cleveland, Ohio 44113   (216) 621-4331
The Studio Foundry repairs bronze sculptures.

Theiss Plating Corporation   9314 Manchester, St. Louis, Missouri 63119   (314) 961-0600
General metal restorations include replating, repairs to silver and other metal articles, and restoration of silver flatware or hollow ware.

Thompsons Studio, Inc.   Back Meadow Road, Damariscotta, Maine 04543   (207) 563-5280
This firm does restorations of any period. It specializes in jewelry and precious and base metals. Hours are weekdays 10:00 A.M. to 5:00 P.M. and Saturdays 9:00 A.M. to noon. A brochure is available for $1.00.

Universal Electro-Plating Company, Inc.   1804 Wisconsin Avenue, N.W., Washington, D.C. 20007   (202) 333-2460
This company does silver plating, polishing and lacquering, hard and soft soldering, dent removal, and

straightening of silver. It also replaces missing pieces; cleans and repairs pewter, silver, brass, and copper; replaces old cutlery with new stainless steel; restores dresser sets; and offers new mirrors, combs, brushes, nail files, and nail buffers. It will repair and restore brass beds, trays, chandeliers, lamps, fireplace andirons, tools, coal scuttles, umbrella stands, bookends, door hardware, plumbing, etc. A brochure is available.

Vermont Plating, Inc.   113 South Main Street, Rutland, Vermont 05701   (802) 775-5759
This firm finishes metal, restores brass, copper, and old wood stove trim parts (nickel plating).

PRICE GUIDES

Duncan, Alastair. *Tiffany at Auction.*
New York: Rizzoli International, 1982.

Horswell, Jane. *Bronze Sculpture of "Les Animaliers": Reference and Price Guide.*
Suffolk, England: Antique Collectors' Club (5 Church Street, Clopton, Woodbridge, Suffolk 1P12 1BR England), 1971. Price revision 1980.

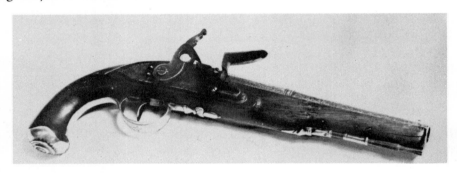

44. MILITARY MEMORABILIA

Collectors of military memorabilia search for everything from toy soldiers to working guns. Many of these souvenirs are dangerous and any military object, gun, hand grenade, etc. that might hold explosives should be checked by the local police or other experts. If you have children in a home with military memorabilia be sure the guns and knives are safely locked up. Old guns should have the barrels filled so it is impossible to accidentally discharge the gun. Old rifles may be unsafe to shoot and often even safe antiques have a recoil that will surprise the inexperienced. Do not sell a gun without checking local laws. Be sure to register any gun.

Repairs to any sort of weapon should be done only by an expert. Many shops that sell modern firearms have staff members who can repair old guns. Other restorers can be located through the publications. Because of the problems of shipping guns, the work usually must be done locally. *See also* Chapter 37, Knives.

CLUBS

The American Model Soldier Society and the American Military Historical Society   1528 El Camino Real, San Carlos, California 94070   (415) 591-8125
DAWK is a quarterly magazine of about 18 mimeographed pages featuring short articles by members.

American Society of Military Insignia Collectors   744 Warfield Avenue, Oakland, California 94610
Trading Post is a quarterly magazine and newsletter for members.

Japanese Sword Society of the United States, Inc.   5907 Deerwood Drive, St. Louis, Missouri 63123   (314) 832-3477
This society's newsletter and bulletin offer information about swords and events of interest to collectors.

PUBLICATIONS

Arms Gazette   13063 Ventura Boulevard, Studio City, California 91604
This is a magazine about guns.

The Doughboy   P.O. Box 3912, Missoula, Montana 59806
This is a quarterly newsletter.

Man at Arms   222 West Exchange Street, Providence, Rhode Island 02903
This is a magazine about weapons.

Military Collectors News   P.O. Box 7582, Tulsa, Oklahoma 74105   (918) 743-6048
This is a monthly magazine.

The MX Military Exchange   P.O. Box 3, Torrington, Connecticut 06790   (203) 482-7667
This monthly international newspaper is for buying, selling, and trading military collectibles.

REPAIR SERVICE

Brandywine Battlefield National Museum, Inc.   P.O. Box 265, Route 1, Chadds Ford, Pennsylvania 19317   (215) 388-1134
The museum specializes in military artifacts such as uniforms, flags, swords, weapons, etc., and offers a restoration service to collectors.

PRICE GUIDES

Byron, David. *The Firearms Price Guide,* rev. ed.
New York: Crown Publishers, 1980.

Flayderman, Norm. *Flayderman's Guide to Antique American Firearms . . . and Their Values,* 2nd ed.
Northfield, Illinois: DBI Books (1 Northfield Plaza, Northfield, Illinois 60093), 1980.

Hawkins, Peter. *The Price Guide to Antique Guns and Pistols.*
Suffolk, England: Antique Collectors' Club (5 Church Street, Clopton, Woodbridge, Suffolk
1P12 1BR England), 1973. Price revision 1980.

Hudgeons, Thomas E., III, ed. *The Official 1981 Price Guide to Antique & Modern Firearms.*
Orlando, Florida: House of Collectibles, 1981.

Kaduck, John M. *World War II German Collectibles.*
Privately printed, 1978 (P.O. Box 02152, Cleveland, Ohio 44102). The 1982–1983 price guide is
available.

The Karl F. Moldenhauer Collection of Remington Arms.
Hyannis Port, Massachusetts: Richard A. Bourne Company (P.O. Box 141, Hyannis Port, Massachusetts 02647), 1980.

Quertermous, Russell and Steven. *Modern Guns: Identification and Values.*
New York: Crown Publishers, 1981.

Rankin, Robert H. *The Official 1982 Price Guide to Military Collectibles.*
Orlando, Florida: House of Collectibles, 1981.

AUCTION HOUSES

Kelley's   553 Main Street, Woburn, Massachusetts 01801   (617) 935-3389 or 272-9167
Kelley's has about 4 auctions a year. It auctions all military items from pre-Revolutionary to current-
day items. An illustrated catalogue is available for $4.00.

Maritime Auctions   P.O. Box 45A, R.R. 2, York, Maine 03909   (207) 363-4247

BUYING BY MAIL

Each of these firms has a catalogue or list available and there is a charge for some. When writing for
information, be sure to include a self-addressed, stamped envelope.

Antique Arms Catalog   Dixie Gun Works, Union City, Tennessee 38261

Brandywine Battlefield National Museum, Inc.   P.O. Box 265, Route 1, Chadds Ford, Pennsylvania 19317   (215) 388-1134
The museum specializes in military artifacts, such as uniforms, flags, swords, weapons, etc. It has a mail order catalogue offering military collectors' items from the Revolutionary War to World War II, including equipment, books, and reproduction clothing.

Collectors Antiquities   Jacques Noel Jacobsen, Jr., 60 Manor Road, Staten Island, New York 10310   (212) 981-0923
Fire, police, and military antiques are offered.

Delta International   P.O. Box 361, Lafayette, California 94549
Delta International sells war souvenirs.

William Fagan   P.O. Box 425, Fraser, Michigan 48026   (313) 465-4637
Write for the *Catalogue of Antique Arms & Armor.*

N. Flayderman & Company, Inc.   Squash Hollow, R.F.D. 2, New Milford, Connecticut 06776
This firm offers antique military arms and many related items including books, uniforms, and equipment.

Peter Hlinka Historical Americana   P.O. Box 310, New York, New York 10028   (212) 369-1660
Militaria and war relics, military books, and military medals are offered.

Quincy Sales   P.O. Box 7792, Tulsa, Oklahoma 74105   (918) 743-6048
Quincy Sales offers military collectibles.

The Soldier Shop, Inc.   1013 Madison Avenue, New York, New York 10021   (212) 535-6788
The largest part of this shop's business is books, but it also sells prints, figures, medals, and other military antiques. A yearly catalogue and supplements are published, $5.00 a copy.

Sydney B. Vernon   P.O. Box 387, Baldwin, New York 11510   (516) 536-5287
Send for the *Catalogue of Military Medals & Decorations.*

APPRAISER
Brandywine Battlefield National Museum, Inc.   P.O. Box 265, Route 1, Chadds Ford, Pennsylvania 19317   (215) 388-1134
The museum offers appraisal services including letters of identification, authentication, and appraisal.

BOOKSELLERS
Books about military memorabilia can be found in every good bookstore or library. Most stores will special order the books for you. Many of these books are available through the mail order antiques book dealers listed in Chapter 91. A few dealers listed here specialize in books about military memorabilia.

Epco Publishing Company   62-19 Cooper Avenue, Glendale, New York 11385

Fairfield Book Company   P.O. Box 289, Brookfield Center, Connecticut 06805   (800) 243-1318

M.C.N. Press   P.O. Box 7582, Tulsa, Oklahoma 74105   (918) 743-6048

The Soldier Shop, Inc.   1013 Madison Avenue, New York, New York 10021   (212) 535-6788

45. MINIATURES

Miniatures can include anything from tiny eighteenth-century silver tea sets to complete dollhouses that are furnished to period. Dollhouses and furnishings are made in several scales ranging from one inch to one foot (one-twelfth scale) to one-eighth or two-fifths scale. Most modern dollhouse pieces are now being made to the scale of one inch to a foot or the latest size, one-half inch to a foot.

There are miniature collector clubs and shows in most parts of the country. Information about these events can be found in the miniature magazines.

CLUBS

Miniature Figure Collectors of America   102 St. Paul's Road, Ardmore, Pennsylvania 19003
(215) 649-4144
This club has 2 publications, *The Guidon* and *The Newsletter*.

National Association of Miniature Enthusiasts   123 North Lemon Street, Fullerton, California
92632   (714) 871-6263
The *Miniature Gazette* is a magazine of over 100 pages filled with illustrated articles about miniatures, ads for shows and sales, and gossip about club events. It is especially good for collectors in the West.

PUBLICATIONS

Miniature Collector   170 Fifth Avenue, New York, New York 10010   (212) 989-8700
This small bimonthly magazine has over 60 pages of articles, pictures, and ads for miniatures, sales, and shows. It is in color on slick paper.

The Miniature Magazine   P.O. Box 700, Newton, New Jersey 07860   (201) 383-3355
This quarterly magazine is about dollhouses and the miniature furnishings used in scale-model houses. It features many articles about antique dollhouses and furnishings and how to make or repair items. Ads offering accessories for sale and listing of events and shows are also included.

Miniature News   1388 Thurell Road, Columbus, Ohio 43229   (614) 885-5307
This newsletter is published as a series, about 100 pages in each series. It is issued approximately every 2 months and contains articles about children's dishes, etc.

Nutshell News   Clifton House, Clifton, Virginia 22024   (703) 830-1000
This monthly magazine is filled with articles and advertisements of interest to the miniature collector and craftsman. Everything needed to make or restore a dollhouse can be found within.

The Scale Cabinetmaker   P.O. Box 87, Pembroke, Virginia 24136-0087   (703) 626-3312
This is a quarterly magazine about the construction of scale miniature period furniture.

Small Talk   P.O. Box 838, Capitola, California 95010   (408) 475-9482
This monthly magazine for collectors of miniatures contains articles about new miniatures, advertisements, articles about how to make miniatures, and other collector information.

BUYING BY MAIL
Hundreds of dealers sell miniatures by mail. Many advertise in the general antiques publications (see Chapter 99) or in the specialized publications listed in this chapter. Some have price lists or catalogues available at a minimal fee. Be sure to include a self-addressed, stamped envelope for a reply.

BOOKSELLER
Books about miniatures can be found in every good bookstore or library. Most stores will special order the books for you. Many other books are available through the mail order book dealers listed in Chapter 91, from the ads in the miniatures publications (Chapter 45), or from the dealer listed here.

Hobby House Press, Inc.   900 Frederick Street, Cumberland, Maryland 21502   (301) 759-3770
Hobby House Press has a selection of patterns and books on miniature making and collecting. Its *Miniature Book Catalog* is free upon request.

46. MIRRORS

An antique mirror consists of a frame and the silvered glass. The value is higher if both parts are original. Unfortunately, old mirrors often lose some of the backing and the reflective qualities are diminished. It is possible to "resilver" the old glass, or to replace the glass entirely, if you do not wish to live with flawed glass.

An inexpensive way to restore some old mirrors with poor "silvering" is to remove the metallic backing from the old glass and put a new mirror behind the old glass. This saves the old glass and gives a mirror that reflects properly.

Some cities have companies that will resilver old glass. These are listed in the Yellow Pages of the telephone book under "Mirrors—Resilvering."

REPAIR SERVICES

All-Tek Finishing Company   355 Bernard Street, Trenton, New Jersey 08618   (609) 695-3644
Mirror resilvering and glass beveling are among the restoration services available from this company.

Atlantic Glass & Mirror Works   439 North 63rd Street, Philadelphia, Pennsylvania 19151
(215) 747-6866
This firm specializes in custom resilvering of antique mirrors and beveled engraved mirror resilvering. Items must be insured by the owner and brought to and picked up from the firm's factory. The process takes 3 weeks.

Century Glass & Mirror, Inc.   1417 North Washington, Dallas, Texas 75204   (214) 823-7773
The firm offers custom beveling, sandblast etching, and glass molding. Send a pattern for quotes.

Joseph DeVoren, Silversmiths   6350 Germantown Avenue, Philadelphia, Pennsylvania 19144
(215) 844-7577
This firm does all types of metal repairs and restores mirror glasses for hand mirrors. Send for a price list.

Estes-Simmons Silverplating Ltd.   1168 Howell Mill Road, N.W., Atlanta, Georgia 30318
(404) 875-9581
Mirrors are restored. A brochure is available.

Bronislaus F. Janulis   6253 North Troy, Chicago, Illinois 60659   (312) 743-7868
Mr. Janulis does hand carving, leafing, and finishing of mirror and picture frames. He also repairs antique ornamental frames.

Keystone   P.O. Box 3292, San Diego, California 92103   (714) 280-1337
Keystone does mirror resilvering and has a general price guide for its services.

New England Country Silver, Inc.   Smith Road, East Haddam, Connecticut 06423
(203) 873-1314
This firm installs new mirrors and refinishes metals. Send your piece for a free estimate and the firm will pay the return postage. A brochure is available.

Universal Electro-Plating Company, Inc.   1804 Wisconsin Avenue, N.W., Washington, D.C.
20007   (202) 333-2460
New mirrors for your antique furniture can be bought from this company. A brochure is available.

47. MOVIE MEMORABILIA

Movie memorabilia is a large field ranging from movie films, sound-track albums, comic materials, toys and dolls representing characters in movies, to ceramics commemorating movie characters and related events. It also includes movie posters, lobby cards, press kits, movie stills, costumes, and memorabilia from the stars, such as Joan Crawford's eyelashes or Judy Garland's ruby slippers and more.

All of this material is rightly considered movie memorabilia and can be found in any shop or show. Specialists should be familiar with the publications and shows that are devoted exclusively to movies. Special fan clubs like the *Star Trek* enthusiasts have regular conventions and meetings. Many dead stars still have fan clubs that exchange information and memorabilia.

See also Chapter 22, Comic Art; Chapter 24, Dolls; Chapter 54, Paper Collectibles and Ephemera; Chapter 57, Photographs and Photographic Equipment; and Chapter 76, Textiles.

CLUBS

Motion Picture Collectibles Association   P.O. Box 33433, Raleigh, North Carolina 27606
(919) 851-4002
Newsreel Magazine is a mimeographed publication with articles and ads.

Old Time Western Film Club   P.O. Box 142, Siler City, North Carolina 27344
Western Film Newsletter is about club activities.

Studio Collectors Club   P.O. Box 1566, Apple Valley, California 92307   (714) 242-8569
Hollywood Studio magazine is published 10 times a year and includes some information about movie collectibles, movies, and movie stars.

PUBLICATIONS

The Big Reel   Drawer B, Summerfield, North Carolina 27358
This is a monthly trading newspaper for the movie collector.

Classic Images   P.O. Box 809, Muscatine, Iowa 52761
This is a newspaper about video and film including articles and buy and sell ads.

Film Collector's World P.O. Box 248, Rapids City, Illinois 61278 (309) 764-8473
This twice-monthly newspaper is a trading paper for collectors featuring buy and sell ads and articles.

Nostalgia World P.O. Box 231, North Haven, Connecticut 06473-0231 (203) 239-4891
This newspaper is published monthly about show business collectibles, photographs, lobby cards, records, magazines, etc.

ADDITIONAL SOURCE

Walt Disney Archives 500 South Buena Vista Street, Burbank, California 91521
This is an additional source for Disneyana. Questions are answered by mail.

REPAIR SERVICE

Ron Stark, S/R Project ASIFA/Hollywood, 1258 North Highland Avenue, Suite 102, Hollywood, California 90038
The Search and Rescue Team is a group of members of the International Animated Film Society (ASIFA/Hollywood) who repair and restore animation artwork. Their service is available to anyone. Charges are made for materials used but the labor is donated by the members. A brochure is available.

PRICE GUIDE

Kaduck, John M. *"Grandma's Scrapbook" of Silent Movie Stars.*
Privately printed, 1976 (P.O. Box 02152, Cleveland, Ohio 44102). The 1982–1983 price guide is available.

AUCTION HOUSE

The Berry Auction Company 8380 Santa Monica Boulevard, Los Angeles, California 90069 (213) 650-1223
Mail and phone bids are accepted. A catalogue is available.

BUYING BY MAIL

Hundreds of dealers sell movie memorabilia by mail. Many advertise in the general antiques publications listed in Chapter 99 or in the specialized publications listed in this chapter. Some have price lists or catalogues available at a minimal fee. Be sure to include a self-addressed, stamped envelope when writing for information.

48. MUSIC BOXES

Mechanical music boxes have been popular for centuries. They range from tiny singing birds in lavish enameled boxes to the large machines that played steel discs 33 inches in diameter. All of the music boxes are delicate, intricate mechanisms that require care. Don't try to repair a music box unless you are an expert. It is a job for a professional. Restorers and parts can be found, but they are rare and expensive. You may be lucky enough to find a local music box devotee who restores. Contact the local chapter of the Musical Box Society to see if there is such a person in your area. Other restorers are listed here, but they have advised us that they are very busy and repairs may take years.

CLUB

Musical Box Society International   P.O. Box 202, Route 3, Morgantown, Indiana 46160
There are 2 publications: *The MBS News Bulletin* has a series of announcements of activities for members and buy and sell ads. *The Musical Box Society International Bulletin* is a small publication sent to members. Articles about repairing, restoring, and history, reprints of old catalogues, and other articles concerning music boxes are illustrated and researched.

PUBLICATIONS

The Music Box   14 Elmwood Road, London W4 England
This magazine is issued 4 times a year.

Jerry's Musical News   4624 West Woodland Road, Edina, Minnesota 55424   (612) 926-7775
This monthly newsletter is for collectors of phonographs, music boxes, radios, and other related items. It includes buy and sell ads.

PARTS AND SUPPLIES

The Musical Box Society International   Mrs. Mark A. Fratti, 2559 Brickyard Road, Warners, New York 13164   (315) 672-3636
For several years the society has offered facsimile tune cards to its members. The price is $1.00 per card.

Panchronia Antiquities   Nancy Fratti, P. O. Box 73, Warners, New York 13164   (315) 672-3636
This company supplies materials for music boxes such as lid pictures, governor jewels, decals, brushes, pads, stops, wheels, etc. A catalogue is available for $4.50.

REPAIR SERVICES

The Antique Phonograph Shop   Dennis and Patti Valente, 320 Jericho Turnpike, Floral Park, New York 11001   (516) 775-8605
This shop restores musical antiques including music boxes.

DB Musical Restorations   Carol and David Beck, 230 Lakeview Avenue, N.E., Atlanta, Georgia 30305   (404) 237-3556
DB Musical Restorations is a small business dedicated to restoration of antique cylinder and disc music boxes. It only does complete restorations. This process includes cleaning, polishing, and lubricating the mechanism. Call for a consultation before shipping your music box. When the Becks receive the machine they will make an estimate.

Gould Piano Craftsmen, Inc.   391 Tremont Place, Orange, New Jersey 07050   (201) 672-4060
Music boxes, phonographs, and pianos are repaired, bought, and sold.

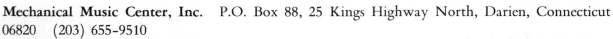

Mechanical Music Center, Inc.   P.O. Box 88, 25 Kings Highway North, Darien, Connecticut 06820   (203) 655-9510
This firm carries antique mechanical musical instruments including music boxes, player pianos, musical clocks, Wurlitzers, etc. It also does repairs and restoration. A catalogue is available.

The Meekins Music Box Company   P.O. Box 161, Collingswood, New Jersey 08108 (609) 858-6421
This company restores music boxes. It can make gears.

Panchronia Antiquities   Nancy Fratti, P.O. Box 73, Warners, New York 13164   (315) 672-3636
Nancy Fratti restores antique music boxes.

Porter Music Box Company, Inc.   Sunset Hill, Randolph, Vermont 05060   (802) 728-9694
This company restores all types of fine antique music boxes, both Swiss and American made. Porter also sells discs and manufactures the New Porter Music Box.

Paul N. Smith   408 East Leeland Heights Boulevard, Lehigh Acres, Florida 33936   (813) 369-4663
This firm repairs clocks, music boxes, and other curious or unusual devices. Send a letter describing the problem and enclose a stamped, self-addressed envelope. Cost estimates are given after examination of the mechanism. The firm makes many special parts such as gears, springs, levers, etc.

PRICE GUIDE

Fredericks, Robert, and Gould, Susan. *The Official Price Guide to Music Collectibles.*
Orlando, Florida: House of Collectibles, 1980.

BUYING BY MAIL

Hundreds of dealers sell music boxes by mail. Many advertise in the general antiques publications listed in Chapter 99 or in the specialized publications listed in this chapter. See also Chapter 49, Musical Instruments and Music-Making Machines.

Eastern Musical Antiques P.O. Box 297, West Orange, New Jersey 07052 (201) 731-3322
This firm sells phonographs, music boxes, nickelodeons, and jukeboxes. When writing for information, be sure to include a self-addressed, stamped envelope.

BOOKSELLERS
Books about music boxes can be found in every good bookstore or library. Most stores will special order the books for you. Many of these books are available through the mail order antiques book dealers listed in Chapter 91.

Vestal Press 320 North Jensen Road (P.O. Box 97), Vestal, New York 13850 (607) 797-4872

49. MUSICAL INSTRUMENTS AND MUSIC-MAKING MACHINES

Music collectibles cover a wide range from old musical instruments to reproducing pianos. The value of each of these items is in the music it makes so each piece must be in good working condition. Repairs of mechanical music-making machines are slow. Many of the restorers have two- and three-year waiting lists. If you can fix this type of antique yourself, you can usually make good buys, but be careful if you buy a machine that needs repairs you can't do yourself.

Large music-making machines are usually not found at the average shops or shows. Old amusement parks, important piano salesrooms, auction galleries, and old stores are the best sources. There are ads in some publications and many mail order dealers. Minor repairs are possible in some cities or through dealers or service shops that are listed in the Yellow Pages of the telephone book under "Musical Instruments—Repairing." *See also* Chapter 48, Music Boxes.

CLUBS

The American Musical Instrument Society   Membership Office, University of South Dakota, P.O. Box 194, Vermillion, South Dakota 57069   (605) 677-5306
This society publishes *AMIS Newsletter* and *Journal of the AMIS*.

Automatic Musical Instrument Collectors Association   P.O. Box 172, Columbia, South Carolina 29202   (803) 738-0567 evenings, 765-2965 days
The AMICA (news bulletin) is a magazine issued 10 times a year featuring notes about meetings and members and a few articles about automatic musical instruments, history, and repair.

The Violin Society of America   c/o Herbert K. Goodkind, 23 Helena Avenue, Larchmont, New York 10538   (914) 834-1448
The Violin Society of America Journal is published quarterly.

Wilhelm Furtwängler Society   6112 West 77th Street, Los Angeles, California 90045
(213) 776-4231
The *Wilhelm Furtwängler Society Newsletter* is a quarterly.

PUBLICATIONS

Jerry's Musical News   4624 West Woodland Road, Edina, Minnesota 55424   (612) 926-7775
This is a monthly newsletter for collectors of phonographs, music boxes, radios, and other related items. It features buy and sell ads.

Mugwumps   15 Arnold Place, New Bedford, Massachusetts 02740   (617) 993-0156
This magazine is published 6 times a year and is for collectors of folk musical instruments such as guitar, banjo, dulcimer, autoharp, etc.

HOW-TO-FIX-IT BOOK

Givens, Larry. *Rebuilding the Player Piano.*
Vestal, New York: The Vestal Press, 1963.

PARTS AND SUPPLIES

Automatic Music Roll Company   P.O. Box 3194, Seattle, Washington 98114   (206) 633-3664
This company offers original rolls for sale, original literature, and parts for player pianos, jukeboxes, phonographs, and radios. A catalogue is available.

Inzer Pianos, Inc.   John and Hazel Inzer, 2473 Canton Road, Marietta, Georgia 30066
(404) 422-2664
Over 3,500 piano rolls are in stock. A catalogue of hard-to-find parts for pianos, player pianos, and reed organs is available for $2.00.

The Musical Museum Deansboro, New York 13328   (315) 841-8774
The Musical Museum offers a choice selection of music rolls for organs. These are mechanically produced from original masters. A list is available.

The Old Lamplighter Shop Route 12-B, Deansboro, New York 13328   (315) 841-8774
This shop sells parts, special felts and fabrics, and information sheets so you can "do it yourself."

Bob Pierce 1880 Termino Avenue, Long Beach, California 90815   Home: (213) 597-7535; office 597-8245
Decals for pianos are offered for $1.50. Send a self-addressed, stamped envelope.

Player Piano Company, Inc. 704 East Douglas, Wichita, Kansas 67202   (316) 263-3241
This company carries approximately 2,450 retail parts, 150 publications, 2,500 piano rolls (Q-R-S and Play-Rite), and 800 raw-stock merchandise items. Orders for parts or catalogues can be taken over the phone. Its toll-free number (except in Kansas) is 1 (800) 835-2911. For technical service call (316) 263-1714. A free introductory catalogue is available. The regular catalogue is $3.50.

REPAIR SERVICES

The Antique Phonograph Shop Dennis and Patti Valente, 320 Jericho Turnpike, Floral Park, New York 11001   (516) 775-8605
This shop rebuilds player pianos and sells piano rolls.

Fisher's Antiques 2010 FM 1960 West, Houston, Texas 77090   (713) 440-9085
This firm restores reed (pump) organs. Write or call for further information.

Jacques Francais 140 West 57th Street, New York, New York 10019 Rene A. Morel, Vice President (212) 586-2607
This firm restores violins. There is a waiting list of at least 2 years.

William D. Gilstrap Route 2, Bevier, Missouri 63532   (816) 385-5338
This firm does player action rebuilding, any make. It specializes in Gulbransen and Schultz. Unavailable piano parts are also made. All work is guaranteed and it furnishes packing crates for stock sent UPS. Call or write for more information.

Gould Piano Craftsmen, Inc. 391 Tremont Place, Orange, New Jersey 07050   (201) 672-4060
This is a full service piano restoration firm specializing in reproducing and player piano and pianocorder installations. It will custom build multi-instrument nickelodeons from antique pianos and offers phonograph and music box repair services. All of the above items are bought and sold as well.

H R String Instruments Peter Horn, Inc., 2570 Superior Avenue, Cleveland, Ohio 44114 (216) 579-1337
This firm repairs all stringed instruments including guitars, gambas, baroque instruments, violins, violas, cellos, and basses. Repairs are available to wholesale and retail customers alike. Instruments may be sent for repair, but please contact the firm first.

Inzer Pianos, Inc.   John and Hazel Inzer, 2473 Canton Road, Marietta, Georgia 30066 (404) 422-2664

Antique keyboard instruments, player pianos, grand pianos, pump organs, and nickelodeons are restored. Other services are custom woodworking, mechanical rebuilding, and refinishing. Restoration of reproducers is a specialty. A catalogue of parts for pianos, player pianos, and reed organs is available for $2.00.

Keyboard Craftsmen, Inc.   350 West 31st Street, New York, New York 10001   (212) 947-0090

This firm restores and rebuilds antique pianos, especially square grand pianos of the 1800s. It will give an appraisal for a fee but there is no fee for mail or phone questions. Services are available to anyone in the U.S. It also has available historical and technical articles on square grand pianos.

Mechanical Music Center, Inc.   P.O. Box 88, 25 Kings Highway North, Darien, Connecticut 06820   (203) 655-9510

Antique mechanical musical instruments including player pianos are repaired and restored. A catalogue is available.

Grant W. Moore   109 North Street, Ypsilanti, Michigan 48197   (313) 485-3244

Mr. Moore's services are limited to seventeenth-, eighteenth-, and nineteenth-century oboes. He does restoration and gives opinions on conservation. He will not answer questions by mail.

Rene A. Morel, Vice President   c/o Jacques Francais, 140 West 57th Street, New York, New York 10019   (212) 586-2607

This firm restores violins. There is a waiting list of at least 2 years.

The Old Lamplighter Shop   Route 12-B, Deansboro, New York 13328   (315) 841-8774

This shop repairs nickelodeons, melodeons, grind organs, parlor-pump organs, and other musical antiques. It can supply you with many of the parts, special felts and fabrics, and information sheets so you can "do it yourself."

Ragtime   1320-C Angie Avenue, Modesto, California 95351   (209) 538-2330

Ragtime does player and nickelodeon repairs as well as conversions. A catalogue is available for $3.50. There are also free brochures.

The Shrine to Music Museum   USD Box 194, Vermillion, South Dakota 57069   (605) 677-5306

Restoration services are available to anyone in the U.S. The museum will answer questions by mail.

Thomas and Barbara Wolf   P.O. Box 40572, Washington, D.C. 20016   (202) 332-3341

The Wolfs specialize in the restoration of harpsichords. Services are available to anyone in the U.S.

PRICE GUIDES

Ehrhardt, Roy. *Violin Identification and Price Guide*, Book 3. Kansas City, Missouri: Heart of America Press, 1978.

Fredericks, Robert, and Gould, Susan. *The Official Price Guide to Music Collectibles.* Orlando, Florida: House of Collectibles, 1980.

BUYING BY MAIL
Each of these firms has a catalogue or list available and there is a charge for some. When writing for information, be sure to include a self-addressed, stamped envelope.

Frank Adams Catalogue   P.O. Box 3194, International Station, Seattle, Washington 98114
This catalogue includes music and musical instruments.

American International Galleries   1802 Kettering Street, Irvine, California 92714   (714) 754-1777
This firm offers automatic musical instruments.

Automatic Music Roll Company   P.O. Box 3194, Seattle, Washington 98114   (206) 633-3664
This firm has a catalogue of publications, service manuals, etc. on player pianos, phonographs, jukeboxes, and so on. It lists various types of rolls, jukeboxes, and player pianos for sale.

David T. Dupree   2392 Mira Sol, Vista, California 92083   (714) 727-5534
Mr. Dupree deals exclusively in player rolls by mail and stocks all the rolls in the catalogues. Two-day service on orders is available. The catalogues are *Q-R-S Player Roll* and *Play-Rite Music Roll*.

Eastern Musical Antiques   P.O. Box 297, West Orange, New Jersey 07052   (201) 731-3322
This firm offers phonographs, music boxes, nickelodeons, and jukeboxes.

The Mekanisk Musik Museum Review   150 Vesterbrogade, Copenhagen, Denmark

Player Piano Company, Inc.   620 East Douglas, Wichita, Kansas 67202   (316) 263-3241
This firm offers player piano parts and accessories.

Record Digest   Music World News, Groom Creek Route, Prescott, Arizona 86301
(800) 453-2400
A sample of this biweekly magazine is available for 50¢ postage.

APPRAISERS
Jacques Francais   140 West 57th Street, New York, New York 10019   (212) 586-2607
This firm appraises and repairs violins.

Herbert K. Goodkind   25 Helena Avenue, Larchmont, New York 10538   (914) 834-1448
Mr. Goodkind appraises violins, violas, cellos, and their bows.

Keyboard Craftsmen, Inc.   350 West 31st Street, New York, New York 10001   (212) 947-0090
This firm restores and rebuilds antique pianos, especially square grand pianos of the 1800s. It will give an appraisal for a fee but there is no fee for mail or phone questions. Services are available to anyone in the U.S. It also has historical and technical articles available on square grand pianos.

Grant W. Moore   109 North Street, Ypsilanti, Michigan 48197   (313) 485-3244
Mr. Moore's services are limited to seventeenth-, eighteenth-, and nineteenth-century oboes. He does appraisals and gives opinions on conservation. He will not answer questions by mail.

BOOKSELLERS

Books about musical instruments and music-making machines can be found in every good bookstore and library. Most stores will special order the books for you. Many of the books are privately printed and can also be ordered by writing to the address listed.

Herbert K. Goodkind   25 Helena Avenue, Larchmont, New York 10538   (914) 834-1448
Mr. Goodkind publishes and sells books on music. A list is available.

Vestal Press   320 North Jensen Road, P.O. Box 97, Vestal, New York 13850   (607) 797-4872
Many specialized books about musical machines and instruments are sold by this company.

50. ODDS AND ENDS

We tried to find a special section for each of these items but they are so unusual we finally had to group them together as "odds and ends."

CLUBS

The American Bell Association   P.O. Box 286, R.D. #1, Natrona Heights, Pennsylvania 15065
The Bell Tower is the newsletter for this group of bell collectors.

Angel Collectors Club of America   11334 Earlywood Drive, Dallas, Texas 75218   (214) 324-1053
Halo, Everybody! is published 4 times a year and contains gossip and news of interest to members.

Candy Containers Collectors of America   Robert Dellaposta, P.O. Box 184, Lucerne Mines, Pennsylvania 15754   (412) 479-9692
The Candy Gram is a monthly newsletter for members, featuring specific information about old candy containers, articles, and old ads.

Cat Collectors   31311 Blair Drive, Warren, Michigan 48092   (313) 264-0285
This is a new club for collectors of cat items. A newsletter is published 6 times a year with articles about cat history, books, and modern figurines and museum pieces that picture cats.

Dionne Quint Collectors   P.O. Box 2527, Woburn, Massachusetts 01888   (617) 933-2219
This club specializes in memorabilia concerned with the Dionne quintuplets. It publishes a newsletter called *The Quint News.*

Flag Research Center   3 Edgehill Road, Winchester, Massachusetts 01890   (617) 729-9410
This is a research and information center specializing in both national and international flags. It publishes a bimonthly magazine, *The Flag Bulletin.*

Golf Collectors' Society   638 Wagner Road, Lafayette Hill, Pennsylvania 19444   (215) 828-4492
The *Golf Collectors' Society Bulletin,* a newsletter, is published about 6 times a year. It contains news, articles, buy, sell, and trade ads, and club gossip.

Hymn Society of America   Wittenberg University, Springfield, Ohio 45501
The Hymn Society publishes a booklet called *The Hymn,* featuring history of hymns, copies of music, words, and other information about this specialized form of music.

International Society of Animal License Collectors   4420 Wisconsin Avenue, Tampa, Florida 33616   (813) 839-6245
Paw Prints is a quarterly newsletter with detailed information about animal tags.

Morse Telegraph Club, Inc.   712 South 49, Lincoln, Nebraska 68510   (402) 489-4062
This club publishes *Dots and Dashes,* a quarterly 10-page paper with information about telegraphers, events, history, and general articles.

National Amusement Park Historical Association   P.O. Box 83, Mount Prospect, Illinois 60056
National Amusement Park Historical News is a bimonthly newsletter about the parks and their rides.

National Fishing Lure Collectors Club   3907 Wedgewood Drive, Portage, Michigan 49008   Home: (616) 382-2190, office: 323-4120
This club publishes *The N.F.L.C.C. Gazette,* a quarterly newsletter.

The Sugar Packet Collectors Club   603 East 105th Street, Kansas City, Missouri 64131   (816) 942-1466
This club publishes *The Sugar Packet—Sweet Collectibles*, a quarterly newsletter.

Texas Date Nail Collectors Association   501 West Horton, Brenham, Texas 77833   (713) 830-1495
This club publishes a bimonthly newsletter called *Nailer News.* It features nail history, membership updates, and buy/sell ads.

The Trivial Group   603 East 105th Street, Kansas City, Missouri 64131   (816) 942-1466
This is a small club specializing in the collection of various forms of trivia such as cigar bands, hornets' nests, business cards, cat cards, and almanacs. The club's purpose is to provide a means of communication for collectors of objects that are unique and unusual but not necessarily valuable. An occasional newsletter, *The Unique and Unusual Collection,* is published for members.

PUBLICATIONS
Gas Station News   P.O. Box 203, Boyce, Virginia 22620   (703) 837-2409
This is a bimonthly magazine about old gasoline stations and accessories. It features buy and sell ads.

The Owl's Nest   P.O. Box 5491, Fresno, California 93755   (209) 439-4845
This is a bimonthly newsletter for owl collectors.

PARTS AND SUPPLIES
Brandywine Battlefield National Museum, Inc.   P.O. Box 265, Route 1, Chadds Ford, Pennsylvania 19317   (215) 388-1134
The museum offers custom framing, hand netting, restoration, identification, authentication, and appraisal of historical flags.

The Popcorn Registry   Ronald E. McBride, 702 South Third Street, Bronson, Missouri 65616   (417) 334-8455
The popcorn registry is attempting to locate and register all popcorn and peanut-roasting equipment produced between the late 1800s and World War II. It also serves as a clearinghouse for spare parts for this equipment. There is no charge for its services.

51. ORIENTAL RUGS

Oriental rugs should always be kept clean and in good repair. This should be a job for the professional, although some minor work can be accomplished at home. A worn spot can be covered temporarily by coloring the exposed beige backing with crayon or colored ink. The full fringe adds to the value of a rug and it should never be trimmed or replaced unless it is absolutely necessary. There are rug dealers in large department stores or shops in many large cities who can do repairs. They can be found in the Yellow Pages. If no local restorer is available, a rug can be shipped to another city.
See also Chapter 76, Textiles.

PUBLICATIONS
HALI: The International Journal of Oriental Carpets and Textiles   P.O. Box 4312, Philadelphia, Pennsylvania 19118   (215) 843-3090
A full-color magazine on slick paper with authoritative articles by experts, this is the most scholarly magazine on the subject and has an international readership. It is important for serious collectors.

Rug News   c/o Museum Books, 48 East 43rd Street, 2nd Floor, New York, New York 10017
This is a monthly newsletter about Oriental rugs featuring goods, events, prices, books, and auctions. It also contains photo essays and details of construction and quality.

REPAIR SERVICES

Aladdin Company Ltd.   221 South Elm Street, Greensboro, North Carolina 27401
(919) 275-6351
This company offers professional cleaning and repairing.

A. Beshar & Company, Inc.   49 East 53rd Street, 2nd Floor, New York, New York 10022
(212) 758-1400
This company repairs antique Oriental rugs and carpets.

Elizabeth Crumley   2208 Derby Street, Berkeley, California 94705   (415) 845-7521
Elizabeth Crumley restores, mounts, and conserves antique textiles and Oriental rugs. Deliveries are UPS. A consultation and written report is available for $25.00. Her consultation fee is $20.00 an hour.

Karekin Beshir Ltd.   1125 Madison Avenue, New York, New York 10028   (212) 838-3763
Oriental rugs are cleaned and repaired.

Michael Leon and John Hegnauer   18 Elm Street, Newport, Rhode Island 02840   (401) 849-3476
or 849-6178
This firm offers Oriental rug restoration.

McMaster Fine & Antique Oriental Carpets   997A Roxwood, Boulder, Colorado 80303
(303) 443-2901
This firm offers hand cleaning and repair of all Oriental carpets.

APPRAISERS

Aladdin Company Ltd.   221 South Elm Street, Greensboro, North Carolina 27401
(919) 275-6351
In addition to its repair and cleaning services, Aladdin appraises Oriental rugs.

Karekin Beshir Ltd.   1125 Madison Avenue, New York, New York 10028   (212) 838-3763
This firm appraises antique Oriental and European rugs and works of art.

John C. Edelmann Galleries   523 East 73rd Street, New York, New York 10021   (212) 628-1700
This firm does appraisals and valuations for estate, tax, and insurance purposes.

McMaster Fine & Antique Oriental Carpets   997A Roxwood, Boulder, Colorado 80303
(303) 443-2901
This firm appraises Oriental carpets.

BOOKSELLERS

Books about Oriental rugs can be found in many bookstores and libraries. Most stores will special order the books for you.

The Textile Museum   2320 "S" Street, N.W., Washington, D.C. 20008   (202) 667-0441
The *Textile Museum Shop Catalogue* offers books, booklets, and items relating to textiles.

52. ORIENTALIA

The art of the Orient has fascinated collectors since the time of Marco Polo. Many Chinese and Japanese porcelains are listed in Chapter 61, Pottery and Porcelain. Other Oriental art may be found here.

CLUBS

The International Chinese Snuff Bottle Society   2601 North Charles Street, Baltimore, Maryland 21218   (301) 467-9400
International Chinese Snuff Bottle Society Journal is a quarterly magazine containing articles about snuff bottles and related Oriental art. Color pictures are featured.

International Netsuke Collectors Society   P.O. Box 10426, Honolulu, Hawaii 96816 (808) 732-1495
Journal of the International Netsuke Collectors Society is a quarterly magazine for serious collectors. Color pictures and scholarly articles are featured.

Netsuke Kenkyukai   P.O. Box 2445, Gaithersburg, Maryland 20879   (301) 762-7500
Netsuke Kenkyukai Study Journal is a quarterly magazine for members.

PUBLICATIONS

Arts Of Asia 1309 Kowloon Centre 29-39 Ashley Road, Kowloon, Hong Kong
This is a fully illustrated, scholarly, slick magazine with much color.

Oriental Art 12 Ennerdale Road, Richmond, Surrey, England
Oriental Art is a quarterly magazine for the student or advanced collector.

Orientalia Journal P.O. Box 94, Little Neck, New York 11363
This is a monthly newsletter about all sorts of Chinese and Japanese collectibles such as cloisonné, Satsuma, and Nippon. Main emphasis is on nineteenth- and twentieth-century items.

Orientations Tung Sun Commercial Centre, 194-200 Lockhart Road, 13th Floor, Hong Kong
This is a monthly magazine with color pictures and erudite articles.

REPAIR SERVICE

Rosene Green Associates, Inc. 1622A Beacon Street, Brookline, Massachusetts 02146
(617) 277-8368
This firm restores Oriental lacquered furniture, caddies, and Coromandel screens. Cracked and blistering pieces are repaired. It also sells cream polish for the care of your lacquer pieces.

PRICE GUIDE

Andacht, Sandra; Garthe, Nancy; and Mascarelli, Robert. *Wallace-Homestead Price Guide to Oriental Antiques.*
Des Moines: Wallace-Homestead, 1981.

BUYING BY MAIL

Hundreds of dealers sell Oriental antiques by mail. Many advertise in the antiques publications listed in this chapter. Some have price lists or catalogues available at a minimal fee.

Bill Egleston, Inc. 509 Brentwood Road, Marshalltown, Iowa 50158 (515) 752-4579
Illustrated lists of Oriental items for sale are sent monthly to subscribers.

APPRAISER

The Oriental Corner 395 Main Street, Los Altos, California 94022 (415) 941-3207
Oriental antiques are appraised. Hours are Tuesday through Saturday, 10:30 A.M. to 5:00 P.M.

BOOKSELLERS

Books about Orientalia can be found in every good bookstore or library. Most stores will special order the books for you.

53. PAINTINGS

Oil paintings require special care. Only lightly dust the surface of a good painting. Never wash a painting. Never try any at-home restoration unless you are trained or care very little about the final results. Never entrust a good oil painting to anyone but a competent restorer or conservator. Many pictures have been completely ruined with overrestoration, too much overpainting, or an overzealous cleaning that "skinned" the picture. They can cause problems that can never be rectified.

If you believe that your painting, no matter how dirty, is valuable, take it to your local museum to learn about the artist. Museums will not appraise but they can tell you if your picture is worth restoring. Most museums can furnish the names of local experts in conservation.

Some cities have restorers listed in the Yellow Pages of the telephone book under "Art Restoration and Conservation" or "Picture Restoring."

We have listed restorers, conservators, and companies using their own descriptions of title, training, and work methods. If you are concerned about the quality of the work or whether the firm is headed by a conservator or a restorer, etc., you must check further on your own. More information can be obtained through the American Institute for Conservation, 1522 "K" Street, N.W., #804, Washington, D.C. 20005.

CLUB

The International Foundation for Art Research   46 East 70th Street, New York, New York 10021   (212) 879-1780
Art Research News is a quarterly newsletter for members. It contains art news and notices of events.

PUBLICATIONS

The ARTnewsletter   750 Third Avenue, New York, New York 10017   (212) 599-6060
This biweekly publication concerns the international fine arts market and features information about paintings and other expensive items sold at auctions in all countries.

Leonard's Index of Art Auctions   30 Valentine Park, Newton, Massachusetts 02165
Paintings, drawings, and sculpture sold at auction are listed in this quarterly.

IDENTIFICATION

Identification of paintings requires study and expertise. First you must determine the age and quality of the painting. Many art museums have an identification service available by special appointment, although appraisals are not given. If the painting is signed, you may be able to determine the age by identifying the artist. *Dictionnaire des Peintres, Sculpteurs, Dessinateurs et Graveurs* by E. Benezit (Librairie Grund, Paris, 1976) is a ten-volume book written in French that lists most major artists. It is found in any good library or museum. Many other books listing artists are also available. Ask your librarian, museum, or bookstore to help.

Massachusetts Materials Research, Inc.   P.O. Box 326, 241 West Boylston Street, West Boylston, Massachusetts 01583   (617) 835-6262
Microscopy and chemical analysis are used to determine genuineness of paint on antique paintings and furniture. The firm can analyze material the size of a dot on an *i,* but larger pieces of material are preferred. For more information on using its services, contact Mr. Doug Shaw or Dr. David Krashes at the above telephone number.

HOW-TO-FIX-IT BOOK
Keck, Caroline K. *A Handbook on the Care of Paintings.*
Nashville: American Association for State and Local History (708 Berry Road, Nashville, Tennessee 37204), 1965.

PARTS AND SUPPLIES
See Chapter 94, Conservation, Restoration, and Preservation Supplies.

CONSERVATORS
See also Part II, Chapter 95, Conservators and Restorers, for further information.

James Alkons   2737 Riverside Boulevard, Sacramento, California 95818   (916) 444-3719
James Alkons conserves and restores paintings. The object must be examined for estimates of restoration costs. There is a fee for written proposals and documentation. He will answer questions by mail if possible but does not appraise.

Art Ltd.   Veronica Burns, Stonecroft 2210, Grafton, Wisconsin 53024   (414) 377-6555
Oil paintings are cleaned, restored, and repaired.

Paul Baron Company   Baron-Rolen Jewelers, 2825 East College Avenue, Decatur, Georgia 30030 (404) 299-1400
Restoration of oil paintings is done by this firm. Pack your pieces well and ship them to the company for an estimate.

Balboa Art Conservation Center   P.O. Box 3755, San Diego, California 92103   (714) 236-9702
The Center conserves paintings and polychromed sculpture only. Consultation is available to the public but treatment services are available only to museum members. Services are offered to the western region of the U.S. Questions are not answered by mail. The fee is $35.00 to $45.00 per hour.

The Broderick Gallery   119 Allandale Street, Jamaica Plain, Massachusetts 02130   (617) 522-1707
This gallery restores oil paintings, watercolors, and pastels as well as frames. Write or call for more information.

Dorothy Baden Elliott   3655 Egerton Circle, Sarasota, Florida 33583   (813) 924-5563
Dorothy Elliott is a conservator and will restore or give an opinion on conservation. There is a fee for an examination and estimate.

Charles E. H. Fenton Workshop & Gallery   Woodstock East, Woodstock, Vermont 05091 (802) 457-3022
This firm restores period items, especially paintings and prints.

Fieux Restoration Laboratory, Inc.   263 Cedar Street, P.O. Box 72, West Barnstable, Massachusetts 02668 (617) 362-3301
This firm offers advanced technological painting restorations. It will answer questions by mail.

Rosene Green Associates, Inc.   1622A Beacon Street, Brookline, Massachusetts 02146 (617) 277-8368
This firm restores oil paintings, miniatures, icons, Oriental paintings on screens and scrolls, and frames.

Emmett Carl Grimm   721 Elati Street, Denver, Colorado 80204   (303) 573-1973, after 6:00 P.M.
Emmett Carl Grimm specializes in restoration of Western paintings, Colonial American and primitives, and contemporary (large modern) paintings. Mr. Grimm is in charge of painting conservation at Rocky Mountain Regional Conservation Center.

Georgette Grosz   4100 Marine Drive, Suite 4-D, Chicago, Illinois 60613   (312) 248-6935
Georgette Grosz restores paintings of all periods. Services are available to anyone in the U.S. and she will answer questions by mail without a fee.

Michael Heslip, Joyce Hill Stoner   Winterthur Museum Paintings Conservation Department
Winterthur, Delaware 19735   (302) 656-8591
Private work in conservation of paintings is done on evenings and weekends only. Call between noon and 1:00 P.M. Services are available to anyone in the U.S. and they will answer questions by mail, usually without a fee.

Yashiro Iguchi   Museum of Fine Arts, 479 Huntington Avenue, Boston, Massachusetts 02115   (617) 267-9300
Yashiro Iguchi restores Asiatic paintings and some other Oriental objects and will answer questions by mail. There is a fee for restoration but not for answering questions. Services are available to anyone in the U.S.

International Antique Repair Service, Inc.   8350 Hickman, Suite 14, Des Moines, Iowa 50322 (515) 278-2518 or (515) 278-2515
This firm repairs and restores oil paintings and watercolors. Damaged canvas is replaced or repaired, varnish is removed and replaced, and missing paint is restored. It also repairs molded picture frames, and regilds old French and Italian gilt frames. All work is guaranteed for 5 years. A brochure is available.

Bronislaus F. Janulis   6253 North Troy, Chicago, Illinois 60659   (312) 743-7868
Services include cleaning and restoration of paintings, and repair of antique ornamental frames.

Just Enterprises   2790 Sherwin Avenue, Unit 10, Ventura, California 93003   (805) 644-5837
Paintings on porcelain and oil paintings on canvas are restored.

Kramer Gallery   229 East Sixth Street, St. Paul, Minnesota 55101   (612) 225-0863
This gallery conserves, restores, and appraises oil paintings and works on paper.

Julius Lowy Frame & Restoring Company, Inc.   Shar-Sisto, Inc., 511 East 72nd Street, New York, New York 10021   (212) 525-5250
This company restores, appraises, and frames fine arts only. It will answer questions by mail and services are available to anyone in the U.S.

Don Manfredi   9010 Main Road, West Bloomfield, New York 14585   (716) 624-3758
Mr. Manfredi's work is solely concerned with the treatment of paintings on fabric (canvas) and wood panels. Restoration work is available to anyone in the U.S.

Duard Marshall   5927 Brookside, Kansas City, Missouri 64113   (816) 363-6111
Duard Marshall's restoration and appraisal services are available throughout the U.S. He will answer questions by mail for a fee.

Mathis Gallery   Emile H. Mathis II, 328 Main Street, Racine, Wisconsin 53403   (414) 637-1111
Restoration and appraisals are available to anyone in the U.S. Questions are answered by mail when possible, although it is better to phone. There is a fee for research and written reports.

Judith A. Meller   Conservation of Paintings, 1338 North Formosa Avenue, Hollywood, California 90046   (213) 876-4650
Judith Meller restores paintings. She will answer technical questions by mail. There is no fee for the first consultation, but there is a fee for the computation of the cost estimate and the proposal for treatment. Services are available to anyone in the U.S.

Charles Munch and Jane Furchgott   1165 Shiloh Road, Sturgeon Bay, Wisconsin 54235
(414) 743-9679
Only oil paintings done before 1920 are restored. Services are available to anyone in the U.S.

Oliver Brothers, Inc.   35 Fairfield Street, Boston, Massachusetts 02116   (617) 536-2323
Restoration services are available to anyone in the U.S. The firm will give an opinion on conservation but prefers not to answer questions by mail.

Louis Pomerantz, Ltd. 6300 Johnsburg Road, Spring Grove, Illinois 60081 (312) 587-6578
Restoration services are available to anyone in the U.S. No cost estimates of cleaning procedures are given without first making a technical examination, including examination with binocular microscope, ultraviolet lamp, infrared viewer, and solubility tests. There is a fee for this. Questions are answered by mail without a fee.

Myrna Saxe Los Angeles, California (213) 273-3161
Myrna Saxe conserves and restores paintings, stone, murals, and monumental artworks. Services are available to anyone in the U.S. She will not answer questions by mail.

Saxon & Clemens, Inc. 979 Third Avenue, New York, New York 10022 (212) 759-5791
This firm will restore and frame antique Oriental scrolls, paintings, etc.

Skylark Studios Paul and Carolyn Berry, 4961 Fayetteville-Manlius Road, Manlius, New York 13104 (315) 682-6642
Skylark Studios conserves and restores oil paintings by appointment only. An analysis of the painting, a written description, its condition, the work to be done, and the exact cost and date of completion are provided. Records are kept and attached to the reverse side of the work. The studio's philosophy is adherence to the original work and all work is reversible. It does work for museums and private collectors.

Southeastern Regional Conservation Center John L. Petty, Conservator, P.O. Box 212, Route 2, Fountain Inn, South Carolina 29644 (803) 862-3597
Services include restoration and appraisals and are available to anyone in the U.S. The Center will answer questions by mail. There is a fee.

Robin Myron Tichane 4220 Army Street, Suite 5, San Francisco, California 94131 (415) 648-2388
Robin Myron Tichane is a conservator and general consultant specializing in paintings. Services include restoration, appraisals, and conservation opinions and are available anywhere in the U.S. Questions are answered by mail and there is a fee.

Richard Trela P.O. Box 934, Clancy, Montana 59634 (406) 443-0071
Richard Trela is a specialist in the treatment of paintings, murals, and decorative objects. Restoration and opinions on conservation are available to anyone in the U.S. He will answer questions by mail. There is a fee.

Twelve Oaks Regional Fine Arts Conservation Center, Inc. Peter Michaels, President, 1922 South Road, Baltimore, Maryland 21209 (301) 367-4380
This firm conserves and appraises fine paintings. Prior appointments are needed during normal business hours. Free estimates of conservation work are given on paintings brought to the studio, otherwise there is a charge based on time and distance. Charges for appraisals are based on time and expenses.

West Lake Studio   Susan Blakney, 97 Jordan Street, Skaneateles, New York 13152
(315) 685-8534
This studio conserves and restores paintings. Services are available to anyone in the U.S. and questions are answered by mail, if possible. Fee depends on the time involved.

PRICE GUIDES

Curtis, Anthony, ed. *The Lyle Official Arts Review, 1982.* New York: Coward, McCann & Geoghegan, 1982.

Hislop, Richard, ed. *Annual Art Sales Index, 1980/81 Season.*
Surrey, England: Art Sales Index (Pond House, Weybridge, Surrey KT13 England), 1982.

————. *Auction Prices of American Artists 1980-1981.*
Surrey, England: Art Sales Index (Pond House, Weybridge, Surrey KT13 England), 1982.

BUYING BY MAIL

Jonesport Wood Company, Inc.   P.O. Box 295, Jonesport, Maine 04649   (207) 497-2322
This firm sells paintings by mail order. A catalogue is issued once a year and is available for $3.00. Lists are issued periodically.

Anthony C. Schmidt Fine Art   112 East Linden Avenue, Collingswood, New Jersey 08108
(609) 858-4719
This firm has a catalogue available. For information send a self-addressed, stamped envelope.

Frank S. Schwarz & Son   1806 Chestnut Street, Philadelphia, Pennsylvania 19103   (215) 563-4887
Illustrated catalogues are available.

APPRAISER

Some conservators also appraise. See Conservators in this chapter and Part II, Chapter 95, Conservators and Restorers. See also Chapter 88, Appraisal Information.

Art Dealers Association of America   Ralph F. Colin, Administrative Vice President, 575 Madison Avenue, New York, New York 10022   (212) 940-8650
The Art Dealers Association of America is a nonprofit organization that offers an appraisal service. Write or call for further details.

54. PAPER COLLECTIBLES AND EPHEMERA

The proper storage, display, and repair of paper collectibles is both difficult and important if you wish to preserve old maps, handwritten documents, sheet music, or other paper items.

For storage, humidity should range between 45° and 65°. If a room is too dry, the paper can become brittle; if it is too wet, various molds and insects can attack. Never glue or paste any paper items. Transparent mending tape can be especially damaging as it will eventually react with the paper and make a stain.

Be sure to display color printed paper away from strong sunlight or direct heat. The sun will fade paper and the heat will cause damage. Unfortunately, the ideal storage conditions for paper are almost impossible for collectors who wish to hang a Currier and Ives print or an old map as decoration.

Consider the value and the possible damage before framing any paper item. Follow these strict rules: use acid-free matting and always leave a space between the paper and the glass. Seal the back to keep it dust free.

Instructions for framing and/or storing valuable paper collectibles can be found in most paper preservation books. If your local art supply shop or frame shop is unfamiliar with the proper materials, you can purchase them by mail through the companies listed in Part II, Chapter 94, Conservation, Restoration, and Preservation Supplies.

See also Chapter 1, Advertising Art; Chapter 12, Books and Bookplates; Chapter 57, Photographs and Photographic Equipment; and Chapter 62, Prints and Woodcuts.

CLUBS

The Ephemera Society   124 Elm Street, Bennington, Vermont 05201
The Ephemerist is a newsletter for members. *The Ephemera News* is issued quarterly.

International Newspaper Collector's Club   P.O. Box 7271, Phoenix, Arizona 85011
(602) 263-8380
The Newes is published occasionally. An 8-page sample copy plus a reprint of a 1690 paper is available for $1.00 postpaid.

National Association of Paper & Advertising Collectibles   P.O. Box 471, Columbia, Pennsylvania 17512
P.A.C. (The Paper and Advertising Collector) is a monthly newspaper for members.

National Sheet Music Society, Inc.   1597 Fair Park Avenue, Los Angeles, California 90041
The *National Sheet Music Society Newsletter* is issued monthly except for July and August. Membership listings and informative articles are featured.

National Valentine Collectors Association   111 East Cubbon, Santa Ana, California 92701 (714) 547-1355
National Valentine Collectors Bulletin is a quarterly newsletter with information and pictures of old valentines.

PUBLICATIONS

Manuscripts   350 North Niagara Street, Burbank, California 91505   (213) 845-3011
This is a quarterly magazine.

Mapline   Hermon Dunlap Smith Center for the History of Cartography, Newberry Library, 60 West Walton Street, Chicago, Illinois 60610   (312) 943-9090
This is a quarterly newsletter for map enthusiasts.

Paper Americana   P.O. Box 334, Baldwin Park, California 91706
This newspaper is issued monthly with buy-and-sell ads and a few articles on paper collecting.

The Paper Station   T.W.E., P.O. Box 684, Sterling Heights, Michigan 48077   (313) 296-0185
This is a bimonthly publication.

HOW-TO-FIX-IT BOOKS

Kane, Lucile M. *A Guide to the Care and Administration of Manuscripts.*
Nashville: American Association for State and Local History (708 Berry Road, Nashville, Tennessee 37204), 1979.

Kovel, Ralph and Terry. *Care and Feeding of Books and Paper Collectibles.*
Des Moines: Register and Tribune Syndicate (715 Locust Street, Des Moines, Iowa 50304), 1975. Leaflet.

Perkinson, Roy L. *Conserving Works of Art on Paper.*
Washington, D.C.: American Association of Museums (Suite 428, 1055 Thomas Jefferson Street, N.W., Washington, D.C. 20007), 1977. Leaflet.

Rare Book and Paper Repair Techniques.
Nashville: American Association for State and Local History (708 Berry Road, Nashville, Tennessee 37204), n.d. Leaflet.

Waters, Peter. *Procedures for Salvage of Water-Damaged Library Materials.*
Washington, D.C.: Library of Congress, 1975.

Williams, John C., ed. *Preservation of Paper and Textiles of Historic and Artistic Value, I and II.*
Washington, D.C.: American Chemical Society (1155 Sixteenth Street, N.W., Washington, D.C.
20036), 1977, 1981.

PARTS AND SUPPLIES

The Book Doctor   984 High Street, P.O. Box 68, Harrisburg, Ohio 43126   (800) 848-7918
This firm offers custom-designed solander boxes. Portfolios and slipcases are made to order.

TALAS   Division of Technical Library Service, Inc., 130 Fifth Avenue, New York, New York
10011   (212) 675-0718
This firm distributes fine tools, supplies, books, and equipment for art restorers, archivists, hand
bookbinders, librarians, museum curators, photographers, etc. Their line of products includes items for
the storage, conservation, and restoration of all sorts of collectibles (photographs, documents, and
works of art). A catalogue is available.

George Theofiles' Miscellaneous Man   P.O. Box 1776, New Freedom, Pennsylvania 17349
(717) 235-4766
A linen mounting service for posters is offered by this company. All posters are carefully cleaned with
no bleaches or abrasives and only soft neutralized water is used. All retouching is done with
watercolor-based pigments for easy removal at any time. Everything used for the backing is of high
quality and, in addition, the backing cloth never touches the poster as there is a layer of Japanese rice
paper between it and the backing cloth. Everything, including all the mounting, is reversible with
water should it ever be desired.

REPAIR SERVICES

American Movie Poster Company   470 Park Avenue South, New York, New York 10016
(212) 686-7744
This company provides linen backing and restoration services for poster art. Paper restoration and
watercolor retouching are also available.

Archival Conservation Center, Inc.   8225 Daly Road, Cincinnati, Ohio 45231   (513) 521-9858
This company repairs, restores, and preserves paper documents, letters, maps, and books. A brochure is
available.

Archival Restoration Associates, Inc.   P.O. Box 353, Blue Bell, Pennsylvania 19422
(215) 686-2249
This firm's services are limited to the preservation of items on paper and parchment and are available
anywhere in the United States. It will answer questions by mail. The fee is $25.00 and it does not
appraise.

W. J. Barrow Restoration Shop, Inc.   State Library Building, Eleventh and Capitol Streets, Richmond, Virginia 23129   (804) 786-2310

Document restoration services include deacidification, deacidification and lamination, deacidification and encapsulation, and treatment of parchment. Recommendations on restoration work are given but not on value. Services are available to anyone in the U.S. and questions are answered by mail.

Marjorie B. Cohn   Center for Conservation and Technical Studies, Fogg Art Museum, Harvard University, Cambridge, Massachusetts 02138   (617) 495-2392

Services are limited to works of art on paper. Restorations are done for institutions only. Questions will be answered by mail if possible, but usually it is necessary to see the object for an extended examination. An hourly rate is charged for this. Examination and conservation recommendations are given to the general public.

George Martin Cunha, Inc.   Conservation Consultants, Tanglewood Drive, Lexington, Kentucky 40505   (606) 293-5703

This firm restores library and archival materials and works of art on paper. It will give an opinion on preservation matters only, not appraisals. Questions are answered by mail. The fee is $175.00 a day plus expenses in the field. There is no fee for correspondence.

Ursula Dreibholz and Paula Jakubiak   Yale Center for British Art, 2120 Yale Station, New Haven, Connecticut 06520   (203) 432-4116

Their specialty is restoring fine works of art on paper and photographs. There is no fee for consultations and answers by mail, if not too time consuming.

Jacqueline Gilliam   The Fort Worth Art Museum, 1309 Montgomery Street, Fort Worth, Texas 76107   (817) 738-9215

Restoration services are available anywhere in the U.S. Work is done on art on paper, historical documents, globes, and articles made of papier-mâché, vellum, and parchment. No estimates are possible without examination.

B. & B. Gimelson, Inc.   Bruce Gimelson, 96 South Limekiln Pike, Chalfont, Pennsylvania 18914 (215) 822-1393

The Paper Restoration Laboratory specializes in the restoration of the old, the rare, and the priceless. Documents, manuscripts, letters, maps, books, prints, photographs, and Bibles are restored. Stains are removed and tears repaired. Estimates are given at no charge. Each fully restored article is accompanied by guidelines for continued care and protection. A brochure is available.

Elizabeth C. Hollyday   110 West Melrose Avenue, Baltimore, Maryland 21210   (301) 433-5378

Elizabeth Hollyday is a conservator of art on paper and graphic arts. Her services are available to those on the East Coast and midatlantic region. Limited services are available to the general public.

Carolyn Horton & Associates, Inc.   430 West 22nd Street, New York, New York 10011 (212) 989-1471
This firm restores books, manuscripts, maps, and works of art on paper. All work must be examined before an opinion can be given. Questions are answered by mail and a fee of $45.00 is charged if the work is not done. Services are available to anyone in the U.S.

Kramer Gallery   229 East Sixth Street, St. Paul, Minnesota 55101   (612) 225-0863
Kramer Gallery conserves and restores works of art on paper.

Murray Lebwohl   411 Cameron Street, Alexandria, Virginia 22314   (703) 836-3339
Mr. Lebwohl restores works on paper only. His services are available to anyone in the U.S. and he will answer questions by mail. There is no fee for a verbal estimate, but there is a fee for extensive examination and a written report. Arrangements must be made beforehand for any examination or conservation estimate.

Harold H. Moore   P.O. Box 11991, 3099 Andrews Drive, N.W., Atlanta, Georgia 30355 (404) 261-6754
Mr. Moore restores paper documents. His services are available to anyone in the U.S. and he will give an opinion on conservation and restoration but will not answer technical questions by mail. A brochure is available.

Northeast Document Conservation Center   Gary E. Albright, Abbott Hall, School Street, Andover, Massachusetts 01810   (617) 470-1010
The Center appraises and restores paper and photographic objects. It will answer questions by mail, but it is usually better to phone. Nonprofit institutions in New England and New York/New Jersey receive a small discount.

PRICE GUIDES

Connolly, Robert D. *A Collectors Identification and Value Guide: Paper Collectibles*, 2nd ed.
Florence, Alabama: Books Americana, 1981.

————. *Paper Collectibles.*
Florence, Alabama: Books Americana, 1979.

Handy, Robin; Narbeth, Colin; and Stocker, Christopher. *Collecting Paper Money and Bonds.*
New York: Mayflower Books, 1979.

Hudgeons, Thomas E., III. *The Official Price Guide to Paper Collectibles.*
Orlando, Florida: House of Collectibles, 1980.

AUCTION HOUSES

Harmers of San Francisco   49 Geary Street, Suite 217, San Francisco, California 94102   (415) 391-8244

Harmers primarily holds stamp auctions, but occasionally auctions autographs, maps, and postcards. Catalogues are available by subscription and include prices realized.

Waverly Auctions   c/o Quill & Brush, 7649 Old Georgetown Road, Bethesda, Maryland 20014 (717) 951-0920
Waverly Auctions holds fine book and paper auctions. It issues detailed catalogues 4 times a year.

BUYING BY MAIL

Each of these firms has a catalogue or list available and there is a charge for some. When writing for information, be sure to include a self-addressed, stamped envelope.

Steven and Linda Alsberg   9580 Kedvale, Skokie, Illinois 60076   (312) 676-9850
A catalogue of historical newspapers and journals is available.

Antique News Documents & News Paper Catalog   29 Parkfield Road, Stourbridge West Midlands DY8 IHD England 5995

John Campbell Poster Catalog   P.O. Box 22974, Nashville, Tennessee 37202

Colbert Gallery   P.O. Box 46601, 8271 Melrose Avenue, Los Angeles, California 90046 (213) 655-0460
Colbert Gallery sells posters.

Collectors Treasures Ltd.   Hogarth House, High Street, Wendover, Bucks HP22 6DU England
At least 3 catalogues a year are published, offering antique maps and prints. Send for rates.

The Exhumation   P.O. Box 2057, Princeton, New Jersey 08540   (609) 921-2339
This firm offers poster art.

Galerie Canadiana   4920 Ouest Boulevard de Maisonneuve, #309, Montreal H3Z 1N1 Canada   (514) 487-9917
This firm sells antique collectibles on paper.

Beverly A. Hamer   P.O. Box 5, East Derry, New Hampshire 03041   (603) 432-3528
A sheet music catalogue is available.

Hughes   2410 North Hills Drive, Williamsport, Pennsylvania 17701   (717) 326-1045
Hughes publishes a mail order catalogue offering early and rare newspapers from 1644 through the Civil War. The catalogue is published 8 times a year. Subscription is $4.00 a year, $1.00 a single copy.

InterCol, London   1A Camden Walk, Islington Green, London N1 8DY England
This company has a mail order business in maps, playing cards, and paper money, and also has a gallery in London. Regular price lists and catalogues are sent free of charge to collectors who write to it. Want lists are maintained. The company will also give valuations for probate and insurance purposes.

Jonesport Wood Company, Inc.   P.O. Box 295, Jonesport, Maine 04649   (207) 497-2322
Books, prints, and paper are sold by mail order. A catalogue is issued once a year and is available for $3.00. Lists are issued periodically.

Miscellaneous Man   P.O. Box 1776, New Freedom, Pennsylvania 17349   (717) 235-4766
Posters and other paper items are offered.

Paper Americana   Ken Elwell, 20 Checkerberry Lane, West Yarmouth, Massachusetts 02673
This semiannual catalogue contains a listing of pre-1900 checks.

Poster America   174 Ninth Avenue, New York, New York 10011   (212) 691-1615
This is a semiannual, illustrated catalogue.

Poster Master   9 North Passaic Avenue, Chatham, New Jersey 07928   (201) 635-6505
A catalogue is available for $5.00.

Poster Plus, Inc.   2906 North Broadway, Chicago, Illinois 60657   (312) 549-2822
Poster art is offered.

Poster World   P.O. Box 1188, Concord, Massachusetts 01742   (617) 369-9088

San Francisco Map House   47 Park Hill Avenue, San Francisco, California 94117   (415) 861-2564

Gordon Totty, Scarce Paper Americana   576 Massachusetts Avenue, Lunenburg, Massachusetts 01462
A catalogue is published 4 times a year. Send $1.00 for the next available catalogue.

APPRAISERS

W. Graham Arader III   1000 Boxwood Court, King of Prussia, Pennsylvania 19406 (215) 825-6570
A grading system for rare maps, books, and prints is offered by this firm. The differences in conceptual importance, the aesthetic quality, condition, and rarity of the material are all considered.

B. & B. Gimelson, Inc.   Bernard Gimelson, 96 South Limekiln Pike, Chalfont, Pennsylvania 18914   (215) 822-1393
This firm appraises old documents, manuscripts, prints, maps, photographs, and books. A brochure is available.

International Newspaper Collector's Club   P.O. Box 7271, Phoenix, Arizona 85011
(602) 263-8380
This club appraises old papers. Send a list of items (*not* the papers), a 50¢ stamp or coin, and a self-addressed, stamped envelope.

55. PAPERWEIGHTS

Advanced paperweight collectors want French, English, or American weights. The most popular are the millefiori, floral, and sulfides of the nineteenth and twentieth centuries. Some of the modern paperweights are being made by artists like Kaziun or Stankard in limited amounts. They are expensive weights with some valued in the hundreds or thousands of dollars. There are less desirable and less expensive American and Chinese weights of similar styles, plus the flat advertising weights, snow weights, and many other types. It is important to be sure the condition of the paperweight is good, although repolishing scratched glass will not lower the value of the item.

CLUBS

American Paperweight Guild   312 North Gladstone Avenue, Margate City, New Jersey 08402

Caithness Collectors Society   225 Fifth Avenue, Room 639, New York, New York 10010 (212) 689-9340
Art in Crystal News is a quarterly newsletter about new paperweights.

Paperweight Collectors' Association   P.O. Box 11, Bellaire, Texas 77401   (713) 668-2745
The *Annual Bulletin of the Paperweight Collectors Association* is a full-color magazine showing new and old paperweights. There is also a mimeographed newsletter sent to members telling about conventions, books, club activities, etc.

PUBLICATIONS

The Gatherer   Wheaton Village, Millville, New Jersey 08332
The Gatherer is a free newsletter about the Wheaton Village glassworks and the paperweights made there.

Glasstique Gaffer Quarterly by George Kamm   406 West Marion Street, Lititz, Pennsylvania 17543   (717) 626-2338
This quarterly newsletter is about modern paperweights and events in the world of paperweight collectors. It contains color pictures of new weights.

REPAIR SERVICES

George N. Kulles   115 Little Creek Drive, Lockport, Illinois 60441   (312) 349-0996
Mr. Kulles restores and polishes paperweights, removing scratches, chips, and "moons." Paperweights, properly packed and insured, may be sent for restoration. Contact Mr. Kulles for further information.

L. H. Selman Ltd.   761 Chestnut Street, Santa Cruz, California 95060   (408) 427-1177
Selman will polish, facet, and repair paperweights.

Studio Hannah   P.O. Box 769, Flemington, New Jersey 08822   (201) 782-7468
Charles Hannah repairs only paperweights that qualify as collectors' items. The minimum charge is
$50.00. Write, explaining the defect or problem, and include a self-addressed, stamped envelope. An
opinion or estimate will be returned.

BUYING BY MAIL
Each of these firms has a catalogue or list available and there is a charge for some. When writing for
information, be sure to include a self-addressed, stamped envelope.

The Glasstique Gaffer   406 West Marion Street, Lititz, Pennsylvania 17543   (717) 626-2338
The firm sells paperweights.

Theresa and Arthur Greenblatt   P.O. Box 276, Amherst, New Hampshire 03031   (603) 673-4401
The Greenblatts offer lists of antique and contemporary paperweights.

L. H. Selman Ltd.   761 Chestnut Street, Santa Cruz, California 95060   (408) 427-1177
Send for *Selman's Catalogue & Price Guide of Collectors' Paperweights.*

56. PEWTER

Pewter is very soft and can easily be damaged or melted. Never put a piece of pewter near a burner on a
stove. Never mechanically buff a piece of pewter. It will permanently change the color of the piece.
Never use harsh scouring powder or steel wool to clean pewter. There are several good commercial
pewter polishes available at jewelry and grocery stores. *See also* Chapter 43, Metal Antiques and
Collectibles, for repair services.

CLUB
Pewter Collector's Club of America   P.O. Box 239, Saugerties, New York 12477
Pewter Bulletin contains scholarly research about American pewter and important information for the
serious collector.

BOOKS OF MARKS
Cotterell, Howard Herschel. *Old Pewter, Its Makers and Marks.*
Rutland, Vermont: Charles E. Tuttle, 1963.

Kovel, Ralph and Terry. *A Directory of American Silver, Pewter and Silver Plate.*
New York: Crown Publishers, 1961.

Laughlin, Ledlie Irwin. *Pewter in America, Its Makers and Their Marks,* vols. I and II.
Barre, Massachusetts: Barre Publishing, 1969.

————. *Pewter in America, Its Makers and Their Marks,* vol. III.
Barre, Massachusetts: Barre Publishing, 1971.

Peal, Christopher A. *More Pewter Marks.*
New York: Glover, 1976.

Stara, D. *Pewter Marks of the World.*
New York: Hamlyn, 1977.

REPAIR SERVICES

Al Bar Wilmette Platers   127 Green Bay Road, Wilmette, Illinois 60091   (312) 251-0187
This firm offers complete metal restoration including plating, polishing, lacquering, and repairing. It also reproduces missing pieces. Hours are weekdays, 8:00 A.M. to 4:30 P.M. and Saturdays, 8:00 A.M. to noon.

Estes-Simmons Silverplating Ltd.   1168 Howell Mill Road, N.W., Atlanta, Georgia 30318 (404) 875-9581
This firm restores, replates, polishes, and repairs pewter and other metals. It replaces missing parts and removes engraving. A brochure is available.

Midwest Burnishing   208 East Main Street, Round Lake Park, Illinois 60073   (312) 546-2200
This firm polishes antique metals including pewter. It also custom makes any needed items. A leaflet is available.

Specialized Repair Service   2406 West Bryn Mawr Avenue, Chicago, Illinois 60659 (312) 784-2800
This firm repairs pewter and other metals.

Universal Electro-Plating Company, Inc.   1804 Wisconsin Avenue, N.W., Washington, D.C. 20007   (202) 333-2460
This company does polishing and lacquering, hard and soft soldering, and dent removal. It will replace missing pieces, clean and repair pewter, silver, brass, and copper. A brochure is available.

BUYING BY MAIL

Robin Bellamy   97 Corn Street, Witney, Oxfordshire OX8 7DL England
Robin Bellamy sells items of pewter.

57. PHOTOGRAPHS AND PHOTOGRAPHIC EQUIPMENT

Photographs became popular with collectors during the 1970s. Because prices have risen into the thousands of dollars for choice pictures, conservation, restoration, and storage have become very important. Many types of photographs can be included in the collector's world. Movies are one special type. The old nitrate film is combustible and it is dangerous to store. If you are fortunate enough to find or own some early movies, have them copied on modern film. The American Film Institute at Kennedy Center for the Performing Arts, Washington, D.C. 20566, can help you with this problem. Walt Disney original art done on celluloid for cartoon features, or what the collectors call "cels," are also collected and require careful framing or flat storage.

All types of photographs from daguerreotypes and glass-plate slides to stereopticon views, cartes de visite, and modern pictures are important as art as well as history. Do *not* try a home remedy restoration. Many old pictures can be saved if the work is done by an expert.

Old cameras can be restored, but once again expertise is required. Sometimes a local camera shop can have the camera repaired but most old cameras need special parts that are no longer available. There are often modern photography club members who are interested in antique cameras and photographic equipment, and it is usually helpful to check with a local professional photographer to see if there is someone in your area who likes to work with old cameras. *See also* Chapter 22, Comic Art; Chapter 47, Movie Memorabilia; and Chapter 54, Paper Collectibles and Ephemera.

CLUBS

National Stereoscopic Association, Inc.   P.O. Box 14801, Columbus, Ohio 43214 (614) 263-4296
The club publishes a bimonthly magazine, *Stereo World*, which features articles about old and new three-dimensional pictures. Each month it publishes unidentified views and asks for help in identifying them. It also features a few buy/sell ads and lists of events.

Photographic Historical Society   P.O. Box 9563, Rochester, New York 14604
This society is primarily interested in photographic equipment rather than photographic images. *The Photographic Historical Society Newsletter* is published 10 times a year and includes current information about the photographic industry.

The Photographic Historical Society of New York, Inc.   Radio City Station, P.O. Box 1839, New York, New York 10101–0075
A magazine, *Photographica,* is published 10 times a year with 12 to 24 pages of news, articles, and columns by experts in specialized fields of photography.

Wallace Nutting Collectors Club   Kampfe Lake, East Shore Drive, Bloomingdale, New Jersey 07403   (201) 838-0799
Wallace Nutting Collectors Newsletter is this club's publication.

Western Photographic Collectors Association (WPCA)   P.O. Box 4294, Whittier, California 90607   (213) 693-8421
The Photographist is a quarterly magazine with articles about cameras and camera parts. Shows and events of interest are listed.

PUBLICATIONS
Graphic Antiquarian   P.O. Box 3471, Wilmington, North Carolina 28401
This is a quarterly magazine.

Photographic Conservation   Rochester Institute of Technology, 1 Lomb Memorial Drive, Rochester, New York 14623
The *Graphic Arts Research Center Newsletter* is a quarterly publication.

Reel 3-D News   P.O. Box 35, Duarte, California 91010   (213) 357-8345
This magazine is about 3-D photography and equipment collecting.

Shutterbug Ads   P.O. Box F, Titusville, Florida 32780   (305) 269-3211
This is a monthly newspaper filled with ads to buy and sell photographic materials.

HOW-TO-FIX-IT BOOKS
Ostroff, Eugene. *Conserving and Restoring Photographic Collections.*
Washington, D.C.: American Association of Museums (Suite 428, 1055 Thomas Jefferson Street, N.W., Washington, D.C. 20007), 1976. Leaflet.

Waters, Peter. *Procedures for Salvage of Water-Damaged Library Materials.*
Washington, D.C.: Library of Congress, 1975.

Weinstein, Robert A., and Booth, Larry. *Collection, Use, and Care of Historical Photographs.*
Nashville: American Association for State and Local History (708 Berry Road, Nashville, Tennessee 37204), 1979.

REPAIR SERVICES

Gary E. Albright   Northeast Document Conservation Center, Abbott Hall, School Street, Andover, Massachusetts 01810   (617) 470-1010
This firm appraises and restores paper and photographic objects. It will answer questions by mail, but it is usually better to phone.

Miles Barth, Curator   Archives and Collections, International Center of Photography, 1130 Fifth Avenue, New York, New York 10028   (212) 860-1750
Services are available to the general public by referral only. There is no fee for estimates of work, only on work completed. Most of the work Mr. Barth does is for people referred to him by auction houses, galleries, or private dealers. He only works on photographic prints, primarily twentieth century.

Ursula Dreibholz and Paula Jakubiak   Yale Center for British Art, 2120 Yale Station, New Haven, Connecticut 06520 (203) 432-4116
The center's specialty is restoring fine works of art on paper and photographs. There is no fee for consultations and answers by mail, if they are not too time consuming.

Grant B. Romer, Peter J. Mustardo   900 East Avenue, Rochester, New York 14607
(716) 271-3361
Services are limited to the restoration of photographic objects and they will answer questions by mail. Services are available to anyone in the U.S.

Ron Stark   S/R Project, ASIFA/Hollywood, 1258 North Highland Avenue, Suite 102, Hollywood, California 90038
The Search and Rescue Team is a group of members of the International Animated Film Society (ASIFA/Hollywood) who repair and restore animation artwork. Their service is available to anyone. Charges are made for materials used but the labor is donated by members.

REPRODUCTIONS

Vintage Images   18 Elm Street, Newport, Rhode Island 02840   (401) 849-3476 or 849-6178
Historical prints from glass plate negatives are done to resemble the original as closely as possible. Images from 1860 to 1930 are available in many categories.

PRICE GUIDES

Falk, Peter H. *The Photographic Art Market.*
New York: Falk-Leeds International, 1981.

McCulloch, Lou W. *Card Photographs, A Guide to Their History and Value.* Exton, Pennsylvania: Schiffer Publishing, 1981.

Witking, Lee D., and London, Barbara. *The Photograph Collector's Guide.* Boston: Little, Brown, 1979.

Wolf, Myron, ed. *Blue Book Illustrated Price Guide to Collectable Cameras, 1839–1981.* Privately printed, 1980 (P.O. Box 351, Lexington, Massachusetts 02173).

BUYING BY MAIL

Each of these firms has a catalogue or list available and there is a charge for some. When writing for information, be sure to include a self-addressed, stamped envelope.

Collectors Cameras   P.O. Box 16, Pinner, Middlesex, HA5 4HN England
Cameras, equipment, daguerreotypes, etc. are available.

Daguerreian Era   Pawlet, Vermont 05761   (802) 325-3360
Photographic Antiques & Literature is its catalogue.

John A. Hess   659 Waverly Road, North Andover, Massachusetts 01845   (617) 686-0549
Fine Photographic Americana is a catalogue about nineteenth-century photography.

Historical Technology, Inc.   6 Mugford Street, Marblehead, Massachusetts 01945
(617) 631-2275
Scientific instruments and cameras are sold by this company.

Janet Lehr, Inc.   P.O. Box 617, Gracie Station, New York, New York 10028   (212) 288-6234
Send for the *19th and 20th Century Photography Catalogue.*

19th Century Photographs   P.O. Box 211, North Haven, Connecticut 06473   (203) 239-5996

Silver Image Antiques   P.O. Box 388, Manchester, Maryland 21102   (215) 678-7234, evenings
Stereo-related photographica and photographic Americana are offered.

Stereo Photography Unlimited   8211 27th Avenue North, St. Petersburg, Florida 33710
(813) 345-1862
This firm has a semiannual catalogue containing buy, sell, and trade ads for stereo cameras.

Tintype Photographica   P.O. Box 35156, Tulsa, Oklahoma 74135   (918) 622-7843
Pre-1900 photographica, images, cameras, and stereo views are offered.

Allen and Hilary Weiner   80 Central Park West, New York, New York 10023   (212) 787-8357
The Weiners' catalogue is *Fine Antique Cameras & Photographic Images.*

BOOKSELLERS
Books about photographic collectibles can be found in every good bookstore or library. Most stores
will special order the books for you. Many of these books are available through the mail order antiques
book dealers listed in Chapter 91.

International Museum of Photography   George Eastman House, 900 East Avenue, Rochester,
New York 14607   (716) 271-3361

58. PICTURE FRAMES

A picture needs a frame, old, new, or restored. Try to reframe any print or painting with a frame in the
same style as the original. It is possible to buy antique frames or copies of antique frames.

PARTS AND SUPPLIES
B & L Antiqurie   6217 South Lake Shore Road, Lexington, Michigan 48450   (313) 359-8623
For information call Tuesday through Saturday, 10:00 A.M. to 3:00 P.M.

Connoisseur Studio, Inc.   P.O. Box 7187, Louisville, Kentucky 40207   (502) 426-6600
This firm sells Treasure Gold, a nontarnishing, metallic wax that comes in 16 different colors. It can be
used to highlight, stain, glaze, antique, stencil, and marbleize. It will not rub off or fade. Call or write
for more information.

John Morgan Baker, Framer   P.O. Box 149, Worthington, Ohio 43085   (614) 885-7040
John Morgan offers custom-made frames of curly maple with either mitered or block corners. Block
corners can be inlaid with brass motifs or carved by special order. Catalogue sheets with photos are
available for a self-addressed, stamped envelope. Order by mail, telephone, or visit by appointment.

REPAIR AND RESTORATION SERVICES

Andrew Hurst   2423 Amber Street, Knoxville, Tennessee 37917   (615) 974-2144 or 523-3498
Andrew Hurst specializes in turning and carving and restoring old frames. He will answer questions by mail.

R. Wayne Reynolds   Restoration of Antique Frames, P.O. Box 28, Stevenson, Maryland 21153 (301) 484-1028
R. Wayne Reynolds conserves and restores gessoed and gold-leafed surfaces including carved wood or cast plaster objects, furniture, mirror frames, picture frames, and architectural gilding of interior or exterior ornamental moldings. Matting and framing are done.

59. POLITICAL MEMORABILIA

Political collectibles include all types of buttons and textiles including such items as banners, large handkerchiefs, pottery, porcelain, glass pieces with appropriate decorations, jewelry, lanterns, boxes, toys, and any other pieces that would relate to a political campaign. The purist collector only saves the buttons and other items that were made for an actual campaign and had not been produced after the campaign for a gift or novelty shop. The American Political Items Collectors (APIC) carefully documents actual campaign material each year in the publications sent to members. Reproductions have been made of many early campaign items.

CLUBS

American Political Items Collectors (APIC)   1054 Sharpsburg Drive, Huntsville, Alabama 35803
This club publishes *Keynoter,* a quarterly magazine, plus a newsletter every 8 weeks.

Nixon Political Items Collectors   55 Warren Avenue, Plymouth, Massachusetts 02360
(617) 746-0344
Checkers is a quarterly newsletter.

Reagan Political Items Collectors   3165 Oak Drive, Bucyrus, Ohio 44820   (419) 562-2006
Reagan Review is a quarterly newsletter for members.

PUBLICATIONS

The Political Collector   444 Lincoln Street, York, Pennsylvania 17404   (717) 846-0418
This is a monthly publication.

The Political Merchant   201 Greenfield Road, Lancaster, Pennsylvania 17601
This is a monthly newspaper.

The Standard   P.O. Box 211, Forest Hills, New York 11375
This magazine is published by the Association for Preservation of Political Americana (not a club).

BUYING BY MAIL

Hundreds of dealers sell political memorabilia by mail. Many advertise in the general antiques publications listed in Chapter 99 or in the specialized publications listed in this chapter. Some have price lists or catalogues available at a minimal fee. A few are listed here.

Be-In Buttons   P.O. Box 35593, Houston, Texas 77035

Richard Bristow   P.O. Box 521, Santa Cruz, California 95061

Callies & Callies   564 Park Lane, Madison, Wisconsin 53711   (608) 233-2657

Frank Enten   5305 Wilson Lane, Bethesda, Maryland 20014

Joyce Harrell   P.O. Box 481, Vermillion, South Dakota 57069

Vernon S. Houston   4101 Hideaway Drive, Tucker, Georgia 30084   (404) 939-4873

The Local Society of Political Item Enthusiasts   P.O. Box 159, Kennedale, Texas 76060
(817) 534-6655

The Political Scientists   P.O. Box 35392, Los Angeles, California 90035

The space above is reserved for postmark.

POSTAL CARD
THE SPACE BELOW IS FOR THE ADDRESS ONLY.

Messrs. Booth, Dailey & Ivins,

13=21 Park Row,

Room 908.   **New York City.**

60. POSTCARDS

Most postcards are made of paper and have all of the storage and care problems of any other paper collectible. They should be kept out of the heat, strong sunlight, away from damp air, and most of all, never glued or taped. There are postcard clubs and shows in many cities. Each card is priced by the condition, age, and rarity, and it takes time and information to understand the market. If you are lucky enough to inherit a box of old cards, don't sell them before you go to the library or some postcard shows to see which cards are the rarities. *See also* Chapter 54, Paper Collectibles and Ephemera.

CLUBS

Deltiologists of America   10 Felton Avenue, Ridley, Pennsylvania 19078
(215) 521-1092
This club publishes a bimonthly magazine, *Deltiology, A Journal for Postcard Collectors & Dealers.*

International Federation of Postcard Dealers   P.O. Box 1765, Manassas, California 22110
No regular publication is available.

The Organization for Collectors of Covered Bridge Postcards   603 East 105th Street, Kansas City, Missouri 64131   (816) 942-1466
A monthly newsletter, *The Bridge,* is published by this group.

Postcard History Society   P.O. Box 3610, Baltimore, Maryland 21214   (301) 483-4778
There is no regular publication, but a newsletter is published before shows.

PUBLICATIONS

American Postcard Journal   P.O. Box 20, Syracuse, New York 13201
American Postcard Journal is published bimonthly. *Picture Postcard News* is published in alternate months.

Barr's Postcard News   Heytman Road, Lansing, Iowa 52151   (319) 586-2424
This is a monthly newspaper.

Picture Postcard Monthly   27 Walton Drive, Keyworth, Nottingham NG12 5FN England
This is an English publication with articles about all types of postcards, clubs, sales and events, and many buy/sell ads.

Picture Postcard News   P.O. Box 20, Syracuse, New York 13201
Picture Postcard News is published bimonthly. *The American Postcard Journal* is published in alternate months.

Postcard Collectors Magazine Annual   P.O. Box 184, Palm Bay, Florida 32905
This is a bimonthly magazine.

The Postcard Dealer   P.O. Box 1765, Manassas, Virginia 22110   (703) 368-2757
This is a bimonthly magazine.

PRICE GUIDES

Kaduck, John M. *Mail Memories.*
Privately printed, 1971 (P.O. Box 02152, Cleveland, Ohio 44102). A 1982–1983 price guide is available.

———. *Patriotic Postcards.*
Privately printed, 1974 (P.O. Box 02152, Cleveland, Ohio 44102). A 1982–1983 price guide is available.

———. *Rare and Expensive Postcards.*
Privately printed, 1974 (P.O. Box 02152, Cleveland, Ohio 44102). A 1982–1983 price guide is available.

———. *Rare and Expensive Postcards,* Book II.
Des Moines: Wallace-Homestead 1979. A 1982–1983 price guide is available from Mr. Kaduck, P.O. Box 02152, Cleveland, Ohio 44102.

———. *Transportation Postcards.*
Privately printed, 1976 (P.O. Box 02152, Cleveland, Ohio 44102). A 1982–1983 price guide is available.

AUCTION HOUSE

Harmers of San Francisco   49 Geary Street, Suite 217, San Francisco, California 94102
(415) 391-8244
This auction house primarily offers stamp auctions, but it occasionally auctions autographs, maps, and postcards. Catalogues are available by subscription and include prices realized.

BUYING BY MAIL

Hundreds of dealers sell postcards by mail. Many advertise in the general antiques publications listed in Chapter 99 or in the specialized publications listed in this chapter. Some have a price list or catalogue available for a minimal fee. A few are listed here.

Charles R. Bray   103 East Central Avenue, East Bangor, Pennsylvania 18013

House of Cards   P.O. Box 31772, Dallas, Texas 75231

Little Red Caboose (The Postcard People)   Alan Weisbord, 2221 82nd Street, Brooklyn, New York 11214

London Postcard Center   21 Kensington Park Road, London W11 England

Mashburn Cards   P.O. Box 118, Enka, North Carolina 28728   (704) 667-1427

BOOKSELLER

Gotham Book Mart & Gallery   41 West 47th Street, New York, New York 10036
(212) 757-0367

61. POTTERY AND PORCELAIN

Pottery and porcelain are found in every home. Dishes, figurines, lamp bases, flowerpots, crocks, and garden ornaments may all be made of ceramics—pottery or porcelain. To care for and repair porcelains properly it is necessary to have some idea of the difference between pottery and porcelain. Pottery is usually heavier than porcelain. It is opaque and chips more easily. Because it is more porous it may

become stained by dark-colored food or dirt. Porcelain is translucent, and if it is held in front of a strong light the light will show through. If it is chipped, the break will be shell-like in shape. Pottery usually cracks on a line. Porcelain is thinner, lighter, more durable, and usually more expensive than pottery. The names stoneware, delft, bone china, majolica, ironstone, etc., all refer to either pottery, porcelain, or similar wares with similar problems.

If your pottery or porcelain dishes are stained, it is possible to bleach them using a household laundry bleach. If the dishes are cracked or chipped, repairs are possible. Waterproof glues are available in most hardware, art supply, drug, and builder supply stores. For a simple break, glue is the best method of repair. If there is further damage and a hole or crack must be filled or if repainting is required, it can still be a do-it-yourself job but special equipment and instructions are necessary. There are many books available to help with this.

Many old sets of dishes have only 11 dinner plates, 10 cups and saucers, and 12 of everything else. It is possible to buy the same pattern of old dishes to fill in the set. Haviland, Castleton, Franciscan, Lenox, Noritake, Oxford, Syracuse, and Wedgwood are all being sold through matching services. To order from a service you must know the pattern of the dish. There are hundreds of patterns listed in books at your library. Many of the patterns have names included on the back as part of the mark. Identify the pattern name from this information or use this easy method: place a plate face down on a photocopying machine and take its picture. Copy the front and the back. Indicate the colors that appear on the plate and send the photocopies to one of the matching services.

To properly identify makers, it may be necessary to check the marks in a special book of marks. For example "H & Co" is one of the marks used by the Haviland Company that can be matched through several services. Some dishes are still being made by some firms and they can be replaced through special orders with firms such as Wedgwood, Royal Doulton, Spode, Royal Worcester, and others that offer this service for some patterns.

Here is just one quick clue for dating your dishes. If the name of the country of origin appears, such as "Spode, England," the dishes were probably made after 1891. About World War I the words "Made in England" or "Made in France," etc. were favored. The term "LTD." as part of a company name for English companies was used after 1880. "RD" in a diamond-shaped cartouche was used in England from 1842 to 1883. The letters "RD" followed by numbers were in use after 1884. The words "22 carat gold" and "ovenproof" were used after the 1930s. "Microwave safe" first appeared in the 1970s. "Made in Occupied Japan" was used only from 1945 to 1952. *See also* Part II, Chapter 100, Matching Services, and Part I, Chapter 52, Orientalia.

CLUBS

Abingdon Pottery Club   Route 6, P.O. Box 59, Galesburg, Illinois 61401   (309) 462-2293
A newsletter is published 3 times a year.

American Art Pottery Association   P.O. Box 714, Silver Spring, Maryland 20901
American Art Pottery is a monthly newsletter for members.

The American Ceramic Circle   55 Vandam Street, New York, New York 10013
A newsletter listing member activities is published.

Belleek Collectors Society   P.O. Box 3179, Jupiter-Tequesta, Florida 33458-0287
(305) 747-0051
The Belleek Collector is a newsletter about recent Belleek.

Blue Willow Collectors Society   4140 Lomo Alto, Highland Park, Dallas, Texas 75219
(214) 521-7800
Willow Talk is a newsletter about blue and white Willow pattern dishes.

The Boehm Porcelain Guild   P.O. Box 5051, 25 Fairfacts Street, Trenton, New Jersey 08638
(609) 392-2207
The Boehm Guild Advisory is a magazine published by the guild.

The Buten Museum of Wedgwood   246 North Bowman Avenue, Merion, Pennsylvania 19066
The BMW Bulletin contains information about the museum and Wedgwood pieces.

Fiesta Collectors & Dealers Association   P.O. Box 100582, Nashville, Tennessee 37210
A newsletter is published 6 times a year.

Goebel Collectors' Club   105 White Plains Road, Tarrytown, New York 10591
Goebel Collectors' Club Insights is a newsletter about new products and events of interest.

Hummel Collectors Club   P.O. Box 257, Yardley, Pennsylvania 19067
Hummel Collectors Newsletter contains information about old and new Hummels.

International Nippon Collectors' Club   c/o Joan Van Patten, P.O. Box 102, Rexford, New York 12148
Nippon Notebook is a folksy newsletter published quarterly containing articles about pieces marked "Nippon" and related Japanese wares, plus chatty articles about collectors and collecting. An annual listing of dealers and collectors is included. The *Canadian Nippon Chronicle,* a bimonthly newsletter, is also an official publication of the International Nippon Collectors' Club. It features information about meetings in Canada and news of Nippon. For more information, write to the club at 129 Bathurst Street, Toronto, Ontario M5V 2R2 Canada or phone (416) 366-3622.

Lithophane Collectors Club   Blair Museum of Lithophanes & Carved Waxes, 2032 Robinwood Avenue, Toledo, Ohio 43620   (419) 243-4115
Lithophane Collectors Club Bulletin is a bimonthly mimeographed newsletter about lithophanes, their history, and recently seen examples. It also has ads for lamps and lithophanes.

National Autumn Leaf Collectors   4002 25th Street, Rock Island, Illinois 61201
This club has a bimonthly newsletter.

Northern Ceramic Society   5 Lynton Court, Lyntown Lane, Alderley Edge, Cheshire, England
Northern Ceramic Society Journal is a biannual publication. *Northern Ceramic Society Newsletter* is issued 4 times a year.

The O.J. Club   c/o Sissie Jackson, 4908 Old Heady Road, Louisville, Kentucky 40299 (502) 267-7427
The Upside Down World of an O. J. Collector is a monthly newsletter with chatty news about Occupied Japan items and members of the club.

The Occupied Japan Collectors Club   18309 Faysmith Avenue, Torrance, California 90504
Occupied Japan Collectors Club Newsletter is a quarterly of 4 pages with articles and buy/sell ads.

Old Sleepy Eye Collectors Club of America, Inc.   P.O. Box 12, Monmouth, Illinois 61462 (309) 734-4933 or 734-2703
Sleepy Eye Newsletter is issued bimonthly.

Phoenix-Bird Collectors of America   18608 Chelton Drive, Birmingham, Michigan 48009
Phoenix-Bird Discoveries is a newsletter about blue and white phoenix pattern dishes.

Precious Moments Collectors Club   ENESCO, 2201 Arthur Avenue, Elk Grove Village, Illinois 60007   (312) 640-5200 or (800) 323-0636
Goodnewsletter is the company publication to promote sales of "precious moments."

Redwing Collectors Society, Inc.   Route 3, P.O. Box 146, Monticello, Minnesota 55362
Redwing Collectors Newsletter is published 6 times a year.

Royal Doulton International Collectors Club   P.O. Box 1815, Somerset, New Jersey 08873
Royal Doulton International Collectors Club Newsletter contains information about old and new Doulton wares. It is published quarterly by the company.

Sebastian Miniatures Collectors Society   321 Central Street, Hudson, Massachusetts 01749
Sebastian Miniatures Collectors Society News is the society's publication.

Sebastian Miniature Exchange Club   1549 Main Street, East Hartford, Connecticut 06108

Stein Collectors International   P.O. Box 463, Kingston, New Jersey 08528
Prosit is a quarterly newsletter about steins, containing events, buy/sell ads, and information.

Tea Leaf Club International   10747 Riverview, Kansas City, Kansas 66111   (815) 547-5128
Tea Leaf Club International Bulletin is a newsletter.

Tiles & Architectural Ceramics Society   c/o Ironbridge Gorge Museum, Ironbridge, Telford, Shropshire TF8 7AW England
A quarterly newsletter, *Glazed Expressions,* contains articles on manufacturers, designers, and buildings, news of exhibitions, and reviews of publications.

The Torquay Pottery Collectors' Society   Mrs. Gerry Kline, 604 Orchard View Drive, Maumee, Ohio 43537
Mrs. Kline is the coordinator for U.S. members of this English collectors' group. A quarterly newsletter, *Torquay Pottery Collectors' Society Newsletter,* is sent to members.

Wedgwood Collectors Society   41 Madison Avenue, New York, New York 10010
This club publishes a newsletter and offers new Wedgwood for sale.

The Wedgwood Society   55 Vandam Street, New York, New York 10013
The American Wedgwoodian is a quarterly.

The Willow Society   6543 Indian Trail, Fallbrook, California 92028   (714) 941-1944
The Willow Notebook is a newsletter published bimonthly about blue willow pattern dishes.

The World Organization of China Painters   3111 N.W. 19th Street, Oklahoma City, Oklahoma 73107
The China Painter is a magazine for members only.

PUBLICATIONS

Amercan Ceramics   15 West 44th Street, New York, New York 10036   (212) 944-2180
This is a quarterly magazine about ceramic art.

American Clay Exchange   800 Murray Drive, El Cajon, California 92020
This is a monthly newsletter devoted to American-made pottery.

The China Decorator   P.O. Box 45375, Los Angeles, California 90045
This is a monthly magazine.

Dishpatch   P.O. Box 106, Buttzville, New Jersey 07829   (210) 453-3491
Dishpatch is a newsletter about twentieth-century dishes.

The Geisha Girl Porcelain Newsletter   P.O. Box 925, Orange, New Jersey 07051
This is a bimonthly newsletter about Geisha girl porcelain, a dinnerware made in Japan in the late nineteenth century. The design featured Japanese ladies and scenery.

The Glaze   P.O. Box 4929, Springfield, Missouri 65804   (417) 831–1320
This monthly newspaper about dinnerwares contains buy/sell ads and articles.

National Blue Ridge Newsletter   c/o Norma Lilly, Highland Drive, Route 5, P.O. Box 298, Blountville, Tennessee 37617   (615) 323–5247
This is a bimonthly newsletter about Blue Ridge dinnerwares.

National Plate Collectors News   10185 River Shore Drive, S.E., Caldonia, Michigan 49316
This is a newspaper.

The Shards Newsletter   The Institute for Ceramic History, 436 West 12th Street, Claremont, California 91711

DECODING ADVERTISING COPY

Reading the ads for antiques and collectibles often takes special knowledge. When looking up general pottery and porcelain, use any of several ceramic dictionaries available. These include: *The Ceramic Collectors' Glossary* by Edwin Atlee Barber (New York: DaCapo Press, 1967) and *An Illustrated Dictionary of Ceramics* by George Savage and Harold Newman (New York: Van Nostrand Reinhold Company, 1974).

For serious research into articles about ceramics see *Pottery and Ceramics,* vol. 7, of *Art and Architecture Information Guide Series* by James Edward Campbell (Detroit: Gale Research, 1978).

For some abbreviations that appear in advertisements for glass and pottery, see the section on decoding advertising copy in Chapter 31.

When looking up Belleek, get to know the terms *first black mark, second green mark,* etc. These refer to the company backstamp that appears on most pieces of Irish Belleek. For a complete explanation as well as pictures of each mark, see *Kovels' Know Your Collectibles* by Ralph and Terry Kovel (New York: Crown Publishers, 1981).

When looking up flow blue china, use the privately printed books by Petra Williams (available from the Strong Museum Shop, 1 Manhattan Square, Rochester, New York 14607): *Flow Blue China: An Aid to Identification* (1981), *Flow Blue China II* (1973), *Flow Blue China and Mulberry Ware* (1975), and *Staffordshire Romantic Transfer Patterns* (1978). Abbreviations, used to indicate patterns and decorations in her books, are often used in ads:

O. Oriental.	*M.* Miscellaneous.	*J.* Juvenile.
S. Scenic.	*B.* Brushstroke painted.	*PC.* Polychrome Chinoiserie.
F. Floral.	*G.* Genre.	*C.* Classical.
AN. Art Nouveau.		

When looking up Hummel get to know the following terms which refer to the factory backstamp: incised bee, full bee, low bee, baby bee, vee bee, new bee, vee over gee, three line mark, stylized bee, small bee, high bee, wide crown, narrow crown, double crown, new mark.

To understand the significance of these terms, the mark each refers to, and the dates when each mark was used, see *Kovels' Know Your Collectibles* by Ralph and Terry Kovel.

When looking up Haviland china it might help to know the books listing the patterns. *Two Hundred Patterns of Haviland China,* books 1 to 5 by Arlene Schleiger, privately printed, 1950–1974 (4416 Valli Vista Road, Colorado Springs, Colorado, 80915) is the most popular. The Schleiger number is found by checking your pattern against the pictures in these books. Also helpful is *Haviland China: Pattern Identification Guide,* vols. 1 and 2, by Gertrude Tatnall Jacobson (Des Moines: Wallace-Homestead, 1979).

When looking up RS Prussia it might help to know the names referred to in some advertisements. They are keyed to books about RS Prussia.

Barlock. *The Treasures of R.S. Prussia* by George E. and Eileen Barlock, privately printed, 1976 (P.O. Box 12, Belle Valley, Ohio 43717).

Schlegelmilch. *The Handbook of Erdmann and Reinhold Schlegelmilch, Prussia-Germany and Oscar Schlegelmilch, Germany: Porcelain Marks* by Clifford J. Schlegelmilch, privately printed, 1973 (P.O. Box 4322, Flint, Michigan 48504).

Sorenson. *My Collection: R.S. Prussia* by Don C. Sorensen, privately printed, 1979 (P.O. Box 57146, Los Angeles, California 90057).

The abbreviations often found in ads are *RM* for "Red Mark," referring to the color of the backstamp, and *RSP* meaning "RS Prussia."

When looking up Royal Doulton it might help to know these terms and abbreviations:

Toby jug. A jug shaped like a full figure of a person.
Character jug. A pitcher shaped like the head and shoulders of a person.
Large jug. A jug about 6 inches high.
Small jug. A jug about 3½ inches high.
Miniature jug. A jug about 2¼ inches high.
Tiny or *teeny.* A jug about 1¼ inches high.
"A Mark." Refers to a special backstamp that included the letter *A.*
Potted. Refers to a special backstamp that included the words "potted by."

BOOKS OF MARKS

Many books are available at your library. These list
the most frequently wanted mark information.

Cushion, J. P. *Handbook of Pottery & Porcelain Marks.*
London: Faber and Faber, 1980.

Godden, Geoffrey A. *Encyclopaedia of British Pottery and Porcelain Marks.*
New York: Bonanza Books, 1964.

Haslam, Malcolm. *Marks and Monograms of the Modern Movement, 1875–1930.*
New York: Charles Scribner's Sons, 1977.

Kovel, Ralph and Terry. *Kovels' Know Your Collectibles.*
New York: Crown Publishers, 1981.

———. *Dictionary of Marks—Pottery and Porcelain.*
New York: Crown Publishers, 1953.

Lehner, Lois. *Complete Book of American Kitchen and Dinner Wares.*
Des Moines: Wallace-Homestead, 1980.

MacDonald-Taylor, Margaret, ed. *A Dictionary of Marks.*
New York: Hawthorn Books, 1962.

Röntgen, Robert E. *Marks on German, Bohemian
and Austrian Porcelain 1710 to the Present.*
Exton, Pennsylvania: Schiffer Publishing Ltd., 1981.

HOW-TO-FIX-IT BOOKS
Evetts, Echo. *China Mending: A Guide to Repairing and Restoration.*
Salem, New Hampshire: Faber & Faber, 1978.

Klein, William Karl. *Repairing and Restoring China and Glass.*
New York: Harper & Row, 1962.

Larney, Judith. *Restoring Ceramics.*
New York: Watson-Guptill, 1975.

Malone, Laurence Adams. *How to Mend Your Treasures: Porcelain—(China)—Pottery—Glass.*
New York: Phaedra Publishers, 1972.

Yates, Raymond F. *How to Restore China, Bric-a-brac and Small Antiques.*
New York: Harper & Brothers, 1953.

PARTS AND SUPPLIES
Atlas Minerals & Chemicals, Inc.   Farmington Road, Mertztown, Pennsylvania 19539
(215) 682-7171
This firm offers a master mending kit for china and glass. All the materials you need to restore or mend china, porcelain, pottery, glass, and other treasures as well as step-by-step instructions are included. There are four basic systems: (1) porcelainate for mending china and porcelain, (2) epoxyglass for mending glass, (3) porcelainizing finish with tints—no firing necessary, (4) new Gloss Glaze for restoring glaze without firing. A brochure is available.

Jonathan Studios, Inc.   Architectural and Decorative Arts, 619 South 10th Street, Minneapolis, Minnesota 55404   (612) 338-0213
This firm offers ceramic tiles, mantels, and murals. Brochures are available.

The Lid Lady   Virginia Bodiker, 7790 East Ross Road, New Carlisle, Ohio 45344
A variety of lids and covers for a number of ceramic and glass vessels and containers are offered.
There is a selection of over 10,000 lids.

REPAIR AND RESTORATION SERVICES

Art Conservation Associates, Inc.   1143 Park Avenue, New York, New York 10028
(212) 427-3523
This company does ceramic restorations.

Paul Baron Company   Baron-Rolen Jewelers, 2825 East College Avenue, Decatur, Georgia 30030
(404) 299-1400
Pack your pieces well and ship them to this company for an estimate.

Berkley, Inc.   2011 Hermitage Avenue, Wheaton, Maryland 20902   (301) 933-4440
Invisible repairs are done on Hummels, figurines, RS Prussia, bisque, ceramics, etc. Send a stamp for
free information.

The Bric-A-Brac, Inc.   8120 Nelson Street, New Orleans, Louisiana 70118   (504) 861-8888
This firm offers restoration services and will answer questions by mail. It specializes in repairing or
restoring antique porcelain including dolls.

Veronica Burns, Art Ltd.   Stonecroft 2210, Grafton, Wisconsin 53024   (414) 377-6555
Veronica Burns does figurine repair and restoration, specializing in the repair of Hummels and
Rockwells and other figurines with a low- or no-gloss finish.

Butterfly Shoppe   637 Livernois, Ferndale, Michigan 48220   (313) 541-2858
This repair business specializes in Hummels, Doulton, Lladro, and Cybis. Estimates are given before
repairing. It has a backlog of 2 or 3 months for most things. Pieces to be repaired should be packed
carefully and shipped UPS. The shop is open Mondays through Wednesdays 10:30 A.M. to 4:00 P.M.,
Thursdays 10:30 A.M. to 7:00 P.M.

Harry A. Eberhardt & Son, Inc.   2010 Walnut Street, Philadelphia, Pennsylvania 19103
(215) 568-4144
This is one of America's oldest repairers of objects of art, primarily porcelains and glass. There is a staff
of 10 artists and craftsmen specializing in various aspects of such repairs.

Ron Fox   416 Throop Street, North Babylon, New York 11704 (516) 669-7232
Ron Fox offers complete stein repair service. He will duplicate missing parts.

Richard George/George Studios   45-04 97th Place, Corona, New York 11368   (212) 271-2506
This firm restores and conserves porcelain. Call for an appointment or make arrangements for the

delivery of the works to be restored. For restoration of large pieces of porcelain, requiring on-location repairs, call or write for information.

Rosene Green Associates, Inc.   1622A Beacon Street, Brookline, Massachusetts 02146 (617) 277-8368
This firm invisibly repairs figurines, earthenware, pottery, Oriental ceramics, and fine contemporary china. Missing parts are duplicated.

Beth Haley   P.O. Box 895, Marblehead, Massachusetts 01945   (617) 631-2267
Beth Haley is an authorized restorer of Sebastian miniatures.

Hess Repairs   200 Park Avenue South, New York, New York 10003   (212) 741-0410
This firm restores porcelains, china, and all kinds of antiques and bric-a-brac. It will fill in chips on china and porcelain.

International Antique Repair Service, Inc.   8350 Hickman, Suite 14, Des Moines, Iowa 50322 (515) 278-2518 or 278-2515
Porcelain, pottery, and ceramics are repaired with missing parts replaced. All work is invisible, black-light proof, and guaranteed for 5 years. It does a mail order business throughout the United States and surrounding countries. A brochure is available.

Mort Jacobs Restorations   Jackson-Green Building, 231 South Green Street, Chicago, Illinois 60607   (312) 648-0009
This nationwide restoration business repairs china and porcelain. There is no charge for estimates. Printed packing and shipping instructions are available for out-of-state inquiries. Business hours are weekdays, 9:00 A.M. to 3:30 P.M.

Ross E. Jasper   2213 West 2nd Street, Davenport, Iowa 52802   (319) 323-0661
Ross Jasper restores china, figurines, bisque, pottery, porcelain, and glass. Prices are quoted upon receipt of material. Send a self-addressed, stamped envelope for a free brochure.

Just Enterprises   2790 Sherwin Avenue, Unit 10, Ventura, California 93003   (805) 644-5837
This firm does restoration and repair.

Levine's Restorations   4801 7th Street North, Arlington, Virginia 22203   (703) 525-4009
Levine's Restorations repairs and restores ceramics, including crockery, stoneware, porcelain, and pottery. Restoration may include repair of cracks, chips, or complete replacement of missing portions. It repairs, paints, and glazes. Mail orders and phone calls are encouraged. The firm will pick up and deliver within a 100-mile radius of its location. Estimates are given and a catalogue is available.

Salvatore Macri   5518 East Pinchot Avenue, Phoenix, Arizona 85018   (602) 959-1933
Salvatore Macri specializes in the restoration of fine art porcelain and Indian artifacts (not rugs or baskets) of a prehistoric, historic, or contemporary nature. Services are available to anyone in the U.S. and he will answer questions by mail.

Laurence A. Malone   The 1749 House, Route 63, Goshen, Connecticut 06756   (203) 491-2141
Mr. Malone mends china and glass and restores missing parts. All work is guaranteed and boil proof.

Mario's Conservation Services   2405 18th Street, N.W., Washington, D.C. 20009
(202) 234-5795
Restoration services are available to anyone in the U.S. and questions are answered by mail. There is a fee for written estimates.

Allen and Ina Brosseau Marx   15 Shadow Lane, Great Neck, New York 11021   (516) 466-4759
The Marxes specialize in the painted and gilded surface with emphasis on the conservation of Oriental lacquer. Their work includes seventeenth- to nineteenth-century inlaid, incised, and carved lacquer on porcelain. They will travel and will answer questions by mail for a fee. A brochure is available.

The Plate Collector's Stock Exchange   478 Ward Street Extension, Wallingford, Connecticut 06492   (203) 265-1722
This firm repairs Hummels and Sebastians. There is a discount for members.

The Porcelain Doctor   Raven and Dove Antique Gallery, 1409 Lake Avenue, Wilmette, Illinois 60091   (312) 251-9550
This firm repairs and restores porcelain and pottery. Missing parts are replaced and chips are filled. All colors are matched. It specializes in figurines, vases, and other strictly decorative objects.

Sierra Studios   P.O. Box 1005, Oak Park, Illinois 60304   (312) 848-2020
This firm will re-create missing parts, fill in chips, cement broken pieces, and paint and glaze. It specializes in matching paints to the colors originally used. RS Prussia is restored. Insured mailing service is available to any area within the United States.

Grady Stewart   Expert China Restoration, 2019 Sansom Street, Philadelphia, Pennsylvania 19103
(215) 567-2888
Grady Stewart does restoration work for collectors, museums, galleries, and dealers on porcelain, pottery, stoneware, enamels, and related antique items. If the article is to be shipped, pack it very tightly in a carton at least twice the size of the piece and wrap each broken section separately in the box so they do not touch one another. Use crumpled newspaper or bubble wrap. Ship it via UPS and insure it. Upon receiving the article, an estimate will be sent.

Donna M. Towle   129 Dexter Avenue, Watertown, Massachusetts 02172
(617) 924-8408 or 924-5213
Donna M. Towle specializes in repairing Hummel and Sebastian figurines. Estimates may be done through the mail or by phone. Work is not started until the price is confirmed by the customer. Prices generally average $15.00 to $40.00 per piece.

Vernal Restorations   Rural Route 1, P.O. Box 152A, Waconia, Minnesota 55387   (612) 442-4984
This firm does invisible repair on bisque and china porcelain. It will only work on items with a minimal value of $300.00. Call or write for more information.

Shirley Vickers   P.O. Box 3428, San Diego, California 92103   (714) 296-4751
Shirley Vickers restores and repairs china, specializing in American art pottery.

FACTORY ADDRESSES
Pottery and porcelain have been marked with trade names since the eighteenth century. Often it is possible to learn about an old pattern or fill in an old set of dishes by contacting the factory. The following list includes many of the firms that have made dishes in the past years and are still working.

If the name you need is not included in this list it may be found in the annual *Buyers Guide and Tableware Directory* published by Giftware News.

Aynsley China Ltd.   225 Fifth Avenue, New York, New York 10010   (212) 481-1978

Bing & Grondahl Copenhagen Porcelain, Inc.   111 North Lawn Avenue, Elsmford, New York 10523   (914) 592-2200

Coalport   2901 Los Feliz Boulevard, Los Angeles, California 90039

Denby Ltd., Inc.   130 Campus Plaza, Edison, New Jersey 08817   (201) 225-4710

Doulton & Company, Inc.   700 Cottontail Lane, Somerset, New Jersey 08873   (201) 356-7880

Franciscan   2901 Los Feliz Boulevard, Los Angeles, California 90039

Richard Ginori Corporation of America   711 Fifth Avenue, New York, New York 10022 (212) 752-8790

Haviland & Company, Inc.   11 East 26th Street, New York, New York 10010   (212) 686-4061

Hummelwerk   250 Clearbrook Road, Elmsford, New York 10523   (914) 592-4050

Hutschenreuther Corporation   41 Madison Avenue, New York, New York 10010 (212) 685-1198

Homer Laughlin China Company   Newell, West Virginia 26050   (304) 387-1300

Geo. Zoltan Lefton Company   3622 South Morgan Street, Chicago, Illinois 60609   (312) 254-4344
Lefton China: An Introductory Guide to Collecting is available upon request.

Lenox China, Inc.   Princeton Pike, Lawrenceville, New Jersey 08648   (609) 896-2000

Martin's Herend Imports, Inc.   1524 Spring Hill Road, McLean, Virginia 22102   (703) 821-8515

J & G Meakin Ironstone   New York Merchandise Mart, 41 Madison Avenue, New York, New York 10010   (212) 532-5950

Nelson McCoy Pottery Company   451 Gordon Street, Roseville, Ohio 43777   (614) 697-7331

Pickard, Inc.   782 Corona Avenue, Antioch, Illinois 60002   (312) 395-3800

Rosenthal USA Ltd.   411 East 76th Street, New York, New York 10021   (212) 570-4600

Royal Copenhagen Porcelain   225 Fifth Avenue, New York, New York 10010   (212) 889-2722 or (800) 223-1275

Royal Worcester Spode, Inc.   26 Kennedy Boulevard, East Brunswick, New Jersey 08816 (201) 846-1227

Wedgwood   New York Merchandise Mart, 41 Madison Avenue, New York, New York 10010 (212) 532-5950

PRICE GUIDES

Altman, Vi and Si. *Price Guide to Buffalo Pottery,* 4th ed.
Privately printed, 1981 (8970 Main Street, Clarence, New York 14031).

Ball, A. *The Price Guide to Pot-Lids and Other Underglazed Multicolor Prints on Ware,* 2nd ed.
Suffolk, England: Antique Collectors' Club (5 Church Street, Clopton, Woodbridge, Suffolk 1P12 1BR England), 1980.

Barry, John. *American Indian Pottery, An Identification and Value Guide.*
New York: Crown Publishers, 1981.

Battie, D., and Turner, M. *The Price Guide to 19th and 20th Century British Porcelain.*
Suffolk, England: Antique Collectors' Club (5 Church Street, Clopton, Woodbridge, Suffolk 1P12 1BR England), 1975; price revision 1981.

————. *The Price Guide to 19th and 20th Century British Pottery.*
Suffolk, England: Antique Collectors' Club (5 Church Street, Clopton, Woodbridge, Suffolk 1P12 1BR England), 1979; price revision 1981.

Bettinger, Charles and Riederer, Lahoma. *Fiesta III: A Collector's Guide to Fiesta, Harlequin and Riviera Dinnerware.*
Monroe, Louisiana: Fiesta Finders (P.O. Box 2733, Monroe, Louisiana 71201), 1980.

Bougie, Stanley J., and Newkirk, David A. *Red Wing Dinnerware.*
Privately printed, 1980 (Route 3, P.O. Box 141, Monticello, Minnesota 55362).

Bradford Book of Collectors Plates, 1981.
Chicago: The Bradford Exchange, 1981.

Chipman, Jack, and Stangler, Judy. *Bauer Pottery 1982 Price Guide.*
Privately printed, 1982 (11057 Ocean Drive, Culver City, California 92030).

Cox, Susan N. *The Collectors Guide to Frankoma Pottery.*
Privately printed, 1979 (800 Murray Drive, El Cajon, California 92020).

Cunningham, Jo. *1979/1980 Update: The Autumn Leaf Story Price Guide.*
Springfield, Missouri: Haf-a-Productions (P.O. Box 4929, G.S., Springfield, Missouri 65804), 1979.

Curtis, Anthony, comp. *The Lyle Antiques and Their Values: China.*
New York: Coward, McCann & Geoghegan, 1982.

Dale, Ronald. *The Price Guide to Black and White Pot-Lids.*
Suffolk, England: Antique Collectors' Club (5 Church Street, Clopton, Woodbridge, Suffolk 1P12 1BR England), 1977: price revision, 1980.

Donahue, Lou Ann. *Noritake Collectibles.*
Des Moines: Wallace-Homestead, 1979.

Eaklor, Thomas W. *A Collector's Guide to Russel Wright Dinnerware and China.*
Privately printed, 1978 (1912 South Street, N.W., #1, Washington, D.C. 20009).

Feeny, Bill, and Robinson, Dorothy. *The Official Price Guide to American Pottery and Porcelain.*
Orlando, Florida: House of Collectibles, 1980.

Florence, Gene. *Collector's Encyclopedia of Occupied Japan Collectibles, Second Series.*
Paducah, Kentucky: Collector Books, 1979.

Gaston, Mary Frank. *The Collectors Encyclopedia of Limoges Porcelain.*
Paducah, Kentucky: Collector Books, 1980.

————. *The Collectors Encyclopedia of R.S. Prussia.*
Paducah, Kentucky: Collector Books, 1982.

Hotchkiss, John F. *Hummel Art II with Current Price List.*
Des Moines: Wallace-Homestead, 1981.

Huxford, Sharon and Bob. *The Collectors Encyclopedia of Fiesta with Harlequin and Riviera.*
Paducah, Kentucky: Collector Books, 1981.

————. *Collectors Encyclopedia of Weller Pottery.*
Paducah, Kentucky: Collector Books, 1979.

Johnson, Glenn S., comp. *Sebastian Miniatures Value Register.*
Worcester, Massachusetts: Commonwealth Press, 1981.

Kerr, Ann. *Russel Wright and His Dinnerware, A Descriptive Price Guide.*
Privately printed, 1981 (P.O. Box 437, Sidney, Ohio 45365).

————. *The Steubenville Saga.*
Privately printed, 1979 (P.O. Box 437, Sidney, Ohio 45365).

Klein, Benjamin. *The Collector's Illustrated Price Guide to Russel Wright Dinnerware.*
Smithtown, New York: Exposition Press, 1981.

Kovel, Ralph and Terry. *The Kovels' Illustrated Price Guide to Depression Glass and American Dinnerware.*
New York: Crown Publishers, 1980.

————. *The Kovels' Illustrated Price Guide to Royal Doulton.*
New York: Crown Publishers, 1980.

Lockett, Terence A. *Collecting Victorian Tiles.*
Suffolk, England: Antique Collectors' Club (5 Church Street, Clopton, Woodbridge, Suffolk 1P12 1BR England), 1979: price revision, 1980.

Luckey, Carl F. *Hummel Figurines and Plates: A Collectors Identification and Value Guide, 4th ed.*
New York: Crown Publishers, 1981.

————. *Norman Rockwell Art and Collectibles.*
Florence, Alabama: Books Americana, 1981.

Miller, Robert L. *Price Guide to M. I. Hummel Figurines, Plates, More . . . No. 1.*
Huntington, New York: Portfolio Press, 1980.

Mount, Sally. *The Price Guide to 18th Century English Pottery.*
Suffolk, England: Antique Collectors' Club (5 Church Street, Clopton, Woodbridge, Suffolk 1P12 1BR England), 1972; price revision, 1981.

Newbound, Betty. *The Gunshot Guide to Values of American Made China & Pottery,* Book 1.
Privately printed, 1981 (4567 Chadworth, Union Lake, Michigan 48084).

Newbound, Bill and Betty. *Southern Potteries, Inc. Blue Ridge Dinnerware.*
Paducah, Kentucky: Collector Books, 1980.

Pine, Nicholas. *The Price Guide to Crested China.*
Portsmouth, Hants, England: Milestone Publications (62 Murray Road, Horndean, Portsmouth, Hants PO8 9JL England), 1981.

———. *The Price Guide to Goss China.*
Portsmouth, Hants, England: Milestone Publications (62 Murray Road, Horndean, Portsmouth, Hants, PO8 9JL England), 1981.

Rehl, Norma. *Abingdon Pottery* (with separate price guide).
Privately printed, 1981 (P.O. Box 556, Milford, New Jersey 08848).

———. *The Collector's Handbook of Stangl Pottery I.*
Privately printed, 1979 (P.O. Box 556, Milford, New Jersey 08848).

———. *Stangl Pottery Part II.*
Privately printed, 1982 (P.O. Box 556-T, Milford, New Jersey 08848).

Roberts, Brenda. *Collector's Encyclopedia of Hull Pottery.*
Paducah, Kentucky: Collector Books, 1980.

Simon, Dolores. *Red Wing Pottery with Rumrill.*
Paducah, Kentucky: Collector Books, 1980.

Tefft, Gary and Bonnie. *Red Wing Potters and Their Wares* (with separate price guide).
Privately printed, 1981 (W174 N9422 Devonwood Road, Menomonee Falls, Wisconsin 53051).

Van Patten, Joan F. *The Collector's Encyclopedia of Nippon Porcelain.*
Paducah, Kentucky: Collector Books, 1981.

Viel, Lyndon C. *1981 Price Guide to the Clay Giants, Book 2.*
Des Moines: Wallace-Homestead, 1980.

Ward, Roland. *The Price Guide to the Models of W. H. Goss.*
Suffolk, England: Antique Collectors' Club (5 Church Street, Clopton, Woodbridge, Suffolk 1P12 1BR England), 1975; price revision 1980.

Weiss, Princess and Barry. *Royal Doulton Discontinued Character Jugs*, 3rd ed.
Privately printed, 1981 (P.O. Box 296, New City, New York 10956).

Wetherbee, Jean. *A Look at White Ironstone.*
Des Moines: Wallace-Homestead, 1980.

Williams, Petra. *Flow Blue China and Mulberry Ware, Similarity and Value Guide,* rev. ed.
Jeffersontown, Kentucky: Fountain House East, 1981.

Worth, Veryl Marie. *Willow Pattern China.*
Oakridge, Oregon: Fact Book Company (P.O. Box 601, Oakridge, Oregon 97463), 1979. The accompanying price guide, *The Collector's Price Guide to Willow Pattern China,* is updated yearly.

AUCTION HOUSE
Woody Auction Company   P.O. Box 618, Douglass, Kansas 67039   (316) 746-2694
This general auction company has special RS Prussia sales.

BUYING BY MAIL
Each of these firms has a catalogue or list available and there is a charge for some. When writing for information, be sure to include a self-addressed, stamped envelope.

American Pottery Enthusiasts   P.O. Box 244, Avalon, New Jersey 08202   (609) 967-5286

B & G Pottery   149 West Park Street, Westerville, Ohio 43081

Cran Antiques   2971 Bremen Street, Columbus, Ohio 43224   (614) 267-5390

The Den of Antiquity   552 Washington Street, Wellesley, Massachusetts 02181   (617) 235-3240
This firm specializes in Wedgwood.

Bill Egleston   509 Brentwood Road, Marshalltown, Iowa 50158   (515) 752-4579

Geisers English Cups/Saucers   Route 1, P.O. Box 426, Rolla, Missouri 65401   (314) 364-8865
Send a self-addressed, stamped envelope for a price list.

Joan and Larry Kindler Antiques   14-35 150th Street, Whitestone, New York 11357
(212) 767-2260
Decorated stoneware is sold by mail.

Tom & Maida Martin   2455 Wilson Avenue, Bellmore, New York 11710   (516) 826-7304
Stoneware is available.

Peter Schriber   P.O. Box 199, Hadley, Massachusetts 01035   (413) 584-3652
Early American stoneware is sold.

Spencer K. House   8240 C North Boundary Road, Baltimore, Maryland 21222   (301) 288-3271
Mettlach, regimental and character steins, early twentieth-century blue historical Staffordshire plates, and ice-cream molds are available.

Tac Antiques   355 Hill Avenue, Etmont, New York 11003   (516) 775-0115
Canton ware is available.

3 Behrs R.D. #8, Horsepound Road, Carmel, New York 10512
Send for the *American Stoneware Catalogue.*

APPRAISERS

Art Conservation Associates, Inc. 1143 Park Avenue, New York, New York 10028
(212) 427-3523

The Bric-A-Brac, Inc. 8120 Nelson Street, New Orleans, Louisiana 70118 (504) 861-8888
Appraisal services are offered and the firm will answer questions by mail.

Henry Pachter 267 East Township Line Road, Upper Darby, Pennsylvania 19082
(215) 789-0999
Mr. Pachter appraises European porcelain and specializes in Meissen.

The Plate Collector's Stock Exchange 478 Ward Street Extension, Wallingford, Connecticut
06492 (203) 265-1711
Appraisals are done by mail. There is a discount to members.

Roundhill's Patterns Unlimited International P.O. Box 15238, Seattle, Washington 98115
(206) 523-9710
This firm offers appraisal service for evaluating discontinued patterns of ceramics. Cost is $30.00 per
pattern, with no limit on the number of pieces.

BOOKSELLER

Books about pottery and porcelain can be found in every good bookstore or library. Most stores will
special order the books for you. Many of these books are available through the mail order antiques
book dealers listed in Chapter 91. If you cannot find the books or if they are privately printed, write to
the address listed to buy a copy.

Keramos P.O. Box 7500, Ann Arbor, Michigan 48107

62. PRINTS AND WOODCUTS

Prints range from the Currier and Ives lithographs of the nineteenth century to the limited edition prints of the 1980s. Each type of print requires special research. Your library should have books such as *Currier and Ives Prints: An Illustrated Check List* by Frederic A. Conningham and Colin Simkin, rev. ed. (New York: Crown Publishers, 1970) or books that show the difference between a lithograph, woodcut, etching, engraving, etc. Restoration of any type of paper is very difficult. It is possible to carefully clean dust from a print by using wallpaper cleaner, wadded fresh white bread, or an art gum eraser. Creases can be carefully ironed out with a very cool iron. More ambitious repairs should always be done by a restorer. Do not tape or glue any paper item. The acids in the adhesive will eventually cause damage.

CLUBS

American Historical Print Collectors Society, Inc.   555 Fifth Avenue, Suite 504, New York, New York 10017   (212) 697–1246
Imprint, a small, quarterly publication has articles about activities, members, historic prints, and book reviews.

Prang-Mark Society   Century House, Old Irelandville, Watkins Glen, New York 14891
Prang-Mark Society Newsletter, published once a year, lists events for members.

Norman Rockwell Memorial Society   P.O. Box 270328, Tampa, Florida 33688   (813) 961–8834
The society has a newsletter published bimonthly for members.

Rockwell Society of America   P.O. Box BC, Stony Brook, New York 11790
Rockwell Society News is a quarterly newsletter about Norman Rockwell art for members.

PUBLICATIONS

American Print Review   P.O. Box 6909, Chicago, Illinois 60680
This is a small bimonthly magazine with auction prices, articles, and a few ads.

Print Review   160 Lexington Avenue, New York, New York 10016   (212) 685-3169
Pratt Graphics Center publishes this twice yearly.

Print Trader   67-62 79th Street, Middle Village, New York 11379
This is a quarterly newsletter about Americana and the work of American artists.

BOOK OF MARKS

Haslam, Malcolm. *Marks and Monograms of the Modern Movement, 1875–1930.*
New York: Charles Scribner's Sons, 1977.

PARTS AND SUPPLIES

See also Chapter 94.

The Book Doctor   P.O. Box 68, 984 High Street, Harrisburg, Ohio 43126   (800) 848-7918
This firm offers custom-designed solander boxes. Portfolios and slipcases are made to order.

REPAIR SERVICES

Archival Conservation Center, Inc.   8225 Daly Road, Cincinnati, Ohio 45231   (513) 521-9858
This firm restores prints. A brochure is available.

International Antique Repair Service, Inc.   8350 Hickman, Suite 14, Des Moines, Iowa 50322
(515) 278-2518 or (515) 278-2515
Prints and lithographs are cleaned and repaired. All work is guaranteed for 5 years. The company does a mail order business throughout the United States and surrounding countries. A brochure is available.

Mr. Robert L. Searjeant   P.O. Box 23942, Rochester, New York 14692   (716) 424-2489
Mr. Searjeant removes water and other stains from prints. He will clean margins and black-and-white or color print plates. Send your prints for a free estimate on the restoration work required.

PRICE GUIDES

Jackson, Denis C. *The Price and Identification Guide to Maxfield Parrish.*
Privately printed, 1980 (Route 2, P.O. Box 246, Phillips, Wisconsin 54555).

Luckey, Carl F. *Norman Rockwell Art and Collectibles.*
Florence, Alabama: Books Americana, 1981.

Pollard, Ruth M. *The Official Price Guide to Collector Prints.*
Orlando, Florida: House of Collectibles, 1979.

AUCTION HOUSE

Sam Yudkin & Associates Booksellers, Book & Print Auctions, 1125 King Street, Alexandria, Virginia 22314 (703) 549-9330
Monthly public and mail order book and print auctions are held on the premises. Items accepted for auction include almost any paper items plus small collectibles including books, prints, maps, postcards, ephemera, stamps, etc. Catalogues are available for $2.50.

BUYING BY MAIL

Each of these firms has a catalogue or list available and there is a charge for some. When writing for information, be sure to include a self-addressed, stamped envelope.

Graphis Larissa 10285 Daystar Court, Columbia, Maryland 21044
This firm offers Audubon prints.

Illustration Collectors Newsletter 53 Water Street, South Norwalk, Connecticut 06854
(203) 838-0486 or 227-6910
This thin magazine comes out 1 to 3 times a year ($2.50 a copy).

Jonesport Wood Company, Inc. P.O. Box 295, Jonesport, Maine 04649 (207) 497-2322
Prints are sold by mail order. A catalogue is issued once a year and is available for $3.00. Lists are issued periodically.

The Old Print Gallery 1212 31st Street, N.W., Washington, D.C. 20007 (202) 965-3777
This firm has a bimonthly, illustrated catalogue.

Maxfield Parrish (Spectrum) Route 2, P.O. Box 246, Phillips, Wisconsin 54555 (715) 339-3663
Only Maxfield Parrish items are offered.

Sierra West 441 El Camino Real, Tustin, California 92680 (714) 832-7417
A catalogue of antique and collector lithographs is available.

APPRAISER

Art Dealers Association of America Ralph F. Colin, Administrative Vice President, 575 Madison Avenue, New York, New York 10022 (212) 940-8650
The Art Dealers Association of America is a nonprofit organization that offers an appraisal service. Write or call for further details.

BOOKSELLERS

See Chapter 91, Booksellers. Many booksellers sell books that are illustrated with prints.

63. RADIO AND PHONOGRAPH COLLECTIBLES

Collectors of phonographs, phonograph records, and radios have little luck in buying at the average antiques shops and shows. It is in the flea market, house sale, and resale shop that most of the radios are found. Early phonographs are stocked in some shops, but the later models are often ignored. The item must be in good working condition to be of value. Repairs can be expensive, slow, and sometimes impossible. If you are able to fix this type of collectible, you can usually make a good buy. Sometimes repairs can cost more than the value of a phonograph in very good condition.

Early phonograph records include many types. Price books for phonograph records have appeared, but there are many record titles that are still unlisted. Radios have gained in interest since the 1970s. Old tubes and other parts are often hard to find but there are dealers, publications, and clubs that make the search a little easier.

CLUBS

The American Phonograph Society   P.O. Box 5046, Berkeley, California 94705
Journal of the American Phonograph Society is a quarterly magazine for members.

Antique Phonograph Society   650 Ocean Avenue, Brooklyn, New York 11226   (212) 941-6835
Antique Phonograph Monthly contains about 20 pages of articles and buy/sell ads each month.

Antique Radio Club of America   81 Steeplechase Road, Devon, Pennsylvania 19333
(215)688-2976
The Antique Radio Gazette is a quarterly magazine with history of the radio and other information of interest to collectors. A brochure is available; send a self-addressed, stamped envelope.

Antique Wireless Association, Inc.   Main Street, Holcomb, New York 14469   (716) 657-7489
Old Timer's Bulletin is a quarterly magazine.

The Association for Recorded Sound Collections   P.O. Box 1643, Manassas, Virginia 22110
(703) 361-3901
ARSC Newsletter is the association's publication.

Association of North American Radio Clubs   557 North Madison Avenue, Pasadena, California 91101   (213) 793-3769
ANARC Newsletter is the club publication.

International Association of Jazz Record Collectors   c/o Eugene Miller, 90 Prince George Drive, Ilsington, Ontario M9B 2X8 Canada

Vintage Radio & Phonograph Society, Inc.   P.O. Box 5345, Irving, Texas 75062
Reproducer offers repair and restoration advice and other interesting articles in an 8-page newsletter.

PUBLICATIONS

Antique Radio Topics   P.O. Box 28572, Dallas, Texas 75228   (214) 321-0927 or 327-8721
This publication contains 4 pages of old advertisements for radios and new buy/sell ads. It comes out 10 times yearly. A subscription includes *The Classic Radio Newsletter*.

The Classic Radio Newsletter   P.O. Box 28572, Dallas, Texas 75228   (214) 321-0927 or 327-8721
This newsletter concerns antique radios. A subscription includes *Antique Radio Topics*. There are 10 issues yearly.

Electronics Trader   P.O. Box 73, Folly Beach, South Carolina 29439
This publication contains buy/sell ads for vacuum tubes, speakers, old catalogues, and equipment. A newsletter is published twice a month.

The Horn Speaker   P.O. Box 53012, Dallas, Texas 75253   (214) 286-1673
This newspaper is about radios and is published monthly except in July and August.

Jerry's Musical News   4624 West Woodland Road, Edina, Minnesota 55424   (612) 926-7775
Collectors of phonographs, music boxes, radios, and other related items will read this monthly newsletter. It contains buy and sell ads.

Kastlemusick Monthly Bulletin   901 Washington Street, Wilmington, Delaware 19801
This is a monthly bulletin with classified ads and articles about recordings. The *Directory for Collectors of Recordings* is also available.

Living Blues   2615 North Wilton Avenue, Chicago, Illinois 60614   (312) 281-3385
Living Blues calls itself a "Journal of the Black American Blues Tradition." It is a quarterly magazine containing profiles of blues performers, record reviews, book reviews, and ads.

Musical Marketplace   561 Washington Street, Santa Clara, California 95050
This monthly newsletter has buy and sell ads for phonographs.

Nostalgia World   P.O. Box 231, North Haven, Connecticut 06473-0231   (203) 239-4891
Articles about show business collectibles, photographs, lobby cards, records, magazines, etc. are in this monthly newspaper.

Radio Age   636 Cambridge Road, Augusta, Georgia 30904   (404)738-7227
This is a monthly newsletter with illustrated articles about old radios and a few classified ads.

The Record Collector's Journal   P.O. Box 1200, Covina, California 91722
This is a monthly newspaper.

Roaring 20's   1545 Raymond, Glendale, California 91201   (213) 242-8961
This quarterly newsletter is free to those sending a self-addressed, stamped envelope. It contains want ads and information about trading, preserving, and collecting vintage radios and radio parts.

HOW-TO-FIX-IT BOOK

McWilliams, Jerry. *The Preservation and Restoration of Sound Recordings.*
Nashville: American Association for State and Local History (708 Berry Road, Nashville, Tennessee 37204), 1981. This book includes detailed information about recordings plus a directory of manufacturers and suppliers, directory of major North American sound archives, and a bibliography of articles about preservation and restoration of sound recordings.

PARTS AND SUPPLIES

Automatic Music Roll Company   P.O. Box 3194, Seattle, Washington 98114   (206) 633-3664
This firm sells parts for phonographs and radios. A catalogue is available.

Sam Faust   Changewater, New Jersey 07831   (201) 689-7020
Mr. Faust sells antique radio tubes that are guaranteed to be good when shipped and will be replaced free if one goes bad (except filament burnout or breakage) within 1 year after purchase. Used but good tubes are available for half the price of new tubes but with no guarantee. Schematic diagrams are also available for $1.00. Please give the model number of the radio. Send a self-addressed, stamped envelope for a free price list.

Musical Americana Talking Machine Company   561 Washington Street, Santa Clara, California 95050   (408) 244-9693
Motor parts, horns and attachments, case hardware, cranks and winding keys, decals, printed material, etc. are available. All parts ordered will be shipped within 5 days of receipt of your order.

Keith Parry   17557 Horace Street, Granada Hills, California 91344   (213) 363-1914
Keith Parry sells authentic replica parts for radios. A flyer is available.

Puett Electronics   P.O. Box 28572, Dallas, Texas 75228   (214) 321-0927 or 327-8721
Antique radio tubes, old-time radio shows on cassettes, schematic diagrams, catalogues, books, booklets, lists, and data are all available from Puett Electronics. Send for a price list.

Radio Shack   1300 One Tandy Center, Fort Worth, Texas 76102   (817) 390-3011
Although it does not make authentic antique replica parts, Radio Shack can supply you with the modern equivalent of the original electrical item. A catalogue is available.

REPAIR SERVICES
The Antique Phonograph Shop   Dennis and Patti Valente, 320 Jericho Turnpike, Floral Park, New York 11001   (516) 775-8605
This shop repairs and restores spring-operated phonographs. It also carries phonograph records, cylinders, needles, and all related parts and accessories.

Harry M. Daniels   35607 Richland Avenue, Livonia, Michigan 48150   (313) 425-1168
Mr. Daniels repairs Edison cylinder phonographs and Victor talking machines. Estimates are free. Write for details.

Al. Gerichten   23 Waldo Avenue, Bloomfield, New Jersey 07003   (201) 748-8046
Antique cylinder and disc phonographs are repaired, bought, and sold. Parts are available. Send for a list.

Gould Piano Craftsmen, Inc.   391 Tremont Place, Orange, New Jersey 07050   (201) 672-4060
Phonographs, music boxes, and pianos are repaired, bought, and sold.

Musical Americana Talking Machine Company   561 Washington Street, Santa Clara, California 95050   (408) 244-9693
This company will repair all types of phonographs, work guaranteed. Send the item in need of repair for an estimate.

Paul N. Smith   408 East Leeland Heights Boulevard, Lehigh Acres, Florida 33936   (813) 369-4663
Mr. Smith repairs phonographs and other curious or unusual devices. Send a letter briefly describing the problem and enclose a stamped, self-addressed envelope for a reply. Cost estimates are given after examination of the mechanism. Many special parts such as gears, springs, levers, etc. are made.

PRICE GUIDES

Docks, L. R. *1915-1965 American Premium Record Guide,* 2nd ed.
Florence, Alabama: Books Americana, 1982.

Fredericks, Robert, and Gould, Susan. *The Official Price Guide to Music Collectibles.*   Orlando, Florida: House of Collectibles, 1980.

Hill, Randal C. *The Official Price Guide to Collectible Rock Records,* 2nd ed.
Orlando, Florida: House of Collectibles, 1980.

Osborne, Jerry. *Popular and Rock Records Price Guide for 45's,* 3rd ed.
Phoenix: O'Sullivan Woodside & Company (2218 East Magnolia, Phoenix, Arizona 85034), 1981.

Osborne, Jerry, and Hamilton, Bruce. *Blues, Rhythm and Blues, Soul.*
Phoenix: O'Sullivan Woodside & Company (2218 East Magnolia, Phoenix, Arizona 85034), 1980.

————. *A Guide to Record Collecting.*
Phoenix: O'Sullivan Woodside & Company (2218 East Magnolia, Phoenix, Arizona 85034), 1979.

————. *Presleyana.*
Phoenix: O'Sullivan Woodside & Company (2218 East Magnolia, Phoenix, Arizona 85034), 1980.

Soderbergh, Peter A. *Olde Records Price Guide 1900–1947.*
Des Moines: Wallace-Homestead, 1980.

BUYING BY MAIL
Each of these firms has a catalogue or list available and there is a charge for some. When writing for information, be sure to include a self-addressed, stamped envelope.

Antique Specialty Company   R.F.D. #1, P.O. Box 404, Norridgewock, Maine 04957
This company sells restored antique radios, parts, and related items.

Arnold's Archives   1106 Eastwood, S.E., East Grand Rapids, Michigan 49506   (616) 949-1398
Arnold's Record Lists is sent on request.

Jeff Barr Records   P.O. Box 7785, Van Nuys, California 91409   (213) 781-6785
Jazz Record Auction List is available by mail.

Eastern Musical Antiques   P.O. Box 297, West Orange, New Jersey 07052   (201) 731-3322
This firm sells phonographs, music boxes, nickelodeons, and jukeboxes.

Laurie Gravino and Henry Hall   82 Sutherland Street, Paddington, Sydney 2021 N.S.W. Australia
Classical Vocal & Instrumental 78 rpm Records, Rare Deleted L.P.s is the mail buyers list.

Jazz House (Division of Charisma Music Corporation Ltd.)   Box 455, Adelaide Street E.P.O., Toronto M5C 1J6 Canada   (416) 368-2381
Records for Sale from Jazz House is its catalogue.

Jazz Record Company   P.O. Box 71, Hicksville, New York 11801   (516) 997-3653
The company's *Rare Record Catalogue* is a list of records for sale.

Mr. Records   P.O. Box 764, Hillside, New Jersey 07205   (201) 688-2693
Catalogues of 78 rpm records and sheet music are available.

Rare Records Unlimited   1723 Lake Street, San Mateo, California 94403   (415) 349-5306
Phonograph records are sold by mail.

Record Collector's Haven   P.O. Box 37215, Los Angeles, California 90037
You can send your want list and a self-addressed, stamped envelope and the store will let you know whether or not it can supply any of the records you are interested in. A catalogue is available.

The Record List   Marc A. Simon, 2815 Barrington, Toledo, Ohio 43606
Records are available.

Records Revived   P.O. Box 302, San Ramon, California 94583   (415) 820-0462

Rose's Collector Records   300 Chelsea Road, Louisville, Kentucky 40207   (502) 896-6233

Serendipity/Record Rarities   P.O. Box 261, Bogota, New Jersey 07603

Shellac Stack   P.O. Box 252, Friendship, Maine 04547

Stereo-Mania   P.O. Box 324, Green Lake, Wisconsin 54941   (414) 294-6458

BOOKSELLERS
Allen Koenigsberg   650 Ocean Avenue, Brooklyn, New York 11226
Mr. Koenigsberg offers books and trade catalogues about antique phonographs and records. A list is available.

McMahon Vintage Radio   P.O. Box 1331, North Highlands, California 95660   (916) 332-8262
This firm sells books about radios.

Vestal Press   P.O. Box 97, 320 North Jensen Road, Vestal, New York 13850   (607) 797-4872
Books about music-making machines are their specialty.

64. RAILROAD COLLECTIBLES

Railroads have a charm that never fades. Collectors are interested in the toy railroads (see Chapter 82, Toys) and the large railroads. You can buy the dining-car silverware or dishes, or even whole train cars if you wish.

CLUB

The National Association of Timetable Collectors   199 Wayland Street, Hamden, Connecticut 06518   (203) 288-3765
The First Edition features informative articles about timetables, trains, and related subjects. It contains photographs.

BUYING BY MAIL

Each of these firms has a catalogue or list available and there is a charge for some. When writing for information, be sure to include a self-addressed, stamped envelope.

The Depot Attic   377 Ashford Avenue, Dobbs Ferry, New York 10522   (914) 693-1832
Send for this shop's *Railroadiana Catalogue and Price Guide,* a bimonthly catalogue of railroad collectibles.

Nostalgia Station   B & O Railroad Museum, 901 West Pratt Street, Baltimore, Maryland 21233 (301) 237-2387
Nostalgia Station is the official gift shop of the B&O Railroad Museum and makes its full line of merchandise available by mail.

65. SALTS

Both saltshakers and open salt dishes were made to hold salt at the table. They come in a vast variety of styles and sizes and were made of porcelain, glass, and silver. Salts are very popular with collectors. *See also* Chapter 31, Glass; Chapter 61, Pottery and Porcelain; and Chapter 70, Silver and Silver Plate.

CLUB

New England Society of Open Salts Collectors   Olson's Way, East Greenwich, Rhode Island 02818   (401) 884-5402
Salt Talk is a newsletter listing events and some articles. It includes information about open salts of ceramic, glass, and metal.

PARTS AND SUPPLIES

Abercrombie & Company   8227 Fenton Street, Silver Spring, Maryland 20910   (301) 585-2385
Abercrombie supplies metal tops for shakers and bottles.

Gem Monogram & Cut Glass Corporation   623 Broadway, New York, New York 10012 (212) 674-8960
Glass liners for salts are available from this company. Send a penciled outline of the container and a photo or sketch of the piece to be matched before sending the piece to be fitted.

Hess Repairs 200 Park Avenue South, New York, New York 10003   (212) 741-0410
Hess Repairs specializes in supplying blue glass liners for silver salts.

The Ross's Antiques Apple Valley Village, Route 6, Milford, Pennsylvania 18337
The Ross's Antiques makes shaker tops from original dies of heavy tinplate as used by the old glasshouses from 1878 to 1926. The line includes silver-plated tops for cut glass and crystal shakers, Pairpoint shaker tops, as well as lead pewter spouts for bottles, glass stoppers for castor bottles and cruets, and antiqued syrup jug lids. Do not send shakers or tops through the mail to be fitted. In cases where exact size is in doubt, invert shaker and rub glass top on a stamp pad and send print of actual size. A brochure is available.

66. SCALES

Information about scales is very scarce. There are a few books and articles and one club to help you with problems with early scales. The later drug store scales that required a penny are discussed in Chapter 21, Coin-Operated Machines.

CLUB
International Society of Antique Scale Collectors   20 North Wacker Drive, Chicago, Illinois 60606
Equilibrium is a quarterly magazine about scales, and includes informative articles, mainly about English and European scales.

REPAIR SERVICES
The Vintage Cash Register & Slot Machine Company   13448 Ventura Boulevard, Sherman Oaks, California 91403
This company specializes in the complete restorations of all types of old ornate scales.

67. SCIENTIFIC COLLECTIBLES

Antique microscopes, telescopes, medical apparatus, and much more are included in scientific collectibles. Of special interest are quack medical machines. *See also* Chapter 66, Scales.

HOW-TO-FIX-IT BOOK
Pearsall, Ronald. *Collecting and Restoring Scientific Instruments.*
New York: Arco Publishing, 1974.

PRICE GUIDES
Fredgant, Don. *Medical, Dental and Pharmaceutical Collectibles.*
Florence, Alabama: Books Americana, 1981.

Turner, Gerard L.E. *Collecting Microscopes.*
New York: Mayflower Books, 1981.

BUYING BY MAIL
The Antiquarian Scientist   P.O. Box 602, Amesbury, Massachusetts 01913   (617) 388-2314
The Antiquarian Scientist specializes in antique scientific and medical instruments and rare books on science, medicine, and technology. A catalogue is available.

68. SCOUT MEMORABILIA

Boy Scout and Girl Scout memorabilia has a special appeal. Old books, uniforms, and badges are of most interest and value.

CLUB

Scouts on Stamps Society International   7305 Bounty Drive, Sarasota, Florida 33581 (813) 924-2006
SOSSI Journal is the periodical for this club.

PUBLICATION

Scout Memorabilia   7305 Bounty Drive, Sarasota, Florida 33581   (813) 924-2006
Scout Memorabilia Magazine, published 5 times a year, contains articles and ads concerning scouting collectibles: badges, books, uniforms, etc.

BUYING BY MAIL

The American Scout Museum   9 Riger Oaks Center, River Road, Route 2, Gatlinburg, Tennessee 37738

69. SCULPTURE

See also Chapter 41, Marble Restoration; Chapter 43, Metal Antiques and Collectibles; and Chapter 61, Pottery and Porcelain.

CLUB

The Rogers Group   4932 Prince George Avenue, Beltsville, Maryland 20705   (301) 937-7899
The Newsletter of the Rogers Group is published twice a year.

REPAIR SERVICES

Balboa Art Conservation Center   P.O. Box 3755, San Diego, California 92103   (714) 236-9702
The center specializes in the conservation of polychromed sculpture. Consultation is available to the public; treatment services are available to museum members. The center will not answer questions by mail. Fees are usually $35.00 to $45.00 an hour.

Georgette Grosz   4100 Marine Drive, Suite 4-D, Chicago, Illinois 60613   (312) 248-6935
Georgette Grosz specializes in the restoration of important sculptures. Her services are available to anyone in the U.S. She will answer questions by mail without a fee.

Georges Radovanovitch   117 Prince Street, New York, New York 10012   (212) 260-5946
Georges Radovanovitch does restoration and conservation of all kinds of sculpture. His services are available throughout the U.S. for a fee plus expenses. A fee is required also for opinions given if the restoration work is not done.

Myrna Saxe   Los Angeles, California   (213) 273-3161
Myrna Saxe conserves and restores stone, murals, and monumental artworks. Services are available to anyone in the U.S. She will not answer questions by mail.

Phoebe Dent Weil, Research Associate/Conservator   Washington University, Center for Archaeometry, P.O. Box 1105, St. Louis, Missouri 63130   (314) 889-6270
Phoebe Dent Weil specializes in the conservation of sculpture, especially outdoor monuments in bronze and stone. Her services are available to anyone in the U.S. A fee for services is required.

Terry Weisser   The Walters Art Gallery, Baltimore, Maryland 21201
Terry Weisser does restoration and conservation and will answer questions by mail.

APPRAISER

Art Dealers Association of America
Ralph F. Colin, Administrative Vice President, 575 Madison Avenue, New York, New York 10022   (212) 940-8650
The Art Dealers Association of America is a nonprofit organization that offers an appraisal service. Write or call for further details.

70. SILVER AND SILVER PLATE

Some notes about silver:

Silver should be kept clean. Use any good commercial polish, and if you keep the silver on display, use a tarnish-retarding polish. For storage, tarnish-retarding cloths and papers are also available. Never use household scouring powder or instant silver polish on your silver. Never store silver in a nonporous plastic wrap, because the wrap may melt or moisture may collect between the silver and the wrap. Silver will tarnish more quickly if displayed on latex paint or near oak trees. If you use camphor (mothballs) to prevent tarnish, don't let the camphor touch the silver.

Knife blades may separate from hollow handles if they are stored in a hot attic or used in a dishwasher. They can be repaired by using a nonmelting filler.

Silver that is kept on display and never used for eating, such as large candelabra, can be lacquered. This will keep the piece clean almost indefinitely. Any good silver plater can lacquer a piece.

Antique plated silver may "bleed." (*Bleeding* is where the copper shows through the silver.) This is not totally objectionable. Resilvering may lower the value so check on the age and type of silver plate before you replate. Very early "rolled-on" silver on copper Sheffield pieces should rarely be replated.

Late nineteenth- and twentieth-century plated silver that was originally electroplated can be re-plated with no loss of value. Local platers are listed in the Yellow Pages under "Plating." For information about silver flatware, *see also* Part II, Chapter 100, Matching Services—Silver. There is a list of books that help to identify your pattern. *See also* Chapter 43, Metal Antiques and Collectibles.

CLUB

American Spoon Collectors   P.O. Box 260, Warrensburg, Missouri 64093   (816) 429-2630
Spooners Forum is the monthly newsletter, which includes buy/sell ads and letters from members about special spoons.

The Scoop Club   84 Oak Avenue, Shelton, Connecticut 06484   (203) 734-4768

This club for souvenir spoon collectors publishes a bimonthly newsletter, *Spoony Scoop Newsletter*. It contains buy/sell ads, history of spoons, chatty news about members, and events.

PUBLICATIONS

The Magazine Silver   P.O. Box 22217, Milwaukie, Oregon 97222

This is a well-illustrated magazine about modern and antique silver. It lists current silver articles appearing in other publications, a bibliography, shows, sales, plus informative articles about silver makers and their products. You can also buy books about silver through the magazine.

The Spooner   R.F.D. #1, P.O. Box 61, Shullsburg, Wisconsin 53586   (608) 965-3179

This is a monthly newsletter about silver spoons. Write for subscription information.

BOOKS OF MARKS

Kovel, Ralph and Terry. *A Directory of American Silver, Pewter and Silver Plate.*
New York: Crown Publishers, 1961.

————.*Kovels' Know Your Collectibles.*
New York: Crown Publishers, 1981.

Rainwater, Dorothy T. *Encyclopedia of American Silver Manufacturers.*
New York: Crown Publishers, 1975.

Wyler, Seymour B. *The Book of Old Silver.*
New York: Crown Publishers, 1937.

————.*The Book of Sheffield Plate.*
New York, Crown Publishers, 1949.

HOW-TO-FIX-IT BOOK

The Care of Antique Silver.
Nashville: American Association for State and Local History (708 Berry Road, Nashville, Tennessee 37204), 1967. Leaflet.

PARTS AND SUPPLIES

Bailey & Walke Enterprises   P.O. Box 6037, Shreveport, Louisiana 71106

Tarnguard, distributed by Bailey & Walke, is a tarnish inhibitor. When placed in an enclosure with metals which normally tarnish, one Tarnguard capsule protects a 3-cubic-foot area for up to a year.

The Carol Company   612 South Hawley Road, Milwaukee, Wisconsin 53214   (414) 771-0342

The Carol Company developed, manufactures, and distributes a gold, silver, and diamond test kit that contains 3 separate tests, each of which can be used for numerous tests. Call or write for more detailed information concerning the kit.

W. J. Hagerty & Sons Ltd., Inc.   P.O. Box 1496, South Bend, Indiana 46624   (219) 623-2923
Hagerty home care products for the care of silver include polish, tarnish preventing spray, a silver care kit, and gloves. A catalogue is available.

The Lid Lady   Virginia Bodiker, 7790 East Ross Road, New Carlisle, Ohio 45344
The Lid Lady carries a variety of lids and covers for ceramic, glass, and silver vessels and containers. She has a selection of over 10,000 lids.

3-M Center   P.O. Box 96661, St. Paul, Minnesota 55101   (612) 778-5586
Silver Protector Strips are especially treated to attract airborne sulfur compounds, a major cause of tarnish. Write for price information.

Wamsutta Specialty Products Group   1430 Broadway, New York, New York 10018
(212) 930-5368
Pacific Silvercloth is a tarnish-preventing material that keeps silver and silver-plated articles clean. It comes in a 31-inch width that can be cut, sewn, or glued to make your own storage pouches, pocketed rolls, and linings for drawers and cabinets. Literature is available.

REPAIR SERVICES
Abercrombie & Company   8227 Fenton Street, Silver Spring, Maryland 20910   (301) 585-2385
Abercrombie repairs metal items including weighted silver candlesticks and compotes. They also replace knife blades, brushes, and other hardware for dresser sets and supply metal tops for shakers and bottles. They polish, buff, and lacquer metal, including gold and silver.

Al Bar Wilmette Platers   127 Green Bay Road, Wilmette, Illinois 60091   (312) 251-0187
This company specializes in complete metal restoration, plating, polishing, lacquering, repairing, and reproducing missing pieces. Its hours are weekdays, 8:00 A.M. to 4:30 P.M., and Saturday, 8:00 A.M. to noon.

Paul Baron Company   Baron-Rolen Jewelers, 2825 East College Avenue, Decatur, Georgia 30030
(404) 299-1400
Paul Baron repairs broken silver pieces. You can send them to him for an estimate.

Bernard Plating Works   660 Riverside Drive, Florence, Massachusetts 01060   (413) 584-0659
Bernard Plating Works specializes in replacing knife and serving blades with stainless steel blades. It gives free estimates.

Butterfly Shoppe   637 Livernois, Ferndale, Michigan 48220   (313) 541-2858
Butterfly Shoppe repairs silver and other items. Estimates are given before repairing. Pieces to be repaired should be packed carefully and shipped UPS. Hours are Monday through Wednesday, 10:30 A.M. to 4:00 P.M., Thursday until 7:00 P.M.

Joseph DeVoren, Silversmiths 6350 Germantown Avenue, Philadelphia, Pennsylvania 19144   (215) 844-7577
Joseph DeVoren specializes in silver plating, metal refinishing, and repairing.

Estes-Simmons Silverplating Ltd.   1168 Howell Mill Road, N.W., Atlanta, Georgia 30318 (404) 875-9581
This company restores, replates, repairs, and polishes silver and other metals. It also replaces missing parts for brushes, combs, mirrors, blades, and sterling handles, and will remove old engraving. A brochure is available.

Martin M. Fleisher's Silversmith Shop   143 North Park Avenue, Rockville Center, New York 11570
This firm does silver plating.

Gem Monogram & Cut Glass Corporation   623 Broadway, New York, New York 10012 (212) 674-8960
Glass liners for salts, mustards, bowls, baskets, and other silver pieces are available. Write giving accurate details, penciled outline of container, and photo or sketch of piece to be matched before sending silver piece to be fitted.

Rosene Green Associates, Inc.   1622A Beacon Street, Brookline, Massachusetts 02146 (617) 277-8368
Restoration of silver pieces is done by this company.

Hess Repairs   200 Park Avenue South, New York, New York 10003   (212) 741-0410
Hess Repairs specializes in the restoration of old silver dresser sets: removing dents; replacing worn brushes, combs, and mirrors; polishing and lacquering the silver. It will also make new velvet easel backs for silver frames and linings for fine boxes, and specializes in supplying blue glass liners for silver salt, condiment, and sugar holders.

Hiles Plating Company, Inc.   2028 Broadway, Kansas City, Missouri 64108   (816) 421-6450
This firm does metal restoration of all kinds, but specializes in replating of silver flatware and hollow ware. They will repair damaged flatware, handles, and spouts; will replace stainless steel knife blades, lost lids and feet. An opinion and/or estimate will be sent upon receipt of pieces to be restored.

International Antique Repair Service, Inc.   8350 Hickman, Suite 14, Des Moines, Iowa 50322 (515) 278-2518 or (515) 278-2515
Prints and lithographs are cleaned and repaired. All work is guaranteed for 5 years. The company does a mail order business throughout the United States and surrounding countries. A brochure is available.

Just Enterprises   2790 Sherwin Avenue, Unit 10, Ventura, California 93003   (805) 644-5837
This firm specializes in the repair of sterling silver, German silver, and silver tableware. It will also do soldering and smithing.

Midwest Burnishing   208 East Main Street, Round Lake Park, Illinois 60073   (312) 546-2200
Antique metals including silver are polished. Any needed item can be custom made. A leaflet is available.

New England Country Silver, Inc.   Smith Road, East Haddam, Connecticut 06423
(203) 873-1314
This firm repairs, refinishes, and replates old silver and other metals or metals plated with silver or gold. It replaces knife blades with stainless steel from Sheffield, England. Repair includes the removal of dents, soldering parts, sealing leaks, or making new parts, as well as buffing, polishing, and plating. Send your piece for a free estimate and the firm will pay the return postage. A brochure is available.

Orum Silver Company   P.O. Box 805, 51 South Vine Street, Meriden, Connecticut 06450
(203) 237-3037
Orum repairs sterling silver and metals plated with silver. It removes dents, installs new insulators, solders, replaces knife blades. Each piece is cleaned and polished. The firm gives free estimates. Send your pieces and it will pay return postage. A brochure is available.

Peninsula Plating Works Inc.   232 Homer Avenue, Palo Alto, California 94301   (415) 326-7825
This firm polishes, plates, and repairs metal. It also repairs brushes, knife blades, pearl handles, salad servers, insulators, sterling, and silver plate. A brochure is available.

The Silver Chest   12 Grafton Street, Greenlawn, New York 11740   (516) 261-2636
Restoration and replating of flatware is done. All requests for information and pricing are answered if accompanied by a self-addressed, stamped envelope.

Theiss Plating Corporation   9314 Manchester, St. Louis, Missouri 63119   (314) 961-0600
This firm repairs silver and other metal articles. Its services include replating, replacement of stainless steel knife blades, removal of dents, straightening bent pieces, etc.

Universal Electro-Plating Company Inc.   1804 Wisconsin Avenue, N.W., Washington, D.C.
20007   (202) 333-2460
Silver plating, polishing, and lacquering; hard and soft soldering; dent removal; straightening of silver are offered. The company will replace missing pieces of cutlery with new stainless steel, restore dresser sets, furnishing new mirrors, combs, brushes, nail files, and nail buffers. A brochure is available.

Vintage Silver   33 Le May Court, Williamsville, New York 14221   (716) 631-0419
Silver-plated flatware is replated.

R & K Weenike Antiques   Route 7, P.O. Box 140, Ottumwa, Iowa 52501   (515) 934-5427
R & K Weenike repairs silver, especially silver-plated bride's baskets and pickle castor frames.

FACTORY ADDRESSES

Some old silver patterns are still being made and new pieces are available. These are factory addresses of silver manufacturers that are making sterling or plated tableware today.

R. Blackinton & Company   Attleboro, Massachusetts 02703

Gorham   333 Adelaide Avenue, Providence, Rhode Island 02907

International Silver Company   Meriden, Connecticut 06450

Samuel Kirk & Son, Inc.   Kirk Avenue at 25th Street, Baltimore, Maryland 21218

Lunt Silversmiths   Greenfield, Massachusetts 01301

Manchester Silver Company   49 Pavilion Avenue, Providence, Rhode Island 02905

National Silver Company   241 Fifth Avenue, New York, New York 10016

The Old Newbury Crafters   Newburyport, Massachusetts 01950

Oneida Ltd.   Oneida, New York 13421

Reed & Barton   Taunton, Massachusetts 02780

The Stieff Company   Wyman Park Driveway, Baltimore, Maryland 21211

Tiffany & Company, Inc.   727 Fifth Avenue, New York, New York 10022

Towle Manufacturing Company   Newburyport, Massachusetts 01950

Wallace Silversmiths   Wallingford, Connecticut 06492

PRICE GUIDES

Curtis, Anthony, comp. *The Lyle Antiques and Their Values: Silver.*
New York: Coward, McCann & Geoghegan, 1982.

De Laperriere, Baile. *Silver Auction Records.*
Norwalk, Connecticut: Hilmarton Manor Press. (This is published annually.)

Frost, T. W. *The Price Guide to Old Sheffield Plate.*
Suffolk, England: Antique Collectors' Club (5 Church Street, Clopton, Woodbridge, Suffolk 1 P12 IBR England), 1971; price revision 1980.

Hagan, Tere. *Silverplated Flatware: An Identification and Value Guide.*
Paducah, Kentucky: Collector Books, 1981.

Harris, Ian. *The Price Guide to Antique Silver.*
Suffolk, England: Antique Collectors' Club (5 Church Street, Clopton, Woodbridge, Suffolk 1P12 1BR England), 1969; price revision 1980.

————. *The Price Guide to Victorian Silver.*
Suffolk, England: Antique Collectors' Club (5 Church Street, Clopton, Woodbridge, Suffolk 1P12 1BR England), 1971; price revision 1980.

Hudgeons, Marc. *The Official Investors Guide: Buying, Selling, Gold, Silver, Diamonds.*
Orlando, Florida: House of Collectibles, 1981.

Merton, Henry A. *Your Gold and Silver.*
New York. Collier Books, 1981.

BUYING BY MAIL
Each of these firms has a catalogue or list available and there is a charge for some. When writing for information, be sure to include a self-addressed, stamped envelope.

Theresa & Arthur Greenblatt   P.O. Box 276, Amherst, New Hampshire 03031   (603) 673-4401
Lists available for coin silver and souvenir spoons.

The Lion Mark   25 Maryland Avenue, Annapolis, Maryland 21401   (312) 446-8448
The Lion Mark specializes in antique English silver.

Whirligig Antiques   P.O. Box 834, Austin, Texas 78767   (512) 327-3182
Whirligig has a coin silver list.

APPRAISERS
Silver flatware values can often be determined from the offerings of antiques dealers and matching services. See Chapter 100, Matching Services.

Leslie C. Brooks   Silver Identification Service, 166-25 Powells Cove Boulevard, Beechhurst, New York 11357   (212) 767-1478
For an appraisal send a detailed description or photograph of sterling or silver-plated object, along with any identifying hallmarks, and include a self-addressed, stamped envelope and $5.00. She will send you a letter in which the piece is identified, dated, and estimated at current market value. When possible, she will provide a history of the piece and background summary of the manufacturer.

Roundhill's Patterns Unlimited International   P.O. Box 15238, Seattle, Washington 98115 (206) 523-9710
Appraisal service for evaluating discontinued patterns of silver. Cost is $30.00 per pattern, with no limit on the number of pieces.

71. SMOKING COLLECTIBLES

Smoking may be bad for the health, but smoking accessories are marvelous collectibles. Included are matchbooks, match holders, cigar boxes, cigar bands and labels, cigarette packs and paper, tobacco tags, pipe stoppers, pipes, cigarette and cigar lighters, cigar cutters, ads for all sorts of tobacco items, and much more.

CLUBS

Australian Match Cover Collector's Society   c/o J. P. Sheddick, 10 Melbourne Avenue, Glenroy, Victoria 3046 Australia
This group has members around the world. An illustrated magazine, *The Observer,* is published every other month.

British Matchbox Label & Booklet Society   c/o Stephen Thompson, 3 Langton Close, Norwich NR5 8RU England
The *Newsletter* is published every 2 months.

Cigarette Pack Collectors Association   61 Searle Street, Georgetown, Massachusetts 01833
Brandstand is the bimonthly newsletter for this club.

International Phillumeny & Hobby Club   Hoogpoort 9-13, Gent 9000 Belgium
A magazine, *Hobby-Post International,* is published 5 times a year. This club has over 5,000 members on 5 continents.

International Seal, Label & Cigar Band Society   8915 East Bellevue Street, Tucson, Arizona 85715   (602) 296-1048
ISL & CBS News Bulletin is a quarterly newsletter for this club.

International Wristwatch & Cigarette Lighter Club   832 Lexington Avenue, New York, New York 10021   (212) 838-4560
Old Flames & Old Timer is the club's monthly newsletter for members.

Lighter Collector's International Society   829 Rockaway Street, Grover City, California 93433
The Flamethrower, a bimonthly newsletter, provides historical facts and news for collectors.

Medway & North Kent Phillumenist Club   24 Poplicans Road, Cuxton, Rochester, Kent, England
The club produces a quarterly newsletter, *MNKPC Newsletter,* "rather spasmodically."

New Moon Match Club   c/o Emily Miller, 3103 South Bristol, #172, Santa Ana, California 92704
A quarterly newsletter, the *New Moon News Bulletin,* is available to members.

Rathkamp Matchcover Society   1311 East 215th Place, Carson, California 90745   (213) 834-9717
Voice of the Hobby, a bimonthly newsletter, provides information about meetings and members. There are many local chapters that have regular meetings and shows.

The Universal Coterie of Pipe Smokers   The Piper's Parlour, 20-37 120th Street, College Point, New York 11356
The Pipe Smoker's Ephemeris, a bimonthly newsletter, provides almost more than you care to know about pipes. Lists of sales, poems, books, clubs, articles, pictures showing pipes, letters from other pipe enthusiasts, and general gossip about pipes and pipe smoking are incuded.

PUBLICATION
Vesta   18 Bain Avenue, Camberley GU15 2RR England
Vesta is a small monthly newsletter for matchbox label collectors.

REPAIR SERVICES
Authorized Repair Service   143 East 60th Street, New York, New York 10022   (212) 759-9765
This firm repairs antique cigarette lighters and will supply a written estimate on all work needed. Work will be done only after customer's approval is received. Missing parts will be made if necessary.

U.S. Tobacco Museum   100 West Putnam Avenue, Greenwich, Connecticut 06830 (203) 869-5531
The museum collects, preserves, and displays items related to tobacco. Its reference library is open to the public.

72. STENCILS

Stenciling was a popular form of decoration during the nineteenth century. Walls, floors, chairs, tinware, and glass clock panels were often painted with stencil decorations. Complete pictures called theorems were made by schoolgirls, who used a variety of appropriate stencils. Most theorems pictured a large bowl of fruit and flowers. This is one of the easier do-it-yourself projects, we have found. An excellent job of stenciling can be done by almost anyone. Our daughter painted a stenciled border in her bedroom when she was 12. Stencils are available that are ready to use. The average art supply store can furnish stencil designs, paper, cutting knives, and paints. Designs not available from a store can be copied from existing stencils or by tracing a stencil from a book. The Dover Publishing Company has printed a series of books offering patterns from the classic to Art Deco. There are also many how-to stencil books. We have listed a few of the best, but your library might have many more.

Stenciling a wall or a floor is very time consuming and you may wish to hire an expert. Most experts work only within easy distance of their homes and we have listed only those who indicated they would travel out of town. The Historical Society of Early American Decoration, Inc. could probably help you find someone in your area. *See also* Chapter 28, Floorcloths and Chapter 76, Textiles.

CLUB

The Historical Society of Early American Decoration, Inc.   19 Dove Street, Albany, New York 12210
The Decorator is published twice a year for members. All types of freehand and stencil decorating for furniture, walls, or tinware are discussed.

HOW-TO-DO-IT BOOKS

Bishop, Adele, and Lord, Cile. *The Art of Decorative Stenciling.*
New York: Viking Press, 1976.

Brazer, Esther Stevens. *Early American Decoration.*
Springfield, Massachusetts: Pond-Ekberg Company, 1947.

Jewett, Kenneth. *Early New England Wall Stencils.*
New York: Harmony Books, 1979.

Sabine, Ellen S. *Early American Decorative Patterns.*
Princeton, New Jersey: D. Van Nostrand Company, 1962.

PARTS, SUPPLIES, AND SERVICES

Adele Bishop. Inc.   P.O. Box 557, Manchester, Vermont 05254   (802) 362-3537
All of Adele Bishop's stencils can be used for hard or fabric surfaces. 18 stencil kits, 2 of which are precut, are available. All stencils are printed on see-through Mylar. Also available is Mylar, unprinted, for those who want to create their own stencils. Other supplies the firm sells include paints (including fabric paints), brushes, and instruction books. A catalogue is available.

Brookstone Company   127 Vose Farm Road, Peterborough, New Hampshire 03458
(603) 924-7181
Brookstone specializes in hard-to-find tools and other supplies for framing, painting, stenciling, etc. Solid brass stencils representing either Victorian or Early American designs are offered, as well as stencil brushes and a handbook. A catalogue is available.

Country Stenciling   1537 York Street, Lima, New York 14485   (716) 582-1369
Country Stenciling has authentic motifs that have been traced from originals found in homes and inns in western New York. The techniques used are the same as those used long ago—treated cardboard stencils and milk-based paint. Most of the fabric stencils are also old motifs, but reduced in size and, in some cases, simplified. A mail order catalogue is available for $1.00.

Craftswomen   P.O. Box 715, Doylestown, Pennsylvania 18901   (215) 822-0721
Authentic New England, Victorian, and Egyptian design wall stencils are offered in addition to eighteenth-century floor stencil patterns and Victorian tile patterns appropriate for walls and/or floors. A brochure is available.

Judith Hendershot   1408 Main Street, Evanston, Illinois 60202   (312) 475-6411
Judith Hendershot does stenciled decorations for ceiling, walls, and floors. An estimate is provided after the initial consultation, arranged by appointment, at no charge to the client. A brochure is available.

Kenneth R. Hopkins   3001 Monta Vista, Olympia, Washington 98501   (206) 943-1118
Furniture stenciling and decoration are done by Mr. Hopkins. His services are available to anyone in the U.S. and he will answer questions by mail.

Sara H. Hopkins   33 S.W. Water Avenue, Portland, Oregon 97201   (503) 222-2903
Sara Hopkins specializes in interior Victorian restoration (1870-1910). Trained in restoration of stenciled ceilings and walls, she will do custom re-creations on a fee-commission basis. References are provided on request, and she will travel. Estimates and opinions are given when asked for.

Milmar Studio   Gina Martin, 359 Avery Street, South Windsor, Connecticut 06074
The studio has authentic theorem patterns, with 72 designs, each consisting of the pattern numbered for cutting, color notes, how-to hints, and a color photograph. These designs are not intended for beginners. You should know the basics of theorem painting. Send a self-addressed, stamped envelope for information.

Megan Parry Wall Stenciling & Murals   1727 Spruce Street, Boulder, Colorado 80302
(303) 444-2724
Stenciling and mural services are available. There is a basic charge for preliminary design work as well as actual painting, plus travel expenses. Call or write and she will send you a selection of slides and her résumé. The slides may be bought at cost or returned.

Silver Bridge Reproductions   P.O. Box 49, New Braintree, Massachusetts 01531
This company supplies authentic precut stencils and manufactures stencil kits. Stencils are precut on oiled stencil board and retail for $9.95 plus $1.50 postage.

The Stencil House   Route 9, P.O. Box 287, Concord, New Hampshire 03301   (603) 225-9121
Individual stencils printed on Mylar may be ordered cut or uncut. The Stencil House specializes in authentic and custom stencils. Some of the old designs were traced off walls. A brochure is available for $1.00.

The Stenciller's Touch   232 Amazon Place, Columbus, Ohio 43214   (614) 263-1420 or 876-4284
Stenciling is done completely by hand using the firm's own designs and copies of New England motifs. Firm members will travel to stenciling jobs with client assuming travel expenses. There is 1 free estimate including design selection, color, and layout.

Ruth S. Szalasny   3048 Belknap Road, Eden, New York 14057
Ruth Szalasny does reproductions of antique theorems by commission. A basic instruction booklet and beginner's kit are offered plus distinctive patterns, work sheets, supplies, and services. A booklet, *Theorem Painting for Beginners,* is available for $1.00.

The Whole Kit and Kaboodle Company, Inc.   8 West 19th Street, New York, New York 10011   (212) 675-8892 or 675-0245
This firm offers designs on clear plastic, precut, that are inexpensive and reusable. Americana, Colonial, and Victorian designs are offered plus stencil supplies. Mail order flyers are available.

Wiggins Brothers   R.F.D. 1, Hale Road, Tilton, New Hampshire 03276   (603) 286-3046
Period interiors, painted and stenciled, are offered plus restoration of existing designs. Wiggins Brothers does freehand work. A brochure is available.

73. STOCKS AND BONDS

Stocks and bonds require special treatment. They are different from any other collectible in this book. *Be sure* to check whether or not the company issuing the paper might still be redeeming it. Call your local stockbroker or one of the services that search for out-of-business companies. The cash value as a stock will be more than the value as a decorative piece of paper. The value of an unredeemable stock is in the engraving or the autograph. The industry pictured, the artistic worth of the picture, the fame of the company, or the signer adds to the value.

Take care of your stocks and bonds like other paper items. Never use glue or tape to mount the paper unless you feel the item is of minimal value. Many rooms that are papered with stock from old companies are valuable collector's items that cannot be sold. *See also* Chapter 54, Paper Collectibles and Ephemera.

PUBLICATIONS
Friends of Financial History   R. M. Smythe & Company, 24 Broadway, New York, New York 10004   (212) 943-1880
This quarterly magazine is written exclusively for serious collectors.

Scrip   58 Inglehurst Gardens, Redbridge, Ilford, Essex 1G4 5HE England
This is a bimonthly magazine for collectors of old bonds and shares.

PRICE GUIDE
Handy, Robin; Narbeth, Colin; and Stocker, Christopher. *Collecting Paper Money and Bonds.* New York: Mayflower Books, 1979.

AUCTION HOUSE
For further information about auction houses and auctions by mail see Part II, Chapters 89 and 90.

NASCA   Numismatic and Antiquarian Service Corporation of America, 265 Sunrise Highway, Suite 53, Rockville Centre, New York 11570   (516) 764-6677
Bids accepted in person or by mail auction on coins, paper money, tokens and medals, bonds, stocks, certificates and related items, and occasionally stamps and autographs. A catalogue is available by subscription.

BUYING BY MAIL

George H. La Barre Galleries   P.O. Box 27, Hudson, New Hampshire 03051   (603) 882-2411
This firm specializes in stocks and bonds. A catalogue is available. Be sure to include a self-addressed, stamped envelope when writing for information.

APPRAISER

Micheline Massé   Stock Market Information Service, Inc., P.O. Box 120, Station K, Montreal, Quebec, H1N 3K9 Canada   (514) 256-9487
Micheline Massé deals with old stocks and bonds. She looks up the background of the companies involved and finds out if the certificate has a redemption value. For a flat fee of $30.00 per company to be traced, along with a photocopy of the certificate, she will undertake the necessary research in any country in the world in order to establish the exact value and present status of stocks and bonds issued since 1850. If, on rare occasion, she is unable to locate a company, she will reimburse the total fee.

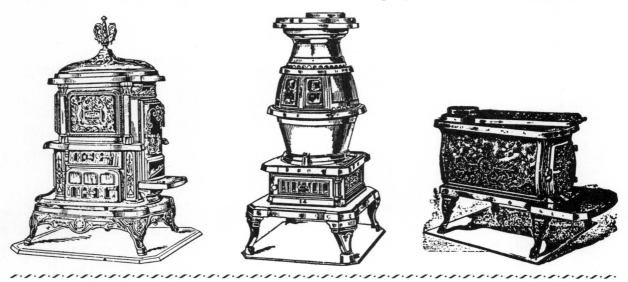

74. STOVES

Antique cooking and heating stoves have gained popularity in the past few years. Be sure that your stove, as well as your chimney, is in safe working condition if you plan to use it. Old parts are available through many of the dealers who sell antique stoves themselves. New parts can be purchased or made for most old stoves.

An amateur should never restore or install an old stove that will be used. Many communities have strict fire code laws that require permits and an inspection of any working stove after installation. Local workmen can safely install your stove; their addresses can be located in the Yellow Pages of your telephone directory.

PARTS AND SUPPLIES

Agape Antiques   P.O. Box 43, Saxtons River, Vermont 05154   (802) 869-2273
Agape Antiques specializes in Glenwood stoves, and has many new castings of grates and liners for the old models.

Custom House   South Shore Drive, Owl's Head, Maine 04854   (207) 594-9281
Custom House carries antique stove replacement parts. Catalogue sheets are available.

Empire Stove & Furnace Company, Inc.   791-797 Broadway, Albany, New York 12207
(518) 449-2590 or 449-5189
This company specializes in replacement parts for all types of wood, coal, gas, and electric ranges, heaters, furnaces, and boilers.

Grampa's Wood Stoves   9 North Street, Ware, Massachusetts 01082   (413) 967-7717
Grampa's Wood Stoves offers accessories, such as lifters, towel rods, pokers, shovels, coal hods, clean-out rakes, and replacement floor grilles. It also carries stove polish and paint. A catalogue is available for $1.00.

Nuhl   2041 Independence, Cape Girardeau, Missouri 63701   (314) 334-5153
Nuhl makes antique reproduction flue covers.

REPAIR SERVICES

Agape Antiques   P.O. Box 43, Saxtons River, Vermont 05154   (802) 869-2273
Agape Antiques specializes in Glenwood stoves. It restores stoves if time permits.

Bryant Steel Works   Thorndike, Maine 04986   (207) 568-3663
Bryant Steel Works specializes in the custom restoration of stoves. (Please allow several months for a restoration.)

Grampa's Wood Stoves   9 North Street, Ware, Massachusetts 01082   (413) 967-7717
This shop restores antique (turn-of-the-century) kitchen ranges, parlor stoves, and base burners. It also repairs stove parts and will renickel. A catalogue is available for $1.00.

The Iron Hearth   Tim and Mary Thompson, Main Street, Addison, Maine 04606   (207) 483-6666
The Iron Hearth specializes in the restoration of antique stoves. Part of its business is located in Connecticut. Write for further information; visit by appointment only.

K & S Supply Company, Inc.   429 North Park Avenue, Indianapolis, Indiana 46202
(317) 637-8267
This company repairs some of the old wood- and coal-burning stoves and ranges. Repairs can be made to the fireboxes and the bottom grates for some of the Round Oak, Kalamazoo, and Majestic ranges.

Preston Stanley   16 Archery Lane, Nashua, New Hampshire 03060   (603) 882-8261
Preston Stanley specializes in the restoration of antique stoves. This service includes dismantling, sandblasting, casting repairs, reassembly, painting with black heat-resistant paint, and nickel plating.

Vermont Plating, Inc.   113 South Main Street, Rutland, Vermont 05701   (802) 775-5759
Vermont Plating restores old wood stove trim parts by nickel plating.

West Barnstable Stove Shop   P.O. Box 472, West Barnstable, Massachusetts 02668
(617) 362-9913
West Barnstable Stove Shop restores antique wood and coal stoves including parlor stoves, oaks, ranges, Franklins, etc. It will nickel-plate trim pieces. You may arrange an appointment by phone.

75. TELEPHONE COLLECTIBLES

Many types of old telephones can be repaired and used. Contact your local phone company for exact information about the types of equipment that will work. Reproduction phones and phone parts are also available from some sources. *See also* Chapter 5, Barbed Wire and Insulators.

CLUB
Antique Telephone Collectors Association   P.O. Box 94, Abilene, Kansas 67410   (913) 263-1757
News and Views is a monthly newsletter for members.

PARTS AND SUPPLIES
Billard's Old Telephones   21710 Regnart Road, Cupertino, California 95014   (408) 252-2104
Billard's maintains a large stock of parts for old telephones and offers same-day service on mail order of brochure or restoration parts, as well as kits to convert old telephones to modern dial usage. A catalogue is available for $1.00, refundable with first order.

Chicago Old Telephone Company   P.O. Box 189, Lemon Springs, North Carolina 28355
(919) 774-6625
Parts for old telephones are available. Send a stamped, self-addressed envelope for literature.

Phoneco   Rural Route #2, Galesville, Wisconsin 54630   (608) 582-4124
Phoneco offers parts for old telephones. A catalogue is available.

REPAIR SERVICES

Chicago Old Telephone Company   P.O. Box 189, Lemon Springs, North Carolina 28355
(919) 774-6625
Chicago Old Telephone Company restores old phones. Literature is available for a self-addressed, stamped envelope.

Larry G. Harmon   1731 Pine Knoll, Caro, Michigan 48723

Phoneco   R.R. 2, Galesville, Wisconsin 54630   (608) 582-4124
Phoneco offers repair services for old telephones. A catalogue is available.

PRICE GUIDE

Knappen, R. H. *Old Telephones Price Guide.*
Privately printed, 1980 (Route 2, Galesville, Wisconsin 54630).

76. TEXTILES

Textiles include all sorts of rugs, coverlets, quilts, lace, and needlework. Care is especially important for the collectibles as they are perishable. The greatest harm to a fabric can come from strong sunlight and dirt. It is often safer to wash or clean a quilt than to store it as it is found. A small piece of fabric can be successfully displayed if it is washed and stitched to unbleached muslin with unbleached pure cotton thread. It should be mounted on acid-free backing and framed under glass. Quilts are too large for this treatment so proper washing and hanging is best if the quilt is not to be used on a bed. Be sure that the quilt is hung from a rod that is held by a tunnel of cloth that supports the entire weight of the quilt and does not cause tears. The Abby Aldrich Rockefeller Folk Art Center (P.O. Box C, Williamsburg, Virginia 23185) identifies quilts and sells books about their care and display. Rugs can also be hung from rods. Instructions for this type of display can be found in how-to books. Lace should be laundered, stretched, and either used or framed.

Cleaning a rug or quilt requires care and the proper supplies. Use Orvus WA Paste or Woolite. Always test the colors first to be sure that they will not run. Rinse thoroughly, dry, and either use or store on rolls. This is not too difficult a project for the careful amateur but be sure to follow directions. Sources of the many types of supplies needed are listed in the book *Considerations for the Care of Textiles and Costumes* by Harold Maitland (Indianapolis: Indianapolis Museum of Art, 1980).

Most rug dealers also clean and repair rugs, so you may be able to find a local expert by checking the Yellow Pages of your local telephone book.

CLUB

International Old Lacers   P.O. Box 1029, Westminster, Colorado 80030-1029   (303) 429-3258
The International Old Lacers are interested in lace and the equipment for making it. They publish a bimonthly magazine.

PUBLICATIONS

Quilter's Newsletter   6700 West 44th Avenue, Wheat Ridge, Colorado 80033   (303) 420-4272
This newsletter is published 10 times a year.

The Textile Museum Newsletter   2320 "S" Street, N.W., Washington, D.C. 20008
(202) 667-0441
This is about the Textile Museum and other museum exhibits of textiles.

BOOKS OF MARKS

A Checklist of American Coverlet Weavers.
Williamsburg, Virginia: Colonial Williamsburg Foundation (Abby Aldrich Rockefeller Folk Art Center, P.O. Box C, Williamsburg, Virginia 23185), 1978.

Haslam, Malcolm. *Marks and Monograms of the Modern Movement, 1875-1930.*
New York: Charles Scribner's Sons, 1977.

Kovel, Ralph and Terry. *Kovels' Know Your Antiques.*
New York: Crown Publishers, 1981 (revised).

HOW-TO-FIX-IT BOOKS

Adrosko, Rita J. *Natural Dyes and Home Dyeing.*
New York: Dover Publications, 1971.

Amini, Majid. *Oriental Rugs, Care and Repair.*
New York: Van Nostrand Reinhold, 1981.

Care of Textiles and Costumes: Cleaning and Storage Techniques. Nashville: American Association for State and Local History (708 Berry Road, Nashville, Tennessee 37204), 1970. Leaflet.

Finch, Karen, and Putnam, Greta. *Caring for Textiles.*
New York: Watson-Guptill Publications, 1977.

Kovel, Ralph and Terry. *Taking Care of Textiles.*
Des Moines: Register and Tribune Syndicate (715 Locust Street, Des Moines, Iowa 50304), 1976.
Leaflet.

Leene, J. E., ed. *Textile Conservation.*
Washington, D.C.: Smithsonian Institution, 1972.

Maitland, Harold F. *Considerations for the Care of Textiles and Costumes: A Handbook for the Non-Specialist.*
Indianapolis: Indianapolis Museum of Art, 1980.

Myers, George Hewitt. *Rugs: Preservation, Display and Storage.*
Washington, D.C.: American Association of Museums (Suite 428, 1055 Thomas Jefferson Street, N.W., Washington, D.C. 20007), 1952. Included with this is another leaflet: *Principles of Practical Cleaning for Old and Fragile Textiles.* Washington, D.C.: American Association of Museums, 1956.

Selection and Care of Rugs and Carpets (Adams and Rector).
Ithaca: Cornell University (Media Services Distribution Center, 7 Research Park, Ithaca, New York 14850), n.d. Leaflet.

Williams, John C., ed. *Preservation of Paper and Textiles of Historic and Artistic Value,* I and II.
Washington, D.C.: American Chemical Society (1155 16th Street, N.W., Washington, D.C. 20036), 1977 and 1981.

PARTS AND SUPPLIES

Country Braid House   Clark Road, Tilton, New Hampshire 03276   (603) 286-4511
Braided rugs are made to order. All are hand laced and reversible in your choice of color and design. The rugs are made in two styles; the hit-miss style where many colors are staggered throughout the rug with no special pattern, or a planned pattern rug made up in rows of circular colored bands.

Country Stenciling   1537 York Street, Lima, New York 14485   (716) 582-1369
This firm manufactures authentic motifs traced from originals found in homes and inns in western New York. It sells treated cardboard stencils and milk-based paint. Most of the stencils for fabrics are also authentic motifs, but are reduced in size and, in some cases, simplified.

J. C. Penney's   Quilt stands to hold a folded quilt can be purchased from the J. C. Penney catalogue for under $40.00. A solid pine model and a brass-plated tubular steel model are available. Contact your local J.C. Penney store for additional information.

Laura Copenhaver Industries, Inc.   "Rosemont," Marion, Virginia 24354   (703) 783-4663
This firm sells hand-tied fishnet canopies for tester beds, as well as coverlets and quilts. It also manufactures reproductions from authentic designs. A catalogue is available.

Pat Nolan   Hand Crafted Rugs, 1437 Herschel Avenue, Cincinnati, Ohio 45208   (513) 871-0890
This firm sells made-to-order, customized braided and loom-woven rugs in wool or cotton, small rag rugs and runners, and materials for do-it-yourself rugcrafters including wool, cotton, and denim fabrics, linen and cotton tufting cord, cotton and linen warp for looms, and all equipment for braiding rugs. Kits for braided rugs and chair mats are also available. Send $2.00 for information and samples of fabrics and cords.

Straw Into Gold   3006 San Pablo Avenue, Berkeley, California 94702   (415)548-5241
This company sells textile art supplies—retail, wholesale, and mail order. It carries fabrics, fibers, tools, dyes, and other supplies for spinning, dyeing, weaving, knitting, and crocheting. It also carries books on the textile arts. Its mail order catalogue is available for $2.50.

Sunflower Studio   2851 Road B½, Grand Junction, Colorado 81503   (303) 242-3883
This firm sells handwoven fabrics by the yard, historical clothing made to measure, and traditional handwoven carpeting available by custom order only. Fabric swatches are available at a minimal cost, refunded when the fabric is ordered. The studio also sells a sampler wall poster of Early American fabric that contains 24 cloth swatches with the historical background of each one. A catalogue is available.

REPAIR SERVICES

Ita H. Aber Company   1 Fanshaw Avenue, Yonkers, New York 10705   (914) 968-4863
This company restores antique needlework.

Noël Bennett   P.O. Box 1175, Corrales, New Mexico 87048   (505) 898-7211
This firm will spin fibers to match original yarns and reproduce dyes to blend with existing colors on Navaho rugs and other textiles. A brochure is available.

Cambridge Textiles   Cambridge, New York 12816   (518) 677-2624
Textiles including tapestries, quilts, samplers, garments, and rugs are conserved and restored. Free estimates are given and a free flyer is available.

Elizabeth Crumley   2208 Derby Street, Berkeley, California 94705   (415) 845-7521
Elizabeth Crumley does restoration and conservation of antique textiles and Oriental rugs. Services also include mounting. You can have a consultation and written report or a consultation by the hour for a fee.

Pie Galinet   New York, New York   (212) 741-3259
This firm restores antique quilts. It will also make custom collapsible stretchers for displaying quilts and rugs.

Havran's Navajo Rug Cleaners   48 West Main, Cortex, Colorado 81321   (303) 565-7977
Professional Navajo rug cleaning and stain removal. Havran's work is fully insured and will be returned promptly. Please note troublesome areas and send rugs insured.

Helen Madeleine Klemm P.O. Box 60, Planetarium Station, New York, New York 10024 (212) 759-3400
Helen Madeleine Klemm restores rugs, tapestries, and textiles. Consultation on preserving your rugs is done in the home or in writing for a fee.

Lacis Jules and Kaethe Kliot, 2990 Adeline Street, Berkeley, California 94703 (415) 843-7178
The Kliots are specialists in antique lace. They do restoration, appraisals, identification, and conservation. Tools and equipment for the textile arts are offered. Their services are available to anyone in the U.S. and they will answer questions by mail.

MacDowell Doll Museum "Oakwood," Aldie, Virginia 22001 (703) 777-6644
This firm will repair antique rugs.

Katy Maty 369 East 62nd Street, New York, New York 10021 (212) 753-5850
Katy Maty does restoration of fine tapestries, needlework, and Aubusson.

Olney Cleaners Stanley L. Smith, 3486 Olney-Laytonsville Road, Olney, Maryland 20832 (301) 774-0789
Olney Cleaners does restoration and appraisal of textiles. It will answer questions by mail. Its services are available to anyone in the U.S.

The Textile Conservation Center 800 Massachusetts Avenue, North Andover, Massachusetts 01845 (617) 686-0191
This firm offers conservation services including cleaning, mounting, and stabilization. There is a fee for an examination, treatment proposal, estimate, and prognosis. The center's services are available to anyone in the U.S. A brochure is available.

The Textile Conservation Workshop 425 Russell Street, Winters, California 95694 (916) 795-4602
The workshop offers conservation of textiles; research and documentation of the artifact's history, materials, and methods of manufacture; and advice on basic care. Treatment proposals and estimates are given after examination of artifacts. There is a fee for this examination and estimate. There is no geographical limit for its services. A brochure is available.

The Textile Museum Clarissa K. Palmai, 2320 S Street, N.W., Washington, D.C. 20008 (202) 667-0442 or (301) 656-6381
This museum specializes in the restoration of textiles. It provides services for anyone throughout the U.S. and will answer questions by mail.

Unique & Art Lace Cleaners, Inc. 5926 Delmar Boulevard, St. Louis, Missouri 63112 (314) 725-2900
This is a specialized cleaner of fine handmade linens. It repairs lace, embroidery, and other textiles requiring special hand attention.

Helene Von Rosenstiel Restorations   382 11th Street, Brooklyn, New York 11215
(212) 788-7909
This is a nationwide restoration and conservation service. It restores quilts, costumes, samplers, wedding dresses, lace, beaded bags, garments, etc. On-site consultation services for individual artifacts as well as entire collections are available. It also carries a selection of textile restoration supplies. Services are available to the public by appointment only. All correspondence is answered. There is a consultation fee.

PRICE GUIDE
Haders, Phyllis. *The Warner Collector's Guide to American Quilts.*
New York: Warner Books, 1981.

AUCTION HOUSE
John C. Edelmann Galleries, Inc.   523 East 73rd Street, New York, New York 10021
(212) 628-1700
The Galleries hold weekly rug and textile auctions. Write for further information. Catalogues are available.

BUYING BY MAIL
Each of these firms has a catalogue or list available and there is a charge for some. When writing for information, be sure to include a self-addressed, stamped envelope.

David and Linda Arman   P.O. Box 3331, Danville, Virginia 24541   (804) 799-6075
Historical textile lists are available free.

Straw Into Gold   3006 San Pablo Avenue, Berkeley, California 94702   (415) 548-5241
This company sells textile art supplies—retail, wholesale, and mail order. It carries fabrics, fibers, tools, dyes, and other supplies for spinning, dyeing, weaving, knitting, and crocheting. Its mail order catalogue is available for $2.50.

APPRAISERS
John C. Edelmann Galleries   523 East 73rd Street, New York, New York 10021   (212) 628-1700
Appraisals and valuations for estate, tax, and insurance purposes are offered.

Olney Cleaners   Stanley L. Smith, 3486 Olney-Laytonsville Road, Olney, Maryland 20832
(301) 774-0789
Appraisals are available. Questions will be answered by mail.

BOOKSELLERS
Straw Into Gold   3006 San Pablo Avenue, Berkeley, California 94702   (415) 548-5241
This company carries books on the textile arts. Its mail order catalogue is available for $2.50.

The Textile Museum   2320 S Street, N.W., Washington, D.C. 20008   (202) 667-0441
The Textile Museum Shop catalogue offers books, booklets, and items relating to textiles.

77. THIMBLES

Thimbles, old and new, are collected by many. The most expensive thimble ever sold was a Meissen thimble that brought $8,500.00 in 1976.

CLUBS

Collector Circle   1313 South Killian Drive, Lake Park, Florida 33403   (305) 845-6075
Collector Circle Gazette is a quarterly newsletter about thimbles with informative articles, pictures, and show listings.

Thimble Collectors International   P.O. Box 143, Intervale, New Hampshire 03845
TCI Bulletin carries articles about old and new thimbles and information about club activities.

The Thimble Guild   Evelyn Eubanks, 315 Park End Drive, Dayton, Ohio 45415
Their newsletter is published every quarter and is available only to members.

Thimble Society of London   C/5, Chenil Gallery, 181 King's Road, Chelsea, London SW3 England
The Thimble Society publishes a quarterly magazine offering antique thimbles at a discount to members. As membership grows they hope to expand the magazine to include letters from members.

PUBLICATION

Thimbletter   93 Walnut Hill Road, Newton Highlands, Massachusetts 02161   (617) 969-9358
This is a bimonthly newsletter.

PRICE GUIDE

Rath, Jo Anne. *Antique and Unusual Thimbles.*
Cranbury, New Jersey: A. S. Barnes, 1979.

BOOKLET

Worldly Thimbles: Getting Started with Your Own Thimble Collection (1977). This booklet is free. Send a self-addressed, stamped long envelope to Belmar Editions Ltd., 1313 South Killian Drive, Lake Park, Florida 33403, (305) 845-6075.

78. TIN AND TOLEWARE

Tin and toleware should be kept dry and free of rust. If the tins are rusty, try removing the rust with 0000 steel wool. If it is painted toleware, just touch up the spot, but *never paint more than is necessary*.

A redecorated piece of toleware is of value as a new item but not as an antique. Once the tin is repainted it has lost its value to the serious collector, but sometimes repainting is the only solution for a severely damaged piece. Serious toleware decorators often look for old pieces with worn paint to redecorate. It is possible to get new tinware made in the same manner as the old. Many restored village museums have tin shops where tin is made and sold.

CLUBS

The Historical Society of Early American Decoration, Inc.   19 Dove Street, Albany, New York 12210
The Decorator is published twice a year for members.

Tin Container Collectors Association   P.O. Box 4555, Denver, Colorado 80204   (303) 755-0800
Tin Type is *the* publication for the collector of old advertising tins. Much original research, buy/sell ads, and gossip about members are included. It is clearly stamped with the personality of the editor, an avid tin collector.

BOOK

Hutchings, Dorothy Dean. *A Quarter Century of Decorating and Teaching Country Painting.*
Privately printed, 1975 (1509 West Delano Drive, Tucson, Arizona 85705).

PATTERN RENTAL

Mrs. Dorothy Hutchings   1509 West Delano Drive, Tucson, Arizona 85705   (602) 888-4541
Rental designs are available for tinware. The rental period is 7 days from the time you receive the pattern. A catalogue of 21 pages of colored designs for rent is available for a stamped, self-addressed envelope with 30¢ for postage plus $1.00.

PARTS AND SUPPLIES

Spindle Top Farm   R.D. 2, P.O. Box 293, Stockton, New Jersey 08559   (201) 996-2885
Made-to-order pierced tin panels suitable for use in a kitchen cabinet, pie safe, or cupboard doors are offered. Some designs are faithful copies of original antique patterns and others are original designs. A catalogue is available.

Victorian Reproductions, Inc.   1601 Park Avenue South, Minneapolis, Minnesota 55404
(612) 338-3636
Tin ceilings are sold. A catalogue is available.

REPAIR SERVICES

Rosene Green Associates, Inc.   1622A Beacon Street, Brookline, Massachusetts 02146
(617) 277-8368
Restoration services on toleware are offered.

REPRODUCTIONS

Dorothy D. Hutchings   1509 West Delano Drive, Tucson, Arizona 85705   (602) 888-4541
Dorothy Hutchings has a variety of handcrafted tin reproductions suitable for decorating, ranging from pourers and teapots to fireplace screens, sconces, and document boxes. A brochure is available for 50¢.

Irvin's Craft Shop   R.D. 1, Box 45, Mount Pleasant Mills, Pennsylvania 17853   (717) 539-8200
Handcrafted tin, copper, and brass reproductions including lamps, chandeliers, lanterns, candleholders, sconces, chambersticks, cookie cutters, molds, candle boxes, etc. are offered. A catalogue is available.

79. TOKENS AND MEDALS

There are many types of tokens that are collected under the general heading of "nonmoney" in coin catalogues. These are special metal or wooden pieces that served as a medium of exchange at a company store or as advertising for a regular store. They were not legal tender produced by a government. This book does not list coins or other legal tender. Information on coin collecting is easily found in any library.

CLUBS

American Tax Token Society   Geo. Van Trump, Jr., P.O. Box 26523, Lakewood, Colorado 80226
The society publishes *The American Tax Token Society Newsletter*.

American Vecturist Association   P.O. Box 1204, Boston, Massachusetts 02104   (617) 277-8111
The Fare Box is a monthly newsletter for collectors of transportation tokens.

American Wooden Money Guild   P.O. Box 3445, Tucson, Arizona 85722
Old Woody Views is a monthly newsletter about wooden money.

Check Collector's Round Table   969 Park Circle, Boone, Iowa 50036   (515) 432-1931
The Check List is a 36-page quarterly newsletter with illustrated articles about checks.

Civil War Token Society   308 Janice Street, Prattville, Alabama 36067   (205) 365-1803
Copperhead Courier is a magazine for civil war token collectors.

Dedicated Wooden Money Collectors   5575 State Route 257, Radnor, Ohio 43066
Timber Lines is a newsletter with membership information, collecting information, and ads.

International Organization of Wooden Money Collectors   900 Stanton, Bay City, Michigan
48706   (517) 892-0396
Bunyan Chips is a monthly newsletter with buy/sell ads and information about wooden money.

Love Token Society   P.O. Box 84, Manquin, Virginia 23106   (804) 769-4145
Love Letter is a bimonthly newsletter with news of events for members.

North Eastern Vecturist Association   P.O. Box 6021, Long Island City, New York 11106
A brief newsletter, *NEVA News*, is published bimonthly. It contains club news and classified ads.

Orders and Medals Society of America   209 West Pittsburg Avenue, Wildwood Crest, New Jersey
08260
The Medal Collector is a magazine.

Society of Ration Token Collectors   P.O. Box 20285, Sacramento, California 95820
This club has a quarterly publication for members.

PUBLICATION

Food Stamp Change Newsletter   P.O. Box 40888, San Francisco, California 94140
(415) 648-8634
This is a quarterly newsletter with information of interest to food stamp and token collectors.

PRICE GUIDE
Rulau, Russell. *Hard Times Tokens.*
Iola, Wisconsin: Krause Publications, 1980.

AUCTION HOUSE
NASCA Numismatic and Antiquarian Service Corporation of America, 265 Sunrise Highway, Suite 53, Rockville Centre, New York 11570 (516) 764-6677
Bids are accepted in person or by mail auction. Coins, paper money, tokens and medals, bonds, stocks, certificates and related items, and occasionally stamps and autographs are offered. A catalogue is available by subscription.

BUYING BY MAIL
Each of these firms has a catalogue or list available and there is a charge for some. When writing for information, be sure to include a self-addressed, stamped envelope.

Merchant Token Collectors Association 752 North 74th, Seattle, Washington 98103 (206) 782-5769

World Exonumia Rich Hartzog, P.O. Box 4143, Rockford, Illinois 61110 (815) 226-0771
Tokens, medals, and exonumia, primarily pre-1920, are offered.

80. TOOLS

Tool collectors are divided on the subject of care and restoration. Some think waxing or treating the wood lowers the value of a tool, while others feel such treatment enhances it. Tools should be kept in clean and working condition. Metal parts should be rust free and will usually require oil or another preservative.

The restoration of tools requires the knowledge of a woodworker, a metalworker, and an expert on the tools. Local shops dealing with tools may be able to help, but many antique tools are beyond the skill and knowledge of the modern toolworker.

CLUB
Early American Industries Association c/o John Watson, Treasurer, Cultural Education Center, P.O. Box 2128, Empire State Plaza Station, Albany, New York 12220
The Chronicle, a monthly magazine, contains serious articles about tool history and use. *The Shavings,* a monthly newsletter, gives news about books, members, and events.

PRICE GUIDE

Cliff Peterson Collection, Vol. 8.
Privately printed, 1982. (2444 Wilshire Boulevard, Santa Monica, California 90403). This is one volume in a series of catalogues featuring United States patent models from 1790 to 1898.

BUYING BY MAIL

Each of these firms has a catalogue or list available and there is a charge for some. When writing for information, be sure to include a self-addressed, stamped envelope.

Arnold & Walker   77 High Street, (Needham Market), Suffolk 1P6 8AN England

Birchland Antiques   P.O. Box 94, Handisville, Pennsylvania 17538

Iron Horse Antiques, Inc.   R.D. 2, Poultney, Vermont 05764   (802) 287-4050

Mechanick's Workbench   Front Street, Marion, Massachusetts 02738   (617) 748-1680

Sign of the Goosewing, Antiques   Singing Brook—79K, Washingtonville, New York 10992 (914) 496-9404

The Toolbox   5005 Jasmine Drive, Rockville, Maryland 20853   (301) 929-1968

Ye Olde Tool Shed   P.O. Box T, Cornwall, New York 12518   (914) 534-2036

BOOKSELLERS

Early American Industries Association   c/o J. Kebabian, Washington Mount Road, Becket, Massachusetts 01223

Iron Horse Antiques, Inc.   R.D. 2, Poultney, Vermont 05764   (802) 287-4050

Ken Roberts Publishing Company   P.O. Box 151, Fitzwilliam, New Hampshire 03447

Charles B. Wood, III   South Woodstock, Connecticut 06267

81. TOOTHPICK HOLDERS

Toothpick holders, often referred to in the ads as just "toothpicks," were made in the late nineteenth century in a variety of shapes and materials. Glass, porcelain, and silver-plated examples are most common. *See also* Chapter 31, Glass; Chapter 61, Pottery and Porcelain; and Chapter 70, Silver and Silver Plate.

CLUB

National Toothpick Holder Collector's Society   P.O. Box 246, Sawyer, Michigan 49125
Toothpick Bulletin is a monthly newsletter with information about glass toothpick holders and a few ads.

82. TOYS

Many toys are found in poor condition because of the love from the children who were the toys' original owners. Collectors judge condition severely and a pristine tin toy is worth a great deal more than the same toy in a damaged or restored condition. Carefully examine an old toy. Has it been repainted? Are there replacement parts? Does it work? It is not advisable for the amateur to make many types of repairs. *Never* repaint or restore a metal toy if there is any way to avoid it. An old toy that is missing its paint is usually worth more than a toy from the same period that has been repainted. If you want a cast-iron bank that looks like a new one, buy a reproduction, but don't paint an old one. The working parts of old toys are very difficult to replace unless you are mechanically inclined. Key-wind mechanisms and power sources for trains are complicated and often must be replaced. Some toys never can be totally repaired. The battery-driven mechanical toys of the 1950s that featured a cigarette-smoking bartender or monkey will never smoke again once the original supply of oil has been used. It was never meant to be repaired.

Many types of toys have been reproduced. Be sure you understand the differences between the old and new toys before you buy. The libraries are filled with books about this subject.

The general rules for buying or selling toys are the same as those for other collectibles and antiques. There are auction houses that specialize in this field. See Part II, Chapter 89, Auction Houses. *See also* Chapter 24, Dolls; and Chapter 48, Music Boxes.

CLUBS

American Bear Club   P.O. Box 179, Huntington, New York 11743
Membership includes a card, badge, price list, newsletter, and copy of *Beggar T. Bear.*

American-International-Matchbox   522 Chestnut Street, Lynn, Massachusetts 01904
(617) 595-4135
A.I.M. is a monthly newsletter.

Antique Toy Collectors of America
This is a small club and you must be sponsored by two members in order to join.

Good Bears of the World   P.O. Box 8236, Honolulu, Hawaii 96815   (808) 946-2844
Bear Tracks is a small quarterly magazine about teddy bears and teddy bear collecting. It features anecdotes about events, books, etc.

Lionel Collector's Club   P.O. Box 11851, Lexington, Kentucky 40578
Lion Roars is a newsletter with articles and pictures. *Interchange Track* is a newsletter with buy and sell ads.

Marble Collectors Society of America   P.O. Box 222, Trumbull, Connecticut 06611
Marble Mania is a quarterly newsletter with articles, anecdotes, news items, editorials, activities information, and current events.

"Matchbox" Collectors Club   141 West Commercial Avenue, Moonachie, New Jersey 07075
(201) 935-3800
A quarterly newsletter about Matchbox toys is published. It features buy/sell ads, articles, and news about coming releases. It is aimed at children who buy new Matchbox toys.

Mechanical Bank Collectors of America   P.O. Box 128, Allegan, Michigan 49010
(616) 673-4509
Mechanical Banker is a newsletter published 3 times a year and is filled with very detailed articles about rare, old, and mechanical banks. Membership is limited to serious collectors of mechanical banks.

Motoring in Miniature Association, Ltd.   147 Pin Oak Drive, Williamsville, New York 14221 (716) 689-9830
This is a club for collectors of miniature vehicles. It holds monthly meetings in the western New York area and does not have a publication at this time.

The National Model Railroad Association   P.O. Box 2186, Indianapolis, Indiana 46206
The NMRA Bulletin is a monthly magazine.

Playing Card Collectors Association, Inc.   3612 Douglas Avenue, Apt. 524, Racine, Wisconsin 53402

Still Bank Collectors Club   c/o Andrew Moore, Beverly Bank, 1357 West 103rd Street, Chicago, Illinois 60643
Penny Bank Post is a newsletter published 3 times a year.

The Toy Train Operating Society, Inc.   25 West Walnut Street, Suite 305, Pasadena, California 91103
T.T.O.S. Bulletin is a magazine with current articles about the train world and some research into the history of toy trains.

The Train Collector's Association   P.O. Box 248, Strasburg, Pennsylvania 17579
Train Collectors Newsletter lists club events and *Train Collectors Quarterly* is a magazine with articles about trains and train collecting.

PUBLICATIONS

The Antique Toy World   3941 Belle Plaine, Chicago, Illinois 60618   (312) 267-8412
This magazine is filled with informative articles about old and new toys of interest to collectors as well as auction and sale reports, and ads of toys for sale. It is important for the serious toy collector.

Collectors' Gazette   30 Brookdale Road, Sutton-in-Ashfield, Nottinghamshire, England
This newspaper about toys is published bimonthly.

Collector's Showcase   P.O. Box 6929, San Diego, California 92107   (714) 222-0386
This is a bimonthly magazine on toys and advertising. It has lavish color illustrations.

International Toy and Doll Collector   P.O. Box 9, Halstead, Essex, England
This is a bimonthly magazine.

Marble Mart   503 West Pine Street, Marengo, Iowa 52301   (319) 642-3891
A buy/sell trade newsletter issued bimonthly, this is the only publication about marbles.

Miniature Tractor & Implement   R.D. 1, P.O. Box 90, East Springfield, Pennsylvania 16411 (814) 922-3460
This monthly newsletter is for collectors of new and old farm toys and models of farm equipment. It lists shows, sales, etc.

Old Toy Soldier Newsletter   209 North Lombard, Oak Park, Illinois 60302
This is a bimonthly newsletter.

Old Toys   Gruttersdreef 541, P.O. 305, Apeldoorn, Netherlands
This international monthly magazine is in full color.

Professor Pug Frog's Newsletter   3 Hillside Avenue, Peabody, Massachusetts 01960
This is a newsletter about antique toys, trains, and collectibles.

The Teddy Tribune   254 West Sidney Street, St. Paul, Minnesota 55107   (612) 291-7571
This newsletter about teddy bears is published 10 times a year.

DECODING ADVERTISING COPY

Reading the ads for antiques and collectibles often takes special knowledge. Two collectors will speak a special language in the same way two doctors have a vocabulary known only to their profession. When looking up still banks it might help to know that some advertisements refer to the following: Cranmer numbers refer to banks shown in the book *Banks: Still Banks of Yesterday* by Don Cranmer (L-W Promotions, P.O. Box 69, Gas City, Indiana 46933); Long numbers refer to banks shown in *Dictionary of Still Banks* by Earnest and Ida Long and Jane Pitman (Long's Americana, P.O. Box 272, Mokelumne Hill, California 95245) 1980; Whiting numbers refer to banks listed in *Old Iron Still Banks* by Hubert Whiting (privately printed, 1968). This book is now available only through libraries. SBC numbers refer to Still Bank Collectors Club numbers; for more information about them contact the club at the address listed in this chapter.

BOOKS OF MARKS

Kovel, Ralph and Terry. *Kovels' Know Your Collectibles.*
New York: Crown Publishers, 1981.

Pressland, David. *The Art of the Tin Toy.*
New York: Crown Publishers, 1976.

White, Gwen. *Toys, Dolls, Automata: Marks and Labels.*
London: B. T. Batsford, 1975.

HOW-TO-FIX-IT BOOKS

Barker, Thomas B. *Greenberg's Operating and Repair Manual for American Flyer Trains.*
Ellicott City, Maryland: Greenberg Publishing (10291 Baltimore National Pike, Ellicott City, Maryland 21043), 1979.

Greenberg, Bruce C. *Greenberg's Repair and Operating Manual for Lionel Trains.* New York: Van Nostrand Reinhold, 1980.

PARTS AND SUPPLIES

Buddy-K Toys   20 Durham Street, Hellertown, Pennsylvania 18055   (215) 838-6446
This firm offers replacement decals for pressed steel toys. A price list is available if you send a self-addressed, stamped envelope.

Mah-Jongg Sales Company   P.O. Box 255721, Sacramento, California 95865
Replacement tiles for Mah-Jongg are available in bone, bamboo, celluloid, plastic, etc. Send the tile you want matched and the company will locate the tiles and advise you of the cost.

Mariani Enterprises   P.O. Box 5126, Lancaster, Pennsylvania 17601   (717) 569-4339
Replacement feet for vest pocket games and stimulators (suction cup or bumper type) are available from this company. Call or write for more information.

George G. Nygren   Route 2, Ashland, Nebraska 68003   (402) 944-2430
Mr. Nygren sells decals and parts for toy tractors and implements. A list is available.

Dennis R. Parker   Route 2, P.O. Box 72, Volga, South Dakota 57071   (605) 983-5987
Replacement parts for toy tractors and other farm toys are available. Send a self-addressed, stamped envelope for a free parts list and brochure.

Plow Boy Toy Crawlers   R.R. 2, P.O. Box 185, Dyersville, Iowa 52040
Parts for Westrak and Terratrak tractor crawlers, Oliver, Minneapolis Moline, and other farm toy models are available.

Thomas Toys   P.O. Box 405, Fenton, Michigan 48430
This firm offers over 100 different rubber tires for old toys, over 1,000 metal parts for cast metal and plastic toys, plastic wheels and parts, and several sheet metal parts. Send a photo or good description of your broken toy accompanied by a self-addressed, stamped envelope for an estimate. It also does some restoring and can make special metal parts, such as a fender, etc.

J. M. Vaughn, Jr.   50 Arland Drive, Pawtucket, Rhode Island 02861   (401) 728-7440
Mr. Vaughn does cast reproductions for MG models. Windshields, steering wheels, radiator and headlight assemblies, bumpers, bumper guards, and wheel hubs are available. Call or write for more information.

Vintage Toy Company   1220 Brookview Drive, Concord, California 94520   (415) 689-4176
Pressure-sensitive decals are reproduced in sizes and colors to match originals. For a price list send a self-addressed, stamped envelope.

Mark Wikner   1420 Parker, Cedar Falls, Iowa 50613   (319) 266-9210
Replacement decals for toy tractors and farm equipment are available. Send a self-addressed, stamped envelope for an illustrated list.

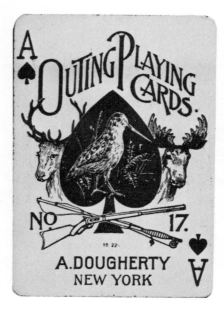

Weldon Yoder   18638 CR 46, New Paris, Indiana 46553

Weldon Yoder sells parts for toy farm tractors. Send a self-addressed, stamped envelope for information and prices.

REPAIR SERVICES

Gary Anderson   Route 2, P.O. Box 102, Mora, Minnesota 55051

Mr. Anderson repairs and repaints toy tractors, Tootsietoys, and die-cast toys in general. Send a self-addressed, stamped envelope for a price list.

Buddy-K Toys   20 Durham Street, Hellertown, Pennsylvania 18055   (215) 838-6446

This firm offers professional restoration services for pressed steel toys. Send a self-addressed, stamped envelope for more information.

Marvin's Crackers   Marv Silverstein, 24 Minton Avenue, Chatham, New Jersey 07928 (201) 635-6260

This firm does restorations of Buddy "L," Keystone, etc. as well as custom-designed toys. It gives free estimates. Write or call.

Dennis R. Parker   Route 2, P.O. Box 72, Volga, South Dakota 57071   (605) 983-5987

Mr. Parker restores and replaces parts for toy tractors and other farm toys. Contact him before sending the toy for restoration. Send a self-addressed, stamped envelope for a free price list and brochure.

Thomas Toys   P.O. Box 405, Fenton, Michigan 48430

This company restores metal toys and can make special metal parts, such as fenders, etc. Send a photo or good description of your broken toy accompanied by a self-addressed, stamped envelope for an estimate.

Weldon Yoder   18638 CR 46, New Paris, Indiana 46553

Weldon Yoder restores toy farm tractors. Send a self-addressed, stamped envelope for information and prices.

PRICE GUIDES

Best, Charles W. *Cast Iron Toy Pistols, 1870–1940: A Collector's Guide.*
Privately printed (Rocky Mountain Arms and Antiques, 6288 South Pontiac, Englewood, Colorado 80110).

Bialosky, Peggy and Alan. *The Teddy Bear Catalog.*
New York: Workman Publishing, 1980.

Conway, Shirley, and Wilson, Jean. *100 Years of Steiff, 1880–1980.*
Berlin, Ohio: Berlin Printing, 1980.

Gardiner, Gordon, and Morris, Alistair. *The Price Guide to Metal Toys.*
Suffolk, England: Antique Collectors' Club (5 Church Street, Clopton, Woodbridge, Suffolk 1P12 1BR England), 1980.

Greenberg, Bruce C. *Greenberg's Price Guide to Lionel Trains 1901–1942.*
Sykesville, Maryland: Greenberg Publishing, 1979.

————. *Greenberg's Price Guide to Lionel Trains: Postwar O and 0-27 Trains.*
Sykesville, Maryland: Greenberg Publishing, 1982.

Kelly, Chad. *Valuable Old Toys with Current Prices of What They're Worth,*
Vols. 1 and 2. Milford, Connecticut: Authentications (7 River Street, Milford, Connecticut 06460), 1981 and 1982.

Mallerich, Dallas J., III. *Greenberg's Price Guide to "N" Gauge Trains.*
Sykesville, Maryland: Greenberg Publishing, 1981.

O'Brien, Richard. *Collecting Toys: A Collector's Identification and Value Guide,* 3rd ed.
New York: Crown Publishers, 1982.

Rubin, Ken. *Drop Coin Here.*
Brooklyn: K & F Publishing, 1979.

Thorpe, John G. *The Playing Cards of the Worshipful Company of Makers of Playing Cards.*
London: Stanley Gibbons Antiquarian (395 Strand, London WC2R OLX England), 1980.

Wieland, James, and Force, Edward. *Corgi Toys: The Ones with Windows.*
Privately printed, 1981 (P.O. Box 2, Osceola, Wisconsin 54020), 1981.

Yorkis, Paul G.; Walsh, James D.; Greenberg, Linda F.; and Greenberg, Bruce C. *Greenberg's Price
Guide to American Flyer "S" Gauge.*
Sykesville, Maryland: Greenberg Publishing, 1980.

AUCTION HOUSE

Lloyd Ralston   447 Stratfield Road, Fairfield, Connecticut 06432   (203) 335-4054 or 366-3399
This auction house specializes in toys. Catalogues are mailed prior to sales. The purchase of a catalogue
is necessary for admittance to a sale.

BUYING BY MAIL

Each of these firms has a catalogue or list available and there is a charge for some. When writing for
information, be sure to include a self-addressed, stamped envelope.

Farm Model Exchange   R.D. 1, P.O. Box 90, East Springfield, Pennsylvania 16411-9739
(814) 922-3460
Miniature tractors and farm implements, 1/32 scale, are offered. A price list is available.

The Miniature Mart   1807 Octavia Street, San Francisco, California 94109   (415) 563-8745

Shamus O. D. Wade   37 Davis Road, Acton, London W3 England
Model soldiers are for sale.

BOOKSELLERS

Antique Toy World   3941 Belle Plaine, Chicago, Illinois 60618

Davison Books   14 Boxwood Drive, Stamford, Connecticut 06906

Greenberg Publishing Company   729 Oklahoma Road, Sykesville, Maryland 21784

John Wilbeck   Route 6, P.O. Box 2, Guntersville, Alabama 35976   (205) 582-8166

83. TRUNKS

Old trunks should be restored to their original condition. If they are in poor condition they can always be refinished in some decorative manner. There are many books about modern decorations for trunks, but there are very few on the correct restoration. Parts are available by mail. *See also* Chapter 32, Hardware.

HOW-TO-FIX-IT BOOKS

Groves, Dorothymae. *Heirloom Treasures from Antique Trunks,* rev. ed.
Privately printed, 1969 (P.O. Box 536, Spearman, Texas 79081). Booklet.

Kovel, Ralph and Terry. *How to Refinish a Trunk.*
Des Moines: Register and Tribune Syndicate (715 Locust Street, Des Moines, Iowa 50304), 1977.
Leaflet.

Labuda, Martin and Maryann. *How to Repair, Decorate, Restore Antique Trunks.*
Privately printed, 1968 (3706 West 169th Street, Cleveland, Ohio 44111).

PARTS AND SUPPLIES

Antique Trunk Company   3706 West 169th Street, Cleveland, Ohio 44111   (216) 941-8618
This company supplies antique trunk restoration parts. Its *Trunk Repair Book* sells for $3.00 postpaid.
Send a large, self-addressed, stamped (30¢ postage) envelope for a parts catalogue.

Charolette Ford Trunks Ltd.   P.O. Box 536, Spearman, Texas 79081   (806) 659-3027
Trunk parts, tools, and books on antique trunks are available. Charolette will answer any questions
you may have. Send for a catalogue. She also has a quarterly publication called *Trunk Talk.*

Furniture Revival and Company   P.O. Box 994, 580 Southwest Twin Oaks Circle, Corvallis,
Oregon 97330   (503) 754-6323
This firm offers trunk hardware. A catalogue is available for $2.00.

Gary's Restorations   P.O. Box 3843, San Bernardino, California 92413   This firm offers replacement hardware for restoring antique trunks. Nails, handles, locks, corners, etc. are available. Send 50¢
for an illustrated catalogue of trunk hardware.

REPAIR SERVICES

R. Bruce Hamilton   Furniture Restoration, 551 Main Street, P.O. Box 587, West Newbury, Massachusetts 01985   (617) 363-2638 or 729-1569
This firm does general restoration. Antique trunks are a specialty. Call for an appointment.

Trunks by Paul   Paul Merritt Jones, 411 Marion Drive, Longview, Texas 75602   (214) 753-8119
Antique trunks are restored. Fees range from $100.00 to $225.00.

PRICE GUIDE

Labuda, Martin and Maryann. *Price and Identification Guide to Antique Trunks.*
Cleveland, Ohio: Antique Trunk Company (3706 West 169th Street, Cleveland, Ohio 44111), 1980.

84. WALLPAPER

Wallpaper can be restored or replaced with new or old paper. Some dealers own stocks of old paper that are available for use on walls, boxes, and screens. A talented artist can do inpainting on damaged paper and it will result in a suitable job of restoration. Check with your local art schools and artists working in your area.

If you want to protect your wallpaper, you can have it professionally treated before it is hung, or you can treat it with a spray after it is on the wall. Wallpaper protector spray can be found in most hardware and wallpaper stores.

PARTS AND SUPPLIES

Avant Garde Division of Crabtree Industries, Inc. 2015 West Race Street, Chicago, Illinois 60612 (312) 243-0898
Avant Garde treats antique wallpaper with a spray that fixes the color, helps retard fading, and gives brittle paper more body. Write for information.

A. L. Diament and Company P.O. Box 230, 309 Commerce Drive, Exton, Pennsylvania 19341 (215) 363-5660
This company offers antique wallpaper and reproductions. They are shown by appointment.

Rejuvenation House Parts 4543 North Albina Avenue, Portland, Oregon 97217 (503) 282-3019
This firm offers anaglypta and supaglypta Victorian wall coverings that have the appearance of heavily embossed paper. Supaglypta is of heavier weight than anaglypta. All patterns come in rolls of 33 feet by 20½ inches. Each roll covers 50 to 55 square feet. Hanging anaglypta is similar to hanging regular wallpaper. Directions are included with each roll. A catalogue is available for $2.00.

San Francisco Victoriana 2245 Palou Avenue, San Francisco, California 94124 (415) 648-0313
This firm offers antique embossed wallpaper borders. Choose from 8 patterns and sizes. These are made available from original rare papers actually manufactured in Germany between 1890 and 1915. The original colors have survived intact and were applied with the "airbrush" technique by European artists of the period. A descriptive price list is available.

Sanderson International P.O. Box 27, 2775 Broadway, Cheektowaga, Buffalo, New York 14240
Included in the selection of wallpapers from Sanderson International are both modern and traditional screen-printed foils and block-printed wallpapers, a collection of embossed papers, German wallpapers, and small-scale wall coverings from Italy.

The Twigs 44 Farnsworth Street, Boston, Massachusetts 02210 (617) 426-4069
This firm produces hand-screened fabrics and wallpapers, and a variety of fabrics and papers. Its primary interest is the production of documentary designs, primarily eighteenth- and nineteenth-century French and nineteenth-century Victorian patterns. Collections are available to professional interior designers, historical societies, museums, antiques dealers, and serious collectors.

Victorian Collectibles Ltd. W66 N394 Kennedy Avenue, Cedarburg, Wisconsin 53012 (414) 377-7608
This firm offers original nineteenth-century wallpapers, made between 1875 and 1925, known as the Brillion Collection. Send exact yardage requirements, style or period of interest, color preference, etc., and a $10.00 sampling fee, deductible from the first order. You will receive photos and a small strip of paper.

REPRODUCTIONS

Bradbury & Bradbury Wallpapers   P.O. Box 155, Benicia, California 94510   (707) 644-0724
This small hand-printing firm deals exclusively with the reproduction of Victorian wall coverings. They are available by mail order. Custom reproduction of wallpapers for historic homes, museums, and private clients is also offered. Send for a brochure and full-color samples.

85. WICKER AND RATTAN

Wicker and rattan baskets, furniture, and other objects should be kept away from direct heat and sunny windows. Any piece can be washed occasionally. Moisture will keep it from becoming dry and brittle. *See also* Chapter 17, Chairs and Chapter 30, Furniture—General.

PUBLICATION

American Indian Basketry Magazine   P.O. Box 66124, Portland, Oregon 97266   (503) 771-8540
This magazine is published irregularly, approximately 4 times a year.

BOOKS

Harvey, Virginia I. *The Techniques of Basketry.*
New York: Van Nostrand Reinhold, 1978.

Stephens, Cleo M. *Willow Spokes and Wickerwork.*
Harrisburg, Pennsylvania: Stackpole Books, 1975.

Stephenson, Sue H. *Basketry of the Appalachian Mountains.*
New York: Van Nostrand Reinhold, 1977.

Tod, Osma Gallinger, and Benson, Oscar H. *Weaving with Reeds and Fibers.*
New York: Dover Publications, 1975.

HOW-TO-FIX-IT BOOK

Saunders, Richard. *Collecting and Restoring Wicker Furniture.*
New York: Crown Publishers, 1976.

REPAIR SERVICES

W. B. Lewis   231 Chatham Avenue, Pooler, Georgia 31322   (912) 748-4094
W. B. Lewis does wicker and rattan restoration.

Wicker King   Jack and Julia Ann Jennings, 8241 Highway 70 South, Nashville, Tennessee 37221
(615) 646-3382
The Jennings are specialists in restoration of Victorian wicker furniture.

The Wicker Shop   Edward Roughton, 2011 Cleveland Road, Sandusky, Ohio 44870
(419) 626-6717
Mr. Roughton has a weaving shop where he repairs old rattan and willow furniture.

BUYING BY MAIL

Patchwork Sampler   9735 Clayton Road, St. Louis, Missouri 63124
The firm sells baskets. A catalogue is available. When writing for information, be sure to include a self-addressed, stamped envelope.

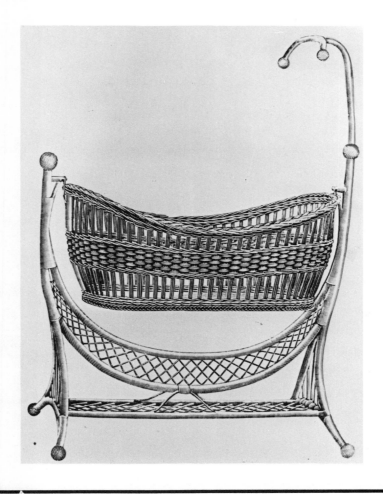

86. WORLD'S FAIRS AND EXPOSITIONS

World's fairs and expositions have created a wealth of collectibles. Items sold at the fairs, advertising materials, and even buildings from the fairs continue to interest the collector.

CLUBS

Expo Collectors & Historians Organization (ECHO)   1436 Killarney Avenue, Los Angeles, California 90065
Expo Info is a newsletter about old fairs.

World's Fair Collector's Society, Inc.   148 Poplar Street, Garden City, New York 11530
Fair News is a bimonthly newsletter with ads and articles.

PRICE GUIDE

Rossen, Howard M., and Kaduck, John M. *Columbian World's Fair Collectibles, Chicago (1892–1893)*. Des Moines: Wallace-Homestead, 1976. The 1982–1983 price guide is available from P.O. Box 02152, Cleveland, Ohio 44102.

87. WRITING UTENSILS

Pens, automatic pencils, ink bottles, inkwells, and many other devices connected with writing are being collected. Early pens and the plastic-cased pens of the 1920s through the 1950s have suddenly become of interest to collectors. The only problems with old pens are stiff or leaky ink sacs or dirty pen points. These can be fixed carefully at home if the proper parts are purchased.

CLUBS

American Pencil Collectors Society   603 East 105th Street, Kansas City, Missouri 64131 (816) 942-1466
The Pencil Collector is a monthly newsletter.

The Pen Fancier's Club   1169 Overcash Drive, Dunedin, Florida 33528
The Pen Fancier's Newsletter is a bimonthly newsletter containing articles on the history of pens, copies of old pen catalogues, club directory, and ads. Members contribute articles and send in questions and are allowed 5 ads per issue of the sell/swap/buy bulletin that is included.

The Society for the Collection of Brand-Name Pencils   603 East 105th Street, Kansas City, Missouri 64131   (816) 942-1466
The Branded Pencil is a monthly newsletter with about 4 mimeographed pages of articles, questions and answers, and news about members.

Society of Inkwell Collectors   5136 Thomas Avenue South, Minneapolis, Minnesota 55410 (612) 922-2792
The Stained Finger, a quarterly newsletter, contains articles on collections, restoration tips, news of events, and a few ads.

PUBLICATIONS

Fountain Pen Exchange   Hudson Valley Graphics, P.O. Box 64, Teaneck, New Jersey 07666 (201)592-9286
The *Fountain Pen Exchange* is a monthly newsletter with articles, repair tips, questions and answers, and ads.

The Typewriter Exchange: A Newsletter for the Writing Machine Collector   P.O. Box 150, 119 South First Avenue, Arcadia, California 91006   (213) 446-5000
This is a quarterly newsletter devoted to old typewriters and typewriter enthusiasts.

DECODING ADVERTISING COPY
Reading the ads for antiques and collectibles often takes special knowledge. Two collectors will speak a special language in the same way two doctors have a vocabulary known only to their profession. When looking up fountain pens it is helpful to know these terms and abbreviations.

GP. 14-karat gold point.	*L L.* Liquid lead.	*TF.* Twist fill.
GF. Gold filled.	*GB.* Gold band.	*LF.* Lever fill.

PARTS AND SUPPLIES
The Fountain Pen Exchange   P.O. Box 64, Teaneck, New Jersey 07666
Parts are available.

R. L. Pribble Company   P.O. Box 728, Hampton Bays, New York 11946
This company offers quill pens with hand-cut tips, as well as quills with ball-point pen tips. It also offers a calligrapher's and Fraktur artist's set, which includes fine-, medium-, and broad-tip quills plus uncut quills for you to cut.

REPAIR SERVICES
Authorized Repair Service   143 East 60th Street, New York, New York 10022   (212) 759-9765
Written estimates are given on all items sent for repair. Work is done only after the customer's approval is received. The company will make up missing parts if unobtainable and also will refinish old fountain pens for an additional charge if requested.

Fountain Pen Hospital   18 Vesey Street, New York, New York 10007
This firm does factory authorized repairs on all makes of fountain pens, desk sets, and pencils. Mail your pen to the pen hospital and it will send you a written estimate before proceeding with the work.

Good Service Pen Shop   1079 Forest Hills Drive S.W., Rochester, Minnesota 55901
(507) 281-1988
This shop maintains a supply of old fountain pen parts and can repair almost any fountain pen. Write for a free catalogue and further information or send your pen to be repaired.

The Pen Store   404 Zack Street, P.O. Box 2780, Tampa, Florida 33601   (813) 223-3865
The Pen Store repairs antique fountain pens and pencils. It collects, sells, and trades inkwells, ink bottles, old quills, and old samples of writing.

Jack H. Plunkett   1067 Latin Way, Los Angeles, California 90065   (213) 255-7641
Mr. Plunkett offers full service pen and pencil repair. Send the item to be repaired by mail or UPS for an estimate.

PRICE GUIDE
Schneider, Stuart L., and Etter, Roberta B. *Collecting and Valuing Early Fountain Pens.*
Teaneck, New Jersey: Hudson Valley Graphics (P.O. Box 64, Teaneck, New Jersey 07666), 1980.

HOW-TO-FIX-IT BOOK
Lawrence, Cliff. *Fountain Pens: History, Repair, Current Values.*
Paducah, Kentucky: Collector Books, 1977.

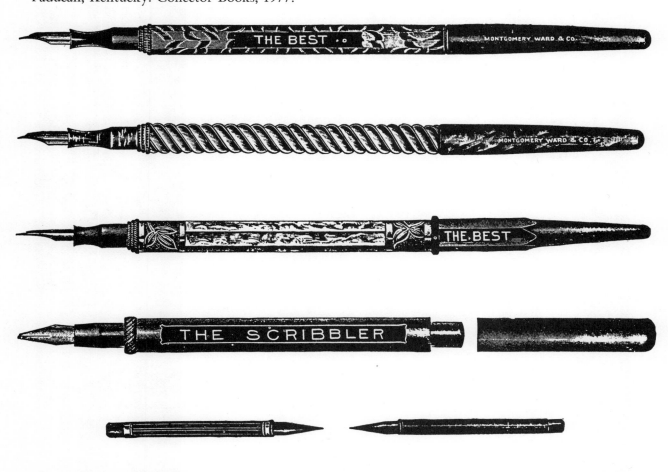

PART II

GENERAL INFORMATION AND SOURCE LISTS

We have made every effort to be complete and accurate in our sources and their addresses. Some sources might not have been included and some addresses might have changed. We will be pleased to make the necessary corrections in any future editions.

88. APPRAISAL INFORMATION

Antique appraising is a specialized field that requires years of experience. There are appraisers listed in the Yellow Pages of the telephone book under "Antiques" or "Appraisal." Be sure that the person you hire is qualified in the field of expertise needed. An appraiser of household goods is not qualified to suggest values for antique silver or rare bottles. Oriental art, guns, jewelry, and many other areas of collecting require specialists. If you cannot find a local person who is qualified, try contacting a major collectors' group in the field. A member may be more familiar with the appropriate prices than a professional appraiser.

When getting an appraisal, you must always be clear about the fee that is to be charged and the form the appraisal should take. A verbal estimate for heirs of an estate who wish to divide household items is far less time consuming and expensive than a written, documented appraisal that may be used with an income tax return. Check to see if the appraiser you hire is a member of a recognized appraisers group. The national groups are listed here. Each has a listing of appraisers and can tell you if there is a member in your area. An appraiser should not offer to buy. It is a conflict of interest for a dealer to buy an item after appraising it. Most organizations feel that it is unethical to appraise for a percentage fee. It should be an hourly rate to avoid influencing decisions.

Specialized appraisers are listed here or in the appropriate chapters in Part I.

NATIONAL APPRAISAL ASSOCIATIONS

American Society of Appraisers (ASA)   Dulles International Airport, P.O. Box 17625, Washington, D.C. 20041   (703) 620-3838

Antique Appraisal Association of America   11361 Garden Grove Blvd., Garden Grove, California 92643 (714) 530-7090

Appraisers Association of America   60 East 42nd Street, New York, New York 10017 (212) 867-9775

International Society of Appraisers   P.O. Box 726, Hoffman Estates, Illinois 60195 (312) 885-2480 or 882-0706   The society requires 5 years experience to be a member.

International Society of Fine Arts Appraisers Ltd.   P.O. Box 280, River Forest, Illinois 60305

Mid-Am Antique Appraisers Association   P.O. Box 981 C.S.S., Springfield, Missouri 65803

New England Appraisers Association   104 Charles Street, Boston, Massachusetts 02114
(617) 523-6272

Registered Appraisers of Florida, Inc.   P.O. Box 15797, Sarasota, Florida 33579
An appraiser must work in Florida to qualify.

Most of the larger auction houses also do appraisals. Some galleries charge by the day, with rates varying from $250.00 to $1,500.00 per day. Some charge by the hour (usually $50.00 to $100.00 per hour) with a set minimum. Others charge a percentage of the total appraised value, usually 1 percent or 1½ percent with a set minimum. Most will give free verbal estimates on objects brought in to their offices. You can also send photographs and get some information by mail, although these appraisals are not valid for insurance or estate purposes. Listed below are some of the larger auction houses that offer appraisals. For more information, see Chapter 89, Auction Houses. You can also contact local auction galleries and dealers to see if they do appraisals.

The addresses and phone numbers for the following auction houses can be found in Chapter 89.

Richard A. Bourne Company, Inc. Fee per day.
Butterfield & Butterfield. Percent of total appraised value.
Christie's. Fee per day.
William Doyle Galleries, Inc. No set rates available; depends on size of estate and time involved.
DuMouchelle Art Galleries Company. Fee per hour.
Robert C. Eldred Company, Inc. Percent of total appraised value.
Samuel T. Freeman and Company. Fee per day.
Garth's Auctions, Inc. Fee per hour.
Milwaukee Auction Gallery. Fee per hour.
Morton's Auction Exchange, Inc. No set rates available.
Phillips. Fee per hour for estates; percent of total value for insurance appraisals.
Robert W. Skinner Gallery. Fee per hour.
C. G. Sloan's and Company, Inc. Fee per hour.
Sotheby's. Fees vary according to size of estate and travel involved.
Adam A. Weschler & Son. Fee per hour.

89. AUCTION HOUSES

Almost every large city has an auction house that sells antiques and household goods. In smaller cities and towns, auctions are held in local barns, houses, or on the premises of a liquidated house or farm.

These local auction houses are listed in the Yellow Pages of the telephone book under "Auctioneers." Some auction galleries offer their catalogues nationally. Subscribers to the catalogue (or anyone else who wishes) can, with proper credit information, bid for any antique either in person or by telephone or mail. Telephone or mail bids are executed by the gallery at the sale.

A helpful book about auctions is *The Auction Companion* by Katharine Kyes and Daniel J. Leab (New York: Harper & Row, 1981).

We have listed only the auction houses that advertise nationally and send out catalogues. There are many, many others.

ABCD Auction Gallery   1 North Clarendon Road, Avondale Estates, Georgia 30002 (404) 294-8264

Auction Center, Kenneth S. Hays & Associates, Inc.   4740 Bardstown Road, Louisville, Kentucky 40218   (502) 499-8942

Richard A. Bourne Company, Inc.   Corporation Street, Hyannis, Massachusetts 02647 (617) 775-0797

Bowers & Ruddy Galleries, Inc. (coins)   6922 Hollywood Boulevard, Suite 600, Los Angeles, California 90028   (213) 466-4595

Butterfield & Butterfield   1244 Sutter Street, San Francisco, California 94109   (415) 673-1362

C. B. Charles Galleries   825 Woodward Avenue, Pontiac, Michigan 48053   (313) 338-9203

Christie's   502 Park Avenue, New York, New York 10022   (212) 546-1000

Douglas Galleries   Routes 5 and 10, South Deerfield, Massachusetts 01373   (413) 665-2877

William Doyle Galleries, Inc.   175 East 87th Street, New York, New York 10028 (212) 427-2730

DuMouchelle Art Galleries Company   409 East Jefferson Avenue, Detroit, Michigan 48226 (313) 963-6255

Early's Antiques & Auction Company   123 Main Street, Milford, Ohio 45150   (513) 831-4833

Robert C. Eldred, Company, Inc.   P.O. Box 796, East Dennis, Massachusetts 02641 (617) 385-3116

Samuel T. Freeman and Company   1808 Chestnut, Philadelphia, Pennsylvania 19103 (215) 563-9275

Kenneth R. French & Company, Inc.   Kenneth French, Auctioneer, 166 Bedford Road, Armonk, New York 10504   (914) 273-3674

Garth's Auctions, Inc.   2690 Stratford Road, Delaware, Ohio 43015   (614) 362-4771

O. Rundle Gilbert   Route 9D, Garrison, New York 10524   (914) 424-3657

Hanzel Galleries, Inc.   1120 South Michigan Avenue, Chicago, Illinois 60605   (312) 922-6234

James D. Julia   Route 201, Skowhegan Road, Fairfield, Maine 04937   (207) 453-9725

Kruse Auction (cars)   Kruse Building, 300 South Union, Auburn, Indiana 46706   (219) 925-4004

Manor House Galleries   8570 Katy Freeway, Houston, Texas 77024   (713) 468-7267

Mid Hudson Galleries   1 Idlewild Avenue, Cornwall-on-Hudson, New York 12520
(914) 534-7828

Milwaukee Auction Gallery   4747 West Bradley, Milwaukee, Wisconsin 53223   (414) 355-5054

Morton's Auction Exchange, Inc.   701 Magazine Street, P.O. Box 30380, New Orleans, Louisiana
70190   (504) 561-1196

Pennypacker Auction Centre   1540 New Holland Road, Kenhorst, Reading, Pennsylvania 19607
(215) 777-6121

Phillips   406 East 79th Street, New York, New York 10021   (212) 570-4830

Bob, Chuck & Rich Roan, Inc.   R.D. 2, Cogan Station, Pennsylvania 17728
(717) 494-0170

Frank Roan, III, Auctioneer   P.O. Box 112, McEwensville, Pennsylvania 17749   (717) 538-9825

Robert W. Skinner Gallery   Route 117, Bolton, Massachusetts 10740   (617) 779-5528

C. G. Sloan & Company, Inc.   715 13th Street, N.W., Washington, D.C. 20005   (202) 628-1468

Sotheby's New York   1334 York Avenue, New York, New York 10021   (212) 472-3400

Stalker & Boos, Inc.   280 North Woodward Avenue, Birmingham, Michigan 48011
(313) 646-4560

Trosby Auction Gallery, Inc.   81 Peachtree Park Drive N.E., Atlanta, Georgia 30309
(404) 351-4400

Adam A. Weschler & Son 905 E Street N.W., Washington, D.C. 20004 (202) 628-1281

Wilson Galleries P.O. Box 102, Fort Defiance, Virginia 24437 (703) 885-4292

Woody Auction Company P.O. Box 618, Douglass, Kansas 67039 (316) 746-2694

90. AUCTIONS BY MAIL

Some auctions are known as mail-order auctions and bids can be made only by letter or phone calls. There is no auction room, no preview, just an illustrated catalogue or list. The catalogue states the date of the auction and bids are accepted until a specified cutoff date. The highest bidder gets the item. Bids are used like actual bids from an audience. Thus, if you bid $500.00 and the bid below you is only $300.00, most of the mail order auctions will sell you the item for $350.00, or $310.00, or whatever was the logical raise for the item.

If you plan to bid by mail, be sure to check on the exact rules for the sale. Some require an advance deposit; all of them require some sort of credit reference. If the condition of the item is not as you expected from the description, most reputable auction houses will accept returns and refund your money. Be careful with mail order. Size can be confusing, so read the descriptions carefully.

Aiglatson P.O. Box 3173, Saxonville Station, Framingham, Massachusetts 01701
Phone bids are not accepted. It auctions gum and other cards; Big Little books; buttons and pins; Cracker Jack prizes; Disneyana; old advertising; radio, TV, cereal, and other premiums; and other items. A free catalogue is published 2 or 3 times a year.

Americana Art Auctions C. E. Guarino, P.O. Box 49, Berry Road, Denmark, Maine 04022 (617) 452-2123
Americana, old prints, maps, etc. are offered.

Americana Collectibles Antiques 702 North Wells, Chicago, Illinois 60610 (312) 787-8027
Political, advertising, cause, and other buttons; radio premiums, and other small collectibles are available.

Anderson Auction Al Anderson, P.O. Box 644, Troy, Ohio 45373 (513) 339-0850
Campaign buttons, political items, and advertising items are available.

Antique Postcard Auction   Mary L. Martin, 231 Rock Ridge Road, Millersville, Maryland 21108   (301) 647-7975 or 647-7976
Want lists are filled. A postcard rarity auction is published every December and a catalogue is published bimonthly: $8.00 annually, $1.50 a single copy.

Auction Americana   P.O. Box 18282, Wichita, Kansas 67218
Political memorabilia, advertising, and Americana are available.

Banjo Dan's Old Sheet Music Auction   50 Grove Street, Apt. 3, New York, New York 10014 (212) 989-6248
Banjo Dan has a vast library and can search for specific items. Active bidders receive a free catalogue 6 to 10 times a year.

Dave and Shirley Beck   P.O. Box 435, Mediapolis, Iowa 52637   (319) 394-3943
An illustrated general catalogue is issued 5 times a year (total of $4.00). Single copies can also be purchased ($1.00 each).

Carolina Collector's Corner, Inc.   Route 2, P.O. Box 378, Fairfax, South Carolina 29827 (803) 632-3406
Carolina Collector's Corner auctions Hummels.

Sally S. Carver   179 South Street, Chestnut Hill, Massachusetts 02167   (617) 469-9175
Sally Carver auctions postcards by mail.

H. W. Cole Enterprises   P.O. Box 201, Woodburn, Oregon 97071   (503) 981-7337
H. W. Cole specializes in sheet music.

Collectors Americana Mail Auction   10 Lillian Road Extension, Framingham, Massachusetts 01701   (617) 872-2229
General and specialized auctions are offered.

The Fox Hole   Ron Manion, Department CN, P.O. Box 9121, Kansas City, Kansas 66109 (913) 299-6692
The Fox Hole offers military relics.

Hake's Americana & Collectibles   P.O. Box 1444, York, Pennsylvania 17405   (717) 843-3731
Political items, radio premiums, and old advertising are auctioned.

Historicana   1632 Robert Road, Lancaster, Pennsylvania 17601   (717) 291-1037 or 291-1038
Historicana auctions political items, nostalgia, and other collectibles.

Iris' Postcard Auction   P.O. Box 368, Rockport, Maine 04856
Postcards are auctioned by mail.

George H. LaBarre Galleries, Inc.   P.O. Box 27, Hudson, New Hampshire 03051   (603) 882-2411
LaBarre Galleries specializes in stocks and bonds. An investment newsletter and a catalogue are available free.

Lazy Day Galleries   26 East Mount Pleasant Avenue, Livingston, New Jersey 07039
Lazy Day Galleries auctions books.

Nancy Levin   3 Sycamore Drive, Great Neck, New York 11021
Movie memorabilia, collectibles, and other items are auctioned.

Lufkin's   P.O. Box 26722, Austin, Texas 77855   (512) 345-9729
Lufkin's mail auctions Hummel items, porcelains, and collector plates. A catalogue is published quarterly that is free to bidders; subscription is $4.00 a year.

M-C Associates Mail Auctions   11910 Lafayette Drive, Silver Spring, Maryland 20902
Historic newspapers, prints, advertising, civil war books, etc. are offered.

Joel L. Malter & Company, Inc.   P.O. Box 777, Encino, California 91316   (213) 784-7772
Coins and ancient art are available.

Joel Markowitz   P.O. Box 367, Port Washington, New York 11050
Mr. Markowitz offers piano rolls.

Midwest Paper Dolls & Toys Quarterly   P.O. Box 131, Galesburg, Kansas 66740
(316) 763-2247 or 336-2491
This quarterly catalogue is $2.00 a single copy, $7.00 per year.

Musical Notes   12 Grafton Street, Greenlawn, New York 11740   (516) 261-2636
Sheet music and music rolls are auctioned. The firm will take music on consignment. Catalogues are published approximately 6 times a year. Send a self-addressed, stamped envelope.

The Nostalgia Company   21 South Lake Drive, Hackensack, New Jersey 07601   (201) 488-4536
The Nostalgia Company offers Coca-Cola collectibles.

Paper Americana Auction   736 North Frazier Street, Baldwin Park, California 91706
This firm has mail auctions of old checks, stocks, letters, magazines, posters, and other paper items.

Pennington's   17104 Hidalgo Drive, Perris, California 92370
Pennington's auctions a wide variety of collectibles.

Recorded Treasures   P.O. Box 5872, Buena Park, California 90622
Music oriented antiques are auctioned.

Rinslands Americana Mail Auction   Box 265, Zionsville, Pennsylvania 18092   (215) 966-5544 or (215) 966-3939
A variety of collectibles is auctioned, including autographs, books, buttons, posters, etc.

Mike and Fred Schwimmer   241 Harbor, Glencoe, Illinois 60022
Mike and Fred Schwimmer offer old piano rolls.

Vi and Si's Antiques   8970 Main Street, Clarence, New York 14031   (716) 634-4488
Vi and Si auction items relating to mechanical music.

World Exonumia   Rich Hartzog, POB 4143PG, Rockford, Illinois 61110
World Exonumia Mail Bid Sales offers sales of tokens, medals, badges, buttons, ribbons, and related items. A catalogue is available by subscription. A free buying list giving prices paid for various tokens and medals is also available. Leaflets on exonumia are free; a stamp is appreciated. Sales concentrate on pre-1940 material.

91. BOOKSELLERS

When researching antiques or trying to learn more about a book, the obvious place to start looking is your local library. Talk to the librarian, learn to use the card catalogue, the indexes, and the inter-library loan systems. If you decide that you want to buy a book, first try your local bookstore. If it is not in stock, ask your bookseller to order it for you. If you are unsuccessful there, write to one or two of the following booksellers.

   We have organized this section into three parts: Sellers of in-print books on antiques, sellers of out-of-print books on antiques, and auctions of out-of-print books. Ask your library if the book you are looking for is in print or out of print. All of the following booksellers sell through the mail. Also, check for specialized booksellers under the specific collectibles chapters in Part I.

   There are many other booksellers. We have listed those that we found through national ads.

SELLERS OF IN-PRINT BOOKS ON ANTIQUES

American Antiques & Crafts Society   Fame Avenue, Hanover, Pennsylvania 17331
The society has a general selection.

American Association for State and Local History   708 Berry Road, Nashville, Tennessee 37204 (615) 383-5991
The association sells their own series of technical books and leaflets.

American Reprints Company   111 West Dent, Ironton, Missouri 63650
This company sells only its own titles.

Antique Collectors' Club 5 Church Street, Clopton, Woodbridge, Suffolk 1 P12 1 BR, England
The club sells only its own titles. Many are price books.

Antique Publications Emmitsburg, Maryland 21727
General books are available.

Apollo Books 391 South Road, Poughkeepsie, New York 12601
Books about art and antiques, new and out of print, are offered.

ARS Libri Ltd. 286 Summer Street, Boston, Massachusetts 02210 (617) 357-5212
Books about art, architecture, painting, sculpture, photography, etc. are offered. A catalogue is available.

Barra Books Ltd. 819 Madison Avenue, New York, New York 10021
This is a general bookseller.

Barron's Art Series 113 Crossways Park Drive, Woodbury, New York 11797
Books on fine arts are available.

Bethlehem Book Company 249 East Street, Bethlehem, Connecticut 06751
General books are available.

Books for Antique Collectors 4656 Virginia, St. Louis, Missouri 63111 (314) 752-3286
Reprints of books about antiques are carried.

The Book Nook P.O. Box 305, Cornwall-on-Hudson, New York 12520
Books on antiques, both new and out-of-print references, are sold.

Collector Books P.O. Box 3009, Paducah, Kentucky 42001
General books are available, many published by Collector Books.

Collector's Shelf of Books 23 Crandall Street (P.O. Box 6), Westfield, New York 14787
General books are available.

Dover Publications 180 Varick Street, New York, New York 10014
This publisher sells only its own titles.

Edmonds Book Sales P.O. Box 143, Ledbetter, Kentucky 42058 (502) 898-6716
A free book list is available for one long self-addressed, stamped envelope.

EPCO Publishing Company 62-19 Cooper Avenue, Glendale, New York 11385
Books on collecting are sold.

Gazette Books   P.O. Box 1011, Kermit, Texas 79745   (915) 586-2571
A selection of books about antiques are offered.

Heritage Books, Inc.   3602 Maureen, Suite 117, Bowie, Maryland 20715
Old and new books on history and genealogy are sold.

Hotchkiss House   18 Hearthstone, Pittsford, New York 14534
A general selection of books about antiques, especially bottles and glass, is available.

Jo-D Books   81 Willard Terrace, Stamford, Connecticut 06903   (203) 322-0568
Book lists are available.

Jonesport Wood Company, Inc.   P.O. Box 295, Jonesport, Maine 04649   (207) 497-2322
A yearly catalogue is available for $3.00. Lists are issued periodically.

Lamplighter Books   Leon, Iowa 50144
A general selection of books about antiques is available.

Lloyd Imig Bird Books   310 Maria Drive, Wausau, Wisconsin 54401   (715) 845-5101
Collector books on birds and natural history are sold through a quarterly mail order catalogue.

Mantelpiece Reflections   1059 Douglas Drive, Wooster, Ohio 44691   (216) 262-3103
This firm sells books on antiques and collectibles. A catalogue is available.

Olana Gallery   Drawer 9, Brewster, New York 10509   (914) 279-8077
Art and artists are the main subjects of books available.

Preservation Shop, National Trust for Historic Preservation   1600 H Street, N.W., Washington, D.C. 20006
Books and pamphlets of interest to the architectural preservationist are available.

PRG   5619 Southampton Drive, Springfield, Virginia 22151
PRG distributes books for the Preservation Resource Group, Inc. It also stocks the preservation briefs prepared by the Technical Preservation Services and the technical leaflets published by the American Association for State and Local History. A brochure is available.

Publishers Central Bureau   1 Champion Avenue, Department 526, Avenel, New Jersey 07131
This firm has a mail order discount catalogue listing many antiques books.

The Reference Rack   P.O. Box 445, Orefield, Pennsylvania 18069   (215) 395-0004
Books on antiques and collectibles are offered.

Riverow Bookshop   204 Front Street, Owego, New York 13827
Books, trade catalogues, and travel guides are available.

Rizzoli International Publications, Inc.   712 Fifth Avenue, New York, New York 10012
A general line of books is available. Many expensive art books can be found in stock here.

Schiffer Publishing Ltd.   P.O. Box E, Exton, Pennsylvania 19341   (215) 363-6889
Schiffer published books are sold.

Seven Hills Books   4620 Spring Grove Avenue, Cincinnati, Ohio 45232   (513) 591-1687
Books on art and antiques are offered. A catalogue is available.

The Shaker Museum   Old Chatham, New York 12136
Books about Shakers and related subjects are sold.

Sieber's   Trexler Road, R.D. #2, Breinigsville, Pennsylvania 18031

Sotheby Parke Bernet Publications   81 Adams Drive, Totowa, New Jersey 17512
Sotheby's sells only its own titles.

Walter J. Sumner   P.O. Box 199, Mentone, Alabama 35984
Mr. Sumner offers old catalogue reprints.

Superintendent of Documents   U.S. Government Printing Office, Washington, D.C. 20402
Government leaflets are sold.

Timothy Trace, Antiquarian Bookseller   Red Mill Road, Peekskill, New York 10566
(914) 528-4074
Timothy Trace specializes in recent and current books on the decorative arts: pottery, porcelain, furniture, glass, silver and other metal objects, American arts and crafts, jewelry, dolls, etc. Antiquarian material on these subjects as early as the sixteenth century is often available. An appointment is advised and inquiries are invited.

Turn of the Century Editions   6 Varick Street, New York, New York 10013   (212) 925-6592
This firm offers facsimile reprints of original catalogues for Mission-style furniture.

Wallace-Homestead Book Company   1912 Grand Avenue, Des Moines, Iowa 50305
This publisher sells its own titles.

Wolf's Head Books   P.O. Box 1048, 198 Foundry Street, Morgantown, West Virginia 26505
(304) 296-0706
Free catalogues are issued periodically.

SELLERS OF OUT-OF-PRINT BOOKS ON ANTIQUES

There are many local out-of-print book dealers listed in the Yellow Pages under Book Dealers—Used & Rare. Some cities have antiquarian book shows. Many dealers who sell out-of-print books sell by mail. Look in the specialized publications for their ads. If you can't find them there, you can place an ad yourself for the books that interest you. We have listed some dealers who advertise nationally.

A Points Northe   3630 N.W. 22nd Street, Oklahoma City, Oklahoma 73107   (405) 949-0675, 9:00 A.M. to noon
This firm sells out-of-print books and magazines. It will locate and quote you the condition and price. There is no obligation until the book is ordered. Mail and telephone service only.

Antiquarian Booksellers Association of America, Inc.   50 Rockefeller Plaza, New York, New York 10020   (212) 757-9395
The ABAA publishes a membership directory which lists antiquarian booksellers geographically, alphabetically, and by specialty. You can get a copy of the directory by sending a stamped, self-addressed #10 envelope with 54¢ postage affixed to the envelope.

The Antiquarian Scientist   P.O. Box 602, Amesbury, Massachusetts 01913   (617) 388-2314
The Antiquarian Scientist specializes in rare books on science, medicine, and technology. A catalogue is available, $5.00 for a single issue, $9.00 per year (2 issues).

Antiques Research Publications   Route 1, P.O. Box 199, Mentone, Alabama 35984
This is a source for out-of-print publications.

Fredrick W. Armstrong, Bookseller   319 North McIlhaney, Stephenville, Texas 76401
(817) 965-7128
Mr. Armstrong offers a search service for any book requested. There is no charge. Send the title and name of the author, if available, as well as edition, publisher, or binding if desired. He specializes in books relating to the Civil War and western Americana. You may see the selection by calling for an appointment.

ARS Libri Ltd.   711 Boylston Street, Boston, Massachusetts 02116   (617) 536-3264
This firm sells books on art and architecture.

Jack Bailes Books Free Search Service   P.O. Box 150, Eureka Springs, Arkansas 72632
(501) 253-9131
This is a free search service with no obligation to buy. It specializes in Harrison Fisher, Coles Phillips, Maud Humphrey, Maxfield Parrish, calendars, and prints.

Bazaar Books   P.O. Box 496, Chico, California 95927
This is a free search service for out-of-print and antiquarian books. Write for further information.

Book Buyer's Guide   P.O. Box 208, East Millstone, New Jersey 08873   (201) 873-2156

The Book Exchange   90 West Market Street, Corning, New York 14830   (607) 936-8536
The Book Exchange specializes in books about glass. It offers a search service for out-of-print books on glass as well as other books. Send title, author, and as much information as possible about the specific company or process of glass production. Catalogues are issued 2 or 3 times a year.

The Book Nook   P.O. Box 305, Cornwall On The Hudson, New York 12520
The Book Nook sells books on antiques, both new as well as out-of-print references.

Books-on-File   P.O. Box 195, Union City, New Jersey 07087
This firm offers a search service for out-of-print titles. Send the name of the author and any other special information such as special edition, publisher, date, etc., to the above address.

The Bookseller, Inc.   521 West Exchange Street, Akron, Ohio 44302   (216) 762-3101
Antiquarian books and magazines are offered.

Caravan Book Store   550 South Grand Avenue, Los Angeles, California 90017   (213) 626-9944
This store buys and sells old and new books, rare books from the sixteenth through the nineteenth centuries, fine bindings, manuscripts, illuminations, maps, and prints. There is a special emphasis on material about California and the West, American Indians, railroads, early aviation, old cookery books, ships and the sea, Americana, children's books, limited editions, and books on antiques and collecting. There is no catalogue.

Collectors Books   14 Brook Bridge Road, Great Neck, New York 11021
A general line of out-of-print books is sold.

Colonial "Out-of-Print" Book Service   P.O. Box 451, Pleasantville, New York 10570
This service is mail order only. All out-of-print books, except foreign language, can be found. There is no service charge and no obligation.

Fantasy Archives   71 Eighth Avenue, New York, New York 10014
This firm carries out-of-print and fine first editions in fantasy and science fiction of the nineteenth and twentieth centuries. Early pulps and original artwork by well-known illustrators of the field are also available. Send a want list and it will quote prices. This is a worldwide search service with no charge. Sales are by mail order and visits are by appointment. Catalogues are issued regularly.

Franklin Publishing Company   P.O. Box 208, East Millstone, New Jersey 08873
This company sells out-of-print books.

Doris Frohnsdorff   P.O. Box 2306, Gaithersburg, Maryland 20879   (301) 869-1256
This is a source for out-of-print books.

Gilded Age Press   Drawer 4, Washington Mills, New York 13479
Out-of-print books are available.

Hillcrest Books   Route 2, P.O. Box 162, Spring City, Tennessee 37381
The *Catalog of Old Catalogs* is actually a list of old catalogues for sale by mail. There is a charge for it, but customers who order old catalogues are sent future lists free.

Hobby House Books   P.O. Box 692-X, Lewiston, Maine 04240
A general line of out-of-print books is available.

Hoffman Research Services   P.O. Box 342, Rillton, Pennyslvania 15678   (412) 863-2367
This is a worldwide book search service. The fee is $3.00 per title, nonrefundable if the book cannot be located. The customer is not obligated to buy the book found if he or she feels the price is too high. A large stock of books are on hand. Satisfaction is guaranteed.

Jean's Books and Folk Art   P.O. Box 264, Hatfield, Pennsylvania 19440
This is an international, rare, and out-of-print book search service. Cost is $2.00 per title. Write for further information.

Lloyd Imig Bird Books   310 Maria Drive, Wausau, Wisconsin 54401   (715) 845-5101
Collector books on birds and natural history are sold through a quarterly mail order catalogue.

Phyllis M. Lumb, Bibliophyl   11725 Larry Road, Fairfax, Virginia 22030
Phyllis Lumb specializes in out-of-print and used books. Send a want list for free search service.

M & S Rare Books, Inc.   45 Colpitts Road, P.O. Box 311, Weston, Massachusetts 02193
(617) 891-5650
This firm's specialties are rare American eighteenth- and nineteenth-century books, pamphlets, and broadsides and European science, philosophy, and economics works. Hours are by appointment. A catalogue is available.

McLaughlin's Books   P.O. Box 3083, Chico, California 95927
This is a free search service for out-of-print books. Send the title, author, and any other information that would help in the search. After the book is located, the service will describe the book including condition and price, postpaid. The book will be sent after payment is received. A general catalogue is offered about twice a year.

Ohio Bookhunters   564 East Townview Circle, Mansfield, Ohio 44907   (419) 756-0655
This firm specializes in Ohio-related material. A catalogue is available.

Olana Gallery   Drawer 9, Brewster, New York 10509   (914) 279-8077
Books are sold by mail. The gallery is open by appointment only. Out-of-print and rare books, new books, catalogues, and reprints devoted to American art are available. Send for a catalogue.

Princeton Antiques Bookservice   2915-17 Atlantic Avenue, Atlantic City, New Jersey 08401 (609) 344-1943

This is a search service. Send the name of the author and the title or subject. If you wish a specific edition, include date, edition, and publisher. There is no fee for the search. You can phone in your request any day (but Sunday) from 10:00 A.M. to 4:00 P.M. EST. Visits by appointment. A brochure is available.

Ron-Dot Bookfinders   4700 Massillon Road, Route 241, Greensburg, Ohio 44232 (216) 896-3482

This is a free search service. There are 30,000 books in stock. Send the title, author, subject, or illustrator wanted. The service will notify you when the work is found as well as its condition and price. Minimum search time is 4 to 5 weeks, but some hard-to-find books take months. Customer wants are kept on file.

Ned J. Rube   68 Marion Drive, New Rochelle, New York 10804

Mr. Rube offers out-of-print books.

Robert Shuhi, Books   R.D. 1, P.O. Box 395, Route 63, Morris, Connecticut 06763 (203) 567-5231

This firm has a used book catalogue.

R.W. Smith, Bookseller   51 Trumbull Street, New Haven, Connecticut 06510   (203) 776-5564

Mr. Smith specializes in books about American art. He has hard-to-find, mostly out-of-print books and exhibition catalogues on American artists, decorative arts, architecture and photographic litera-ture, as well as books on nineteenth-century European painting. His specialty is art reference. Cata-logues on various topics in American art are available; send $2.00 for a sample copy or $7.50 for 6 issues.

R. Sorsky, Bookseller   3845 North Blackstone, Fresno, California 93726

R. Sorsky offers new and out-of-print books on woodworking exclusively. Catalogues are available for $1.50.

Timothy Trace, Antiquarian Bookseller   Red Mill Road, Peekskill, New York 10566 (914) 528-4074

Timothy Trace specializes in recent and current books on the decorative arts: pottery, porcelain, furniture, glass, silver, and other metal objects and American arts and crafts, jewelry, dolls, etc. Antiquarian material on these subjects as early as the sixteenth century is often available. An appoint-ment is advised and inquiries are invited.

Sam Yudkin & Associates Booksellers, Book & Print Auctions   1125 King Street, Alexandria, Virginia 22314   (703) 549-9330

This is a general bookstore. There are used books in stock in most categories. It specializes in monthly book and print auctions. Out-of-print book searches and appraisals are also offered. Book lists are available for $1.00.

OUT-OF-PRINT BOOKS SOLD AT AUCTION

Books can be sold at any general auction. There are many book auctions other than those listed here. We have listed those that advertise nationally.

California Book Auction Galleries, Inc.   358 Golden Gate Avenue, San Francisco, California 94102   (415) 775-0424
Monthly catalogues and post-sale price lists are available. Catalogue subscriptions are $35.00 per year; price lists, $15.00.

Fortunate Finds Bookstore   16 West Natick Road, Warwick, Rhode Island 02886
(401) 737-8160
This is a book auction, in person or by mail. The book auction catalogue is $3.50 and prices realized are available for $1.00. There are free catalogues for children's books and natural history trade catalogues, and specified lists of interest to collectors and dealers.

Plandome Book Auctions   113 Glen Head Road, Glen Head, New York 11545   (516) 671-3209
Auctions include rare books and literary property. Mail and telephone bids are accepted. Catalogues are available by subscription, 10 per season.

Swann Galleries, Inc.   104 East 25th Street, New York, New York 10010   (212) 254-4710
Auction sales are conducted weekly from September through June, with occasional summer sales. There are approximately 40 sales per year. Catalogues are sent 3 to 4 weeks prior to sale. Swann specializes in rare book auctions. Catalogue subscriptions are $65.00 per year for catalogues only, $75.00 with price lists.

Waverly Auctions   c/o Quill & Brush, 7649 Old Georgetown Road, Bethesda, Maryland 20014
(717) 951-0920
Waverly runs fine book and paper auctions. Detailed catalogues are issued 4 times a year and cost $10.00 with prices realized. Single copies are available for $2.75.

Sam Yudkin & Associates Booksellers, Book & Print Auctions   1125 King Street, Alexandria, Virginia 22314   (703) 549-9330
Monthly public and mail order book and print auctions are held on the premises. Items accepted for auction include almost any paper items plus small collectibles including books, prints, maps, postcards, ephemera, stamps, etc. Catalogue subscriptions are $15.00 per year, $25.00 with prices realized. Single copies are available for $2.50.

92. BUYING BY MAIL

There is no need to leave home to buy antiques and collectibles—you can order by mail! There are dozens of mail order catalogues that list items and prices. Also some of the general mail order gift catalogues sell antiques by mail. Because there are such strict laws about defrauding through the mails, most of these transactions work out to everyone's satisfaction. Most catalogues offer return privileges if there is a reasonable objection to an item. There can be unhappy incidents because of misunderstandings, so exercise caution when buying by mail.

There are hundreds of dealers who sell by mail. This is a list of some of those who advertise in the national antiques publications.

The following catalogues sell only antiques; they do not deal in reproductions.

The American Scout Museum   9 River Oaks Center, River Road, Route 2, Gatlinburg, Tennessee 37738

Antique & Curio Catalogue   93 Whitmore Road, Nottingham NG6 OHJ, England

Antique Search, Inc.   P.O. Box 724, Cooperstown, New York 13326   (315) 858-0315
This is a new organization bringing together individuals or organizations who wish to buy or sell antiques and works of art. An illustrated catalogue is sent to members each month showing items advertised for sale and listing items sought by members. The organization forwards inquiries to the advertiser.

Scott Arden's Railroad Dispatch   20457 Highway 126, Noti, Oregon 97461   (503) 935-1619
Monthly lists of railroad memorabilia are available.

Berkeley-Lainson   Brown Palace Hotel, Denver, Colorado 80202   (303) 893-3224
A yearly catalogue is published and is available for $3.00. Art Deco is a specialty.

N. Bloom & Son Ltd.   40/41 Conduit Street, London W1 England
Jewelry and silver are featured in this color illustrated catalog.

The Caledonian   P.O. Box 793, 22 Court Street, Sussex, New Brunswick EOE 1PO Canada
An illustrated catalogue of books and ephemera is published twice a month. The cost of a subscription is $12.00, but a free sample copy may be obtained by writing the company.

Christopher Sykes Antiques   11 Market Place, Woburn, Milton Keynes Bedfordshire MK17 9PZ England
Illustrated catalogues on pottery and porcelain; tavern signs; metalware, scientific collectibles; dolls; oil paintings and watercolors; wooden articles; furniture; glass, bronzes, and silver are offered.

Collectors Gallery   P.O. Box 24126, Columbus, Ohio 43224   (614) 267-5390

Collectors Treasures Ltd.   Hogarth House, High Street, Wendover, Bucks HP22 6DU England
Maps, prints, and Oriental art are offered.

Consolidated Artists   1848 North Oakland Avenue, Milwaukee, Wisconsin 53202
What's Next? The Age of Atomic Art is a catalogue about twentieth century, Art Deco, etc.

Coup's Collectibles   1632 Robert Road, Lancaster, Pennsylvania 17601   (717) 393-4977

Criswell's Fort McCoy, Florida 32637
This mail order business sells paper Americana: currency, bonds, stocks, documents, song sheets, souvenir sheets, books, checks, railroadiana, paper memorabilia, etc. A catalogue is issued once a year.

Distinctive Documents P.O. Box 1523, Cedar City, Utah 84720 (801) 586-2682
Old stocks, bonds, and other historical paper Americana are offered for framing, collecting, and investing. A catalogue is available at $2.00 for 3 issues.

Doll and Craft World 125 8th Street, Brooklyn, New York 11215 (212) 768-0887

L. K. Donaldson 871 Plymouth Road, Norristown, Pennsylvania 19401

Jim Ducote 21112 East Cypress Street, Covina, California 91724 (213) 967-3257
Citrus labels, pinup art, advertising items, and calendar prints are offered wholesale and retail.

East Coast Casino Antiques 98 Main Street, Fishkill, New York 12524 (914) 896-9492
Gambling antiquities are offered.

Finders Keepers Agness B. Powers, 561 Old Plantation Road, Jekyll Island, Georgia 31520
(912) 635-2837
Lists available may vary, but they include postcards, medals and badges, keys and locks, vintage clothing and furs, books, sheet music, and ephemera.

Fine Art & Antique Offerings 3320 Red Rose Drive, Encino, California 91436

M. Friedman Specialty Company P.O. Box 5777, Baltimore, Maryland 21208 (301) 922-9450

Stanley Gibbons, Antiquarian 395 Strand, London WC2R OLX England
Old and new playing cards and books on collectibles are offered.

The Girl Whirl P.O. Box 7244, Washington, D. C. 20044
Pinups and glamour art, prints, and magazines are offered.

Theresa and Arthur Greenblatt P.O. Box 276, Amherst, New Hampshire 03031 (603) 673-4401
Lists are available on coin silver, souvenir spoons, antique paperweights, and contemporary paperweights.

The Horchow Collection 4435 Simonton, Dallas, Texas 75234 (800) 527-0303, except in Texas
(800) 442-5806, and Dallas 385-2719
One special catalog in 1982 offered only antiques.

House of Oldies 267 Bleecker Street, New York, New York 10014 (212) 243-0500

Spencer K. House   100K Waldon Road, Abingdon, Maryland 21009   (301) 676-6553
This firm offers steins, ice cream and candy molds, glass, plates, etc.

Ivy Galleries, Inc.   2121 North Akard, Dallas, Texas 75201   (800) 527-9250

Jay's Nostalgia World   P.O. Box 5806, Baltimore, Maryland 21208   (301) 296-6556
Baseball cards, movie, music, and miscellaneous items are offered. A catalogue is available.

Leonard Antiques   P.O. Box 127, Albertson, New York 11507   (516) 742-0979
This firm specializes in mechanical antiques.

Martin's Memorabilia   610 North Detroit Avenue, Toledo, Ohio 43607

Montague Sales   7919 Grant, P.O. Box 4059, Overland Park, Kansas 66204-0059   (800) 255-6064

Moran's Memorabilia   P.O. Box 371, Vally Park, Missouri 63088

The Paper Pile   P.O. Box 337, San Anselmo, California 94960   (415) 454-5552
Paper Pile Quarterly is a sales publication devoted to old paper items and advertising: military and political items, documents, postcards, trade cards, movie memorabilia, photos, prints, old checks, assorted advertising, and ephemera. The Paper Pile also publishes the *Paper Pile Catalog,* an illustrated and descriptive catalogue of over 400 collectible items.

Patricia Anne Reed   5 Pump Street, Newcastle, Maine 04553   (207) 563-5633
Toys and folk art are offered.

Walter Reuben, Inc.   910 American Bank Tower, Austin, Texas 78701   (512) 478-3338
Old maps and atlases and rare books pertaining to travel and Americana are offered.

Robin Bellamy Antiques   97 Corn Street, Witney, Oxfordshire OX8 7DL England
This catalogue offers antique pewter. A subscription is $5.00 for 5 catalogues issued over a 2-year period. Cost of the catalogues is deductible from first purchase.

Howard & Gail Rogoesky   P.O. Box L-1102, Linden Hill Station, Flushing, New York 11354
(212) 723-0954
Comics, movie posters, bubble gum cards, etc. are offered.

Rooks' The Locator   880 Washington Boulevard, Baltimore, Maryland 21230   (301) 539-8550
Paper items, books, and prints are available by mail.

Rustco, Inc.   P.O. Box 742 x 4, Lima, Ohio 45802-0742   (419) 229-2662
Postcards, covers, sheet music, valentines, and books on collectibles are offered as well as postcard albums. Postcards and covers are sold on approval. Lists are available.

Sampler's Annex   P.O. Box 298, Venturary, California 93001
Toys, comics, and books are offered.

Saulsbury Antiques   Highway 23, Spicer, Minnesota 56288

The Soldier Shop, Inc.   1013 Madison Avenue, New York, New York 10021   (212) 535-7688
This firm offers yearly catalogues and supplements.

Team Antiques   P.O. Box 52, Great Neck, New York 11023   (516) 487-1826
Tiffany and Art Nouveau are offered in *Team's Tiffany Treasures List.*

Ciay Tontz   4043 Nora, Covina, California 91722
Primitives are offered.

Treasure Trove   19 Village Road, Manhasset, New York 11030   (516) 627-7296
Collectibles such as toys, dolls, and nostalgia are offered.

21st Century Antiques   Hadley, Massachusetts 01035   (413) 549-6678
Catalogues containing collections of Arts and Crafts, Art Nouveau, Art Deco, and modern objects are offered: *First Collection; Second Collection, Minilog I; Booklog,* a catalogue of books about these fields of collecting; and *Retrolog,* featuring replicas of these past decorative styles. The firm is planning to issue *Spacelog,* offering space-related items and gear.

Woodcraft Supply   313 Montvale Avenue, Woburn, Massachusetts 01801   (617) 935-5860

Wurtsboro Wholesale Antiques, Inc.   P.O. Box 386, Wurtsboro, New York 12790
(914) 888-4411
Primitives are offered.

Yesterday's Paper, Inc.   P.O. Box 294, Naperville, Illinois 60566   (312) 355-4855
Old stocks, bonds, and paper Americana are offered. Lists are available.

93. THE COLLECTOR'S RESEARCH LIBRARY

The questions we hear most often about antiques and collectibles are "Who made it?" and "What is it worth?" These are questions that any appraiser, dealer, or serious collector must be prepared to answer. A little knowledge can make a big difference in money.

This is a basic bibliography of 128 books we consider essential for identifying and evaluating antiques. Of our 7,000-volume reference library, these are the books we consult most often. They are not necessarily the newest, or the ones with the prettiest pictures, but they have the most useful information.

Because of the economics of the book trade, it is unlikely that most books on the list will be in stock at local bookstores. But they are still in print and can be ordered. They may also be available for reference at the public library. If not, titles can be obtained via interlibrary loan.

GENERAL

American Heritage History of American Antiques, from the Revolution to the Civil War, The. New York: American Heritage, 1968.

American Heritage History of Antiques, from the Civil War to World War I, The. New York: American Heritage, 1969.

Comstock, Helen, ed. *The Concise Encyclopedia of American Antiques.* 2 vols. New York: Hawthorn Books, 1958.

Drepperd, Carl W. *A Dictionary of American Antiques.* Garden City, New York: Doubleday, 1952.

Haslam, Malcolm. *Marks and Monograms of the Modern Movement, 1875–1930.* New York: Charles Scribner's Sons, 1977.

Hornung, Clarence P. *Treasury of American Design.* 2 vols. New York: Harry N. Abrams, 1976.

Kovel, Ralph and Terry. *Kovels' Know Your Antiques,* 3rd ed. New York: Crown Publishers, 1981.

————. *Kovels' Know Your Collectibles.* New York: Crown Publishers, 1981.

Random House Collector's Encyclopedia, Victoriana to Art Deco, The. New York: Random House, 1974.

Robertson, Patrick. *The Book of Firsts.* New York: Clarkson N. Potter, 1974.

GENERAL-PRICE BOOKS

Kovel, Ralph and Terry. *The Kovels' Antiques & Collectibles Price List,* 15th ed. New York: Crown Publishers, 1982.

Rinker, Harry, ed. *Warman's Antiques and Their Prices,* 16th ed. Elkins Park, Pennsylvania: Warman Publishing Company, 1982.

BRONZE

Berman, Harold. *Bronzes: Sculptors & Founders, 1800–1930.* Chicago: Abage Publishers (6430 North Western, Chicago, Illinois 60645), 1974.

————. *Bronzes: Sculptors & Founders, 1800–1930,* vol. 2. Chicago: Abage Publishers (6430 North Western, Chicago, Illinois 60645), 1976.

————. *Bronzes: Sculptors & Founders, 1800–1930,* vol. 3. Chicago: Abage Publishers (6430 North Western, Chicago, Illinois 60645), 1977.

————. *Bronzes: Sculptors & Founders, 1800–1930,* vol. 4. Chicago: Abage Publishers (6430 North Western, Chicago, Illinois 60645), 1980.

————. *Index, Abage Encyclopedia—Bronzes: Sculptors & Founders, 1800–1930.* Chicago: Abage Publishers (6430 North Western, Chicago, Illinois 60645), 1981.

CLOCKS AND WATCHES

Baillie, G. H. *Watchmakers & Clockmakers of the World,* vol. 1. London: N.A.G. Press (London EC1V 7QA England), 1947.

Baillie, G. H. et al. *Britten's Old Clocks and Watches and Their Makers.* New York: Bonanza Books, 1956.

Loomes, Brian. *Watchmakers & Clockmakers of the World,* vol. 2. London: N.A.G. Press (London EC1V 7QA England), 1976.

Palmer, Brooks. *The Book of American Clocks.* New York: Macmillan, 1950.

———. *A Treasury of American Clocks.* New York: Macmillan, 1967.

CLOCKS AND WATCHES—PRICE BOOK

Shugart, Cooksey. *The Complete Guide to American Pocket Watches.* Cleveland, Tennessee: Overstreet Publications (780 Hunt Cliff Drive N.W., Cleveland, Tennessee 37311), 1981.

DECORATING PERIODS

Battersby, Martin. *The Decorative Twenties.* New York: Walker, 1969.

Johnson, Diane Chalmers. *American Art Nouveau.* New York: Harry N. Abrams, 1979.

19th-Century America: Furniture and Other Decorative Arts. New York: Metropolitan Museum of Art, 1970.

DOMESTIC INTERIORS

Cooper, Nicholas. *The Opulent Eye: Late Victorian and Edwardian Taste in Interior Design.* New York: Billboard Publications (1515 Broadway, New York, New York 10036), 1976.

Old House Journal, 69A 7th Avenue, Brooklyn, New York 11217. (Periodical)

Peterson, Harold L. *Americans at Home: From the Colonists to the Late Victorians.* New York: Charles Scribner's Sons, 1971.

Seale, William. *The Tasteful Interlude: American Interiors through the Camera's Eye, 1860–1917,* 2nd ed. Nashville: American Association for State and Local History (708 Berry Road, Nashville, Tennessee 37204), 1981.

FURNITURE

Aronson, Joseph. *The New Encyclopedia of Furniture.* New York: Crown Publishers, 1967.

Bishop, Robert. *Centuries and Styles of the American Chair, 1640–1970.* New York: E. P. Dutton, 1972.

Downs, Joseph. *American Furniture: Queen Anne and Chippendale Periods.* New York: Macmillan, 1952.

Kovel, Ralph and Terry. *American Country Furniture, 1780–1875.* New York: Crown Publishers, 1965.

Montgomery, Charles F. *American Furniture: The Federal Period.* New York: Viking Press, 1966.

Nutting, Wallace. *Furniture Treasury*. New York: Macmillan, 1961.

GLASS—GENERAL

Arwas, Victor. *Glass: Art Nouveau to Art Deco*. New York: Rizzoli International, 1977.

Gardner, Paul V. *The Glass of Frederick Carder*. New York: Crown Publishers, 1971.

Grover, Ray and Lee. *Art Glass Nouveau*. Rutland, Vermont: Charles E. Tuttle, 1967.

————. *Carved & Decorated European Art Glass*. Rutland, Vermont: Charles E. Tuttle, 1970.

Hollister, Paul, Jr. *The Encyclopedia of Glass Paperweights*. New York: Clarkson N. Potter, 1969.

Kamm, Minnie Watson. *Two Hundred Pattern Glass Pitchers*. Watkins Glen, New York: Century House, 1968.

Lee, Ruth Webb. *Early American Pressed Glass*. Wellesley Hills, Massachusetts: Lee Publications (105 Suffolk Road, Wellesley Hills, Massachusetts 02181), 1933.

Lindsey, Bessie M. *American Historical Glass*. Rutland, Vermont: Charles E. Tuttle, 1967.

McKearin, George S. and Helen. *American Glass*. New York: Crown Publishers, 1948.

Newman, Harold. *An Illustrated Dictionary of Glass*. London: Thames and Hudson, 1977.

Oliver, Elizabeth. *American Antique Glass*. New York: Golden Press, 1977.

Pearson, J. Michael. *Encyclopedia of American Cut and Engraved Glass (1880–1917)*, Vol. I: Geometric Conceptions. Privately printed, 1975 (402844 Ocean View Station, Miami Beach, Florida 33140).

————. *Encyclopedia of American Cut and Engraved Glass (1880–1917)*, Volume II: Realistic Patterns. Privately printed, 1977 (402844 Ocean View Station, Miami Beach, Florida 33140).

————. *Encyclopedia of American Cut and Engraved Glass (1880–1917)*, Volume III: Geometric Motifs. Privately printed, 1978 (402844 Ocean View Station, Miami Beach, Florida 33140).

Revi, Albert Christian. *Nineteenth Century Glass: Its Genesis and Development*. Camden, New Jersey: Thomas Nelson, 1967.

GLASS—PRICE BOOKS

Florence, Gene. *The Collector's Encyclopedia of Depression Glass,* 5th ed. Paducah, Kentucky: Collector Books, 1982.

Kovel, Ralph and Terry. *The Kovels' Illustrated Price Guide to Depression Glass and American Dinnerware.* New York: Crown Publishers, 1980.

GLASS—BOTTLES

Baldwin, Joseph K. *A Collector's Guide to Patent and Proprietary Medicine Bottles of the Nineteenth Century.* New York: Thomas Nelson, 1973.

McKearin, Helen, and Wilson, Kenneth M. *American Bottles & Flasks and Their Ancestry.* New York: Crown Publishers, 1979.

Munsey, Cecil. *The Illustrated Guide to Collecting Bottles.* New York: Hawthorn Books, 1970.

Ring, Carlyn. *For Bitters Only.* Wellesley Hills, Massachusetts: Pi Press, 1980.

Toulouse, Julian Harrison. *Bottle Makers and Their Marks.* Camden, New Jersey: Thomas Nelson, 1971.

————. *A Collectors' Manual: Fruit Jars.* Camden, New Jersey: Thomas Nelson, 1969.

GLASS—BOTTLES—PRICE BOOKS

Creswick, Alice M. *The Red Book of Fruit Jars No. 4.* Privately printed, 1982 (0-8525 Kenowa S.W., Grand Rapids, Michigan 49504).

Kovel, Ralph and Terry. *The Kovels' Bottle Price List,* 6th ed. New York: Crown Publishers, 1982.

JEWELRY

Gere, Charlotte. *American & European Jewelry, 1830–1914.* New York: Crown Publishers, 1975.

JEWELRY—PRICE BOOK

Poynder, Michael. *The Price Guide to Jewellery, 3000 B.C.–1950 A.D.* Suffolk, England: Antique Collectors' Club (5 Church Street, Clopton, Woodbridge, Suffolk 1P12 1BR England), 1976.

KITCHENWARE

Lantz, Louise K. *Old American Kitchenware, 1725–1925*. Camden, New Jersey: Thomas Nelson, 1970.

LIGHTING DEVICES

Darbee, Herbert C. *Technical Leaflet 30: A Glossary of Old Lamps and Lighting Devices*. Nashville: American Association for State and Local History (708 Berry Road, Nashville, Tennessee 37204), 1965.

Early Lighting, A Pictorial Guide. Talcottville, Connecticut: The Rushlight Club (P.O. Box 3053, Talcottville, Connecticut 06066), 1972.

Thuro, Catherine M. V. *Oil Lamps: The Kerosene Era in North America*. Des Moines: Wallace-Homestead, 1976.

Thwing, Leroy. *Flickering Flames: A History of Domestic Lighting through the Ages*. Rutland, Vermont: Charles E. Tuttle, 1958.

MISCELLANEOUS METALS

Coffin, Margaret. *The History and Folklore of American Country Tinware, 1700–1900*. Camden, New Jersey: Thomas Nelson, 1968.

Gould, Mary Earle. *Antique Tin and Tole Ware: Its History and Romance*. Rutland, Vermont: Charles E. Tuttle, 1958.

Kauffman, Henry J. *American Copper and Brass*. Camden, New Jersey: Thomas Nelson, 1968.

Schiffer, Herbert, Nancy, and Peter. *The Brass Book: American, English and European, Fifteenth Century through 1850*. Exton, Pennsylvania: Schiffer Publishing (P.O. Box E, Exton, Pennsylvania 19341), 1978.

MUSIC

Bowers, Q. David. *Encyclopedia of Automatic Musical Instruments*. Vestal, New York: Vestal Press, 1972.

Reblitz, Arthur A., and Bowers, Q. David. *Treasures of Mechanical Music*. Vestal, New York: Vestal Press, 1981.

NEEDLEWORK

Checklist of American Coverlet Weavers, A. Williamsburg, Virginia: Colonial Williamsburg Foundation (Abby Aldrich Rockefeller Folk Art Center, P.O. Box C, Williamsburg, Virginia 23185), 1978.

Groves, Sylvia. *The History of Needlework Tools and Accessories.* New York: Arco Publishing, 1973.

Montgomery, Florence M. *Printed Textiles: English and American Cottons and Linens, 1700–1850.* New York: Viking Press, 1970.

Safford, Carleton L., and Bishop, Robert. *America's Quilts and Coverlets.* New York: E. P. Dutton, 1972.

PEWTER

Cotterell, Howard Herschel. *Old Pewter: Its Makers and Marks.* Rutland, Vermont: Charles E. Tuttle, 1963.

Laughlin, Ledlie Irwin. *Pewter in America: Its Makers and Their Marks,* vol. I and II. Barre, Massachusetts: Barre Publishers, 1969.

————. *Pewter in America: Its Makers and Their Marks,* vol. III. Barre, Massachusetts: Barre Publishers, 1971.

Montgomery, Charles F. *A History of American Pewter.* New York: E. P. Dutton, 1978.

PHOTOGRAPHY

Coe, Brian. *Cameras: From Daguerreotypes to Instant Pictures.* New York: Crown Publishers, 1978.

PHOTOGRAPHY—PRICE BOOK

Witkin, Lee D., and London, Barbara. *The Photograph Collector's Guide.* Boston: Little, Brown, 1979.

POTTERY AND PORCELAIN

Boger, Louise Ade. *The Dictionary of World Pottery and Porcelain: From Prehistoric Times to the Present.* New York: Charles Scribner's Sons, 1971.

Ehrmann, Eric. *Hummel: The Complete Collector's Guide and Illustrated Reference.* Huntington, New York: Portfolio Press, 1976.

Evans, Paul. *Art Pottery of the United States: An Encyclopedia of Producers and Their Marks.* New York: Charles Scribner's Sons, 1974.

Eyles, Desmond. *Royal Doulton Character and Toby Jugs.* Carlstadt, New Jersey: Royal Doulton Tableware (400 Paterson Plank Road, Carlstadt, New Jersey 07072), 1979.

Eyles, Desmond, and Dennis, Richard. *Royal Doulton Figures Produced at Burslem c. 1890-1978.* Carlstadt, New Jersey: Royal Doulton Tableware (400 Paterson Plank Road, Carlstadt, New Jersey 07072), 1978.

Godden, Geoffrey A. *British Porcelain: An Illustrated Guide.* New York: Clarkson N. Potter, 1974.

————. *British Pottery: An Illustrated Guide.* New York: Clarkson N. Potter, 1975.

————. *Encyclopaedia of British Pottery and Porcelain Marks.* New York: Bonanza Books, 1964.

Haslam, Malcolm. *English Art Pottery, 1865-1915.* Suffolk, England: Antique Collectors' Club (5 Church Street, Clopton, Woodbridge, Suffolk 1P12 1BR England), 1975.

Kovel, Ralph and Terry. *Dictionary of Marks—Pottery and Porcelain.* New York: Crown Publishers, 1953.

————. *The Kovels' Collector's Guide to American Art Pottery.* New York: Crown Publishers, 1974.

Lehner, Lois. *Complete Book of American Kitchen and Dinner Wares.* Des Moines: Wallace-Homestead, 1980.

Mankowitz, Wolf. *Wedgwood.* New York: E. P. Dutton, 1953.

Poche, Emanuel. *Porcelain Marks of the World.* New York: Arco Publishing, 1974.

Ray, Marcia. *Collectible Ceramics: An Encyclopedia of Pottery and Porcelain for the American Collector.* New York: Crown Publishers, 1974.

Savage, George, and Newman, Harold. *An Illustrated Dictionary of Ceramics.* New York: Van Nostrand Reinhold, 1974.

Stitt, Irene. *Japanese Ceramics of the Last 100 Years.* New York: Crown Publishers, 1974.

POTTERY AND PORCELAIN—PRICE BOOKS

Kovel, Ralph and Terry. *The Kovels' Illustrated Price Guide to Royal Doulton.* New York: Crown Publishers, 1980.

————. *The Kovels' Price Guide for Collector Plates, Figurines, Paperweights, and Other Limited Editions.* New York: Crown Publishers, 1978.

Robinson, Dorothy, and Feeny, Bill. *The Official Price Guide to American Pottery and Porcelain.* Orlando, Florida: The House of Collectibles (773 Kirkman Road, No. 120, Orlando, Florida 32811), 1980.

SILVER

Fales, Martha Gandy. *Early American Silver for the Cautious Collector.* New York: Funk & Wagnalls, 1970.

Kovel, Ralph and Terry. *A Directory of American Silver, Pewter and Silver Plate.* New York: Crown Publishers, 1961.

Rainwater, Dorothy T. *Encyclopedia of American Silver Manufacturers.* New York: Crown Publishers, 1975.

Rainwater, Dorothy T. and H. Ivan. *American Silverplate.* Nashville: Thomas Nelson, 1968.

Sterling Flatware Pattern Index. Radnor, Pennsylvania: Jewelers' Circular—Keystone (Chilton Way, Radnor, Pennsylvania 19089), 1977.

Wyler, Seymour B. *The Book of Old Silver.* New York: Crown Publishers, 1937.

————. *The Book of Sheffield Plate.* New York: Crown Publishers, 1949.

STORE AND ADVERTISING

Anderson, Will. *The Beer Book.* Princeton, New Jersey: Pyne Press, 1973.

Johnson, Laurence A. *Over the Counter and on the Shelf: Country Storekeeping in America, 1620–1920.* Rutland, Vermont: Charles E. Tuttle, 1961.

Munsey, Cecil. *The Illustrated Guide to the Collectibles of Coca-Cola.* New York: Hawthorn Books, 1972.

STORE AND ADVERTISING—PRICE BOOK

Munsey, Cecil, and Petretti, Allan. *Official Coca-Cola Collectibles Price Guide, 1980–1981 Edition.* Hackensack, New Jersey: Nostalgia Publishing (21 South Lake Drive, Hackensack, New Jersey 07601), 1980.

TOYS AND DOLLS

Coleman, Dorothy S., Elizabeth A., and Evelyn J. *The Collector's Encyclopedia of Dolls.* New York: Crown Publishers, 1968.

King, Constance Eileen. *The Encyclopedia of Toys.* New York: Crown Publishers, 1978.

Pressland, David. *The Art of the Tin Toy.* New York: Crown Publishers, 1976.

TOYS AND DOLLS—PRICE BOOKS

O'Brien, Richard. *Collecting Toys: A Collector's Identification and Value Guide,* 3rd ed. New York: Crown Publishers, 1981.

Smith, Patricia R. *Modern Collector's Dolls.* Paducah, Kentucky: Collector Books, 1973.

————. *Modern Collector's Dolls,* Second Series. Paducah, Kentucky: Collector Books, 1975.

————. *Modern Collector's Dolls,* Third Series. Paducah, Kentucky: Collector Books, 1976.

————. *Modern Collector's Dolls,* Fourth Series. Paducah, Kentucky: Collector Books, 1979.

WOODENWARE

Gould, Mary Earle. *Early American Wooden Ware.* Rutland, Vermont: Charles E. Tuttle, 1962.

MISCELLANEOUS

Lesser, Robert. *A Celebration of Comic Art and Memorabilia.* New York: Hawthorn Books, 1975.

MISCELLANEOUS—PRICE BOOKS

Beckett, J., and Eckes, D. W. *The Sport Americana Baseball Card Price Guide.* Laurel, Maryland: Den's Collectors Den (P.O. Box 606, Laurel, Maryland 20910), 1981.

Conningham, Frederic, and Simkin, Colin. *Currier and Ives Prints: An Illustrated Check List.* New York: Crown Publishers, 1970.

Overstreet, Robert M. *The Comic Book Price Guide #12.* New York: Harmony Books, 1982.

Sugar, Bert Randolph. *The Sports Collectors Bible,* 3rd ed. New York: Bobbs-Merrill, 1979.

94. CONSERVATION, RESTORATION, AND PRESERVATION SUPPLIES

There are some supplies needed for the proper care of antiques that are very difficult to locate, including such products as acid-free paper-backing materials, special soaps, special waxes, etc. These are used primarily by the professional restorer or conservator, but collectors will often need these products. This is a list of such parts and supplies. Many of these companies only sell to wholesale accounts and will not sell to individuals but will direct you to the store or dealer nearest you that carries the products. Special items for use with one type of antique, such as clock parts, doll eyes, etc., are listed in the appropriate chapters.

We have also included a few general books and pamphlets that are helpful to collectors. Again, look in specific chapters for books on a particular subject.

CONSERVATION SUPPLIES

American Association for State and Local History   708 Berry Road, Nashville, Tennessee 37204 (615) 383-5991
The AASLH is the major publisher of professional literature for local historians and historical organizations. It offers books and pamphlets on the care of various items of interest to collectors. Catalogues of its books and technical leaflets are available.

American Association of Museums   1055 Thomas Jefferson Street, N.W., Washington, D.C. 20007
This association offers reprints on the conservation and care of objects of interest to collectors. Send for its folder *Books & Reprints*.

Barap Specialties   835 Bellows, Frankfort, Michigan 49635
This firm offers odorless liquid hide glue which needs no mixing or heating. Moderate set speed permits an unhurried assembly before clamping. It comes in a 4-ounce, pint, or quart size. A catalogue is available for 50¢.

Dovetail, Inc.   P.O. Box 1569, Lowell, Massachusetts 01853   (617) 454-2944
This firm offers authentic reproductions of Federal and Victorian ceiling medallions, cornices, and entire cornucopian ceilings and door panels. A brochure is available.

Furniture Revival and Company   P.O. Box 994, 580 Southwest Twin Oaks Circle, Corvallis, Oregon 97330   (503) 754-6323
This company carries furniture and cabinet hardware including pulls, keyholes, knobs, hooks, hinges, kitchen and icebox hardware, casters and feet, trunk hardware, etc. Cane webbing, reed spline, accessories, replacement chair seats, curved china cabinet glass, wood replacement parts, and finishing products are also offered. A catalogue is available for $2.00.

The Hollinger Corporation   P.O. Box 6185, 3810 South Four Mile Run Drive, Arlington, Virginia 22206   (703) 671-6600
This firm offers storage materials including Mylar sleeves, folders, envelopes, storage boxes, document cases, etc. A catalogue is available.

Len's Country Barn Antiques, Inc.   9929 Rhode Island Avenue, College Park, Maryland 20740 (301) 441-2546
This firm offers a complete line of refinishing supplies including paint removers, brass hardware, chair cane, solvents, dowels, locks, and hard-to-find items.

New York State College of Human Ecology and New York State College of Agriculture and Life Sciences   Cooperative Extension, Cornell University, Ithaca, New York 14850
The Know How Catalog is a list of free or inexpensive bulletins, leaflets, booklets, packets, and other printed material from the New York State College of Human Ecology and the New York State College of Agriculture and Life Sciences. Pamphlets of interest to collectors include *Cane Seats for Chairs, Furniture Restoration, Glazed Finish over Enamel, Rush Seats for Chairs, Splint Seats for Chairs,* and others.

Process Materials Corporation   301 Veterans Boulevard, Rutherford, New Jersey 07070 (201) 935-2900
This firm offers products for conservation, framing, mounting, bookbinding, and restoration. A catalogue and price list are available.

Restoration Systems, Inc.   14 Wexford Street, Needham, Massachusetts 02194   (617) 444-8950
Restoration Systems' Trefler Restoration Kit will help you restore damaged objects made of china, glass, and other materials. The kit contains two adhesive glazes, liquid colors, tools, and accessories required for restoration, and a copy of *Professional Restoration Manual,* which gives directions for mending, filling chips, sealing cracks, and otherwise restoring the object.

TALAS Division of Technical Library Service, Inc.   130 Fifth Avenue, New York, New York 10011   (212) 675-0718
This is a major distributor of fine tools, supplies, books, and equipment for art restorers, archivists,

hand bookbinders, librarians, museum curators, photographers, etc. Its services include the storage, conservation, and restoration of all sorts of collectibles (photographs, documents, and works of art). It carries Orvus WA Paste. TALAS's catalogue is available for $5.00.

University Products, Inc. P.O. Box 101, South Canal Street, Holyoke, Massachusetts 01041 (413) 532-9431
This company offers conservation, restoration, and preservation materials. Included are acid-free storage materials, acid-free paper, mounting materials, conservation products, film storage supplies, and more. A catalogue is available for $2.00.

BOOKS ON CONSERVATION

Conservation of Decorative Arts. Washington, D.C.: American Association of Museums (Suite 428, 1055 Thomas Jefferson Street, N.W., Washington, D.C. 20007), 1976–1977. Series of leaflets.

Doussy, Michel. *Antiques: Professional Secrets for the Amateur.*
New York: Quadrangle/The New York Times Book Co. 1971.

Grow, Lawrence. *The Brand New Old House Catalogue.*
New York: Warner Books, 1980. A source book for house restoration supplies.

Guldbeck, Per E. *The Care of Historical Collections: A Conservation Handbook for the Nonspecialist.*
Nashville: American Association for State and Local History (708 Berry Road, Nashville, Tennessee 37204), 1972.

Keck, Caroline. *On Conservation.*
Washington, D.C.: American Association of Museums (Suite 428, 1055 Thomas Jefferson Street, N.W., Washington, D.C. 20007), 1971–1972. Series of articles.

Kinard, Epsie. *The Care and Keeping of Antiques.*
New York: Hawthorn Books, 1971.

Kovel, Ralph and Terry. *Daily Care and First Aid to Antiques.*
Des Moines: Register and Tribune Syndicate (715 Locust Street, Des Moines, Iowa 50304), 1974. Leaflet.

McGrath, Lee Parr. *Housekeeping with Antiques.*
New York: Dodd, Mead, 1971.

Mills. John Fitzmaurice. *The Care of Antiques.*
New York: Hastings House, 1964.

————. *Collecting & Looking After Antiques.*
London: Hamlyn, 1974.

Official Museum Products and Services Directory, 1981, The. Washington, D.C.: The American Association of Museums (1055 Thomas Jefferson Street, N.W., Washington, D.C. 20007), 1981.

Old-House Journal 1982 Catalog: A Buyers' Guide, The. Brooklyn, New York: The Old House Journal, 1981. A source book for house restoration supplies.

Organ, R. M. *Design for Scientific Conservation of Antiquities.*
Washington, D.C.: Smithsonian Institution Press, 1969.

Plenderleith, H. J. *The Conservation of Antiquities and Works of Art.*
London: Oxford University Press, 1956.

Plenderleith, H. J., and Werner, A.E.A. *The Conservation of Antiquities and Works of Art: Treatment, Repair and Restoration,* 2nd ed.
London: Oxford University Press, 1971.

Young, Dennis. *Encyclopedia of Antique Restoration and Maintenance.*
New York: Clarkson N. Potter, 1974.

BOOKLETS ON CONSERVATION

American Association for State and Local History   708 Berry Road, Nashville, Tennessee 37204 (615) 383-5991
The AASLH is the major publisher of professional literature for local historians and historical organizations. It offers books and pamphlets on the care of various items of interest to collectors. Catalogues of its books and technical leaflets are available.

American Association of Museums   1055 Thomas Jefferson Street, N.W.,   Washington, D.C. 20007
This association offers reprints on the conservation and care of objects of interest to collectors. Send for its folder *Books & Reprints.*

New York State College of Human Ecology and New York State College of Agriculture and Life Sciences   Cooperative Extension, Cornell University, Ithaca, New York 14850
The Know How Catalog is a list of free or inexpensive bulletins, leaflets, booklets, packets, and other printed material from the New York State College of Human Ecology and the New York State College of Agriculture and Life Sciences. Pamphlets of interest to collectors include: *Cane Seats for Chairs, Furniture Restoration, Glazed Finish over Enamel, Rush Seats for Chairs, Splint Seats for Chairs,* and others.

Victoria and Albert Museum Conservation Department, South Kensington, London SW 7 England
The museum offers pamphlets under the general title Technical Notes on the Care of Art Objects: *The Care of Portrait Miniatures, The Care of Wax Objects,* and *The Deterioration of Art Objects by Light.*

95. CONSERVATORS AND RESTORERS

Listed here are restorers and conservators together with a description of the subjects in which they specialize. Many conservators are connected with museums or galleries and can work on several types of antiques. The men and women listed here and in the other sections of the book are listed as they requested. Each filled out a form furnishing their name and title (either restorer or conservator) and a description of the work they will perform. This is only a partial listing of the conservators in America. There are many others, but we only included those who responded to our questionnaire. Other conservators are listed in the appropriate chapters.

There are rules of ethics for conservators and restorers, as well as professional organizations with strict requirements. The following is only a reference, not a recommendation of quality, because we have not seen the work done by most of the conservators listed here. Be sure to check further if you decide to hire someone to restore a valuable work of art.

All-Art Restorers Patricia Hammel, 140 West 57th Street, New York, New York 10019 (212) 957-1074
This firm restores and repairs antiques including bronze and metal, ceramics, enamels, gilding, glassware, ivory, icons, marble, porcelain, stone, tortoiseshell, wood, etc. Missing parts are replaced. Free estimates are given on pieces brought in. It does no mail order business and no appraisals.

American Center for Conservation of Art & Antiquities, Inc. 165 West End Avenue, Suite 5K, New York, New York 10023 (212) 580-9874
This firm does restoration and conservation of ethnographica, paintings, statuary, objets d'art, photographs, paper, furniture, drawings, prints, and documents. Other services include technical authenticity analysis of art and antiquities and appraisals. The American Center for Conservation is a multidisciplinary group of professionals who have joined together to offer a comprehensive spectrum of support services to the art community. Contact them by phone or mail, but a call is preferable since it enables them to ask pertinent questions. A brochure is available.

American Museum of Natural History Department of Anthropology, Gary Sawyer and Marie de Troostembergh, Central Park West at 79th Street, New York, New York 10024 (202) 873-1300, Ext. 367 or 278

Services include restoration and conservation of items of anthropological, ethnographic, and archaeological interest.

Antique Restorations   1001 High Street, Burlington, New Jersey 08016   (609) 386-2666
This firm restores fine art such as china, porcelain, bisque, pottery, Orientals, objets d'art, etc. All work is guaranteed. Customers may forward their items by UPS. The firm will examine the piece and mail a cost quotation. The normal time required to complete the work is 8 to 10 weeks.

Art Conservation Laboratory, Inc.   Dudley Homestead, Raymond, New Hampshire 03077 (603) 895-2639
The laboratory is open by appointment only, weekdays 9:00 A.M. to 5:00 P.M. There is an appointment fee. The lab will answer questions by mail but does not do appraisals.

Dorothy Briggs   410 Ethan Allen Avenue, Takoma Park, Maryland 20012   (301) 270-4166
Dorothy Briggs specializes in the restoration of painted clock dials, reverse painted clock door glass, painted wood art objects, oil paintings and Santos. She also restores other objects. Phone or write for information.

Roger D. Broussal   Fine Art Conservators, Inc. 18 Parrott Court, San Mateo, California 94402 (415) 574-2259
Mr. Broussal restores paintings and decorative arts (stone, metal, wood, ceramic), and Asian art. He does not accept mailed work without prior approval. New clients are required to make a 20 percent deposit with each item left for conservation.

Geoffrey I. Brown   7000 Stockton Avenue, El Cerrito, California 94530   (415) 524-9500
Mr. Brown's services include repair; stabilization; restoration of dimensional objects of historic, artistic, or archaeological origins such as ceramics, stone, metal, wood, fiber, porcelain figures or vessels, tapa cloth/bark cloth, baskets, artifacts, etc. He does not work on furniture, paintings, or paper. He will answer questions by mail, consults on the care and maintenance of collections, and offers instruction on preventive conservation, etc. There are no fees for inquiries or examination in his studio unless shipping is involved. There is a fee for on-site examination. Work is done by appointment.

Center Art Studio   149 West 57th Street, New York, New York 10019   (212) 247-3550
This firm restores and appraises porcelain, pottery, ceramics, glassware, chandeliers, picture frames, furniture, marble, bronze or other metalwork, ivory, tortoiseshell, wood carvings, gold leafing, hand-painted screens, scrolls, murals, and wallpaper. Missing parts are replaced.

R. R. Donnelley & Sons Company   Graphic Conservation Department, Robert C. Wiest, Manager, 350 East 22nd Street, 1-D-8, Chicago, Illinois 60616   (312) 326-8525 or 326-8426
This company specializes in restoration. There is an examination fee in addition to regular conservation charges. Please call or write before sending anything.

Robert O. Downing   P.O. Box 24, Allenwood, New Jersey 08720   (201) 518-6132
Mr. Downing does appraisals, restoration, and conservation of objets d'art. The restoration workshop will work with oil paintings and frames (cleaning, relining, and restoring), porcelain, ivory, pottery, and stone. It repairs objets d'art and replaces missing pieces. It also does repairs on European and Oriental antiques. A brochure is available.

Harry A. Eberhardt & Son, Inc.   2010 Walnut Street, Philadelphia, Pennsylvania 19103
(215) 568-4144
This firm specializes in the repair of porcelains, glass, ivory, jade, etc. It does appraisals and will answer questions by mail. There is no fee for an estimate.

Fine Arts Center, Inc.   1639 Bissonnet, Houston, Texas 77005   (713) 529-9411
This firm restores paintings on canvas or wood; prints; watercolors, pastels; murals; sculpture in wood, metal, stone, or ceramic; and books and fabrics from clothing to tapestries. It offers a framing service and will repair damaged frames and reproduce classic frames. It also tests for authenticity. For additional information, call or write for a brochure.

St. Julian Fishburne   48 Jenkenstown Road, New Paltz, New York 12561   (914) 255-1042
Restoration services are available and questions will be answered by mail.

Foland Restoration Studio   304 2nd Avenue South, St. Petersburg, Florida 33701   (813) 894-5576
This studio does restoration and appraisals. Services are available to anyone in the U.S. and it will answer questions by mail.

Warner G. Friedman   P.O. Box 622, Sheffield, Massachusetts 01257   (413) 229-8076
Mr. Friedman conserves and restores works of art. He will answer questions by mail, if possible. Services are available to anyone in the U.S.

Georgette Grosz   4100 Marine Drive, Suite 4-D, Chicago, Illinois 60613   (312) 248-6935
Georgette Grosz restores paintings of all periods and important sculptures. Services are available to anyone in the U.S. and she will answer questions by mail without a fee.

Hess Repairs   200 Park Avenue South, New York, New York 10003   (212) 741-0410
This firm repairs a wide variety of items but not furniture, mechanical devices, or electrical appliances. Some of the items it repairs are: alabaster, boxes, brass, bronze, candelabra, carvings, china, crystal, cutlery, dresser sets, fans, figurines, glassware, gold plating, handbags, ivory, jade, jewelry, lamps, metalwork, miniatures, mirrors, music boxes, onyx, pepper mills, pewter, picture frames, porcelain, pottery, quartz, reed, screens, sculpture, silver, silver plating, tortoiseshell, vacuum bottles, wood, and wrought iron.

Julius Lowy Frame & Restoring Company, Inc.   Shar-Sisto, Inc., 511 East 72nd Street, New York, New York 10021   (212) 525-5250
Services include restoration, appraisals, and framing of fine arts only. It will answer questions by mail and services are available to anyone in the U.S.

Just Enterprises   2790 Sherwin Avenue, Unit 10, Ventura, California 93003   (805) 644-5837
This firm does antique restoration and repair. It works on metal, paintings, gilding, woodwork, porcelain, bronze, clock cases, furniture, pewter, enamelware, cameo glass, silver, jewelry, cloisonné, marble, etc.

Salvatore Macri   5518 East Pinchot Avenue, Phoenix, Arizona 85018   (602) 959-1933
Mr. Macri is a conservator specializing in, but not limited to, the restoration of fine art porcelain and Indian artifacts (not rugs or baskets) of a prehistoric, historic, and contemporary nature. Services are available to anyone in the U.S. and he will answer questions by mail.

Ms. Billie Milam   c/o 8350 Hillview Avenue, Canoga Park, California 91304   (213) 340-2847, 5:00 to 8:00 P.M. Sundays and 937-4250 Ext. 381 7:00 A.M. to 4:00 P.M. weekdays
Ms. Milam is a conservator of 3-D art objects and sculpture including metals, ceramics, stone, wood, etc. There is a consultation fee.

Nordstern Service International (U.S.), Inc.   116 John Street, Suite 406, New York, New York 10038   (212) 227-2224
Nordstern selects the appropriate conservator and coordinates the conservation process on behalf of its clients. A flat fee is charged for this service. Consultation is available on security, packing, shipping, framing, and all information regarding the fine arts. Estimates of fees will be quoted based on time of specialists involved and costs of processing. A brochure is available.

Old World Restorations, Inc.   705 Wooster Pike, Route 50, Terrace Park, Ohio 45174 (513) 831-2724
This company specializes in art form restoration and conservation of paintings, frames, porcelain, gold leafing, ivory, china, sculpture, pottery, and glass. Complimentary estimates are given.

Larry Price   R.D. 1, P.O. Box 372, Craryville, New York 12521   (518) 851-6541
Mr. Price is a conservator of gilded objects of art, picture frames, and mirrors. Services are available to anyone in the U.S. and he will answer questions by mail and give opinions on conservation. There is a fee.

Georges Radovanovitch   117 Prince Street, New York, New York 10012   (212) 260-5946
Mr. Radovanovitch does restoration and conservation of all kinds of sculptures. Services are available throughout the U.S. for fee plus expenses. There is a fee for opinions given if the restoration work is not done.

Restorers of America   126 Main Street, Ravena, New York 12143   (518) 756-9600
This firm restores all works of art, such as fine porcelain, marble, ivory, oil paintings, Hummel figurines, cloisonné, etc. Work is black-light proof, invisible, and guaranteed. Kits are available for the amateur to make minor repairs to their keepsakes.

R. Wayne Reynolds   Restoration of Antique Frames, P.O. Box 28, Stevenson, Maryland 21153 (301) 484-1028
This firm offers complete conservation and restoration of gessoed and gold-leafed surfaces including carved wood or cast plaster objects, furniture, mirror frames, picture frames, and architectural gilding of interior or exterior ornamental moldings. Matting and framing are done to museum standards.

Rikki's Studio, Inc.   2256 Coral Way, Miami, Florida 33145   (305) 856-6741
Services include restoration, conservation, and appraisals of all art forms (not furniture) including paintings, porcelain, paper, metal, wood carvings, lacquer, ivory, hardstone, glass, etc.

Sender's Galerie Nouvelle   3482 Lee Road, Shaker Heights, Ohio 44120   (216) 752-2435
Sender's offers repair and restoration services for paintings, china, porcelain, and art objects.

Ann Shaftel Conservator, Fine Arts Conservation   P.O. Box 1306, Boulder, Colorado 80306
Ann Shaftel prefers to work on 3-dimensional objects, and usually specializes in Oriental art. Her specialty is Tibetan thangka paintings and she also works on textiles, ceramics, wood, metal, etc. Restoration services are available to anyone in the U.S. Questions are answered by mail, usually at no fee.

George Walter Vincent Smith Art Museum   Emil G. Schnorr, General Conservator, 222 State Street, Springfield, Massachusetts 01103   (413) 733-4214
Services include restoration of any work of art, available to anyone in the U.S. Questions are answered by mail. The fee is based on the amount of work involved.

Sotheby's Restoration   440 East 91st Street, New York, New York 10028   (212) 472-3463
Services include care and repair of furniture and on-site restoration for large collections or in cases where it is inadvisable to move the property. Preventive maintenance programs are designed to help maintain the condition of extensive collections. Pre-auction restoration estimates are given. Sotheby's Restoration workshop is divided into two specialized areas: the Cabinet Shop with complete restoration facilities, and the Finishing Center for gilding, polishing, japanning, and lacquer work. There is a fee for restoration estimates, which is deductible if you use Sotheby's services. Fees for estimate visits made outside metropolitan New York will be quoted. A brochure is available.

Wiebold, Inc.   Art Conservation Lab, 413 Terrace Place, Terrace Park, Ohio 45174 (513) 831-2541
This firm works on paintings (conservation, restoration, cleaning, varnish removal, etc.); sculpture (china, glass, porcelain, quartz, jade, ivory, wood, marble, bronze, plastic, stone, etc.); and frames (custom framing, gold leafing, gesso repair, resilvering and beveling mirrors). Other services include metal repair; jewelry repair; and repairs on clocks, music boxes, leaded shades; and papier-mâché.

96. DISPLAYING COLLECTIBLES

There are some special problems in displaying antiques properly. Rough porcelain or glass bases should not scratch furniture tops, picture hooks should be strong enough, and collectibles should be displayed to their greatest advantage.

Many display items can be purchased at local giftware, hardware, and art supply stores, but we have listed items that are not always found with ease. Other supplies can be found in Chapter 94, Conservation, Restoration, and Preservation Supplies.

Bard's Products, Inc.   1825 Willow Road, Northfield, Illinois 60093   (312) 446-9548
Round glass domes, vitrines, shadow boxes, curio cabinets, bases, plate stands, wall accessories, plate frames, shelves, thimble trees, etc. are offered. Bard's products are sold through retailers. Call or write for the dealer nearest you. A catalogue is available.

The Book Doctor   984 High Street, P.O. Box 68, Harrisburg, Ohio 43126   (800) 848-7918
The Book Doctor offers custom-designed solander boxes. Portfolios and slipcases are made to order.

Center Art Studio   149 West 57th Street, New York, New York 10019   (212) 247-3550
Display pieces are made to order for works of art in 6 model variations: with plain or illuminated platform bases, with or without walnut cap, see-through case, or mirrored background; in wood, metals (except stainless steel), Lucite and glass, or marble and alabaster. There is a choice of American or Oriental classic styles. A brochure is available.

Collectors Cabinet   1023 Connecticut Avenue, Washington, D.C. 20036   (202) 785-4480
This firm offers Mexican glass-and-brass cases, vitrines and decorative boxes including front-opening cases on ball feet and wall cabinets with 3 shelves and a mirror back. The store has a variety of glass domes including watch domes with an inside hook at top with a wooden base. Send for full details and shipping instructions.

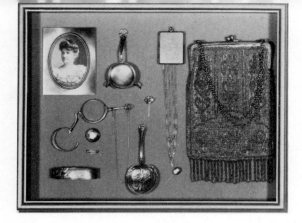

The Collectors' Store   P.O. Box 22200 K, Beachwood, Ohio 44122   (216) 752-3115
This store carries black lights, cup and saucer holders, tabletop easels, felt pads, special picture hooks, diamond-tipped markers, polishes, and other material of use in household display of collections. A catalogue is available.

Family Tree Antiques   P.O. Box 93, Merrick, New York 11566
This firm has glass domes for clocks, dolls, figurines, watches, toys, etc. They are available in large (11 inches tall by 5½ inches) or small (4¼ inches tall by 3 inches) sizes. A wooden base is available if desired. Write for further information.

Hamlin Overton Frame Company, Inc.   South Haven, Michigan 49090   (616) 637-5266
This firm offers quality cases, shelves, and frames specifically designed for collectors. Call or write for the name and address of the nearest dealer.

The Magazine Silver   P.O. Box 22217, Milwaukie, Oregon 97222   (503) 654-4155
This firm offers all-wood display racks in which you can display your spoon and thimble collections.

Putnam Rolling Ladder Company, Inc.   32 Howard Street, New York, New York 10013
(212) 226-5147
Oak rolling library ladders are made to order. They are finished in oak, walnut, mahogany, or to a sample supplied. The ladder runs on a slotted track. This company also offers other types of ladders and library carts. A catalogue is available.

Replica Products   610 57th Street AI, Vienna, West Virginia 26150   (304) 295-7239
Replica Products makes collector display frames for convenient and compact storage of small objects: coins, buttons, badges, jewelry, etc. Boxes are made of heavy chipboard with sturdy glass windows in 6 different sizes. Minimum order is 5 frames.

Rogay, Inc.   4937 Wyaconda Road, Rockville, Maryland 20852   (301) 770-1700
This firm designs and makes special display facilities. It accepts custom orders from private collectors for wall cabinets, vitrines, and counter and freestanding displays of all shapes and sizes in wood, glass, metal, and plastic (including Lucite). Write for information on ordering. Specify kinds of art objects, dimensions, and display space as well as any associated artwork and accompanying furnishings.

Saxon & Clemens, Inc.   979 Third Avenue, New York, New York 10022   (212) 759-5791
This is a specialty workshop that sells and frames Oriental art and artifacts, shadow boxes, and Oriental scrolls. No catalogue is available.

97. GENERAL INFORMATION FOR DECODING ADVERTISING COPY

Reading the ads for antiques and collectibles often takes special knowledge. Two collectors will speak a special language in the same way two doctors have a vocabulary known only to their profession. It might help to know these terms and abbreviations that often appear in the ads.

If you are reading ads for clocks, dolls, Depression glass, and other specialized subjects, you will find helpful abbreviations in the appropriate chapters.

amb. Amber.
app. Applied.
b. or *bl.* Blue.
b & b. Bread and Butter.
blk. Black.
BM. Black mark.
B.P. Buffalo Pottery.
br. Brown.
bs. Backstamped.
bul. Bulb, bulbous.
bxd. Boxed.
C & I. Currier & Ives.
Carn. Carnival.
c. gl. Cut glass.
c.i. Cast iron.
ck. Check.
cl. Clear.
cr. Creamer.
crm. Cream (color).
c.s. Cup, saucer.

d. or *dia.* Diameter.
D & B. Daisy & Button.
D & M. Duncan & Miller.
dbl. Double.
dec. Decoration.
des. Design.
dia. Diamond.
diag. Diagonal.
diam. Diamond.
dq. Diamond quilted.
EAPG. Early American Pattern Glass.
emb. Embossed.
ex. Extra.
exc. Excellent.
f. Flint.
fgmn. Forget Me Not.
fig. Figurine.
fl. Flashed, flint, flake, or flute(d).
fl. b. Flow Blue.
flr. flower(s).

F.O.B. Free on board. (delivered free of charge to city named in ad)

ft. Feet.

ftd. Footed.

gld. Gilding, gold.

GM. Green mark.

gr. Green.

h. High.

Hav. Haviland.

hdle. Handle(d).

hex. Hexagonal.

hldr. Holder.

h.p. Hand painted.

i. or *I.* Insurance.

ill. Illustration(s).

inst. Instrument(s).

iri. or *irid.* Iridescent.

K.G. Kate Greenaway.

l. Long, length, liter.

LCT. Louis Comfort Tiffany.

lg. Large.

lt. Light.

m. Mint or marigold.

mari. Marigold.

m.g. Milk glass.

MIE. Made in England.

min. or *mini.* Miniature.

mk. or *mk'd.* Mark(ed).

m.o. Mail or money order.

M.O.P. Mother-of-pearl.

msng. Missing.

m/t. Marble top.

N. Trademarked N for Northwood glass.

nbs. Not backstamped.

n.f. or *non-f.* Non-flint.

n.h. No harm.

n.m. Near-mint.

o. Oval.

op. or *opal.* Opalescent(ce).

org. Orange.

P & I. Post and insurance.

pat. Pattern or patent.

pc(s). Piece(s).

ped. Pedestal.

per. or *perf.* Perfect.

pfgmn. Paneled Forget Me Not.

pk. Pink.

pl. or *plt.* Plate(s).

pol. pon. Polished pontil.

pon.(t) Pontil(led).

porc. Porcelain.

pot. Pottery.

pp. Parcel post.

ppd. Postpaid.

pr. Pair.

Ptld. T. of L. Portland Tree of Life.

PUG. Painted under glaze.

pur. Purple.

r. Round.

R.B. Royal Bayreuth.

rd. Red.

rec. or *rect.* Rectangular.

ref. Refer, reference.

res. Resilvered.

ret. Retail or return.

rev. Reverse.

RM. Red mark.

rnd. Round.

R.S.G. R.S. Germany.

R.S.P. R.S. Prussia.

Sand. Sandwich, Sandwich Co.

SASE or *SSAE.* Self-addressed, stamped envelope.

Sat. Guar. Satisfaction guaranteed.

sg. or *sgn.* Signed.

sil. Silver.

s-p. Salt, pepper.

sp. Spoon, spooner, spout.

s-pl. Silver plate.

sq. Square.

st. Stained.

sug. Sugar.

t. Tall.

Tif. Louis Comfort Tiffany.

tpk. Toothpick (holder).

tr. Transfer.

tri. or *tria.* Triangular.
UPS. United Parcel Service.
V. & B., Met. Villeroy & Boch, Mettlach.
v.g. Very good.
v.n.m. Very near mint.

w- or *w.* With.
wgt. or *wht.* Weight.
wh. White.
WW. Wedgwood.
yl. Yellow.

98. GENERAL PRICE GUIDES

Price guides are just that—guides to current prices. Some list estimated prices; some show the actual reported prices. Others just list prices offered from many years and some only list prices from the previous year. The accuracy depends on the method of obtaining the prices shown in the book.

Specialized guides are listed in the appropriate chapter; this is just a list of the *general* guides. Of course, we like our *Kovels' Antiques & Collectibles Price List* (New York: Crown Publishers, 1982) the best.

Art and Antique Auctions World-wide 1981. Netherlands: Vonk Publishers, 1981.

Colt, Charles C., Jr., ed. *Antique Trader Price Guide to Antiques & Collectors' Items.*
Dubuque, Iowa; Babka Publishing. Published quarterly.

————. *The Official Sotheby Parke Bernet Price Guide to Antiques and Decorative Arts.*
New York: Simon & Schuster, 1980.

Coombs, David, ed. *The Antique Collector's Picture Guide to Prices.*
London: Ebury Press, 1979.

Hammond, Dorothy. *Pictorial Price Guide to American Antiques and Objects Made for the American Market,* 1982–1983 ed.
New York: E. P. Dutton, 1981.

Herbert, John, ed. *Christie's Review of the Season 1981.*
New York: Rizzoli International Publications, 1981.

Herzog, David Alan. *Collecting Today for Tomorrow.*
New York: Arco Publishing, 1980.

Hislop, Richard, ed. *Annual Art Sales Index 1979–1980 Season.* 2 vols.
Surrey, England: Art Sales Index, 1980.

Hothem, Lar. *A Collector's Identification and Value Guide to Antiques.*
Florence, Alabama: Books Americana, 1980.

Kaduck, John M. *Sleepers that Have a Future (Small Collector's Items).*
Privately printed, 1970 (P.O. Box 02152, Cleveland, Ohio 44102). A 1982–1983 price guide is available.

Ketchum, William C. Jr. *The Catalog of American Collectibles.*
New York: Mayflower Books, 1981.

————. *The Catalog of World Antiques.*
New York: Rutledge Press, 1981.

————. *Western Memorabilia: Collectibles of the Old West.*
Maplewood, New Jersey: Hammond, 1980.

Kovel, Ralph and Terry. *The Kovels' Antiques & Collectibles Price List,* 15th ed.
New York: Crown Publishers, 1982.

Lyle Official Antiques Review, The, 1982.
Glenmayre, Galesheils, Scotland: Lyle Publications, 1981.

McFarland, Grace. *Official Price Guide to Antiques & Other Collectibles.*
Orlando, Florida: House of Collectibles, 1979.

McNerney, Kathryn. *Primitives, Our American Heritage.*
Paducah, Kentucky: Collector Books, 1979.

Mackay, James. *The Price Guide to More Collectable Antiques.*
Suffolk, England: Antique Collectors' Club (5 Church Street, Clopton, Woodbridge, Suffolk 1P12 1BR England), 1980; price revision list, 1981.

Miller, Robert W. *Wallace-Homestead Flea Market Price Guide,* 3rd ed.
Des Moines: Wallace-Homestead, 1981.

————. *Wallace-Homestead Price Guide to Antiques and Pattern Glass,* 8th ed.
Des Moines: Wallace-Homestead, 1982.

Quertermous, Steve, ed. *Flea Market Trader,* rev. 3rd ed.
Paducah, Kentucky: Collector Books, 1979.

Raycraft, Don and Carol. *Wallace-Homestead Price Guide to American Country Antiques,* 2nd ed. Des Moines: Wallace-Homestead, 1981.

Rinker, Harry L. *Warman's Antiques and Their Prices,* 16th ed.
Elkins Park, Pennsylvania: Warman Publishing Company, Inc., 1982.

Skinner Auctions Catalogue: The 1975–1980 Reorganized Edition.
Privately printed, 1980 (John W. Cooper, 605 N.E. 170th Street, Seattle, Washington 98155).

Sugar, Bert Randolph. *Collectibles: The Nostalgia Collector's Bible.*
Privately printed, 1981 (33 West 60th Street, New York, New York 10023).

99. GENERAL PUBLICATIONS

General information about antiques, collectibles, shows, sales, clubs, books, sources to buy and sell, repairs, and more can be found in the general antiques publications. They range from slick color magazines filled with articles by museum-trained experts to mimeographed sheets listing events by dedicated collectors. If you are a serious collector, you should read at least one of the national publications and one of the general regional newspapers or magazines that tell about shows and sales close to home. Specialized publications are included in the appropriate chapters in Part I.

American Art Journal   40 West 57th Street, 5th Floor, New York, New York 10019
(212) 541-9600
Quarterly fine arts magazine.

American Art Review   P.O. Box 65007, Los Angeles, California 90065
Fine arts magazine issued 6 times a year.

American Collector   Drawer C, Kermit, Texas 79745
Monthly newspaper.

The American Collector's Journal   P.O. Box 407, Kewanee, Illinois 61443   (309) 852-2602
Bimonthly newspaper.

American Heritage Magazine   381 West Center Street, Marion, Ohio 43302
This monthly magazine deals with history and historic memorabilia.

American Preservation   P.O. Box 2451, 620 E. 6th Street, Little Rock, Arkansas 72203
This is a bimonthly magazine with full-color illustrated stories about neighborhood preservation and articles about buildings and interiors.

Americana   475 Park Avenue South, 28th Floor, New York, New York 10016   (212) 686-6810
Monthly magazine.

Andex, A Market Place   1700 Walnut Street, Philadelphia, Pennsylvania 19103   (215) 735-0778
This is a monthly newsletter for buying and selling art and antiques. It features classified ads.

Antique & Collectables   P.O. Box 551, South Pasadena, California 91030   (213) 682-1786
Newspaper issued twice monthly.

Antique & Collectors Mart   15100 West Kellogg, Wichita, Kansas 67235
Monthly newspaper.

Antique Collecting   5 Church Street, Clopton, Woodbridge, Suffolk 1P12 1BR England
Monthly magazine about the English market.

Antique Collector   c/o Expediters of the Printed Word, 527 Madison Avenue, New York, New York 10022
Monthly magazine about the English market.

The Antique Dealer & Collectors Guide   165-177 The Broadway, Park House, 5th Floor, Wimbledon, London SW19 1NE England
Monthly magazine about the English market.

The Antique Gazette   929 Davidson Drive, Nashville, Tennessee 37205   (615) 352-0941
Monthly magazine.

Antique Market Tabloid   10305 Calumet Drive, Silver Spring, Maryland 20901   (301) 681-9090
Monthly newspaper with ads, articles, and events of interest to readers in the midatlantic states.

Antique Monthly   P.O. Drawer 2, Tuscaloosa, Alabama 35401   (205) 345-0272
Monthly newspaper.

Antique Show & Auction Calendar   9 Raymond Lane, Shelton, Connecticut 06484
(203) 929-5238
Monthly newspaper listing antiques shows and auctions.

Antique Trade Gazette   Langley House, 116 Long Acre, London WC2E 9PA England
Weekly newspaper.

Antique Trader Weekly   P.O. Box 1050 Dubuque, Iowa 52001   (319) 588-2073
Weekly newspaper featuring buy and sell ads and a few articles.

Antiques (The Magazine Antiques)   551 Fifth Avenue, New York, New York 10017
(212) 922-1818
Monthly magazine.

Antiques & Art Monitor   9 Great Newport Street, London WC2E 9PA England
Newspaper.

Antiques & Collectibles   525 North Barry Avenue, Mamaroneck, New York 10543
(914) 698-1500
Monthly want-ad publication.

The Antiques Dealer   1115 Clifton, P.O. Box 2147, Clifton, New Jersey 07015   (201) 779-1600
Only dealers can subscribe to this monthly magazine.

Architectural Antiques & Artifacts Advertiser   P.O. Box 31, 459 Rockland Road, Merion, Pennsylvania 19066   (215) 664-4559
Monthly newspaper with ads for architectural antiques.

Architectural Digest   5900 Wilshire Boulevard, Los Angeles, California 90036
Although this bimonthly magazine is primarily about decorating it may interest antiques collectors.

Art & Antique Auction Review   IFM Building, Old Saybrook, Connecticut 06475
(203) 388-4647
Monthly newsletter with auction reports.

Art & Antiques   1515 Broadway, New York, New York 10036   (212) 764-7300
Monthly magazine.

The Art/Antiques Investment Report   120 Wall Street, New York, New York 10005
Newsletter for investors issued biweekly.

Art & Auction   250 West 57th Street, New York, New York 10019   (212) 582-5633
Magazine issued 10 times a year consisting mainly of auction reports.

Arts & Antiques Antiquarian   P.O. Box 798, Huntington, New York 11743   (516) 271-8990
Monthly newspaper with show and shop ads and events.

The Auction Bottom Line   1 AMN Park, New Paris, Ohio 45347   (513) 437-7071 or 437-0263
Monthly newspaper for auctioneers.

The Auctioneer   112 Street, Clair Avenue West, Toronto, Ontario M4V 2Y3 Canada
Monthly newsletter.

The Australasian Antique Collector 1PC Business Pty Ltd., Queen Street, Chippendale, Sidney NSW 2008 Australia
Magazine about the Australian market.

Barron's 420 Lexington Avenue, New York, New York 10017 (212) 285-5373
Arts and Antiques sections appear 4 times a year. *The Sotheby Index* appears weekly and gives price trends in the art and antiques market.

California Art & Antiques Monthly P.O. Box 706, Lodi, California 95240 (209) 334-5533
Monthly newsletter.

Canadian Collector 27 Carlton Street, Suite 406, Toronto, Ontario M5B 1L2 Canada
Monthly magazine.

CanadiAntiquer P.O. Box 250, 39 1st Avenue South, Chesley, Ontario N0G 1LO Canada
(519) 363-3313
Monthly newspaper.

Collect America International P.O. Box 777, Waynesboro, Tennessee 38485 (615) 722-3338
Monthly newspaper.

Collectibles Illustrated Depot Square, Peterborough, New Hampshire 03444 (603) 563-8111
Monthly magazine featuring memorabilia and collectibles.

Collector Editions Quarterly 170 Fifth Avenue, New York, New York 10010 (212) 989-8700
Quarterly magazine concerned with limited editions and modern collector items.

The Collector-Investor 740 Rush Street, Chicago, Illinois 60611 (312) 649-5280
An investment-oriented monthly magazine for the high-priced market.

Collectors Journal P.O. Box 601, Vinton, Iowa 52349
Weekly newspaper.

Collector's News P.O. Box 156, Grundy Center, Iowa 50638 (319) 824-5456
Monthly newspaper.

Collectors' Showcase P.O. Box 6929, San Diego, California 92107 (714) 222-0386
Bimonthly magazine on toys, advertising, and memorabilia.

Colonial Homes P.O. Box 10160, Des Moines, Iowa 50350
Bimonthly decorating magazine for the "country look" enthusiast.

The Connoisseur   250 West 55th Street, New York, New York 10019
Monthly magazine about fine arts and decorating arts.

Country Americana Magazine   R.D. 1, P.O. Box 228, Washington, New Jersey 07882
(201) 689-7512
Bimonthly magazine.

Early American Life   P.O. Box 1607, Marion, Ohio 43302   (717) 255-7720
This bimonthly magazine contains history, decorating, and some collector information.

Everything Has a Value   27 Wilfred Street, London SW1E 6PR England
Monthly magazine about collectibles.

Finders Keepers   Old Bottle Emporium, Herriotts Lane, Wellingborough, Northants, United Kingdom
Bimonthly magazine about postcards, cigarette cards, advertising, ephemera, etc.

The Gray Letter   P.O. Drawer 2, Tuscaloosa, Alabama 35401
Weekly newsletter about high ticket antiques and art.

The Herald   Friends of Greenfield Village & Henry Ford Museum, Dearborn, Michigan 48121
(313) 271-1620
Quarterly magazine about antiques in the Henry Ford Museum.

Hobbies   1006 South Michigan Avenue, Chicago, Illinois 60605
Monthly magazine containing ads, a few articles, and show listings.

Home Restoration   P.O. Box 327, Gettysburg, Pennsylvania 17325   (717) 624-7586 or 624-4105
Bimonthly magazine about home restoration. Some how-to articles and success stories.

The Jersey Devil   P.O. Box 202, Lambertville, New Jersey 08530
Monthly newspaper.

Joel Sater's Antiques and Auction News   P.O. Box B, Marietta, Pennsylvania 17547
(717) 426-1956
Biweekly newspaper.

Journal of the Museum of Early Southern Decorative Arts   Drawer F, Salem Station, Winston-Salem, North Carolina 27108   (919) 722-6148
One must be a member of MESDA to receive this semiannual magazine. Members also receive *The Luminary,* a newsletter, in February and August, which falls between the usual publication dates of the MESDA journal.

Kovels on Antiques and Collectibles   P.O. Box 22200, Beachwood, Ohio 44122
Illustrated monthly newsletter for dealers and collectors. Up-to-date price information.

Maine Antique Digest (M.A.D.)   P.O. Box 358, Jefferson Street, Waldoboro, Maine 04572
(207) 832-7534
Monthly national newspaper reporting on U.S.A. and eastern Canada.

National Auction Report   15100 West Kellogg, Wichita, Kansas 67235   (316) 722-9750
Monthly newsletter listing auction results.

National Journal   P.O. Box 3121, Wescosville, Pennsylvania 18106   (215) 432-1090
This monthly magazine just changed from a newspaper format. It contains articles and ads about
antiques and collectibles with emphasis on twentieth-century glass and china.

The New York Antique Almanac   P.O. Box 335, Lawrence, New York 11559   (516) 371-3300
Monthly newspaper.

The New York-Pennsylvania Collector   4 South Main Street, Pittsford, New York 14534
(716) 381-3300
Monthly newspaper.

The Newtown Bee   Bee Publishing Company, Newtown, Connecticut 06470
This weekly newspaper features articles, sales, and shows in New England.

Nineteenth Century   The Athenaeum, East Washington Square, Philadelphia, Pennsylvania 19106
This quarterly magazine is distributed to members of The Victorian Society in America and contains
information about Victorian decorative arts and buildings.

Ohio Antique Review   72 East North Street, Worthington, Ohio 43085   (614) 885-9757
Monthly newspaper about Midwestern antique events and interests.

The Old-House Journal   69A Seventh Avenue, Brooklyn, New York 11217
This is a monthly newsletter with detailed information on how to restore an old house, from wiring
and painting to basements and leaks. Back issues are available and the material is dateless.

Old Stuff   P.O. Box 230220, Tigard, Oregon 97223
Old Stuff is published quarterly and is distributed free at antiques shows and shops in the Northwest. It
is also offered by subscription. Shop and show ads and events are listed.

Ontario Showcase   1567 Sedlescomb Drive, Mississauga, Ontario L4X 1M5 Canada
(416) 625-4700
Monthly magazine about Canadian antiques.

Portfolio: The Magazine of the Fine Arts   171 Madison Avenue, New York, New York 10016
(212) 686-2112
Bimonthly magazine.

Provenance 2227 Granville Street, Vancouver, British Columbia V6H 3G1 Canada (604) 734-4944
Magazine about fine arts in Canada.

Rarities 17337 Ventura Boulevard, Encino, California 91316   (213) 788-7080
Bimonthly magazine.

The Register Lock Box C, Minden Lane, Yarmouth Port, Maine 02675   (617) 362-2111
Monthly newspaper.

Smithsonian Membership Data Center, P.O. Box 2953, Boulder, Colorado 80321
Monthly magazine with some articles about antiques.

Southern Antiques—The Southeast Trader P.O. Box 1550, Lake City, Florida 32055
(904) 752-3167
Monthly newspaper.

Spinning Wheel Fame Avenue, Hanover, Pennsylvania 17331   (717) 653-8401
Monthly magazine.

Swap Meet USA P.O. Box 272, Saginaw, Michigan 48606   (517) 793-4704
Semiannual magazine containing show listings.

Tri-State Trader P.O. Box 90, Knightstown, Indiana 46148
Weekly newspaper about Ohio, Indiana, Pennsylvania, Illinois events.

The Upper Canadian P.O. Box 1171, Kingston, Ontario K7L 4Y8 Canada   (613) 542-6111
Bimonthly newspaper.

Victorian Homes P.O. Box 61, Millers Falls, Massachusetts 01349   (413) 659-3785
Magazine published quarterly featuring articles on restoration, sources for products and services, and how-to advice.

West Coast Peddler P.O. Box 4489, Downey, California 90241
Monthly newspaper.

Winterthur Portfolio 11030 South Langley Avenue, Chicago, Illinois 60628
Quarterly magazine featuring scholarly articles.

Yankee Dublin, New Hampshire 03444
Monthly magazine with occasional articles on antiques.

100. MATCHING SERVICES

Now that you have inherited that set of dishes from your mother or silverware from your great aunt, you should use them. But what to do about the four broken cups or the two missing teaspoons? Matching services can help. Many patterns of dishes, silverware, and glassware can be found through these matching services. Learn the name of your pattern by researching in books at the library or take a very clear picture and send it to the appropriate matching service. Dinnerware can be pictured easily by placing the dish face down on a photocopying machine. List the pieces you want and the service will write back with information regarding prices and pieces available. You may have to wait a few months while the service hunts for the pieces you need, or sometimes you may not be able to locate the pieces you need. Usually, though, these services are successful. See Chapters 31, 61, and 70 for factory addresses.

Manufacturers sometimes offer specials on out-of-stock china, glass, and silver. These offers occur once a year, usually in January, and you can order to fill in a set. Only a small number of patterns can be matched this way. Some porcelain factories will take an order for an out-of-date pattern when they are making a similar pattern, but this may take several years and is very expensive.

Of course, you might be lucky and find your missing pieces at shows or sales. Ask the dealers. There are many matching services; the ones included here are only those that answered our questionnaire. These matching service lists also help you to determine the value of a set for insurance. If the vocabulary used by the dealers in their instructions confuses you, see Chapter 61, Pottery and Porcelain, for an explanation.

CHINA

Auld Lang Syne   Yosemite Junction, 7600 Highway 120, Jamestown, California 95327 (209) 984-DISH
This is a locating service that specializes in Haviland dinnerware. Send a list and identify the pattern desired using the Schleiger number, Jacobson number, or photocopy of three flat plates with the colors identified and backstamps. Send a self-addressed, stamped envelope with all inquiries.

Ernestine R. Bell   423 S.E. 17th Place, Ocala, Florida 32670   (904) 622-3953
This is a matching service for French and American Haviland china. Send the pattern number or a photocopy of the front and back of a plate with the colors written in, along with a self-addressed, stamped envelope.

The Blue Plate Antiques   P.O. Box 124, Sherborn, Massachusetts 01770   (617) 655-3971
This is a Flow Blue china matching service. Complete sets and individual pieces are available. Send the pattern name and the pieces desired. Include a self-addressed, stamped envelope for reply. A catalogue of patterns, prices, and photos is available for $2.50.

Blue Willow   P.O. Box 601, Oakridge, Oregon 97463
Blue Willow china is available. Send a self-addressed, stamped envelope for a list.

Mildred G. Brumback   P.O. Box 21, Route 2, Middletown, Virginia 22645   (703) 869-1261
This is a matching service for Syracuse, Castleton, and American Haviland. Write concerning your needs.

The China Corner   P.O. Box 7745, Colorado Springs, Colorado 80933   (303) 598-4210
This firm offers a matching service for discontinued patterns of French and American Haviland china. Postage is required with any sample that is sent for identification if you want it returned; postage is also required with the first inquiry.

The China Match   9 Elmford Road, Rochester, New York 14606   (716) 426-2783
Replacement pieces for Minton, Royal Doulton, Lenox, Syracuse, and other fine china are offered. The company does not carry Haviland or Noritake. Send stamps for a reply.

Marian Church   P.O. Box 255A, Road #6, New Castle, Pennsylvania 16101   (412) 924-2271
This matching service specializes in Castleton, Franciscan, Lenox, Oxford, and American Haviland.

Coalport   2901 Los Feliz Boulevard, Los Angeles, California 90039
This is a matching service. Coalport china is matched.

Mrs. Robert Conner Matching Service for Haviland China   "Dishes Like Grandma Used to Break," 1060 Crestline Drive, Crete, Nebraska 68333   (402) 826-2622
This is a matching and identification service for French and American Haviland patterns. This service is free, but please include a self-addressed, stamped envelope with a request for instructions on how you can obtain replacements for your pattern.

Eileen's Elite Haviland China Service   2300 Van Dorn, Lincoln, Nebraska 68502   (402) 475-6868
Send the Schleiger number or a photocopy along with a self-addressed, stamped envelope.

Fran Jay   24 Minton Avenue, Chatham, New Jersey 07928   (201) 635-6260
Fran Jay deals with Stangl, Russel Wright, Hall, and other American-made china (no Castleton). Send a self-addressed, stamped envelope with specific wants.

Franciscan   2901 Los Feliz Boulevard, Los Angeles, California 90039
Franciscan china is matched.

Galerie de Porcelaine   520 Hillside, Glen Ellyn, Illinois 60137   (312) 858-9494 or 834-5846
This is a matching service for French and American Haviland patterns. A self-addressed, stamped envelope is appreciated with all mail inquiries.

Gayle's   606 4th Avenue S.E., Jamestown, North Dakota 58401   (701) 252-4544
This is a French Haviland china matching service, pieces or sets. Send the Schleiger number or a sample plus a self-addressed, stamped envelope.

Geiser's English Cups/Saucers and Dinnerware   Route 1, P.O. Box 426, Rolla, Missouri 65401
(314) 364-8865
Many brands of English-made china are matched. Send a 30¢ stamp for a price list of items available.

Judi Giangiuli   Road #6, P.O. Box 152, New Castle, Pennsylvania 16101   (412) 924-9052
Judi Giangiuli offers Castleton china replacements. Send a self-addressed, stamped envelope for a reply.

Grace Graves   3959 North Harcourt Place, Milwaukee, Wisconsin 53211   (414) 964-9180
Grace Graves specializes in identifying and matching old French and American Haviland patterns. Use the Schleiger number or send a sample with a self-addressed, stamped envelope.

Jacquelyn B. Hall   10629 Baxter Avenue, Los Altos, California 94022   (408) 739-4876
This is a china pattern matching service dealing with Lenox and Oxford dinnerware (no Lenox crystal and no Lenox Temper-ware). Refer to your pattern by name and/or number. Send a self-addressed, stamped envelope for a reply.

Larry Hamm   2265 Hamilton-Middletown Road, Hamilton, Ohio 45011
This is a French and American Haviland matching service. Send Schleiger number or a photocopy of your china and a self-addressed, stamped envelope for a reply.

Haviland Corner Matching Service   P.O. Box 82, Belmont, California 94002   (415) 591-2818
This is a matching service for Haviland patterns. Send the Schleiger number or a photocopy, front and back, of a saucer or a plate to identify the pattern.

Mildred Holdeman   P.O. Box 585, Auburn, Indiana 46706   (219) 925-4567
This is a matching service for French Haviland. Send the Schleiger number and a self-addressed, stamped envelope.

Marvetia Jack   Noritake and Lenox China Matching, 148 12th Street, Silvis, Illinois 61282
(309) 792-0818
Marvetia Jack matches discontinued Noritake and Lenox dinnerware. List the brand name, pattern name, numbers, and measurements of the items needed. If the pattern name and numbers are both unknown, either a clear picture or a sample of the pattern (perhaps from a damaged item) is necessary. Written requests should include a stamped, self-addressed envelope and a phone number. Phone calls are preferred.

Jacquelynn's China Matching Service 4770 North Oakland Avenue, Milwaukee, Wisconsin 53211 (414) 962-7213
This firm has over 5,000 pieces of discontinued and custom order Lenox and Oxford china in stock. It may have your pattern or it can locate it for you. Send a self-addressed, stamped envelope with your pattern request.

The Jewel Box P.O. Box 145, Albertville, Alabama 35950 (205) 878-3301
This is a matching service for discontinued china. Send the pattern name and brand with a self-addressed, stamped envelope.

Lillian Johnson Antiques 405 Third Street, San Juan Bautista, California 95045 (408) 623-4381
This is a Haviland matching service for sets or single pieces. Send the Schleiger number or a sample with a self-addressed, stamped envelope.

Judy's House of Hope 2968 Appling Drive, Chamblee, Georgia 30341 (404) 458-JUDY or 458-5839
This is a mail and phone matching service for discontinued china. List your exact needs, the manufacturer, the pattern name and/or number, a description of the shape, color, trim, and dimensions. With all unknown patterns a good clear photograph must accompany your request and will not be returned. Send a self-addressed, stamped envelope for a reply.

Locator's, Inc. 908 Rock Street, Little Rock, Arkansas 72202
This is a matching service for out-of-production patterns of china. It specializes in American and English manufacturers. Give the name of the manufacturer and the pattern name or number and include a self-addressed, stamped envelope for a reply.

The Matchmakers 1718 Air Port Court, Placerville, California 95667 (916) 626-5672
The Matchmakers deal in Haviland and Noritake discontinued patterns. Send a copy of the backstamp which includes the pattern name and/or number and a photocopy of the plate with colors indicated and a list of needed pieces. Please enclose a long, self-addressed, stamped envelope with requests.

L. D. (Les) McGinnis P.O. Box 3411, 129 North Goliad Street, Amarillo, Texas 79106 (806) 353-2782
This is a Syracuse china replacement center carrying discontinued patterns. Mail order only.

Dirck and Sjoeke Meengs P.O. Box 578, Woodland Hills, California 91365
This is a Spode replacement service. All requests are kept on file and all inquiries are answered. Frequent buyers and dealers receive a discount. They are also interested in purchasing full or partial sets of Spode dinner services. You can obtain a wallet-size list of patent dates, helpful in determining the oldest possible date of manufacture of any antique, for $1.00 plus a self-addressed, stamped envelope.

Virginia J. Miller 302 North Main Street, Bloomdale, Ohio 44817 (419) 454-2651
Virginia Miller offers a Haviland matching service. A sample or Schleiger number is necessary. Send a self-addressed, stamped envelope for a reply.

Old China Patterns Ltd.   P.O. Box 250, West Hill, Ontario M1E 4R5 Canada
This is a matching service for dinnerware patterns. Send all necessary information for the desired pieces. Enclose coins rather than a stamp for a reply.

The Old Toll Gate Antiques   600 North Avenue, Milan, Illinois 61264   (309) 787-2392
This is a Haviland china matching service. Use the Schleiger number or send a saucer as a sample, as well as a self-addressed, stamped envelope.

Patterns of Yesterday   139 York Avenue, Battle Creek, Michigan 49015   (616) 968-1205
This firm carries discontinued tableware replacements, china, and collectible dinnerware. Send the complete brand and pattern name, description, plus any markings. List the pattern pieces desired. A free request register and search service are available on request. Color photos and an associated price list are available for over 50 patterns. Send a self-addressed, stamped envelope for a free phone list and 2 extra stamps if a search is desired.

Peggy's Matching Service   P.O. Box 476, Ocala, Florida 32670   (904) 629-3954
This service deals in Noritake china exclusively. It answers all requests accompanied by a self-addressed, stamped envelope.

Vera L. Phillips   6427 South Prince Street, Littleton, Colorado 80120   (303) 794-4135
Vera Phillips offers a matching service for French and American Haviland china. She must know the pattern number so use a sample or have a clear photo or photocopy made to determine the pattern.

Popkorn Antiques   137 Main Street, Flemington, New Jersey 08822   (201) 782-9631
Items handled include Stangl, Fiesta, Russel Wright, Franciscan, and other American china. Hall china is a specialty. Send a photo or drawing along with a self-addressed, stamped envelope.

Replacements   1510 Holbrook Street, Greensboro, North Carolina 27403   (919) 275-7224
This firm buys and sells discontinued china, mostly by mail. It specializes in Lenox, Spode, Oxford, Minton, Doulton, Franconia, Syracuse, Castleton, Noritake, Worcester, Flintridge, Franciscan, American Haviland, Wedgwood, etc. Enclose a self-addressed, stamped envelope with your inquiry.

Dorothy N. Robinson   P.O. Box 180, Trenton, New Jersey 08601   (215) 295-1023
Dorothy Robinson specializes in finding Lenox china liners or inserts for sterling holders (sherbets, bouillons, demitasse cups, etc.).

Roundhill's Patterns Unlimited International   P.O. Box 15238, Seattle, Washington 98115
(206) 523-9710
This firm deals in discontinued patterns of tabletop items. Call or write inquiries. An appraisal service for evaluating discontinued patterns of ceramics, crystal, and silver is available. Cost is $30.00 per pattern, with no limit on the number of pieces.

Sandra's China Gallery Ltd.   4209 Hunt Club Lane, Westlake Village, California 91361 (213) 889-5699
Sets and pieces of Haviland china are identified and located. Send the Schleiger number or a sample with a self-addressed, stamped envelope.

The Side Door   P.O. Box 573, 181 Depot Street, Dennisport, Massachusetts 02639   (617) 394-7715
This matching service specializes in Flow Blue, Mulberryware, and Staffordshire. Send a self-addressed, stamped envelope for a list. Flow Blue is updated monthly. Mulberryware and Staffordshire transfer patterns are updated bimonthly.

Sophia's China   141 Sedgwick Road, Syracuse, New York 13203   (315) 472-6834
This is a matching service for discontinued china. Sales are solely by mail order. Provide a self-addressed, stamped envelope for reply. Customer wants are maintained on file; therefore, it is important that an exact listing of all items needed be made with the initial query.

Stonewall Antiques   230 Franklin, Selma, Alabama 36701   (205) 872-9632
This is a Haviland matching service. Send the Schleiger number or a sample.

Straw Flowers, Inc.   801 West Eldorado, Decatur, Illinois 62522   (217) 428-7212 or 423-8303 or 864-2938
This is a matching service for Haviland china. Write or call with inquiries.

Tabletop Matching Service and Collectors Items   China and Crystal Replacements, Mrs. Betty H. Allen, P.O. Box 205, Cookeville, Tennessee 38501   (615) 526-4303
This firm carries replacements for discontinued lines of most companies in china and pottery. Inventory is new, never used, usually store stock, mint condition, and guaranteed to the buyer. Send a self-addressed, stamped envelope for a reply.

Topex Company   58 Linda Lane, Tiffin, Ohio 44883   (419) 447-7939
This company carries discontinued patterns of china. There is no charge for its location service, only for pieces you purchase. Send complete identification including manufacturer's name, pattern name, china backstamps or markings, and the items you are seeking. Pattern and shape photos help and are usually required. Please include a self-addressed, stamped envelope for a reply.

Treasure Hunt   Margaret Head, 758 Nadeau Road, Monroe, Michigan 48161   (313) 241-7430
Matching Haviland china is easy: Inventory your china, listing the needs desired to complete your set. Have a photocopy made of a bread-and-butter plate, or send a damaged piece. Send a self-addressed, stamped envelope.

Unique Antiques and Gifts   7119 Navajo Road, San Diego, California 92119   (714) 461-7780
This firm offers china matching for old French Haviland, Lenox, and Oxford. It buys and sells by the piece or by the set.

Varner's Matching Service   1439 N.E. 13th Avenue, Rochester, Minnesota 55901   (507)289-2938
This firm specializes in French and American Haviland china. Include a self-addressed, stamped envelope with inquiries.

The Victorian Antique Shop   3720 6th Avenue, Sioux City, Iowa 51106   (712) 276-6141
This is a matching service for old French Haviland. Send the Schleiger number or sample along with a self-addressed, stamped envelope.

Vintage Patterns Unlimited   3571 Crestnoll Drive, Cincinnati, Ohio 45211   (513) 662-2543
This firm specializes in Rosenthal and other fine lines such as Wedgwood, Spode, Franciscan, Flintridge, Noritake, etc. Send a self-addressed, stamped envelope for a reply.

Walker's Haviland China   P.O. Box 357, 21 Utah Place, Athens, Ohio 45701   (614) 593-5631
This is a matching service for discontinued French and American Haviland china. Send a photocopy of a plate noting colors and back markings, a piece of your china packed well with return postage included, or a photo clear enough to show pattern details. Include a listing of the pieces needed to fill out your set. A stamped, self-addressed envelope is most appreciated.

Mildred E. Webster   P.O. Box 37114, 1110 West 50th Street, Los Angeles, California 90037
(213) 758-4353
Mildred Webster specializes in French Haviland china. Send a sample or the Schleiger number.

The Wedgewood China Cupboard   740 North Honey Creek Parkway, Milwaukee, Wisconsin
53213   (414) 771-0966
This is a matching service for discontinued Wedgwood dinnerware. Written inquiries must include a self-addressed, stamped envelope.

Wesche's Antiques   480 North Orange, Orlando, Florida 32801   (305) 425-6481
China matching services are offered.

White's Collectables & Fine China   P.O. Box 680, 104 South College, Newberg, Oregon 97132
(503) 538-7421
This firm deals in discontinued china patterns with Lenox and Spode its specialty. Some Royal Worcester, Royal Doulton, Syracuse, Franciscan, Castleton, and Minton are also handled. Each request must give a pattern name, not just a number or description. If the pattern is not known, send a picture or photocopy of a plate along with the company name, dimensions, and a self-addressed, stamped envelope.

FURNITURE
Roder's Antiques   160 Cokato Street East, Cokato, Minnesota 55321   (612) 286-5081
This firm specializes in antique pressed back chairs. Send a photo of the chair you would like to match. A large selection is in stock.

GLASS

Bishop-White's, Inc.   P.O. Box 52414, Atlanta, Georgia 30355   (404) 231-8708
This firm matches discontinued crystal stemware. Send a self-addressed, stamped envelope.

China House Antiques   Madeleine Pastor, Proprietor, 20 6th Avenue, Tiffin, Ohio 44883
(419) 447-4714
This is a Tiffin glass matching service. Send a photo or sketch of the pattern needed and a self-addressed, stamped envelope for a reply.

The Hawkes Hunter   5384 Pennock Point Road, Jupiter, Florida 33458   (305) 746-6382
This firm deals in Hawkes glass with an emphasis on matching stemware patterns. Send two stamps for a brochure.

Fran Jay   24 Minton Avenue, Chatham, New Jersey 07928   (201) 635-6260
This is a matching service for Depression glass, Fostoria, Cambridge, etc. (no Early American pattern glass). A self-addressed, stamped envelope with specific wants is appreciated.

The Jewel Box   P.O. Box 145, Albertville, Alabama 35950   (205) 878-3301
This is a crystal matching service. Send your pattern name and brand in with a self-addressed, stamped envelope.

Judy's House of Hope   2968 Appling Drive, Chamblee, Georgia 30341   (404) 458-JUDY or 458-5839
This is a mail and phone order service which helps locate discontinued china and crystal. List exact needs, manufacturer, pattern name and/or number, and a description of the shape, color, trim, and dimensions. If the pattern is unknown a good clear photograph must accompany your request and it will not be returned. Also send a self-addressed, stamped envelope.

Margaret Lane Antiques   2 East Main Street, New Concord, Ohio 43762   (614) 826-4418
This is a Cambridge glass matching service of all patterns produced by the company between 1901 and 1957. Send a self-addressed, stamped envelope and you will be notified of any pieces in your pattern.

Lil-Bud Antiques   141 Main Street, Yarmouth Port, Massachusetts 02675   (617) 362-6675
This is a matching service for Early American pattern glass. To ensure a reply send a self-addressed, stamped envelope.

Locator's Inc.   908 Rock Street, Little Rock, Arkansas 72202
This is a matching service for out-of-production crystal patterns. It specializes in American and English manufacturers of china and crystal. When writing, please give the name of the manufacturer and the pattern name and/or number and include a self-addressed, stamped envelope for a reply.

Lynne-Art's Glass House   P.O. Box 54-6014, Miami Beach, Florida 33154   (305) 861-7700
This firm specializes in unusual pieces of Heisey glass.

Marcy's Antiques & Gifts   6777 Dumeny Road, Greencastle, Pennsylvania 17225   (717) 328-2573
This firm deals in Early American pressed glass.

Nadine Pankow   207 South Oakwood, Willow Springs, Illinois 60480   (312) 839-5231
Nadine Pankow offers a matching service for Depression glass, etched Cambridge, Fostoria, and Heisey. Write for specific wants.

Patterns of Yesterday   139 York Avenue, Battle Creek, Michigan 49015   (616) 968-1205
This firm offers discontinued tableware replacements including crystal and Depression glass. Send the complete brand and pattern name and description plus any available markings. List the pieces desired. A free request register and search service are available upon request. Color photos and corresponding price lists for over 50 patterns are also available free with a self-addressed, stamped envelope. Send 2 extra stamps for a search.

Popkorn Antiques   137 Main Street, Flemington, New Jersey 08822   (201) 782-9631
This firm offers Depression glass, Cambridge, Fostoria, Fenton, etc. Send a self-addressed, stamped envelope with inquiries on specific glass wants. Also send a photo or drawing.

Replacements   1510 Holbrook Street, Greensboro, North Carolina 27403   (919) 275-7224
This firm buys and sells discontinued crystal and china, mostly by mail. It specializes in Tiffin, Heisey, Duncan, Fostoria, Cambridge, etc. Enclose a self-addressed, stamped envelope with your inquiry for a reply.

Dorothy N. Robinson   P.O. Box 180, Trenton, New Jersey 08601   (215) 295-1023
Dorothy Robinson specializes in finding crystal liners or inserts for sterling holders (sherbets, bouillons, demitasse cups, etc.).

Roundhill's Patterns Unlimited International   P.O. Box 15238, Seattle, Washington 98115   (206) 523-9710
This firm deals in discontinued patterns of tabletop items. Call or write. There is an appraisal service for evaluating discontinued patterns of ceramics, crystal, and silver. Cost is $30.00 per pattern, with no limit on the number of pieces.

Sophia's China   141 Sedgwick Road, Syracuse, New York 13203   (315) 472-6834
This is a matching service for discontinued crystal. Sales are by mail. Provide a self-addressed, stamped envelope for a reply. Customer wants are maintained on file; therefore, it is important that an exact listing of all items needed be made with the initial query.

Tabletop Matching Service and Collectors Items   China and Crystal Replacements, Mrs. Betty H. Allen, P.O. Box 205, Cookeville, Tennessee 38501   (615) 526-4303
This firm offers replacements for discontinued lines in crystal and glassware. The inventory is new, never used, usually store stock, mint, and guaranteed to the buyer. Send a self-addressed, stamped envelope for a reply.

Topex Company   58 Linda Lane, Tiffin, Ohio 44883   (419) 447-7939
This company locates discontinued patterns of crystal. There is no charge for location service, only for pieces you purchase. Send complete identification material including manufacturer's name, pattern name, markings, and the items you are seeking. Patterns and shape photos help and are usually required. Include a self-addressed, stamped envelope for a reply.

Trafalgar Antiques   P.O. Box 562, 2122 California Street, N.W., Washington, D.C. 20008
This is a search service for American pressed glass. Send a list of the specific pieces wanted including pattern and color. A self-addressed, stamped envelope is required for a reply.

Varner's Matching Service   1439 N.E. 13th Avenue, Rochester, Minnesota 55901   (507) 289-2938
This firm specializes in Heisey glass. Please include a self-addressed, stamped envelope with all inquiries.

Vintage Patterns Unlimited   3571 Crestnoll Drive, Cincinnati, Ohio 45211   (513) 662-2543
This is a replacement center for fine crystal. Include a self-addressed, stamped envelope with all inquiries.

SILVER

IDENTIFICATION

The first step in successfully matching items of silver is proper identification. The following books will enable you to identify almost any silver pattern.

Davis, Fredna Harris and Deibel, Kenneth K. *Silverplated Flatware Patterns.*
Dallas: Bluebonnet Press, 1981.

Hagan, Tere. *Silverplated Flatware: An Identification and Value Guide.*
Paducah, Kentucky: Collector Books, 1981.

Osterberg, Richard F., and Smith, Betty. *Silver Flatware Dictionary.*
San Diego: A. S. Barnes, 1981.

Snell, Doris. *American Silverplated Flatware Patterns.*
Des Moines: Wallace-Homestead, 1980.

————. *Art Nouveau & Art Deco Silverplated Flatware.*
Des Moines: Wallace-Homestead, 1976.

————. *Silverplated Flatware.*
Des Moines: Wallace-Homestead, 1971.

Sterling Flatware Pattern Index.
Radnor, Pennsylvania: Chilton Publications, 1977.

MATCHING SERVICES

Antiques Olde and Nue   6960 North Interstate, Portland, Oregon 97217   (503) 289-2922
This firm offers silver plate pattern matching and hollow ware. Call or write for more information.

As You Like It   3929 Magazine Street, New Orleans, Louisiana 70115   (504) 897-6915
This firm offers sterling and silver-plated flatware, active, obsolete, and inactive patterns. A want list is maintained. Mail orders are welcome.

Bennett Antiques   Silverplate Matching Service, 417 Marina Boulevard, Suisun City, California 94585   (707) 425-2994
This firm carries about 200,000 pieces in stock from 1845 to the present. It has active, inactive, and obsolete patterns. A want file is maintained. A list is available for an envelope and 2 stamps.

Beverly Antiques, Inc.   8827 Beverly Boulevard, Los Angeles, California 90048   (213) 271-8517
This is a matching service for sterling silver flatware and sterling and Sheffield hollow ware. Want lists are kept. Send a self-addressed, stamped envelope with any inquiries.

Robert D. Biggs   1155 East 58, Chicago, Illinois 60637
This is a matching service for silver-plated flatware. A want list is kept. Send a self-addressed, stamped envelope with all inquiries and for a list.

Beverly Bremer Silver Shop   2424 Piedmont Road N.E., Booth 328, Atlanta, Georgia 30324
(404) 261-4009
This is a matching service for American sterling silver flatware. Write for pattern inventory.

Buschemeyer's Fine Jewelry Since 1865   515 South 4th Avenue, Louisville, Kentucky 40202
(800) 626-4555
This firm carries active, inactive, and obsolete patterns. Write explaining your needs and enclose a self-addressed, stamped envelope, or call for quotes, toll free.

Carman's Collectables   P.O. Box 258, Levittown, Pennsylvania 19059   (215) 946-9315
This firm offers silver plate pattern matching and unusual pieces. Want lists are kept active. There is no charge for shipping in the U.S.

Carol's Silver Exchange   P.O. Box 11133, Indianapolis, Indiana 46201   (317) 353-8870
This firm matches obsolete and discontinued silver plate flatware patterns. Inquire with a self-addressed, stamped envelope. Your name is kept on file and you will be notified when your piece is available.

The Clark's   P.O. Box 434, Oceanside, California 92054
This is a silver plate matching service. Send a self-addressed, stamped envelope with your wants for an inventory list.

Edward G. Wilson Antiques 1802 Chestnut Street, Philadelphia, Pennsylvania 19103
(215) 563-7329
This firm matches active, inactive, and obsolete sterling patterns. Coin silver, flatware, and hollow ware are available. Send $1.00 for a list.

Eulah's Silverplate Flatware Matching Service P.O. Box 2760, Anderson, Indiana 46018 (317) 643-5773
This is a silverware matching service. Inquiries are answered if a self-addressed, stamped envelope is enclosed.

Fisher Silver Exchange P.O. Box 90611, 2010 FM 1960 West, Houston, Texas 77090
(713) 440-9085
This is a silver matching service for sterling and silver-plated flatware featuring inactive and obsolete patterns. Its specialty in silver plate is old "grape" patterns. For a free identification guide for silver plate send a self-addressed, stamped envelope.

Flat Facts: Flatware Facts Exchange 64 Ponus Avenue, Norwalk, Connecticut 06850
(203) 847-8217
Flat Facts is a newsletter published every 3 months listing silver-plated flatware patterns alphabetically with the names of dealers and collectors wanting to buy or sell them. Special requests such as hollow ware and special services such as restoration and replating are also listed. A copy can be obtained by sending $1.00 to *Flat Facts*. This includes one free listing of a pattern or item you are looking for.

Charles H. Fuller P.O. Box 4325, Main Station, San Francisco, California 94101 (415) 626-2300
This is a matching service for discontinued American and sterling flatware patterns. Also available are English Georgian and Victorian flatware. A self-addressed, stamped envelope with inquiries ensures a reply.

Georgetown Silver Shoppe 1261 Wisconsin Avenue, N.W., Washington, D.C. 20007
(202) 337-0011
This firm has hundreds of active, inactive, and obsolete patterns of sterling silver flatware and sterling hollow ware.

The Gold Exchange P.O. Box 1678, Florence, South Carolina 29503 (800) 845-4360
This is a sterling flatware matching service. Everything is sold by the ounce. Thousands of pieces are in stock. Active, inactive, and obsolete items are carried. Call toll free.

Julius Goodman & Son 113 Madison Avenue, Memphis, Tennessee 38103 (901) 526-8528 or 526-8529
This firm specializes in antique, obsolete, inactive, and active sterling flatware and hollow ware.

Theresa & Arthur Greenblatt   Amherst, New Hampshire 03031   (603) 673-4401
A coin silver flatware list is available.

House of Antiques   202 North 5th Street, Springfield, Illinois 62701   (217) 544-9677
This is a sterling flatware matching service. It has a large stock of active, inactive, and obsolete patterns. Send wants or a tracing along with a self-addressed, stamped envelope.

Karen Kronimus   P.O. Box 300B, Jefferson, New York 12093   (607) 652-6237 or 652-6231
Karen Kronimus does silver plate matching. Send the name of your pattern and the backstamp, or a photocopy or drawing if the name is unknown, and you will be answered and your request placed in a want file. Send 2 stamps for a large list. A catalogue is available to dealers upon request.

La Mona's   73 Colonial Park Drive, Santa Rosa, California 95401   (707) 838-4911
Send a self-addressed, stamped envelope for a reply. A list is available.

The Lampost Silver Company   8312 East 11th Street, Tulsa, Oklahoma 74112
This company matches sterling flatware, all patterns, with rare exceptions. Coin silver, English, Georgian, and Victorian silver are available as purchases permit. Always include a self-addressed, stamped envelope for an answer.

Helen Lawler   Route 1, P.O. Box 334, Blytheville, Arkansas 72315   (314) 720-8502
Helen Lawler matches silver-plated flatware. Interested persons should send a self-addressed, stamped envelope for a listing of her patterns. Send a photocopy if you are unable to identify the pattern.

Locator's Inc.   908 Rock Street, Little Rock, Arkansas 72202
This is a matching service for out-of-production silver. When writing to it, please give the name of the manufacturer and the pattern name and/or number and include a self-addressed, stamped envelope for a reply.

Marleda's   P.O. Box 2308, San Bernardino, California 92406   (714) 882-1716
This is a matching service for silver-plated flatware. Stock ranges from patterns made in the late 1800s to the present time. All inquiries are answered. A self-addressed, stamped envelope is appreciated.

Matchmaker of Iowa   142 Hampshire Road, Waterloo, Iowa 50701   (319) 233-0578
This firm specializes in current, discontinued, and obsolete patterns of silver-plated flatware. A rubbing, drawing, or photocopy of a pattern may be sent for pattern identification. A self-addressed, stamped envelope is appreciated. A want file is kept.

Maxwell's House Antiques, Inc.   612 West 4th Street, Sioux Falls, South Dakota 57104
(605) 334-3640
This is a sterling silver matching service. Want lists are kept. Send a self-addressed, stamped envelope for a list of available pieces.

Marilyn McCann   300 South 18th, Quincy, Illinois 62301   (217) 223-6919 evenings
Marilyn McCann will try to find pieces of silver-plated flatware for individuals or dealers. Those interested in her services should write including a self-addressed, stamped envelope.

Martin M. Fleischer's Silversmith Shop   143 North Park Avenue, Rockville Centre, New York 11570
The Silversmith Shop specializes in old flatware patterns and souvenir spoons. It is open by appointment only.

Miscellargeny (J. E. Mettler)   P.O. Box 11077, Govans Station, Baltimore, Maryland 21212 (301) 547-1013
This firm matches sterling silver flatware, mostly inactive and obsolete patterns. It also deals in sterling silver hollow ware. Send wants and include a self-addressed, stamped envelope for a reply.

Mitchell Enterprises   157 Mineola Avenue, Roslyn Heights, New York 11577   (516) 484-1200
This is a sterling flatware matching service. Want lists are kept and inquiries are answered.

Amy Monsen   34401 Road 140, Visalia, California 93291   (209) 733-4441
Amy Monsen specializes in silver plate patterns from 1880 to 1915. Send a large self-addressed, stamped envelope for a list, or write giving the pattern name and pieces you are looking for. A want list is maintained. There is a 5-day return privilege.

Munn's Silver Shop   209 West Wilson Avenue, Glendale, California 91203   (213) 241-2776 or 241-1909
This shop matches sterling and silver-plated lines, active, inactive, and obsolete. Flatware patterns are available. Coin silver flatware and sterling hollow ware are available by catalogue.

Dale A. Nelson   P.O. Box 35 DN, Kenilworth, Illinois 60043   (312) 262-4042
This firm matches silver plate. A permanent want file is maintained. Send a self-addressed, stamped envelope with inquiries and a photocopy of the pattern.

Patterns of Yesterday   139 York Avenue, Battle Creek, Michigan 49015   (616) 968-1205
This firm matches discontinued silver plate. Send the complete brand and pattern name, description, and any markings. List the pattern pieces desired. A free request register and search service are available. Send 2 extra stamps if a search is desired.

Perfect Hostess Company   P.O. Box 173, Miami Springs, Florida 33166   (305) 887-9709
Over 1,900 patterns since 1828 are available. Steak knives, sterling salad sets, berry spoons, and obsolete items are available in some patterns.

Rolling Wheels Antiques   18661 Lancashire, Detroit, Michigan 48223   (313) 836-7933
This is a silver plate matching service. Send a self-addressed, stamped envelope with inquiries.

Roundhill's Patterns Unlimited International   P.O. Box 15238, Seattle, Washington 98115 (206) 523-9710
This firm deals in discontinued patterns of tabletop items. Call or write with inquiries. It offers an appraisal service for evaluating discontinued patterns of silver. Cost is $30.00 per pattern, with no limit on the number of pieces.

Rubye Barber Antiques   P.O. Box 521, Hot Springs, Arkansas 71901   (501) 623-5788
This firm matches sterling silver flatware and sterling serving pieces. Send a self-addressed, stamped envelope with inquiries.

Scavenger's Den   P.O. Box 142, R.D. #4, Muncy, Pennsylvania 17756   (717) 584-4921
This is a sterling and silver plate matching service. Hollow ware, flatware, coin, and souvenir pieces are also dealt with. Want lists are kept and there are layaway and search services. Include a phone number with your inquiry.

Silver Antiquities   Mrs. Roz Mouber, P.O. Box 6137, Leawood, Kansas 66206   (816) 333-1361
Mrs. Mouber specializes in antique and unique sterling silver as well as old Baltimore flatware and hollow ware. There is a pattern matching service for the ornate patterns introduced before 1910. A card file is kept.

The Silver Chest   12 Grafton Street, Greenlawn, New York 11740   (516) 261-2636
This is a matching service for silver-plated flatware and serving pieces. Send a pattern or photocopy for a quote. All requests for information and pricing are answered if accompanied by a self-addressed, stamped envelope.

The Silver Lady   P.O. Box 792, Friday Harbor, Washington 98250   (206) 378-5512
This firm matches silver plate, both flatware and hollow ware. Inquiries must be accompanied by a self-addressed, stamped envelope for a reply. If the pattern is not known send a photocopy or sketch of the flatware. For hollow ware, send the trademark on the bottom of the piece and the number below the trademark.

The Silver Queen Inc.   778 North Indian Rocks Road, Belleair Bluffs, Florida 33540 (813) 581-6827
This firm offers sterling silver pattern matching. A want list is kept.

Silver Season   64 Ponus Avenue, Norwalk, Connecticut 06850   (203) 847-8217
This firm matches silver-plated flatware from 1860 to the present, with particular interest in the patterns of the 1920s and 1930s. It will also identify patterns if a rubbing or photocopy is sent, along with whatever markings appear on the piece. Send a self-addressed, stamped envelope for a list.

Silverplate Flatware Matching Service by Eulah Kemp   2526 Walton Street, Anderson, Indiana 46011   (317) 643-5773
This firm matches silver-plated flatware dating from about 1860 to 1975. Write or phone for information on patterns. If a pattern is not known, send a sketch and the company name on the back. For information on patterns and pieces send a self-addressed, stamped envelope.

Simply Sterling   829 Walt Whitman Road, Melville, New York 11747   (516) 423-2969
This company offers a pattern matching service for sterling flatware.

The Sterling Fox   P.O. Box 398, Richmond, Kentucky 40475   (606) 623-5868
This is a sterling silver flatware matching service for both active and inactive patterns. A want list is kept. Include a self-addressed, stamped envelope with inquiries.

The Sterling Shop   P.O. Box 595, Silverton, Oregon 97381   (503) 873-6315
The Sterling Shop matches sterling and silver-plated flatware. Send a request for the patterns and pieces needed along with a self-addressed, stamped envelope.

Jeremy Street   850 West First South, Salt Lake City, Utah 84104   (801) 363-2441
Silver-plated flatware is matched.

Tabletop Matching Service and Collectors Items   China and Crystal Replacements, Mrs. Betty H. Allen, P.O. Box 205, Cookeville, Tennessee 38501   (615) 526-4303
This is a matching service for silver-plated flatware. All inventory is new (usually store stock), in mint condition, and guaranteed to the buyer. Send a self-addressed, stamped envelope for a reply.

Tere Hagan Silverplated Flatware Matching Service   P.O. Box 26004, Tempe, Arizona 85282
(602) 966-8838
This firm matches silver-plated flatware. An availability list in the customer's pattern is sent free of charge.

Topex Company   58 Linda Lane, Tiffin, Ohio 44883   (419) 447-7939
This company locates discontinued patterns of silver. There is no charge for its location service, only for pieces you purchase. Send complete identification material such as patterns and shape photos. Please include a self-addressed, stamped envelope for a reply.

Vintage Silver   33 Le May Court, Williamsville, New York 14221   (716) 631-0419
This is a silver-plated flatware matching service. A listing of available pieces is free with a self-addressed, stamped envelope, and customers' want lists are maintained. This service specializes in old patterns (pre-1920).

Vroman's Silver Shop   1748 South Grand Avenue, Glendora, California 91740   (213) 963-0512
This shop matches and sells American-made patterns of sterling and stainless patterns of flatware that are obsolete, discontinued, or inactive.

Walter Drake Silver Exchange   Drake Building, Colorado Springs, Colorado 80940
(303) 596-3140
This firm matches sterling and silver plate flatware and hollow ware.

Wesche's Antiques　480 North Orange, Orlando, Florida 32801　(305) 425-6481
A silver matching service is offered.

William & Mary's Antiques, Inc.　P.O. Box 20041, San Jose, California 95160　(408) 268-4797
This is a matching service for sterling. An inventory list is available with a self-addressed, stamped
envelope.

101. PROFESSIONAL ASSOCIATIONS AND PRESERVATION SOCIETIES

There are many national clubs and organizations for collectors, dealers, or students of antiques. Some
organizations are primarily for the professional museum or decorative arts personnel but they offer
special memberships for collectors. The membership permits you to go to their conventions, meetings,
and to receive the publications. There are a few clubs for collectors that are national but most of them
require an invitation by the local chapter members. Ask about this at antiques shows and sales and you
may be able to learn more about the local groups.

Specialized collector clubs exist on a national basis with local chapters. Groups such as the Federation
of Historic Bottle Clubs are listed in their appropriate chapter in Part I of this book. Each national club
will tell you about its closest local activity. The *Encyclopedia of Associations* (Detroit: Gale Research,
1982) is a helpful guide to both general and specialized organizations.

American Association for State and Local History　708 Berry Road, Nashville, Tennessee 37204
(615) 383-5991
History News is a monthly magazine for members. The association is for people working in museums,
libraries, archives, and historical societies. Seminars are offered.

American Association of Museums   1055 Thomas Jefferson Street, N.W., Washington, D.C. 20007
A national convention is held annually.

The American Federation of Arts   41 East 65th Street, New York, New York 10021
(212) 988-7700
The American Federation of Arts organizes traveling art exhibitions and provides films, publications, and other services to museums and their audiences. It publishes a newsletter listing exhibits, meetings, and buildings.

Antiquarian Society   185 Salisbury Street, Worcester, Massachusetts 01609

The Decorative Arts Society of the Society of Architectural Historians   c/o Ms. Deborah D. Waters, Secretary, 341 Clinton Street, Brooklyn, New York 11231
The Decorative Arts Newsletter is for members only. Meetings are open to members and guests.

The Decorative Arts Trust   P.O. Box 1226, Camden, South Carolina 29020   (803) 432-7864
The Decorative Arts Trust Newsletter contains information about members, meetings, and museum events. Seminars are offered each year.

Museum of Early Southern Decorative Arts   Drawer F, Salem Station, Winston-Salem, North Carolina 27108   (919) 722-6148
There are 2 publications: *Journal of Early Southern Decorative Arts* and *The Luminary,* a newsletter. The *Journal* and *The Luminary* are published twice yearly. *The Luminary* is published in summer and winter and the *Journal* in spring and fall. *The Luminary* reports on "behind the scenes matters that the *Journal* doesn't concern itself with."

National Trust for Historic Preservation   740-748 Jackson Place, N.W., Washington, D.C. 20006
Historic Preservation is a monthly newspaper with the latest news about which buildings have been saved or destroyed, where preservationists have found new jobs or had meetings, and book reviews.

Questers, Inc.   210 South Quincy Avenue, Philadelphia, Pennsylvania 19107
Questers, Inc. has many local chapters. Antiques are studied. A newsletter is available for members. Membership is by invitation.

The Victorian Society in America   The Athenaeum, East Washington Square, Philadelphia, Pennsylvania 19106
The society's publication, *Nineteenth Century,* is a slick illustrated color magazine for the Victorian enthusiast. It contains articles about objects and houses. Seminars are offered each year.

DIRECTORY
Encyclopedia of Associations. Detroit: Gale Research Company, 1982.

102. RECORD-SETTING PRICES

Record-setting prices are of interest to collectors for many reasons. It's always fun to be able to shine in party conversation with facts like: "A candy container just sold for $1,700" or "A doll that is only 50 years old went at auction for $2,700." There is also a serious reason for checking the record prices. Each year some antiques or collectibles gain in favor and prices go up. The records show the collecting interest of the moneyed buyer.

United States auction records from January 1, 1980 to January 1, 1981 went from the sublime to the ridiculous. A painted bed sold for $23,000, a 1914 dress for $5,500, a set of Dionne Quintuplets dolls for $4,200, and a pair of ruby slippers worn by Judy Garland in *The Wizard of Oz* for $12,000.

The most expensive work of art was a Picasso self-portrait for $5,300,000; the most unexpected record prices were $30,000 for a Cox-Roosevelt campaign button and $1,790 for a golf ball.

AUTOMOBILES
Bentley automobile: $90,000 for a 1931 Bentley 8-liter Sport Sedan, sold February 15, 1981 at Christie's, Los Angeles.

BEDS
Painted bed: $23,000 for a Federal grain-painted tall-post tester bed, American, c. 1800, gray with black graining, 74 inches high; sold April 24, 1981 at Robert Skinner, Inc., Bolton, Massachusetts.

BOOKS
Medieval manuscript: $225,000 for *The Tacuinum Sanitatis,* a fifteenth-century northern Italian handbook on good health practices, manuscript on vellum, illustrated with 132 full-page miniature paintings; sold October 30, 1981 at Sotheby's, New York.

Western illuminated manuscript: $1,468,250 for the twelfth-century Ottobeuren Sacramentary, sold in 1981 at Sotheby's, London.

BOTTLES
Candy container: $1,700 for a glass soldier in World War I uniform standing beside a tent, 3⅜ inches, chip under foot; sold April 3, 1981 at a Lloyd Ralston auction in Fairfield, Connecticut.

CLOTHING

Fortuny cape: $5,000 for a hooded cape, c. 1930, of muted teal blue velvet striped with gilt; sold May 20, 1981 at Christie's, New York.

Fortuny coat: $7,800 for a deep green velvet coat designed by Mariano Fortuny; sold October 14, 1981 at Christie's East, New York.

Fortuny dress: $7,000 for a black double delphos tea gown by Mariano Fortuny; sold September 15, 1981 at Sotheby's, New York.

Paul Poiret evening dress: $5,500 for an evening dress of violet and ivory silk charmeuse, c. 1914; sold May 20, 1981 at Christie's, New York.

DECOYS

Decoy: $23,000 for a lesser yellowlegs by William Bowman of Bangor, Maine; sold November 18, 1981 at William Doyle Galleries, New York.

Duck or goose decoy: $14,000 for a swimming Canada goose by Nathan Cobb of Cobb Island, Virginia; sold October 23, 1981 at Richard A. Bourne, Hyannis, Massachusetts.

DOLLS

Bru doll (U.S. auction record): $16,500 for an Oriental Bru, c. 1875, by Casimir Bru; sold February 23, 1981 by Auctions by Theriault in West Palm Beach, Florida.

Googly-face doll: $8,400 for a doll sold in May 1981 by Auctions by Theriault in Boston.

Lenci doll: $2,700 for a blue-eyed, cloth Lenci "polo player" from the "Sports Series"; sold February 23, 1981 by Auctions by Theriault in West Palm Beach, Florida.

Twentieth-century composition dolls: $4,200 for a set of Dionne Quintuplets celebrity dolls made in 1935 and sold June 1981 by Auctions by Theriault in Chicago.

FOLK ART

Gus Wilson folk art carving: $30,000 for a 30-inch wooden tiger, carved and painted by Gus Wilson, Maine lighthouse keeper and decoy carver (1864–1950); purchased in a private sale in late 1981.

FURNITURE (GENERAL)

Belter settee: $38,130 for a mid-nineteenth-century settee by John Henry Belter; sold in October 1981 at Phillips, Knowle, England.

Connecticut furniture: $145,000 for a Chippendale cherrywood bookcase; sold January 30, 1981 at Sotheby's, New York.

English furniture, single piece: $860,000 for a Queen Anne black japanned bureau bookcase, 39 inches wide by 95 inches high; sold October 17, 1981 at Christie's, New York. The bookcase had formerly belonged to Queen Mary, then to the Duke of Windsor, who sold it in 1957 for $4,352. It was auctioned most recently for $95,000 in 1973.

Highboy: $105,000 for a Kittredge family Queen Anne carved mahogany bonnet-top highboy, sold September 26, 1981 at Sotheby's, New York.

New York furniture: $170,000 for a Chippendale tea table, sold January 30, 1981 at Sotheby's, New York.

Suite of English furniture: $340,000 for a 15-piece suite of George II carved mahogany furniture, c. 1755, including a settee, pair of armchairs, and 12 side chairs, with period needlework upholstery; sold April 25, 1981 at Sotheby's, New York.

Gustav Stickley furniture: $21,000 for a rare, unsigned oak spindle-back settle, c. 1905, 47 inches wide; sold May 15, 1981 at Sotheby's, New York.

Walnut furniture: $230,000 for a small George I burr walnut bureau bookcase, c. 1725, 84½ by 25 by 20½ inches; sold March 31, 1981 at Christie's, New York.

GLASS
Emile Gallé glass: $261,363 for an applied, engraved, intercalaire, overlay and marqueterie-de-verre vase; sold November 16, 1981 at Christie's, Geneva.

JEWELRY
Price per carat for a sapphire: $28,421 when a 9.50-carat sapphire ring sold for $270,000, April 14, 1981 at Sotheby's, New York.

Watch: $165,000 for a Swiss gold hunting case watch, minute repeating, split-second Grande Sonnerie clockwork with perpetual calendar and moon phases by L. Gallopin & Company, Geneva, c. 1890, 2 inch diameter; sold April 9, 1981 at Sotheby's, New York.

Yellow diamond: $700,000 for a 23-carat diamond ring, also established a record price per carat for a yellow diamond at $30,434; sold April 14, 1981 at Sotheby's, New York.

MILITARY MEMORABILIA
Colt revolver: $75,000 for "The Cox Navy," a cased factory engraved model 1861 navy revolver, no.

233711P, presentation model, unfired condition, ivory grips, 7½-inch barrel, presented to New York banking executive William H. Cox; sold October 7, 1981 at Christie's, New York.

Kentucky rifle: $50,000 for the Toffolon-Armstrong rifle, with .46-caliber browned octagonal barrel rifled with seven grooves, carved curly maple stock with brass and silver mounts, signed "J. Armstrong," eighteenth-century gunsmith, sold October 7, 1981 at Christie's, New York.

MOVIE MEMORABILIA
Pair of shoes: $12,000 for a pair of "ruby" slippers worn by Judy Garland in *The Wizard of Oz*; sold October 1981 at Christie's East, New York.

ODDS AND ENDS
Engine model: $31,360 for an exhibition standard 6 inch-to-1 foot scale model of a Burell "Devonshire" single-crank compound two-speed, three-shaft general purpose traction engine, 60 by 96 inches, built by South Dorset Engineering Company, Weymouth, 1978; sold April 6, 1981 by Christie's at the British Engineerium, Great Britain.

ORIENTALIA
Chinese wood sculpture: $170,000 for a large carved wood figure of Guanyin, twelfth century; sold November 6, 1981 at Sotheby's, New York.

Japanese inro: $54,000 for an inro by Oyama Koshida depicting a whale amid crashing waves; sold March 11, 1981 at Sotheby's, New York.

Netsuke (world record): $78,000 for a nineteenth-century ivory netsuke of a reclining horse with crossed front legs by Kaigyokusai Masatsuga of Osaka; sold January 8, 1981 at Sotheby's, Honolulu, Hawaii. (In 1962, the horse sold for £165 at Sotheby's, London, then a world record.)

Oriental work of art: $1,372,382 for an early Ming blue and white ceramic jar, painted with a single flying dragon; sold December 15, 1981 at Sotheby's, London.

PAINTINGS
American illustrator: $230,000 for the original oil painting for the 1945 *Saturday Evening Post* cover, *The Homecoming Marine,* 45¼ by 41¼ inches, by Norman Rockwell; sold April 2, 1981 at Phillips, New York.

American Impressionist painting: $820,000 for *Gravesend Bay,* a pastel by William Merritt Chase, depicting his wife, sister, and daughter Alice; sold May 29, 1981 at Sotheby's, New York.

Latin American art: $250,000 for *The Smile* (1964) by Rufino Tamayo of Mexico; sold December 2, 1981 at Sotheby's, New York.

Work by any living American artist: $420,000 for *Marsh Hawk* (1964) by Andrew Wyeth; sold December 10, 1981 at Sotheby's, New York.

Twentieth-century painting: $5,300,000 for Picasso's *Self-portrait,* executed during his first trip to Paris, before his "Blue Period"; sold May 1981 at Sotheby's, New York.

Francis Bacon painting and work by any living English artist: $350,000 for a triptych, *In Memory of George Dwyer* (1971), each panel 78 by 58 inches; sold May 18, 1981 at Christie's, New York.

Pompeo Batoni painting: $139,000 for *Portrait of Charles Crowle of Fryston Park,* 100 by 66½ inches; sold June 26, 1981 at Christie's, London.

William Baziotes painting: $130,000 for *Primeval Landscape* (1953); sold November 18, 1981 at Christie's, New York.

James Henry Beard: $15,000 for *Reflections on Darwin,* 32½ by 26¼ inches; sold September 23, 1981 at William Doyle Galleries, New York.

Max Beckmann painting and any German Expressionist artist: $600,000 for *Self Portrait in Sailor Hat,* 39⅜ by 27¾ inches; sold May 18, 1981 at Christie's, New York.

Etienne Prosper Berne-Bellecour: $7,000 for *On the Duelling Ground,* 52½ by 39⅜ inches; sold September 23, 1981 at William Doyle Galleries, New York.

Sandro Botticelli painting: $280,000 for *Virgin and Child with the Infant St. John;* sold January 8, 1981 at Sotheby's, New York.

Pieter Brueghel the Younger: $250,000 for *Summer;* sold January 8, 1981 at Sotheby's, New York. (It sold for $450 in 1925.)

Jack Bush painting: $48,000 for *On Purple,* by the contemporary Canadian artist; sold November 18, 1981 at Christie's, New York.

James E. Buttersworth: $45,500 for *The Sloops Approaching Nun #8,* American; sold October 3, 1981 at Butterfield's, San Francisco.

Niccolo Cannici painting: $70,000 for *Le Retour de la Fete,* a nineteenth-century oil; sold December 11, 1981 at Stalker & Boos, Birmingham, Michigan.

Gerald Cassidy: $8,500 for *Indian Chief,* sold October 3, 1981 at Butterfield's, San Francisco.

William Merritt Chase: $820,000 for a pastel, *Gravesend Bay,* depicting his wife, sister, and daughter Alice; sold May 29, 1981 at Sotheby's, New York.

George Chinnery painting: $129,350 for *Portrait of a Chinese Lady,* 24¾ by 19¼ inches; sold June 26, 1981 at Christie's, London.

Howard Chandler Christy: $18,000 for *By the Pond in Summer,* 40 by 45 inches; sold September 23, 1981 at William Doyle Galleries, New York.

Salvador Dali work: $813,600 for *Le Sommeil,* painting signed and dated 1937, 19¾ by 30¼ inches; sold March 30, 1981 at Christie's, London.

Thomas Daniell painting: $91,200 for *The Delhi Gate of the Agra Fort,* 40½ by 50¼ inches, signed and dated 1808; sold March 3, 1981 at Christie's, London.

Henri-Pierre Danloux painting: $218,900 for *The Masters Foster: Portrait of the Sons of Constantia and Richard Foster,* signed and dated 1792, 45½ by 37½ inches; sold June 26, 1981 at Christie's, London.

Melchior d'Hondecoeter painting: $290,000 for *A Menagerie: a Pelican, a Flamingo, a Heron, a Cockatoo, with Ducks and Other Birds in a Park,* 60½ by 73½ inches; sold June 12, 1981 at Christie's, New York.

Willem de Kooning painting: $220,000 for *Untitled III* (1977), 88 by 77 inches; sold May 13, 1981 at Christie's, New York.

Pieter de Neyn painting: $26,000 for *A Wooded Landscape with a Horseman and Other Figures on a Path;* sold January 8, 1981 at Sotheby's, New York.

Maurice de Vlaminck painting: $316,400 for *Les Barques* (1907), signed on the reverse, 18 by 21¾ inches; sold March 30, 1981 at Christie's, London.

Edgar Degas painting: $2,200,000 for his 1876 portrait of Eugene Manet, 25⅝ by 31⅞ inches, sold May 19, 1981 at Christie's, New York.

Robert Delaunay painting: $290,000 for *The Three Graces* (1912), Paris, 83 by 68¼ inches; sold May 19, 1981 at Christie's, New York.

Charles Edouard Delort: $37,500 for *Wedding Party at Fontainebleau,* 35¼ by 51 inches; sold September 23, 1981 at William Doyle Galleries, New York.

Charles Demuth painting: $75,000 for *At the Golden Swan,* a self-portrait with Marcel Duchamp, watercolor; sold May 29, 1981 at Sotheby's, New York.

André Derain painting: $380,000 for *Pont de Londres;* sold May 19, 1981 at Christie's, New York.

Richard Diebenkorn work on paper: $28,000 for *Untitled, 1974,* in acrylic and charcoal; sold November 19, 1981 at Christie's, New York.

Thomas Doughty: $25,000 for *Fisherman by a Mountain Stream,* American; sold October 3, 1981 at Butterfield's, San Francisco.

Arthur Dove: $160,000 for *Dancing Tree* (1930), oil painting; sold October 6, 1981 at Sotheby's, Los Angeles.

Sir Russel Drysdale painting: $53,190 for *Bottle Tree* (1950), 26 by 40 inches; sold June 12, 1981 at Christie's, London.

Govaert Flinck painting: $75,000 for *Portrait of a Rabbi;* sold January 8, 1981 at Sotheby's, New York.

Tsuguji Foujita painting: $379,600 for *Woman Writing,* signed, 30½ by 26 inches; sold February 14, 1981 at Christie's, Tokyo.

Caspar David Friedrich: $323,000 for *A Mountain Peak with Drifting Clouds,* a 9¼-by-11½-inch Alpine view; sold November 26, 1981 at Sotheby's, London.

Sawrey Gilpin painting: $80,000 for *White Horse in a Wooded Landscape,* sold May 1, 1981 at Christie's, New York.

Spencer Frederick Gore painting: $47,280 for *Mornington Crescent* (1911), signed, 16 by 20 inches; sold June 12, 1981 at Christie's, London.

John Graham painting: $140,000 for *The Horse of the Apocalypse;* sold November 18, 1981 at Christie's, New York.

Armin Carl Hansen: $25,000 for *Making Her Easting;* sold October 3, 1981 at Butterfield's, San Francisco.

Lawren Harris: $240,000 for *South Shore Baffin Island,* large landscape oil; sold May 26, 1981 at Sotheby's, Toronto.

George Peter Alexander Healy: $20,000 for a portrait of George Inness, 23¼ by 18¼ inches; sold September 23, 1981 at William Doyle Galleries, New York.

William Hogarth painting: $400,000 for *Portrait of The Jeffreys Family* (1730); sold January 8, 1981 at Sotheby's, New York.

Edward Hopper painting: $300,000 for *Summer in the City* (1949); sold December 10, 1981 at Sotheby's, New York.

Ellsworth Kelly painting: $80,000 for *Orange Blue I,* sold May 13, 1981 at Christie's, New York.

Frederick Leighton painting: $178,000 for *The Painter's Honeymoon,* 33 by 30¼ inches; sold June 5, 1981 at Christie's, London.

Illustration by J. C. Leyendecker: $26,000 for *Yule,* the original oil painting for the December 1931 cover of the *Saturday Evening Post;* sold April 2, 1981 at Phillips, New York.

George Luks painting: $235,000 for his 1909 portrait of the child Lily Williams; sold December 10, 1981 at Sotheby's, New York.

Brice Marden work on paper: $12,000 for an untitled work in white crayon, watercolor, and graphite; sold November 19, 1981 at Christie's, New York.

Master of the Naumburg Madonna painting: $57,500 for *The Madonna and Child;* sold January 8, 1981 at Sotheby's, New York.

Otto Mueller painting: $140,000 for *Badende* (c. 1917), signed with initials, on burlap, 47½ by 37½ inches; sold May 18, 1981 at Christie's, New York.

Andrew Nicholl watercolor: $7,000 for *Daisies, Foxgloves, Poppies and Other Flowers at Kingston,* signed, 18½ by 27 inches; sold June 9, 1981 at Christie's, New York.

James Peale painting: $280,000 for *Fruit in a Chinese Basket,* signed and dated 1822, 16⅝ by 21¾ inches; sold April 24, 1981 at Christie's, New York.

Picasso painting: $5,300,000 for Picasso's *Self-portrait,* executed during his first trip to Paris, before his "Blue Period"; sold in May 1981 at Sotheby's, New York.

Alexander Pope painting: $170,000 for *Sportsman's Still Life;* sold November 5, 1981 at Richard Oliver, Kennebunk, Maine.

Edward Potthast painting: $160,000 for *Bathers by the Sea;* sold December 10, 1981 at Sotheby's, New York.

Maurice Prendergast painting: $410,000 for *Flying Horses;* sold May 29, 1981 at Sotheby's, New York.

Robert Rauschenberg combine painting: $190,000 for *Coexistence* (1961), made of oil, fabric, metal, and wood on canvas, 60 by 42 by 13¾ inches; sold May 13, 1981 at Christie's, New York.

Rembrandt Harmenszoon van Rijn drawing: $576,000 for *Study of a Nude Woman as Cleopatra,* red and white chalk on cream paper, 9¾ by 5⅓ inches; sold July 7, 1981 at Christie's, London.

Wilhelm Reuter painting: $57,500 for *A Roman Market;* sold January 8, 1981 at Sotheby's, New York.

Armando Reveron painting and any Venezuelan artist: $43,000 for *Port Near La Guaira;* sold December 2, 1981 at Sotheby's, New York.

Sir Joshua Reynolds painting: $250,800 for *Portrait of the Hon. George Seymour Conway in Van Dyck Costume,* 24½ by 18¼ inches; sold March 27, 1981 at Christie's, London.

William Trost Richards: $20,000 for *Low Tide Along the New Jersey Coast,* 8 by 14 inches; sold September 23, 1981 at William Doyle Galleries, New York.

Georges Rouault print: $15,075 for *Fille au Cafe* (1910), monotype printed in colors, signed in pen and brown ink, 12⅜ by 7½ inches; sold June 18, 1981 at Christie's, London.

John Singer Sargent painting: $260,000 for *Portrait of Dorothy* (1900); sold December 10, 1981 at Sotheby's, New York.

Egon Schiele drawing: $200,000 for *Liegender akt mit Grunen Strumpfen;* sold May 19, 1981 at Christie's, New York.

Oskar Schlemmer drawing: $100,000 for *Blau-Rot-Gelb am Gelander;* sold May 19, 1981 at Christie's, New York.

Charles Sheeler painting: $170,000 for *Amoskeag Mills #2;* sold December 10, 1981 at Sotheby's, New York.

Frank Stella work: $180,000 for *Laysan Millerbird* (1977), a wall relief, 83 by 123 by 15 inches; sold May 13, 1981 at Christie's, New York.

Rufino Tamayo painting: $250,000 for *The Smile* (1964); sold December 2, 1981 at Sotheby's, New York.

Henry Ossawa Tanner painting: $250,000 for *The Thankful Poor;* sold December 10, 1981 at Sotheby's, New York.

Wayne Thiebaud painting: $130,000 for *Four Pinball Machines* (1962), 68 by 72 inches; sold May 13, 1981 at Christie's, New York.

Walter Ufer: $17,000 for *Juanita,* by the Taos, New Mexico, artist; sold October 3, 1981 at Butterfield's, San Francisco.

Jacob Van Oolen painting: $21,000 for *Trompe L'Oeil Still Life with Game and Hunting Implements;* sold January 8, 1981 at Sotheby's, New York.

Remedios Varo work: $47,000 for *Trasmundo;* sold December 2, 1981 at Sotheby's, New York.

John William Waterhouse work: $123,750 for *Flora and the Zephyrs,* a color sketch, 41 by 80¼ inches; sold March 6, 1981 at Christie's, London.

Worthington Whittredge: $280,000 for *Indian Encampment on the Platte River, Colorado* (1868), 23 by 34 inches; sold September 23, 1981 at William Doyle Galleries, New York.

Andrew Wyeth painting: $420,000 for *Marsh Hawk* (1964); sold December 10, 1981 at Sotheby's, New York.

PEWTER

American pewter: $15,000 for a flat-top quart tankard, William Bradford, Jr., New York (1719–1758), 7⅛ inches high, record for American pewter; sold April 11, 1981 at Christie's, New York.

English pewter: $16,848 for a Charles II English pewter broad-rimmed commemorative charger, 22 inches; sold April 30, 1981 at Christie's, London.

PHOTOGRAPHS

Single photograph: $71,500 for *Moonrise, Hernandez, New Mexico, 1941,* by Ansel Adams; large size print 40 by 60 inches, one of about 6 in that size, c. 1960–1961; sold in early 1981 at the G. Ray Hawkins Gallery, Los Angeles.

Color photograph: $12,000 for *Roses and Clouds,* by Paul Outerbridge, Jr.; sold May 14, 1981 at Christie's, New York.

Ansel Adams photograph: $71,500 for *Moonrise, Hernandez, New Mexico, 1941,* large size print 40 by 60 inches, one of about six in that size, 1960–1961; sold in early 1981 at the G. Ray Hawkins Gallery, Los Angeles.

Edward S. Curtis photograph: $6,000 for *Before the Storm—Apache* (c. 1910), orotone; sold May 14, 1981 at Christie's, New York.

Pietro Devizielli photograph: $1,700 for *The Cascate delle Ferriere, Tivoli* (1850s), salt print; sold May 14, 1981 at Christie's, New York.

Roger Fenton photograph: $19,095 for *Westminster Cathedral, Interior Study* (1850s), albumen print; sold June 18, 1981 at Christie's, London.

French daguerreotype: $15,000 for a French postmortem daguerreotype by A. Le Blondel, c. 1849; sold May 14, 1981 at Christie's, New York.

David Octavius Hill and Robert Adamson photograph: $4,500 for *Study of a Tree, Colinton Wood* (1846–1847), calotype; sold May 14, 1981 at Christie's, New York.

Work by George Hurrell: $9,000 for a 1930 gelatin silver print of Ramon Navarro by George Hurrell, inscribed on the back: "this is my first original vintage print of Ramon Navarro which launched my career in Hollywood. . . ."; sold May 14, 1981 at Christie's, New York.

Nevil Maskelyne photograph: $7,235 for *Group of Hands* (mid–1850s), a salt print from a collodion negative; sold June 18, 1981 at Christie's, London.

Work by Paul Outerbridge, Jr.: $12,000 for *Roses and Clouds;* sold May 14, 1981 at Christie's, New York.

POLITICAL

Political campaign button: $30,000 for a 1920 Cox-Roosevelt button, a 1¼-inch black and white jugate, the only one known of its size and type; sold April 4, 1981 by New England Rare Coin Auctions in New York.

PORCELAIN AND POTTERY

Pre-Columbian art: $125,000 for a pair of Mayan molded cache vessels from the Classic period, A.D. 350–450, decorated earthenware; sold December 5, 1981 at Sotheby's, New York.

Rookwood iris glaze vase: $2,750 for a 10½-inch Classic form vase in dark blue shading to pale green, with narcissus blossoms; sold January 16, 1981 at Robert Skinner's, Inc., Bolton, Massachusetts.

Sebastian Miniature figurines: $1,500 for pair, *Swedish Boy and Swedish Girl,* sold on September 26, 1981 by Don Culbertson Auction of Urbana, Illinois.

Snuffbox: $91,347 for a Meissen royal topographical gold-mounted snuffbox, painted with views of Dresden, Moritzburg, and Warsaw, c. 1749, 3 by 2 inches; sold May 11, 1981 at Christie's, Geneva.

Teacup and saucer: $44,100 for a white porcelain teacup and saucer decorated with white swans and yellow and orange flowers, made by J. J. Kaendler in Meissen, Germany, in 1740; auctioned in 1981 at Christie's in Geneva.

POSTCARDS

Postcard: $761 for a Diamond Jubilee of Queen Victoria card, with written message, mailed June 21, 1897; sold February 26, 1981 by Neale's of Nottingham, England.

PRINTS AND WOODCUTS

Any print: $160,800 for *La Minotauromachie* (1935) by Pablo Picasso, etching with scraper work, signed and numbered 5/50, 19¾ by 27⅜ inches; sold June 18, 1981 at Christie's, London.

SCULPTURE

Sculpture by Marcel Bouraine: $19,000 for *Harlequin,* a silvered, enameled, and cold-painted bronze, ivory, and glass table lamp, 21¾ inches high; sold December 5, 1981 at Christie's, New York.

Albert Giacometti sculpture: $340,000 for *The Glade* (1950), Paris, bronze grouping, 25⅝ by 24⅞ by 18⅞ inches; sold May 19, 1981 at Christie's, New York.

Giacomo Manzu sculpture: $175,000 for a bronze statue of a seated cardinal; sold May 18, 1981 at Christie's, New York.

Elie Nadelman sculpture: $145,000 for *Dancing Lady,* a polychrome wood sculpture; sold December 10, 1981 at Sotheby's, New York.

Sculpture by Ferdinand Preiss: $23,000 for *Flame Leaper,* a female figure of an acrobat, made of cold-painted bronze, ivory, and Bakelite, 14¼ inches high including base; sold December 5, 1981 at Christie's, New York.

William Henry Rinehart sculpture: $50,000 for a white marble sculpture of Harriet Newcomer; sold June 16, 1981 by Christie's, New York.

Veracruz work of art: $95,000 for a large Veracruz seated female figure; sold December 5, 1981 at Sotheby's, New York.

Francisco Zuniga sculpture: $55,000 for *Mexican Woman;* sold December 2, 1981 at Sotheby's, New York.

SILVER

Silver spoon: $17,480 for a single silver teaspoon, bearing the English hallmark for 1465, during the reign of King Edward IV, the earliest cycle of date letters on English silver; sold in November 1981 at Sotheby's, London.

STOCKS AND BONDS

Antique bond: $14,000 for an 1898 Chinese 500-pound sterling bond for a 4½ percent gold loan, countersigned by the Deutsche Asiatische Bank of Berlin. The defunct bond was sold on March 6, 1981 at Stanley Gibbons Auction Galleries, New York.

TEXTILES

American Indian textile: $54,000 for a Navajo serape, c. 1850; sold April 25, 1981 at Sotheby's, New York.

Needlework: $45,000 for an unsigned Boston School needlework, 1750–1760, *The Fishing Lady;* sold on August 25, 1981 by Richard A. Bourne Galleries, Hyannis, Massachusetts.

Needlework sampler: $38,000 for a Pennsylvania needlework sampler embroidered with the figure of a young girl, inscribed *Matilda Filbert her work in the twelfth year of her age, 1830,* from the Theodore Kapnek collection; sold January 31, 1981 at Sotheby's, New York.

Quilt: $10,500 for a pieced, appliquéd, and embroidered pictorial quilt, signed *F. Cochran,* American, twentieth century, depicting the family farm, complete with livestock, gardens, farming activities, 72 by 92 inches; sold July 9, 1981 at Sotheby's, New York.

Tapestry: $1,198,175 for a Swiss medieval tapestry; sold in 1981 at Sotheby's, London.

TOKENS AND MEDALS

English merchant token: $1,800 for a Lancaster halfpenny, 1794; sold December 8, 1981 at Sotheby's, New York.

TOOLS

Sandusky Tool Company molding-type plane: $3,500 for a multiform molding-type plane with the handle; sold in late 1981 by Richard A. Crane, Your Country Auctioneer, Inc., Hillsboro, New Hampshire.

Nicholson wood plane: $2,200 for a molding-type plane; sold in late 1981 by Richard A. Crane, Your Country Auctioneer, Inc., Hillsboro, New Hampshire.

TOYS

Capshooter: $3,400 for "Two Dogs on a Bench," one of two known; sold April 4, 1981 at a Lloyd Ralston auction in Fairfield, Connecticut.

Celluloid Mickey Mouse: $1,350 for a 1930s, working windup from Japan, 7⅜ inches; sold April 4, 1981 at a Lloyd Ralston auction in Fairfield, Connecticut.

Golf ball: $1,790 (£950), for a feather ball stamped *Wm. Robertson,* size 26; sold in July 1981 at Christie's, South Kensington, England.

Lead soldier, single: $560 for a Britains Camel Corps figure from set no. 131, made in 1910, 3¾ inches high; sold October 1, 1981 at Christie's East, New York.

Military toy miniature: $820 for a Britains scale working model of a Direct Control Auto-Gyro; sold October 17, 1981 at Phillips, New York.

Pedal car toy: $5,700 for a classic 1931 Packard rumble seat sports roadster; sold April 4, 1981 at a Lloyd Ralston auction in Fairfield, Connecticut.

103. SECURITY INFORMATION

SECURITY, BURGLAR ALARMS, AND OTHER PROBLEMS

Theft and fire are two of the biggest worries to antiques collectors. There are many ways to lessen these dangers—some inexpensive, some expensive. Consider the monetary value of your collection and the vulnerability of your home; then decide how to handle the problems.

FIRE

The normal safety precautions against fire are of added importance if you are a collector. Be sure to remove all extra burnable trash, don't store inflammable materials in the house, and periodically check all appropriate safety features on furnaces, heaters, etc. If you refinish furniture, be very careful with the used rags. Rags soaked with linseed oil and turpentine mixtures can easily ignite by spontaneous combustion. If you have a collection of inflammable items like movie film, photographs, books, or paper items, try to keep them away from the furnace, fireplace, any open flame, or cigarette ashes.

A smoke detector is the one single investment that is probably most important to a collector. Buy several and place them at the top of stairs, near any library or collection of easily ignited articles, and, of course, near the bedrooms to warn you of fire at night. The alarms make a loud noise and wake you or, with some extra equipment, notify the fire department even if you are not at home.

Also, it is a good idea to keep small fire extinguishers in the house. Do not install a sprinkler system. The water can often do more damage than a small fire.

THEFT PREVENTION

The least expensive form of protection is common sense. Don't talk about your collection in strange places. Check on the workmen you hire to repair your house. Be sure your household help is reliable. Don't give anyone a key to the house if it can be avoided. Don't tell the local paper, beauty parlor, gas station, or anyone else you meet casually that you will be away. Don't put your house key on the car key ring. Never let an unknown collector who calls to see your collection enter the house. Get some sort of reference first.

If you see a strange car near your home, write down the license number and a description of the car.

PROTECTION

Another inexpensive protection for your collection is the complete set of records and photographs you keep. It gives the police enough information to look for stolen items. A taped TV record is another alternative.

To add to this protection, write your social security number or driver's license number (check first to see if your state assigns a number on a permanent basis) on the antique with one of the new marking devices. There are two types of markers. One is an electric pencil, much like a dentist's drill, that etches the number into the piece. This is suitable for a limited number of antiques. Some cities have a program called "Operation Identification." See if your town has one. The material needed to mark your collection can be borrowed from the program.

The other type of marker is a special pen filled with "invisible" ink that will fluoresce under a black (ultraviolet) light.

BETTER PROTECTION

After you have marked, photographed, and recorded your antiques, stop to consider how a thief would gain entry to your house. Every house has a weak spot.

Perhaps it is glass patio doors. You can't keep anyone from breaking the glass and entering, but you can make it difficult. Put dead bolt locks on the door, where they can't be easily reached through the broken glass. This way the burglar will have to make some noise to enter and won't be able to just push open an easily jimmied key lock. Use poles to "lock" sliding patio doors.

Lock all windows. Be sure the milk chute either locks from the inside or is too small for someone to enter. Put lights outside the house so the neighbors will notice intruders. Don't leave ladders outside the house.

Be sure the flat-roofed garage is not next to an open window. Be sure your garage door is closed and locked. Put bars over the basement windows or window wells. Don't put your name on your mailbox or doormat. A burglar often looks up the name in the phone book, calls to see if you are home, and then uses the empty house as an invitation. Keep lights on in the house when you are away.

An inexpensive timer is excellent, as you can arrange to turn on lights or a television set at a specified time. This makes the house seem occupied. There are special timers that can be set to turn lights on at a different time each night.

Tell the neighbors and police if you plan to be gone for a while. Be sure to do the obvious, such as stopping paper delivery, arranging for mail delivery, having the grass cut, or shoveling the snow, etc. Don't disconnect your phone, even temporarily. A phone-answering machine can be a help, as it can give a message that says you are unable to come to the phone and will call back. The message should never say that you are away from home. If possible, have a neighbor put some trash in the trash cans each week. It is a good idea to leave a car in the driveway to block the way of a burglar with a truck.

BEST PROTECTION

Burglar alarm equipment is one of the best deterrents to robbery, but it must be the proper equipment for the job. Talk to people who own such systems, check with several suppliers, and then study the problems of your house and your collection before you decide on which alarm system to purchase.

The best protection for your family and your antiques is placed outside the house. No one ever wants to meet a burglar inside the house. He is nervous and so are you. Outside defenses should include lights in the yard, driveway, and garden; fences; bars on basement windows; good locks; and an automatic garage door opener or a locked garage door.

The next line of defense is at the door. There are several systems that set off bells, gongs, or silent alarms when a door is opened improperly or even when a window is broken. Many of these systems also notify police if a phone or power line is cut.

The next line of defense is up the stairs or across the halls. Detectors can be strategically placed in the home to warn you if anyone is moving in the house. This detector is useless if you have young children, dogs, cats, or sleepwalking family members.

The last hope for help is the "panic button." This is an alarm that can be pushed to silently call for help. It is either installed by a door or bed or is a portable unit.

Each type of installed alarm is designed for special conditions and special purposes. There are several brands of "tripalarms" that can be installed. These set off a loud noise when the window or door is opened. (Always be sure to buy the type that has to be turned off with a key. If the turnoff can be made with a switch, a burglar will have no trouble stopping the noise.) One of the major problems with this type of alarm is that each door and window must be wired with a separate unit. It is even possible for a clever burglar who knows the alarm system to go through a wall or remove the window in a special way that will not set off the alarm.

A more complex and expensive alarm is one with sensors attached to the windows and doors. This type sends a message to a control box that emits a noise, calls the police, turns on the lights, or whatever combination you choose.

Some of the expensive alarm systems have silent door and window alarms that alert the police or a listening station that your house is being entered. There is no noise and no visible sign because the theory is that the police will catch the burglar with the loot before he leaves the house.

If these fail, there are several types of alarms available that go off once a burglar is in the house.

Ultrasonic devices can be installed that will set off an alarm if anything is moving in the room. These alarms are usually placed in different zones throughout the house. For example, one may cover the living room, another the front stairs, and still another the basement stairs.

These alarms alert the police or a listening station and do not make any noise. This system cannot be used if you own dogs or cats. A good system will be activated if just a mouse runs across the floor.

Another type of alarm placed in specific zones is the electric eye. This is an almost invisible beam of infrared light that, when crossed, activates the silent alarm.

A similar type of alarm uses microwave installation and covers larger areas, such as an entire room.

A pressure-sensitive type of alarm installed under the rug is another device that detects people in the house. Many of these alarms can be purchased at retail stores and installed by an amateur.

One of the most popular alarms for private homes is a "bugging" system. This system is installed inside the walls or in inconspicuous spots throughout the house. Microphones will pick up any noise in the house. The system is usually installed with the addition of several of the door-opener alarms. If someone enters the home the noise is heard. The listening station can tell if the burglar is walking from room to room, packing antiques, or talking to a friend. The owners of a home with this system turn it off when they are in the house to maintain their privacy. Panic buttons are strategically placed throughout the house and can be activated instantly even if the system is off.

All of these alarms require a form of check-in and check-out with the alarm company. Some use keys; some have special combinations of buttons that must be activated in the proper sequence. Others require a phone call and a turnoff switch. All of the check-in procedures are a nuisance, but there is no way to have an alarm system without it.

The only way to decide which alarm you should use is by carefully considering how it will affect your daily life. The consideration should include the size of the area to be covered, the number of people entering the house on a daily basis who must check in and out, the physical problems of installation, whether or not you have pets, and the type of police service available. Sometimes the best alarm is a large dog.

ADVANTAGES AND DISADVANTAGES OF ALARMS

Be sure to deal with a reliable burglar alarm company. There are cases on record where the alarm installation was done by the man who later robbed the house.

The "bugging" alarm has several good features. A smoke alarm can be installed that will give you full fire protection even when you are away. The alarm will pick up any signal of smoke or fire and transmit the sound to the main alarm center. The alarm service quickly calls the fire department. The installation is almost invisible.

You have personal contact with the alarm system company on a daily basis as you call in and out; so in case of exceptional problems, long trips, or other high-risk times, you can advise them.

Taped windows and zone coverage in the house are ideal for some homes. If your collection is displayed in a single area, this type of protection can be easily and inexpensively installed.

There are advantages to any system if you live alone. We know a collector who has told her alarm system company that if she does not check in each day by ten o'clock, they should send the police. She has no relatives nearby and this is a sort of insurance program for her in case of illness. Some services have their own security men who check out each alarm call. Most send the local police.

There are a few insurance companies that will lower fire and theft rates if you have an alarm. Many insurance companies will not insure a collection without proper protection.

UNSOLVED QUESTIONS

There are some questions about alarms that have never been answered satisfactorily. Should you put a sign in front of your house advising the world that you have an alarm? Should you tie in directly to the police station, or is it best to use a listening service?

The sign in front alerts a burglar to the type of alarm and may give him the opportunity of working around it. Also, it suggests there are valuables inside. It could also suggest that the house next door without an alarm might be a better place to enter. If you have *no* alarm, the window decals saying you are protected by an alarm might help. If you are a known collector and the burglar is a professional, the sign probably will make little difference.

Some cities permit private homes to have a direct link to the police station. This means prompt service; but if you have a series of false alarms because you are checking in improperly (and this seems inevitable the first few months), the police may become very uncooperative. It is always a good idea to send a donation to the local police fund if you start having too many false alarms.

Some alarm owners prefer to use the listening station because the alarm people keep tabs on the progress of the police with continued follow-through until the attempted break-in is resolved.

Check with your local police department and ask about rules for alarms in your area. Call those alarm companies that offer the best protection.

One last note, all the alarm expense may be tax deductible in some way. Keep records because it could be a cost that can be added to the base price of your collection when it is sold. This will lower the taxes paid on any profit gained from the sale of the collection.

If you have questions about insurance rates, filing a claim, appraising your collection, etc., you can call the Insurance Information Institute's hotline toll free at (800) 221-4954. In New York call (212) 669-9200. Your questions will be answered over the phone and you can also order free brochures.

INSURANCE AND SECURITY SYSTEM COMPANIES

ADT Security Systems   155 Avenue of the Americas, New York, New York 10013
(212) 777-3300
This is a national security system with local branches. Look in the Yellow Pages for a nearby office.

Chubb Group of Insurance Companies,   51 John F. Kennedy Parkway, Short Hills, New Jersey 07078
This group writes policies for fine arts.

Dictograph Security Systems   26 Columbia Turnpike, Florham Park, New Jersey 07932   (201) 822-1400 or (212) 267-1994
This firm offers burglar alarm systems and/or fire and smoke detection systems both linked to a central monitor or the police or fire department.

Fred S. James & Company of California   Carl G. Allen, Robin Dutton, 3435 Wilshire Boulevard, Los Angeles, California 90010   (213) 385-0545 TELEX: 677353
Fine-arts insurance for museums and collectors of fine arts. This firm currently insures approximately 85 museums and individual collectors across the United States. It provides a special Collectors Insurance Certificate through American and London underwriters for the individual whose collection amounts to $800,000.00 or more. An appraised schedule of the objects to be insured done by a qualified appraiser needs to be provided. A secure premise is required, including central station burglar and smoke alarms.

Flather and Company, Inc.   888 Seventeenth Street, N.W., Washington, D.C. 20006
(202) 466-8888
Flather and Company, Inc. will write insurance on a fine-arts form for the following types of collections: antique dolls, antique toys, antique pewter, antique glass, first editions and rare books, antique maps and documents, antique weapons and tools. It will also consider writing insurance for bottles, phonographs, music boxes, and slot machines.

Great Northern Brokerage Corporation   950 Third Avenue, New York, New York 10022 (212) 371-2800

This firm offers a special coverage form for antiques dealers and collectors subject to the client meeting the company's underwriting criteria. It offers special loss prevention and loss control services to assist its clientele in the protection and preservation of their valuable property. It is in the business of insuring art dealers, art collectors, coin dealers and collectors, and various other clients involved in the art world. It also insures some very large art and antiques auction houses.

Huntington T. Block Insurance   2101 L Street, N.W., Washington, D.C. 20037   (800) 424-8830

This firm carries fine arts insurance and special insurance for appraisers and auctioneers.

Protection Services Division, Honeywell, Inc.   Honeywell Plaza, Minneapolis, Minnesota 55408 (612) 870-5483

This firm sells security systems.

J & D Security Corporation   P.O. Box 15642, Seattle, Washington 98115   (206) 523-2746

This corporation offers a theft-deterrent kit which includes 2 pens: 1 for marking porous and 1 for marking nonporous items. Also, it has warning seals and signs, a detector solution, instructions, and a property ledger sheet. This invisible engraving system protects property and expendables without devaluing or defacement.

National Burglar & Fire Alarm Association   1730 Pennsylvania Avenue, N.W., Washington, D.C. 20006   (202) 857-1130

The association offers a list of recognized alarm dealers.

Nordstern Service International (U.S.), Inc.   116 John Street, Suite 406, New York, New York 10038   (212) 227-2224

Nordstern offers a comprehensive fine-arts insurance program for private collectors, corporate collections, dealers, and museums. Nordstern provides insurance on an agreed-value basis with current appraisals ensuring that there is a concise valuation record in the event of a loss. A brochure is available.

NuTone Housing Products   Madison and Red Bank Roads, Cincinnati, Ohio 45227 (513) 527-5100

NuTone offers a variety of fire and security alarms. These are available nationwide.

Radio Shack   2617 West 7th Street, Fort Worth, Texas 76107   (817) 336-4684

Radio Shack sells security systems. See phone book for local store.

John P. Slade & Son Insurance Agency, Inc.   199 Pleasant Street, Fall River, Massachusetts 02722   (617) 676-8283

This firm offers an insurance program for members of United Federation of Doll Clubs only. This program is limited to the United States at this time.

Sonitrol Security Systems   1100 Cleveland Street, Clearwater, Florida 33515
This is a national system. See your local phone book for a nearby office.

3M Security Products   3M Center, St. Paul, Minnesota 55101   (612) 733-1110

United Security Products   2171 Research Drive, Livermore, California 94550   (415) 455-8866
United Security Products manufactures several security devices including the Fence Guard system, Telsar and Window Bug, a glass breakage detector. Brochures are available.

Value-tique, Inc.   111 Irving Street, Leonia, New Jersey 07605   (201) 461-6500
This firm sells Sentry home and office safes. The company pays all freight charges to any location within the continental United States. A catalogue is available.

Westinghouse Security Systems, Inc.   4721 McKnight Road, Pittsburgh, Pennsylvania 15237 (412) 931-5160
This is a national company. See the Yellow Pages for a local office.

PUBLICATIONS ON SECURITY

Eastman Kodak Company   Consumer Markets Division, Rochester, New York 14650 (716) 724-4440
For 35¢ Eastman Kodak will send you a booklet explaining the importance of photographing your belongings in case of disaster. The booklet also offers suggestions as to how to go about taking a photo inventory.

The International Foundation for Art Research   46 East 70 Street, New York, New York 10021   (212) 879-1780
The foundation publishes a newsletter entitled *Stolen Art Alert* 10 times a year. It is an illustrated list of thefts and most wanted art that has been stolen.

INDEX